THE STATE OF THE JEWS

THE
STATE
OF
THE
JEWS

Marie Syrkin

New Republic Books
Washington, DC

Many of the essays in this book originally appeared in *The Jewish Frontier, Midstream, Commentary* and *The New Republic*. The author is grateful for permission to reprint them.

Published in 1980 by

New Republic Books
1220 19th Street, NW
Washington, DC 20036

Library of Congress Cataloging in Publication Data

Syrkin, Marie, 1900-
  The state of the Jews.

      1. Jews—Politics and government—1948-—Addresses, essays,
lectures. 2. Refugees, Jewish—Germany, West—Addresses, essays, lectures. 3. Israel—Addresses, essays. 4. Zionism—Addresses, essays, lectures. 5. Jews in the United States—Politics and
government—Addresses, essays, lectures. 6. United States—
Ethnic relations—Addresses, essays, lectures. I. Title.
DS143.S94   909'.04924'009045   80-13991
ISBN 0-915220-60-1

Printed in the United States of America

Remembering Golda

CONTENTS

THE STATE OF THE JEWS

INTRODUCTION

These essays and reports reflect a life-long concern with the riddle of Jewish experience in our times. I first encountered the riddle in its crudest form as a child of six in Czarist Russia. There I learned the meaning of "pogrom" from friendly village children who counseled me to paint a cross on our cottage should the killing start. But when I brought these tidings of salvation to my father I discovered that this was not the right solution. The answer, I was taught and grew up believing, lay in a Socialist society and a Socialist Jewish state. My Zionist roots went even further back. My parents, young Russian Jews who attended a Swiss university because of quotas against Jews in Russia, had met in Basle at the second Zionist Congress summoned by Herzl in 1898. I was born a year after their marriage in Bern. By the time my father's peripatetic career as the theoretician of Socialist Zionism had brought his family to the United States in 1908 the solution had resolved itself into three simple theses: the good world to come would be Socialist; it would have a homeland for the persecuted Jewish people; and this homeland would be Socialist.

Brought up in a quixotically idealistic and dogmatically atheistic home— no religious observance compromised my father's ideological consistency—I was thoroughly imbued with a sense of belonging to a people whose endurance of suffering was willed. Readily escaped by acceptance of the cross recommended by those peasant children, the persecution, therefore, could never be demeaning, any more than could our poverty, suffered, I was given to understand, because of my father's dedication to a great though unprofitable cause. At the Socialist-Zionist meetings to which my parents, too impecunious for baby-sitters, zealously took me I was to hear the Internationale sung in a variety of languages (depending on where we lived) by small groups of devotees. In time I.was assured it would be sung openly in every tongue, including Hebrew.

These childhood certainties, reinforced by the rhetoric of the American public school which still proclaimed the democratic creed with conviction, were inevitably to crumble. World War I was the watershed. The

Marie Syrkin

enlightened twentieth century was beginning to dim, though the ultimate darkness was still some decades away. Gradually the baggage of illusion which had been my heritage grew lighter. As a teacher, first in a New York highschool, later in a liberal college, unsuspected social issues whose remedies violated former assumptions came to the fore. The horror of the Nazi rise to power had to be faced. And for those who were Socialists as well as Zionists the Moscow Trials would be the first in a bitter series of shocks and disappointments. The shift from the romantic Zionism of pioneer Palestine to the reality of an embattled, fallible state, from confident understandings about the nature of social justice in a democracy to the challenges of the sixties, was a revolution that would profoundly affect American Jewry. The essays in this book, written at various stages of this process, mirror changing attitudes in response to these developments.

What did it mean to grow up in the kindest diaspora Jews have known in their tormented history, and from that privileged spot to witness and in some measure experience not only the greatest catastrophe of that history but the greatest triumph as well? Since the thirties the overriding concerns of American Jews have been the holocaust of European Jewry, the establishment of Israel, and social change in the United States. This triad cannot be disentangled; the three concerns interact to form a composite— the state of the Jews. Though chronologically, organized Zionism preceded the Nazi regime and its consequences by half a century, the impact of the latter transformed American Zionism from a small, peripheral movement to a major force animating and uniting the American Jewish community. The gas chambers effected the ideological conversion of previously indifferent American Jews. For this reason these reports begin with the survivors of the Nazi extermination scheme. Their plight galvanized Jewish Palestine and American Jewry—the only diaspora left with the means and ability to influence events.

In the summer of 1933 I took my first trip to Palestine. The ship's radio carried news of fresh measures enacted by Hitler, newly come to power. Yet the Nazi menace in its initial unfolding seemed somehow unreal. It was too preposterous; it would blow over. More real were the kibbutzim that I saw in the Valley of the Jordan and Galilee, the rapture of a young woman who ran up to me with the first radish grown in her settlement, the _hora_ danced on the Sabbath on the streets of still uncrowded Tel Aviv along whose shore camels slowly made their way. Each accomplishment was still a victory to be celebrated in the popular pioneer songs of the time.

In 1933 European Jews showed little eagerness for the ascetic life of the agricultural settlements, and American Jewry, except for small enclaves, had only a slight, sentimental interest in the remote Zionist experiment. An example of this emotional and intellectual distance was an encounter with Max Lerner which he has no reason for remembering and which I

2

trust he will forgive me for citing. In 1934 I had joined the staff of *The Jewish Frontier*, a new Labor Zionist journal whose ambitious objective was to bring the teaching of Socialist Zionism to English-speaking readers. It occurred to our enterprising editors that Max Lerner, then on *The Nation*, might (in view of the magazine's liberal stance) be interested in the social experiment in Palestine. When I approached Lerner he informed me with utmost kindness that he had never heard of a kibbutz. I still remember the pall that fell on our editorial collective. If Lerner was uninformed, what liberal American intellectual might be expected to be interested in the cooperatives of Palestine?

By the summer of 1936, when I again went to Palestine, portents of the future were more perceptible. Arab disturbances, inspired by the pro-Nazi Mufti, had broken out; the ship carried few tourists. But my fellow travellers included a Youth *aliyah* group (an organization founded to rescue young people from Germany and settle them in Palestine). These boys and girls had no illusions about their German past or the likely ease of their Palestinian future, yet they sang the poignant songs of the Emek and danced the *hora* with pioneer confidence. Other passengers were more troubled at the prospect of disembarking in a country where any vehicle might become the target of bombs or gunfire. Four American ministers eager to visit the Holy Land worried as to whether they would get to see the Church of the Holy Sepulchre in Jerusalem, the dream of a lifetime. At first the ministers, seeing the spirited youth group, felt instant sympathy for their trials and admiration for their courage. In a flush of enthusiasm one of them compared the ship to the Mayflower and the young *halutzim* (pioneers) to the Puritan forefathers. But the enchantment was short-lived. Within two days they had been taken over by an English Quaker missionary who was returning to an Arab school of which he was the principal.

To the Quaker's usual anti-Zionist arguments, which no statistical data I offered could affect, the missionary added an objection in which the American ministers sadly concurred: the smart Jews would exploit the simple Arab, make him work while they enjoyed the profits. When I countered with "self-labor," the cardinal tenet of the settlements, and with the Histadrut's (the trade union of Palestine) insistence on Jewish productive work, he came up with a contrary grievance: by demanding that all physical work in reclaiming the soil be done by Jews, Zionists were failing to employ Arabs. Despite the baffling logic of these grievances, the ministers had been won. Only when the ship reached Haifa and we stood on deck to look at the long, bare stretch of hills and the small cluster of houses at the base of Mount Carmel—scant evidence of habitation or cultivation as far as the eye could see—one minister whispered to me, "I guess they could use some more of these Jewish ploughboys." The debate on the displaced Arab was beginning.

That year I could see at first-hand the practice of *havlaga*, the much debated, self-imposed "restraint" of the *Yishuv*, the Jewish community of Palestine: Haganah, the Jewish defense force, would not answer terrorist outrages with indiscriminate retaliation but would limit itself to defense. This policy was assailed as cowardly by the Revisionists and subsequently violated by the Revisionist Irgun; however, anyone who observed the unspectacular fortitude of Jewish Palestine, the matter-of-fact determination to carry on the orderly routines of existence without being provoked into emulating terrorism or being reduced to panic would not doubt the people's courage. Here too were the seeds of a division as to ends and means that would deepen progressively in the future.

A grimly ironic note to this journey was struck on the return trip. On the ship were some German Jews, businessmen who had decided to survey the economic opportunities of the Jewish homeland. They had concluded that organized labor was too strong in Palestine; private enterprise was trammeled by Socialist notions. So they were going back to Germany to consider other alternatives.

This complacency was soon to change. By the end of the thirties, as the virulence of Nazi persecution increased, even the blindest were to see that escape to Palestine was their sole refuge. The fearful drama of leaky ships bearing illegal immigrants to Palestine in defiance of British quotas and blockade had begun. And American Jews were fast losing their composure. To their shock at the Nuremberg laws was added something new—fear for themselves.

The forties represented the coming of age of American Jewry. Until then, despite the hardships of the immigrant experience and sporadic instances of brutal anti-Semitism in the United States, progress had seemed steady. Manifestations of prejudice in centers with large Jewish concentrations were more likely to be insult than injury. Each decade since the years of mass immigration had marked not only political freedom but continuing economic and professional success. The forties were to introduce old terrors into the consciousness of American Jewry. For the first time native-born American Jews were nervous. Home-grown rabble-rousers, emboldened by Nazi victories, had come out of the closet. Pro-Nazi Father Coughlin rallied his disciples in popular radio broadcasts that influenced a periphery extending far beyond the circles of such rabidly anti-Semitic groups as the Christian Front or the Silver Shirts. The German American Bund strutted openly in full stormtrooper regalia in Madison Square Garden at huge meetings called to demonstrate against American involvement in World War II, and just as openly against American Jews scheming to inveigle the United States into the conflict.

Until December 1941, blatant pro-Nazi and anti-Semitic agitation, no matter how scurrilous or incendiary, was protected by the right of free speech. In the highschool in which I taught, pro-Nazi pupils propounded their creed during the current events period with little objection from their classmates; "It's their opinion" would be the nonchalant response. Few teachers ventured to challenge this tolerance. Indoctrination was taboo in the pedagogic lexicon. After Pearl Harbor the patriots of the Bund retreated into the unwelcome role of enemy alien, and students in American public schools prudently stopped proclaiming their allegiance to Hitler's doctrines. Jews breathed more easily; they were on the right side.

But American entry into the war did not exorcise the specters that had been summoned. Jews were on the world scene as victims and targets; even second generation American Jews, supposedly ensconced behind the bulwark of their country's cause, were on the defensive. The furies unleashed across the sea had shaken their recently attained sense of security. More than one decent Jew found himself shamefacedly scanning lists of wartime casualties for obviously Jewish names, though he knew from ancient experience that libels were data-proof. No multitude of corpses would persuade. The dreaded charge, loudly proclaimed before Pearl Harbor, then whispered, was that the struggle against the Nazis was a Jewish war from which Jews managed to absent themselves. ("The Case of Jacob Goldstein" describes this state of mind.)

There was another large question: what, for American Jews was primary, concern for American interests or for their fellow Jews? Because of the stated determination of the American government to keep the war effort free of "extraneous" issues such as the fate of European Jewry—a resolution abetted by the notable indifference of the media—suspicious disapproval met attempts made by American Jews to move the government to act in behalf of Nazi victims. Each appeal had to carry the pathetic caveat that aid for Hitler's hostages was in the spirit of American democracy and an integral part of the struggle against its foe.

Nevertheless, American Jews held somber protest meetings, sent delegations to the White House and Congress, and placed full-page advertisements in the *New York Times* in hopes of kindling public indignation. Space for such purposes had to be bought. Only obscure Anglo-Jewish journals and Yiddish papers viewed what was happening as major or wholly credible. The Bermuda Conference on Refugees meeting in 1943 took no measure to admit refugees even within the immigration quotas permitted by United States regulations. All pleas were met with the standard answer, "The solution is to win the war" (see "Conferring in Bermuda").

In view of the magnitude of the catastrophe the activities of American Jews seem pitiful in retrospect. But to accuse American Jews of apathy or indifference is unjustified. *Post facto* critics too readily forget that the forties were not the sixties. In a country engaged in a desperate war those concerned with anything other than the prime goal—winning the war— were in the way. Suggestions by the Jewish Agency that the crematoria of Auschwitz and Birkenau be destroyed by direct bombing were dismissed by the War Department as impracticable. Proposals for the bombing of railway lines leading to Auschwitz met the same fate. Chaim Weizmann was informed that there were too many "great technical difficulties." In any case these discussions were not for public consumption. Most important, World War II was not an unpopular conflict like Vietnam but one in which the country and certainly its Jewish citizens were passionately involved. Roosevelt was the democratic savior who had fought off the America Firsters and come to the aid of Britain. No rationale for civil disobedience, for any obstructionist act likely to strengthen the secret opponents of the war who, like Lindbergh, had retired into obscurity, existed at the time. The technique of mass protest was a generation away; the totally different climate of the forties provided no soil for such growth. So the American Jewish community could do little more than clamor to closed ears. Individual American Jews joined Jewish Palestinians who in various ways tried to break into the Nazi charnel house for the specific rescue of Jews. Not until victory and Eisenhower's entrance into the death camps did the extent of the Holocaust become apparent to a skeptical world.

In 1945, at the close of the war, I was again in Palestine. The sore question of the "passivity" of Jews in ghettos and concentration camps had already arisen and I went specifically to gather material for a book on Jewish resistance (*Blessed Is The Match*). Palestine was the place where surviving ghetto fighters and partisans, as well as Palestinian parachutists and organizers of the illegal immigration could be found. The central role of Palestinian Jewry in whatever rescue attempts were made distinguished that small community from American Jewry. The explanation given to me for the difference was brief and simple: "We are a people and act like a people when in peril." Teddy Kollek, now mayor of Jerusalem, could give first-hand information about those who broke the British blockade. Abba Kovner, a partisan leader from Vilna, Chayka Grossman and others who were to achieve international reputations, were fresh from the ghetto battles.

While there I saw the beginnings of the armed struggle against the British. The scruples that had inhibited reprisals against Arab terrorism in the thirties were again in evidence. Determined to "open the gates" of the Jewish homeland to survivors in defiance of British restrictions, the Haganah nevertheless adopted a strict code: military action to bring in refugees reaching the shores of Palestine and to aid in their settlement should be taken wherever necessary; however, indiscriminate violence such as characterized the dissident Irgun and Stern was opposed. Those who witnessed the heart-searchings and qualms of visionary Socialists whose pacifist dreams had to make way for the realities of armed battle know how profound was the spiritual crisis undergone by young kibbutzniks who made up the bulk of the Haganah. The tough years ahead were to bring pride in military prowess, but Golda Meir and others of her generation never stopped mourning the original vision: "We wanted to be good farmers, not good soldiers."

The plight of the survivors finally became an international issue. In view of British policy and Arab hostility Palestinian Jews accepted the painful compromise of the Partition Resolution and the establishment of a Jewish state in a small part of Palestine. The reports dealing with this familiar history offer glimpses of the situation as it was lived, with no foreknowledge of happy or unhappy endings. Those sharing in the euphoria of 1948 assumed that the opposition of the Arab states would prove temporary. Above all they were not prepared for the successive abandonments of the young state by the international community that had sanctioned its creation as an act of historic justice. The polemics with Toynbee and others marked the beginning of a still-continuing debate on the morality of Zionism—a debate whose initial terms have been altered by the rewriting of history to include an Arab-Palestinian nationalism not in existence in the forties. For this reason in essays dealing with this period "Palestinian" refers to Jews.

Since 1948 American Jews have demonstrated their deep emotional involvement in the fate of the Jewish state by unprecedented financial and political support. They fell short of Zionism's ultimate demand—large-scale immigration to help build the young country—largely because their sense of being at home in America was authentic, and, for most Jews, stronger than the wonder of a Jewish homeland. At the same time, pressures to which Jews were particularly vulnerable began to appear in the fabric of American society. These did not signify a recrudescence of gross anti-Semitism but something more subtly threatening.

Since the sixties a new gospel as to what constitutes justice in a democracy has been proclaimed. Equality of opportunity, once interpreted as the right of the individual to advance without regard for race and religion, has become more associated with group rights. What once would have been viewed as the failure of democracy in the new ideology has become its triumphs. When in the twenties I was appointed to a New York highschool purely on the basis of rank in the examination lists, despite the ethnic or religious preferences of my principal, this was hailed as progress. But today "meritocracy" is a fashionable word of contempt; the form of the good society is being cast in a different mold. In such a transvaluation, American Jews— who constitute only 2½ percent of the population—are bound to be among the chief losers.

I have made no attempt to reconcile these evolving attitudes. For example, the essay on "The Arab Refugees" states the problem as it appeared at the time. "The Palestinians" analyzes the next stage. The same holds true for other issues discussed. It is my hope that this method has not only historic merit but provides a better perspective on the fundamental questions still being argued.

I.
IN
THE
DP
CAMPS

Historical Note for Section 1

At the close of World War II, camps, officially designated as Assembly centers, were set up by the Allies in the occupied zones of Germany, Austria and Italy for persons displaced by the war. These camps were administered by UNRRA, the United Nations Relief and Rehabilitation Administration.

Jewish survivors began flocking to these camps in 1945. The British closed their camps to survivors in June 1946; consequently the bulk of Jewish DPs found their way to camps in the American Zone of Germany. The refugees elected a "Central Committee of Liberated Jews in the United States Zone of Germany" with headquarters in Munich. The American authorities gave this body official recognition as the representative of Jewish DPs.

The camps became a center of Zionist sentiment and a source of Aliyah Bet, *the "illegal" immigration to Palestine. The Central Committee issued a proclamation demanding the abrogation of the 1939 British White Paper that curtailed immigration into the Jewish homeland. The proclamation also called for the establishment of a Jewish state.*

In January 1947, I received permission to visit the DP camps in the American Zone for the purpose of gathering first-hand information on the DP problem. An additional purpose was to screen suitable candidates for admission to American colleges, who would be allowed to enter the United States above and beyond the restrictions of the immigration quotas.

IN THE CAMP FOR
DISPLACED PERSONS

"**D**isplaced Person" is a savage euphemism. By now a DP is an almost forgotten term; so is DP camp. Yet the period between liberation and the establishment of Israel, during which survivors of the Nazi death camps became DPs, represents a grim epilogue to the holocaust and a coda to its meaning. Jews who emerged from hiding places and concentration camps discovered that there was no place for them in their countries of origin: their families and homes were gone; and the hostility of the local population broke out in pogroms against the Jewish remnant, particularly in Eastern Europe. The survivors were indeed "displaced," not only from Europe but, it seemed, from the globe. They streamed to the camps set up in Western Europe by the Allies, largely in the American Zone. Some hoped for a visa to the New World; most were fiercely determined to reach the "Jewish homeland" whose gates were barred by the British. The young and strong periodically made the dangerous underground journey to Palestine on decrepit "illegal" ships. The others waited.

When I visited the DP camps of the American Zone in January 1947, the Jewish survivors seemed to have sunk into hopelessness. Not only because physical conditions were bad—and they were wretched. The Jewish DPs were no longer the gaunt figures with tragic, hollow eyes we had seen in newsreels immediately after liberation; the graveyard look was gone. They could walk freely in and out of the former SS barracks that housed them. Yet the men and women I met were more bitter than in May 1945. They talked constantly about the days when Eisenhower's troops had liberated them and the GIs had showered the starvelings of Buchenwald and Dachau with sympathy, chocolate and cigarettes. *Then* the American soldiers were friendly and the Germans afraid if not ashamed; and *then* the survivors of the Nazi holocaust were sure that the world would be eager to make good the wrongs they had suffered. "We thought all doors would be opened to us," person after person said to me.

Now they knew better. Their early naive hopefulness had given way to a mixture of despair, cynicism and resolution. Sick of visitors, skeptical of

Committees of Inquiry, abandoned and betrayed, they were somehow determined to get out.

They understood that Germany was a trap as well as a dead end. The savage irony by which German soil had become a haven for hundreds of thousands of Jews fleeing from anti-Semitic outbreaks in Eastern Europe was not lost on the DPs. Of the 153,000 Jews in the American Zone only 29,000 had been liberated in Germany proper. The rest were "infiltrees" who sought the shelter of the American Zone, particularly after the massacre of Kielce. They had come believing that the sojourn would be brief. In the words of the Hebrew slogan blazoned on every camp, they were *bderech* ("on the way") to Palestine. None expected the temporary asylum provided by the American army to become virtual imprisonment on German soil.

Everything pointed up the irony. Huge figures of stormtroopers were carved on their living quarters, and quotations from *Mein Kampf* over doors and in assembly rooms. And though the DPs had hung the blue and white flag of Zion over the entrance of each camp, and had tacked on placards, bravely designating the forbidding barracks as "Herzl House" or "Sholem Aleichem House," they could not escape the feeling that they were in the territory of the enemy.

An evil paradox pervaded each aspect of DP existence: German earth provided the only available asylum and an SS barrack the only available dwelling. Yet, in a deeper sense, the DP camp was a self-contained world with no fixed locality. The banner of Palestine inspired it; the American flag guarded it. The Germany to which it found itself attached was a sardonic postscript to their tragedy.

"We are not in Bavaria," one DP said to me. "We are nowhere, suspended between heaven and earth."

It may have been "nowhere" but very near Landsberg lay Dachau. A survivor showed me the sights. I had read so many descriptions of the Nazi extermination technique that the crematorium wore a specious air of familiarity. Here was the room where the victims had been stripped. Here was the door deceptively marked *Brause-bad*, the supposed shower room where the lethal gas was turned on. On the walls I saw the peepholes through which the Nazi guards could watch the contortions of the dying. Finally, here were the huge ovens where the bodies were burned—a larger one for adults, and a smaller one for children. The long forks and the shovels for putting in the bodies still hung neatly at the side. The mill for grinding the bones into phosphate was intact. The quiet of recognition surrounded the place. It was exactly as described. Then I saw something new, something which I had not noticed in any of the numerous accounts I had read. Directly behind the ovens, painted on the wall, was a German inscription which had been left untouched. It was a set of instructions to the Nazi guards. *Reinlichkeit ist pflicht hier*, it began. "Cleanliness is a duty here. Be sure to wash your hands."

In the cellar below were rows of little red flower pots, used as containers for the human ashes, valuable fertilizer for the surrounding fields. The pots looked clean and attractive. Farmers from the neighboring countryside would be glad to own them.

The American army did not relish its role of unwilling guardian. The occupation officers were understandably eager to be rid of the DP headache, and many had neither the patience nor the understanding for a problem at once so simple and apparently so insoluble. Some were more perceptive. One high-ranking officer, with a sensitive face and scholarly manner which did not jibe with the conventional picture of a professional soldier, said sadly: "Whatever we do, the picture is hopeless unless these human beings can get out and live again."

A baffled colonel spoke of the army's efforts in behalf of the DPs. "We kept the borders open," he said with dignity. "We did our best for these unfortunates."

I felt his pride in America's generosity. Alone of countries it had let the flood of refugees stream over the borders to the American haven in Germany. It had fed and sheltered "the unfortunates."

Then he added: "However, some solution must be found. If they do not emigrate, they will have to become self-sustaining."

"In the German economy?" I asked. "Will they have to work for the Germans and rebuild Germany?"

"It's not a pleasant prospect," he admitted, "but unless there are emigration possibilities, they will remain in Germany. The United States can't maintain these camps forever. If they won't work in the Germany economy, perhaps they can form an enclave here. After all, since Germany and Japan are the only countries over which the United States has control, perhaps the DPs should be settled in enclaves in these countries. As long as the American army is stationed there, they will be safe."

"And then?"

He shrugged his shoulders.

If army officers, UN officials and relief workers were discouraged, the despair of the DPs themselves was beginning to produce pathological symptoms. I think of the "professor," so-called not because he had held a chair in a university but because he had been a highschool teacher in Vienna in the days before Hitler. He was one of the small number of Jewish intellectuals who had escaped extermination. We met a short time after my arrival in Germany in one of the first DP camps I visited. It was a dreary January day and we sat in one of the cold rooms of the barracks which served as an administration building. The small wood-burning stove gave hardly any heat. The window was tightly shut to prevent the escape of any bit of warmth, and the air was heavy with the smell of acrid smoke and damp clothing.

The professor was obviously a man of refinement and culture and just as obviously in a state of high nervous tension. He gave me some general information about the history of the camp, and then he looked out of the streaked window at the dismal courtyard, across which people were hurrying to get out of the cold, and said mournfully: "We need a Judas Maccabeus, or a Herzl to lead us out of here. Somebody must come and start an exodus out of this desert."

His eyes lit up, and he thumped the table, not vigorously but with a swift, soft motion. He went on: "A Moses must come and liberate our people from the worship of the golden calf. If they stay in Germany, a terrible catastrophe will befall them. They will return to the golden calf."

The barracks I had seen did not look like promising quarters for the golden calf and I decided that the professor was suffering from an acute nervous disturbance. He was overwrought, as a sensitive person with his experiences might well be; he was probably a psychiatric case.

"It is a scheme," he continued, "a fiendish scheme. The Great Powers have shut up the Jewish survivors in these camps so as to degrade them. They will rot here. They will change and become corrupt and evil. Then the Germans will point at them, and clamor: "You see, we were right.""

"But why should the world conceive such a diabolical plan?" I wanted to know.

"To justify themselves and the Germans. To free themselves from the crime of the murder of six million and to free themselves from the responsibility for those who remain. Otherwise the sense of guilt is too heavy."

I remained silent; hypochondria, persecution complex, I assumed. "Dear lady," he went on; his voice shook and to my consternation tears filled his eyes, "You think perhaps that I exaggerate. But it is not so. I have seen what has been happening month after month. The people grow hopeless. They lose faith in any future or any goodness and then they begin to worship the golden calf. Already the Germans are beginning to nudge each other and whisper to the American soldiers: 'You see, they are lazy, tricky; our Hitler was right.' You think that I exaggerate?"

I admitted that I did.

"But it is so plain. Why else have they kept these few hundred thousands in these prisons for two years? Why don't they let them go somewhere? Our young people have no chance to study, to work. Our children grow thinner and paler from month to month. What is there left to dream of— except the golden calf? Hitler's work is being finished in the most dreadful way. This is the last phase of the extermination program, only instead of crematoriums and SS men, it has been disguised into these camps. And the

SS men are masquerading as UNRRA workers, as Joint officials, as consuls. Expose the scheme, dear lady, tell everyone before it is too late."

Afterwards I made inquiries about him. To my astonishment, he was not considered nutty. His name, in fact, elicited generous praise in regard to his learning, kindness and devotion to his fellows.

Among other things I learned that he had been offered an opportunity to emigrate to the United States. The visa was his for the asking. But he had refused; he could not bear to abandon the flock of which he was a self-constituted shepherd in Germany.

I kept looking for the golden calf after that; it was possible to stumble upon it. It was not of gold, of course; that precious metal was rarely to be seen in the DP camps. But one might glimpse a grimy horn in the midst of the scrounging for daily needs, in the dreary barter for necessities that was stupidly called the black market, in the enervating despondency which made all effort and a continued will to struggle seem a cynical joke.

And the so-called "plot?" I never got around to believing that the victorious Allies concocted a scheme in cohoots with the Germans according to which the original *Schwarze Korps* scheme would be fulfilled. But as I went from camp to camp, and heard the reiterated bitter question: "How long will we rot here?" and the still more bitter question, "Why?," the professor's notion began to appear increasingly less far-fetched. At any rate, it offered a working hypothesis. To the DP the situation in which he still found himself, in the shadow of Dachau and Buchenwald, was far more incomprehensible and crazy than the professor's saturnine plot.

One homespun fellow with whom I had been discussing the professor's fantasies smiled sardonically and told me: "After the crematoriums, nothing will astonish me any more. You are sorry for the professor because he has such wild ideas. Maybe you should be sorry for yourself for not understanding what's so simple. Forget the word *plot*. So it's not a plot. But they don't want us to live like human beings, do they? They are treating us like animals and forcing us to die or to become like animals. So what's the difference what names you call it?"

The Palestinian emissaries (*shlichim*) who had reached the camps to aid the DPs in various capacities as teachers, social workers, or officials of the Jewish Agency emigration bureau, were aware of this state of mind. First, they tried to sustain the morale of the children. The DP schools were among the most extraordinary expressions of the will to live.

THE DP SCHOOLS

Anyone accustomed to the munificent physical plant provided by the American school system in most large cities might find the word "school" inordinately ambitious when used to describe the DP classrooms I visited in Germany. Depending on the size of the DP camp, a whole or a part of a barracks would usually be set aside for the school. The equipment varied with the resources of the camp. Sometimes the children sat on the crudest of stools or benches, and used any kind of makeshift boards for desks. In other places, the furniture more closely resembled that of the conventional schoolroom. The benches were firm, the tables stout, and adapted to their purpose. Blackboards, of course, were at a premium. A small blackboard at the front of the room was the maximum a teacher could hope for. Such treasures as chalk, pencils, notebooks were extremely scarce though attempts were being made to secure school supplies.

On the January days when I made my rounds, many of the rooms would be bitterly cold. The small wood stove which burned in a corner did not give enough warmth to heat the room, and I would find teacher and children bundled in whatever shabby coat or sweater they happened to own.

The first impression was invariably of dinginess, cold and poverty. Afterwards, the practised eye would begin to notice other details. The floors were not littered. The snow of paper scraps which drifts down relentlessly beside the desks of American pupils, and seeps into drawers and every available cranny the moment a teacher's watchfulness is relaxed, was noticeably absent. There were no bulging waste paper baskets placed strategically around the room. That bane of every classroom janitor, wads of gum, broken pencils, crumbling chalk, the endless clutter produced by active youth in more fortunate environments, was non-existent. These children were either neat, or they simply lacked the wherewithal for litter. Chalk and pencil stubs were luxuries to be hoarded. So was paper.

The next impression was that of extraordinarily good discipline. The size of the classes ranged between 20 to 30, and whatever the age group the class would rise as soon as a visitor entered, and welcome the newcomer with the Hebrew greeting: *Shalom.* The children would remain standing, erect and attentive, until directed to sit down. The same automatic, orderly rising would take place when the visitor left.

Seeing the children at work—well-behaved, studious and attentive— one had the momentary illusion that, as far as the scholars rather than the equipment were concerned, one had wandered into a normal classroom which enjoyed the guidance of an exceptionally efficient teacher. It was only after one had visited many such rooms that one realized that the good behavior was part of a general pattern. The animal spirits of the children required little checking. Their responsiveness to orders was immediate.

However, when one starts looking at the children individually, one observes that despite the superficial air of good spirits, they are thin, pale and undersized. I did not appreciate how terribly stunted in growth many of the children were until I learned their ages. The child who looks like a six-year-old is ten; the one who seems to be ten is actually 14. After a while one readjusts one's standards, but the shock of surprise is never quite lost.

A class is not a homogeneous group from the point of view of age. The great bugaboo of sound educational practice—serious disparity in age levels—cannot be avoided in the DP school. The children's histories have been such that no correlation between age and schooling can be established. Since 1939, most of the children have had no opportunities for regular schooling, with a consequent great diversity of educational background. In the ghettos some attempts at secret instruction had been made. In the concentration camps, the few children who survived were obviously not provided with books and teachers. Nor were the months in the woods, with the partisans, better guarantees of schooling. Children who had been hidden as Christians in Catholic convents, or who had lived as Aryans, generally had some education, though not along Jewish lines. Those repatriated from Russia had usually attended Soviet institutions where they learned their three Rs in Russian.

This conglomerate mass, with no common language and no common educational background, had to be organized into workable classroom units. The difficulties inherent in such a situation were enormous.

By 1947, 66 Jewish DP schools had been established in the American Zone of Germany. The initial problem had been met, and methods and curriculum were being worked out. The school in the DP camp of Landsberg was a good example of the course of development. Since Landsberg was one of the earliest camps to be established with inmates largely composed of concentration camp survivors, it had few children when first organized. Though one of the largest camps in the American Zone with a fluctuating population of over 5,000, the school started with only a handful of children. In September 1945 two classes were formed with a total of 40 pupils. As the "infiltree" movement from Poland came into swing, families with children began to arrive. These were largely repatriates from Russia, among whom a normal age distribution existed. The usual spectacle of old men and women, frequently complete family units with grandparent and grandchild, began to be seen. Due to this rapid influx, the school had as many as 300 children by January 1946. Later, families were transferred to other camps with a consequent shrinkage of the child population. At the time that I visited the school it had an enrollment of 110 children.

W hen the school opened the language of instruction was at first Yiddish. The native tongues of the children were heterogeneous—Polish, Hungarian, Russian or French. The language most familiar to the majority was Yiddish, though this was true chiefly of the children from Poland. Hungarian children, or those who had been brought up in the Siberian tundras, were not likely to know Yiddish. It became clear that the children had to be taught a common language, which would serve as a bond of union as well as a means of intelligibility. Hebrew was the obvious choice.

The emotional tone of the DP camps was preponderantly Zionist. With practically no exceptions, the children dreamt of Palestine. The slogan blazoned on the classroom walls was *bderech* (on the way) and everything learned had to be a preparation for this future.

The Hebrew-speaking school was a retreat. Outside was the courtyard of the DP camp, and the cold, dirty barracks. If a child ventured beyond the gate, he found himself in hostile Germany along whose streets he could hear the dreaded sound of German speech and encounter blond, blue-eyed children who stared curiously at the strangers they had been taught to fear and hate. But in the classroom no alien influence intruded. The illusion of "belonging" was complete. The classroom was an extension of Palestine not only in speech but in spirit. The homeland had sent a ship to rescue the wayfarers; and the children were aboard waiting for the journey home, learning the poems of Palestine, and singing its songs.

In every classroom, the decorations consisted of variants of the *leit-motif* of the "return." Streamers and placards with Hebrew slogans carefully lettered and decorated with Stars of David announced in one way or another that the homeless children had a land of their own which awaited them. *Artzenu* (our land) was the fairy-land world which had a reality more compelling than the disastrous present. On the walls hung pictures in colored crayon, simply conceived and crudely executed, showing the blooming fields and sunlit hills of *Artzenu*, the land of Israel. The shivering, ill-clad children gazed at the pictures of brown-limbed, radiant Palestinian boys and girls and dreamed of the moment when they could join the players in the valley of the Emek or the Sharon.

In the kindergartens the thin little tots sang Palestinian nursery songs and played games following instructions in Hebrew: *Ekhad, Shnayim, Sholosh* (one, two, three). A pretty little girl stood up and recited a poem, *degel, degel* (the flag). Of course, the flag she described was that of Zion.

In the upper classes, the children studied the history of their people, the Bible, and the geography of Palestine with more than ordinary industry: these were subjects in which many of them had had no previous instruction. They had arrived destitute, stripped of the shreds of East-European background which had once been theirs—the national heroes of the countries in which they had been born and tortured. In the DP school, the raiment of tradition was being returned. The naked were again clothed.

I happened to enter a room during Bible study. The text for the day dealt with the glories of Solomon's temple. The children were enthusiastically describing its size and splendor. This was no usual Sunday school class where the verses about Solomon's grandeur seem as remote in time and space as they actually are. In the dismal DP barracks, Solomon was more real than the Nazi stormtroopers some of them remembered, perhaps because Solomon made more sense. The children had to awaken from the barbaric nightmare they had known to the true world of Solomon's temple and the valley of Esdraelon if they were to survive. Instinctively they sought this reality.

In a fifth-grade class where the median age of the children was 12, we discussed life in the DP camp. The children were outspoken in their criticism. They did not like Landsberg. Why? The first answer given was: "We want to be in Palestine. Why should we be in Germany? We have a land of our own." That was the chief objection. Then came another characteristic answer: "We do not want to eat the bread of charity."

One boy told me: "The people here are sick of Auntie UNRRA. They'd like to have a chance to work and make their own living." "Auntie UNRRA" was a nickname I was to hear applied often with a mixture of derision and gratitude.

Complaints about the quality of the food, clothing, and shelter followed, but the complaints of the children were never as bitter as those of their elders. In fact, the younger the children the less exacting were their demands. Many of them had never known adequate food and decent surroundings. They had no basis for comparison.

I wanted to know whether life in Landsberg offered any advantages. Wasn't there a brighter side which they had failed to mention?

One little girl said, "Yes, there are opportunities to learn." The children agreed that education was something they were acquiring and they showed me their notebooks with lessons in algebra, English, and, of course, Hebrew. The notebooks were marked "War Relief Services, National Catholic Conference, U.S.A."

In a class for younger children, where the average age was ten, I asked the same questions. Here the children were more kindly disposed to life in Landsberg. They went to school, they told me, they played, they had clubs. It wasn't at all bad. But, they didn't want to stay here.

"Why not?" I wanted to know, "Landsberg sounds like a nice place from what you tell me."

A small, dark boy with a thin sweet face raised his hand. He whispered his answer so faintly that I could hardly hear him.

"Talk louder, Yankele," urged the teacher.

Yankele repeated his answer: "It is a sin to stay in a land where so much Jewish blood has been shed."

The child's voice was so earnest, that even the teacher, to whom such answers were surely familiar, was affected. She told me later that Yankele had been hidden for a year and half in a cellar. That was why he still whispered. He had almost lost the use of his voice. Yankele wore a skull-cap; he came of orthodox parents. Perhaps that is why he had begun his answer with the words: "It is a sin."

In another class, where the children were in their teens, I again walked in upon Bible study. The youngsters had just read the passage in *Numbers* which dealt with Cities of Refuge. (According to the Mosaic Law certain cities were to be designated as places of asylum for those who had unintentionally killed a fellow man. The involuntary homicide could flee to one of these cities to seek refuge from the vengeance of the victim's kinsmen.)

The class discussion of the concept of the "innocent" murderer and his rights under old Judaic law was ideally calculated to lead to subjects nearer home. "Relate it to life," is a cardinal pedagogic precept, so without forcing the issue unduly I was able to ask the children a question which for them was by no means academic: "Do you think there were any innocent Germans?" The question was being discussed constantly in the American press, and supposed experts were offering their views. I wanted to hear the judgment of these children, old enough already to have opinions and certainly more deeply involved in the problem than most of those whose views were before the public.

Child after child said: "They knew, of course, they knew what was happening."

The question of retribution was raised. "If the Germans all knew should they be punished?"

I expected an outburst of general vengefulness. In an American classroom, I had often heard the simple counsel: "They should get a taste of their own medicine." But the reaction was unexpected.

A little girl got up and said: "They should be punished, too." When I asked her to be more specific, should they be treated as Jews had been treated by Germans, she said with genuine shock:

"No, no. Jews can't do those things; maybe they should be treated the way the Russians treat them, not pampered."

A boy stood up: "They should pay for what they've done. But even if we had the power we wouldn't put them in gas chambers. How could Jews do such things?"

The majority agreed with this sentiment. I was amazed at the generosity of the victims, and to make sure that my poll was accurate I asked if there were no dissenting opinions.

A boy who had previously taken no part in the discussion raised his hand. He said slowly: "If I could find the man who killed my father and mother, I would kill him." But he stressed the fact that he wanted to kill not any German, but the particular guilty German.

The discussion was becoming uncomfortably personal. I looked about the room. A dark girl in a front seat was weeping. The teacher whispered to me, "Her whole family was killed." In another part of the room, a child was dabbing at her eye with a handkerchief. And to my horror, I noticed that the teacher was on the verge of tears, too.

I knew that in another moment, a general wave of hysteria might break out in the room. I quickly shifted the subject. English came to the rescue. Would the children like to know something about American schoolchildren before I left? Yes, the children would like to know.

I learned something from that experience. The blundering idiocy with which I had embarked on the practice of the prime pedagogic tenet "relate it to life," was not likely to be repeated by me in these surroundings where everything sooner or later related to death.

At the end of the period, the teacher, a young woman in her very early twenties, went out with me. She started to apologize for her lack of self-control, and then she began to weep openly. "I can't bear to see the children cry," she said.

"One has to be so careful," she told me. Once she had begun to write "Honor thy father and mother" on the blackboard. And then she remembered in time. Most of the children in her class had no father and mother. She hastily wrote another commandment for the children to copy.

And when the holidays came, she wanted to teach the children how to write notes of greeting to their families, but when she started to show them how to spell "Dear Mother" in Hebrew, she substituted, "Dear friend."

I learned something about the teachers also from this incident. Despite their apparent self-possession and exemplary discipline, the undercurrent of tension was strong. It could hardly be otherwise. The young woman before me had spent the war years in a ghetto, and then in the torture-chamber of Ravensbruck. Her wounds were even deeper and rawer than those of the children, because though she had an adult's greater self-control she had none of childhood's resilience.

One had to walk warily in this world of graves and ghosts. The apparent calm and ease with which children and adults alike spoke of the gas-chambers and the "chimneys" was deceptive. At any moment the great anguish might break through.

The supply of illustrative material drawn from experience was inexhaustible. No teacher could have desired richer sources to tap, and the children did not have to cudgel their brains in order to produce frighteningly appropriate similes. The more far-fetched, fantastic the situation under discussion the more likely it was to evoke the response of recognition. I don't know how fabulous an account of a normal, average child's life in some American town might have seemed to these children. I had no occasion to watch the effect of such a wonder-tale. Here the commonplaces were of another kind.

A Bible class was studying the life of Moses; they were reading the part where the infant Moses is left by his mother among the bulrushes. The teacher wanted to know if the mother was justified in abandoning her child to an unknown woman, the Egyptian princess. Was that how a real mother would act? This was no problem for the children. They had to make no effort of the mind and imagination beyond their years in order to produce replies. Of course, agreed the children, that's how a real mother would act. One little girl mentioned mothers whom she had seen throwing children out of trains to save them from certain extermination. Perhaps a compassionate passer-by would pick up the child. Another child had been present when a baby had been thrown over a fence during an "action." And, finally, a boy got up and said, "Some of us in this class were given by our mothers to Poles. That's how we escaped."

In another class Jewish holidays were being studied. Many of the children had forgotten their religious training or had been too young to receive any when the deportation began. The teacher was explaining the significance of the prayer of *Kol Nidre,* in which which Marranos, secret Jews who accepted Christianity in fear of the Inquisition, pray for forgiveness for the false vows they must make. Here, too, the children had no lack of parallels to offer. Had not their parents done the same thing if they lived on "Aryan" papers? And what about those Jews in Poland who had baptized their children to save them from death? Everything the teacher was saying was familiar—Egypt, the Inquisition. It was just like today.

The Cities of Refuge appeared again when I visited an orthodox school, maintained by a strictly religious group in a camp in Ulm. In the secular schools, called the "people's schools," modern methods of instruction were used in so far as the teachers were acquainted with them. The orthodox school, however, was a perfect replica of an old-fashioned Polish Yeshivah. Little boys with earlocks, wearing skull-caps, sat bending over their books, swaying back and forth. They were studying the *Torah,* intoning the passages in the traditional sing-song. A knotty problem had arisen in connection with the Cities of Refuge! If a man accidentally strikes a pregnant woman who is passing by while he is engaged in a fight with a man whom he wants to kill, and she should die, what should be his punishment? Is he to be sent to the asylum for involuntary homicides? The verdict of the Law was that this refuge was to be denied him because, though he had had no homicidal impulse toward the actual victim, the desire to kill had been the cause of the fight. Since he had murder in his heart, he could not qualify as an unwilling killer.

The boys discussed the *pros* and *cons* of this problem in crime and punishment with zeal and obvious appreciation of the fine points involved. In the Yeshivah I maintained a discreet silence, as befits an ignorant woman, but the students themselves offered their experiences as illustrative material. One boy said "That's how it is in Russia; they exile you to Siberia for a crime." Another boy grew indignant at the comparison, "Siberia is a punishment," he remonstrated. "The City of Refuge was an asylum, not a prison." On consideration, the class agreed that the ethical plane of Biblical Law was superior to that of modern legislation.

The Yeshivah I observed was not likely to make a favorable impression on a casual visitor. Quite apart from the earlocks and costumes of the students, the modern ear was bound to be outraged by the sing-song, the shouted answers, the irritating swaying, the abominable posture. But if intellectual energy and a high regard for the ethical implications of the issues so eagerly dissected were virtues, these were to be observed in abundance despite the unpromising exterior.

One of the most poignant moments in the course of my visits—perhaps because the pathos was so unconscious—was my encounter with Yossele in DP school in Berlin. Yossele was a round-faced cherub who looked like a four-year-old but was actually six. He had been hidden for two years in the forests near Poland where his parents had perished. An acquaintance took charge of him and brought him to Berlin when the flight to the American Zone started. Yossele, despite his experiences, was wonderfully precocious and the pride of the class when visitors came. For my benefit he was urged to display his talents, which he did by declaiming a long Yiddish poem about a wolf and a lamb. In the poem, the wolf who is about to devour the lamb, offers all kinds of specious excuses for his intention. The lamb keeps pleading his case, pointing out plaintively the falsity of each accusation. Some of the acts with which the wolf charges him happened before he was born; he had never been in the locality where another alleged crime was committed, and so forth for a number of stanzas. Finally, the wolf tires of the futile discussion, and announces brusquely: *"Du must nit vergessen, as ich will fressen."* Yossele, and the other lambs, laughed merrily.

The majority of the teachers who work in these schools have had no professional training. Educators, like all intellectuals, enjoyed a high priority in the Nazi extermination program. Many of the younger teachers had as their sole qualification the fact that they had managed to graduate from one of the Jewish seminaries or *gymnasiums* of Poland before the war started. They knew Hebrew well—that was a prime requisite—and with the aid of a single textbook and their natural intelligence they taught the children as best they could. A few—to be found particularly among those who had been evacuated to Russia—were professional teachers who had studied and taught in the world famous institutions of Polish Jewry. The experienced guided their colleagues and assisted in the management of the school—the working out of programs and of curricula.

I was tremendously impressed by the results they obtained as well as by their *esprit de corps*. Not all observers shared my estimate. I had occasion to see the report of a young American voluntary agency worker who was describing the poor physical conditions of the school in the camp to which she had been assigned. She wrote: "The teaching staff is very poor. Most of them are not graduated teachers; they are very selfish and ask for things for themselves only and very rarely for the school. The principal is a very disagreeable man. He always puts his personal needs above the school. He demanded weekly packages from Joint, 4 packs of cigarettes a week from A.J.D.C., suits, coats, etc."

Possibly the experiences of this reporter were particularly unfortunate, but even if her indictment were accurate, it is interesting to note its terms: the members of the faculty want some return for their work. The apex of this greed is exemplified by the principal's demand for four packs of cigarettes a week, and for some clothing. I came upon the complaint of "selfishness" among the DPs repeatedly. As it was generally made by individuals who were themselves amply rewarded for their philanthropic efforts in good American dollars, not to mention their abundant supply of American food and cigarettes, it was a little hard to see the point. Neither the military nor the personnel of UNRRA and the voluntary agencies were contributing their services *gratis*. But a DP who had the indecency to ask for better rations—pitiful at best—or a few cigarettes in return for his extra work would be freely criticized as lazy, ungrateful, and lacking in social responsibility.

The teachers who worked in the DP camps were putting in a difficult and nerve-racking day's work, yet in class after class, the first request that I heard from the instructors was for more books and writing materials for the children. "Won't America send us books?" Only later did questions of the teachers' personal needs arise. Several times during my stay in Germany I heard dark rumors of teachers' strikes. The teachers would not come to classes unless they received a better "category" in the distribution of Joint packages—the sole pay for work. It seemed a very modest objective, but the sense of shock at the notions of teachers "striking" was acute. Even the teachers were divided in their score; many refused to "desert" the children. Nothing came of one such threatened strike and the sense of responsibility towards the children proved to be the prime consideration.

A teachers' organization had been formed for the purpose of enabling the teachers to acquaint themselves with pedagogic procedure in other camps and to profit from whatever trained educators could be found in their midst. I attended a teachers' meeting in the Chaplain's center in Berlin. Teachers from all the DP camps in the American sector of Berlin were represented. The gathering was very much like one of the countless department meetings with which I am familiar, except that here attendance was voluntary, and the meeting took place in the evening instead of immediately after school hours.

The teachers, men and women, presented their classroom problems. They discussed the relative merits of the literature books that could be obtained. Should they try to order Mendele or Peretz? Anyone who has ever been present at an English teachers' meeting where the faculty discusses the advisability of dropping *Travels with a Donkey* but is told by the head of the department that there are 500 good copies in stock, therefore the teachers will please continue with the *Travels,* would recognize the nature of the problems raised.

The question of the Prophets was next on the agenda. Would it be better for the children to study the early or later prophets? Which would give them more spirit?

The principal, faithful to the doctrine of "relate it to life," suggested that since spring was in the offing there should be a project on spring. True, the DP camps were not ideal places for nature study, but it would be well for the children to learn something about flowers and birds. Perhaps they could plant a garden somewhere. That's what they used to do in Poland in the spring. In May the children used to plant beautiful gardens on the school grounds. Children should learn and work—that would prepare them for Palestine.

A teacher suggested the advisability of a vacation in the summer months. It was hard for the children to keep their minds on schoolwork in the heat. I could sympathize with the teachers' longing for a vacation; however, another teacher arose and stated that though schoolwork in the summertime left much to be desired, it might not be wise to abandon the children to their own devices for two months. "After all," she said, "we are not in a vacation resort but a DP camp." The teachers agreed; there would be no vacation.

W hen the meeting was over, the teachers expressed a desire to hear from the American colleague. I expected the request. No matter how tired the audience was of greetings from the "great Jewish community overseas," of commendations for their valor, and of expressions of hope for their speedy deliverance, courtesy demanded that each visitor arise and proceed with his piece. Something had been tormenting me in all of my contacts with the children in the DP camps—their simple faith, their absolute assurance that the end of their bitter road was Palestine, and that nothing could happen to keep them from the promised land. The completeness of this conviction frightened me. The children had already suffered blows and shocks beyond the human mind to imagine. Supposing political developments prevented their reaching *Artzenu,* were they able to endure another major blow? Every element in the school fed and stimulated their natural longing for "home." Was this wise from the point of view of the child's interests? Should they not be prepared for other eventualities?

I knew that to raise this question was heresy. I ran the danger of giving serious offense, in addition to being viewed as a traitor to Zionism. None of these prospects was pleasant but I decided to chance it. I used the pedagogic lingo suitable to the occasion in the hope of making the issue more palatable. Was indoctrination a sound educational method—even indoctrination for Zionism? In view of the present political picture were not the children being raised in an unreal world? What about the danger of further psychological injury if other eventualities were not taken into account?

From the heat of the discussion that followed, I realized that I had hit on a vital issue.

"Maybe it's not good pedagogy to present only one side of a case," said one young woman passionately, "but we can't afford such luxuries. The children have nothing, nothing. What should we talk about—the blessings of Poland? They know them. Or the visas for America? They can't get them. The map of *Eretz* is their salvation."

There was much talk along these lines, but I remember most vividly a tired-looking, middle-aged man who spoke with less vehemence than most of his colleagues.

"I have been a teacher all my life, and I also know about modern methods. Indoctrination may not be good for normal children in normal surroundings. But what is normal here? How can you make the same demands of us in the DP camps in Mariendorf as you do of your colleagues in a free American highschool? *Auf a krumme fuss passt a krumme shuh.* (A crooked foot needs a crooked shoe.)"

(March 1947)

THE HARDEST EXAMINATION

One of the tasks assigned me when I left for Germany to visit DP camps was to find suitable applicants for Hillel scholarships. The successful candidates would have their transportation paid to the United States and would be maintained at an American university. When their studies would be completed, they would be obliged to return to Germany or leave for some country for which they obtained a visa. But in the meantime a respite from DP existence would be granted and opportunities for a college education given. As the maximum program for all of Europe called for only several hundred scholarships, and a number of these had already been filled, I could recommend no more than approximately 50 students to be chosen from the entire American Zone in Germany. It was a heartbreaking as well as responsible assignment in the course of which I became intimately acquainted with another sector of DP life—that of the young students, and the problems peculiar to them.

In addition to the financial outlay involved, several other factors served to limit the number of scholarships that could be offered. American universities were badly overcrowded. Returning veterans naturally had the first claim on the educational facilities of the country. Nevertheless, colleges in every part of the United States managed to allot a place for one or two DP students. But even taking into account the generous and helpful attitude of many American universities the grand total of openings was small. Furthermore, after a candidate had been accepted by an American university, he still had to pass through the consular mill before he could be granted a visa as a non-quota immigrant. Despite the fact that recipients of Hillel scholarships were to receive only temporary student visas outside the regular quota, the consul insisted that they meet the residence requirement demanded of all immigrants to the United States according to the Truman directive: they had to bring proof of residence in the American Zone since December 23, 1945. This automatically disbarred a large number of able young people with exceptional educational backgrounds who had arrived after the given date.

My first problem was to devise some method of gauging the qualifications of the countless applicants. It stood to reason that many boys and girls confined in a DP camp would welcome the chance to study at an American university. Each could adduce need; each had a past so tragic that it became impossible as well as presumptuous to seek to measure the extent of suffering or to use that as a criterion. The determining consideration had to be the individual's ability to meet the academic demands of an American university. It would have been misguided kindness to award a scholarship to someone who would fail in the first semester. "You must not be emotional," I had been warned.

My first steps were the conventional ones, and, as such, foredoomed to failure. No matter how much theoretical knowledge of conditions in DP camps one was equipped with, it was hard to keep the realization that one was in a special world with its own special conditions. At the first camp I visited, I asked that all those interested in a scholarship should come for an interview bringing their credentials. There was no dearth of applicants. People of various ages appeared. Then the ludicrousness of my request became apparent. If the youth was of normal college-entrance age, 17 to 20, then he had had no preparatory schooling. In the years when he should have been attending highschool he had been in a ghetto or a concentration camp. Those in the middle twenties had been old enough to graduate from a *gymnasium* by the time the war had broken out. But when I asked for diplomas, they smiled. How could they have diplomas? Everything was burned, destroyed together with their homes and families. The schools they had attended were razed. Their teachers had fed the crematoria. Where were they to get records? Could they pass an entrance examination? Most of them looked troubled. Geometry, physics—so many years had passed since they had looked at a school textbook. "We didn't memorize formulas in Dachau," one boy said to me angrily. There was no countering that answer, yet its truth did not relieve me of the need of instituting some objective standard of judgment.

Finally, with the assistance of the educational adviser of the Joint Distribution Committee, it was decided to give an examination general enough in its scope to permit its answering by students of various nationalities and academic backgrounds, and yet concrete enough to enable the examiner to estimate intelligence as well as performance. Standard IQ tests could not be used because of the language difficulties involved and the varieties of previous experience.

We decided that comprehensive questions in literature, history, mathematics and physics would be feasible. Every country had a literature and a history, and mathematics was international. Such vague questions as: "Discuss three important writers who influenced your thinking" offered equal opportunities to one boy who had studied in a Polish Yeshiva and another in a Hungarian *gymnasium*. The same helpful latitude was offered by requests to compare two historical epochs in regard to social, economic and political institutions. General knowledge and native intelligence were bound to get their innings even though specific dates might no longer be remembered.

After the questions were formulated, another problem arose to stump us. What language should be used? We did not have a staff of translators on hand who could give us accurate renderings of the variety of languages that might be used if we permitted a free choice. We had to limit the number of languages to those known by the two examiners—French, German, Yiddish, Hungarian, Polish, Russian and English. Furthermore, the candidates had to have some knowledge of English if they proposed to study in an American college. They could not be complete novices upon arrival in the United States. We therefore gave the following instructions. The questionnaire giving essential data as to birth, education, experience, etc., had to be answered in English. The literature and history questions— which I was to mark—had to be answered in German, Yiddish, French or Russian. Mathematics and physics could be answered in Polish or Hungarian, since these would be marked by my colleague who knew both languages.

The mere listing of the problems connected with the preparation of a simple examination indicates something of the complex and tortured world into which this academic paraphernalia was making its somewhat incongruous entrance. Further developments shed added light on the life of the young DP.

The announcement that an examination would be held at once discouraged a sizeable number of applicants. If the number of openings at American colleges had been unlimited, I should have viewed this as a serious indictment of the procedure. But, unfortunately, we were under the tragic necessity of choosing, and since all were equally needy, we had to try to find those most likely to profit from the opportunity. However, despite the drop in candidates, there were still plenty from whom to choose. These were mainly young people who had already qualified formally as "students" by enrolling in German universities.

The first impulse of my committee was to debar those who were already studying at German universities and to make scholarships available only to those who had not been admitted to any higher institution. But, again, the notion, though theoretically sound, proved not feasible. We had to face the fact that the small number of genuine students among the Jewish survivors had, for the most part, already managed to be admitted to the German universities. Immediately after liberation, German universities, as they re-opened, accepted Jewish students freely. That seemed the minimum restitution "democratic," de-Nazified German colleges could make. However, with the passage of time, German academic institutions like other sectors of Germany became less sensitive to their moral obligations and more insistent on technical requirements which, as in the past, were an effective means of excluding "non-Aryans." Nevertheless, by January 1947, there were 570 Jewish students enrolled in the German universities. They could be found in Heidelberg, Marburg, Frankfurt and other places, but the great majority—408—were in the Technische Hochschule and University of Munich. Over a third of the students were women.

The students were organized into a union, and I had occasion to meet with the Munich chapter. We discussed the problems of study in the United States. The inevitable objection was raised: why should any student go to the United States? The majority wanted to settle in Palestine. Why weren't the scholarships being awarded for study at the Hebrew University? I was in the curious role of opposing a 100 percent Zionist position and defending the right of those who wished to settle in the United States to make that choice. Besides, this was study, not emigration. I had been assured by a number of candidates that when their permitted student period in the United States expired, they would leave for Palestine. In fact, they would train themselves for Palestine.

The question of Palestine had appeared periodically during my interviews. Some very bright boys had refused to consider the offer of a scholarship; nothing was going to deflect them from their goal of Palestine even temporarily. They were skeptical of the assurances of those of their colleagues who claimed that they would be pioneers "later." These were the "deserters," who permitted personal advantage to obscure the national struggle. Naturally, it was not my business to de-convert the zealots. They had my affection as well as my admiration. But, despite the preponderant tide toward Zion, there was still no scarcity of applicants among whom the choice had to be made.

On the day of the examination, the rooms of the Jewish highschool in Munich assigned for the purpose were filled to overflowing. Despite the difficulties of transportation, students had come from as far as Frankfurt. Food and shelter were being provided by the Students' Union on the elementary basis that every Munich student who had a bed on which to sleep would share it with a comrade who had to stay overnight. The Joint and the Central Committee of DPs had promised to provide rations, for it must be remembered that neither lodging nor food were obtainable in Germany without travel orders and ration cards. Even the simple mechanics of getting the students together and receiving a day's provision for them was a complex affair, involving endless negotiations about every step from the moment of departure to obtaining the necessary writing paper.

I have proctored many examinations in the course of my teaching career but never with the concern with which I approached this one. After the questions were distributed, and translated into the several languages, a few glanced at the paper for a few minutes, got up and walked out. "I thought I remembered more," was the explanation. One tall, attractive, fair-haired girl of twenty-three, whom I knew to be exceptionally intelligent, walked out despite my urging her to "stay." She had been a bright science and mathematics student in Poland. But she had forgotten in Ravensbruck. The shock of seeing the familiar diagrams and terms without being able to place them in their correct relationship was a painful one. "I did not realize how much I had lost," she said to me, her fine gray eyes filling with tears.

But the majority remained and wrote doggedly. The tell-tale beads of sweat appeared on many foreheads. One of the characteristic features of concentration camp survivors was their tendency to break out into a profuse sweat, often in the midst of an apparently calm conversation. The three hours allowed for the test passed. Most of the students were only half-finished. I was astonished at the slowness of pace, for the time allotted had been liberal according to ordinary standards. I knew with what debonair speed the average New York highschool class would have galloped through the questions, but these boys and girls protested: they couldn't write fluently in foreign languages and, besides, the habit of formulating ideas in writing had to be reacquired. But they kept on with something of the slow, painstaking persistence of conscientious illiterates. I decided to drop one question of the original four. They could choose any three.

When the amputated examination finally dragged to an end, I collected the papers with many misgivings. Despite the agonizing slowness with which the questions had been answered, my trepidation turned out to be uncalled for. The results of the examination proved to be exceptional from several points of view. The average paper had been answered in three languages: English for the questionnaire, German, French or Russian for the literature and history, and the student's native tongue for science. The English varied from rudimentary to good, and the German or equivalent from good to excellent. It was an extraordinary exhibition of stamina as well as ability, for the knowledge had either been acquired years before or more recently in German concentration camps or German universities. As might be expected, the content varied from average to excellent, except that the number of mature and able discussions was higher than the norm. My colleague's report on his part of the test was as satisfactory as mine.

But perhaps the most poignant and revealing aspect of the examination was the *curriculum vitae* which had to be answered in English. One of the questions included was the inevitable: "Why do you think you should receive a scholarship?" I quote some of the replies exactly as they were written.

Some wrote laconically: "My parents perished in Auschwitz. Have nobody to help me." Others were more explicit. A young girl whose mother had been killed in Treblinka, and who herself had been in Maidanek, wrote: "It is very hard for me right now to explain why should I be one of the few who will receive the permition of studying in America. I would probably have to tell my war stories and how and in what conditions I survived the hell of the war. I think it was a wonder so I keep hoping maybe you will understand what I am trying to say. Maybe I shall be lucky once. . . ."

A boy described the influence of his home life: "My father was a director of textil factory. My mother finished commercial school. Their greatest purpose was to give me and my two year younger brother a thorough education. They gave me a quiet, happy childage, with all necessities to a perfect youth. I learned from my father the diligent in work, the feeling of duty, and learned from my mother the beauty and pleasure of life, to keep smiling and got my ongoing activity which leads me on the best way." The family was deported and exterminated. The boy, the sole survivor, was liberated in Germany by the American Army. His account continues: "My parents and brother were killed by the Nazis and I didn't have mood to go back to a land where I was managed in such a way. The society turned me out of itself; allowed me its citizen deport to a foreign land in the certain death. I didn't go back there where the people were so wrong and remained so wrong. I'm staying here in Germany since 1945 and am waiting for the opportunity to start a productive, worthy life in free democratic land. In a free country where the men, spirit, mention is free, and there is reason to work and amuse the fruits of it."

A youth from Rumania wrote: "From my childhood I wanted to study bacterology. One of my uncles was a bacterologist. I was early influenced by his work. Paul de Kruif's books were like the Bible to me as I was sixteen. . . . I have no family and no wealth on earth; only a strong will to study that for which I'm waiting since my early years."

A chemistry student described his feeling in the German University at Munich: "The life here, in the former capital of the Nazi movement is, besides the material shortcomings, hard. It is easy to imagine what I feel when I am day by day surrounded by my German colleagues in the same room and chambers where some of the chemists who performed such clean work at the gas-chambers of Auschwits got their technical instruction."

One of the most brilliant boys in the group, a gifted mathematician, born in Rumania, answered at length in faultless German which I translate: "It is hard to answer the question: Why should I receive a Hillel scholarship? One is full of hesitations for fear of seeming immodest. Besides, every such answer is subjective . . . but I feel justified in assuming that I am among those who have drawn fundamental conclusions from the agony of the last years, and have succeeded in fashioning a *Weltanschauung* which bears the mark of suffering. It is my present hope that in surroundings adapted for a human being who wishes to devote himself wholly to scientific work, I shall be able to recreate the state of mind which will enable me to devote my whole spirit and energy for the idea of mankind, knowledge and progress."

But perhaps the most wistful note was struck by a handsome Hungarian boy, whose entire family had been killed in Auschwitz, who wrote: "I have no money and help to study farther. I am going in little chamber on the German rations. I try to concept my situation with humor, but the winter was terrible. More hunger and cold as I waited (than I expected). But I did not lost my time. Now I am going in my fourth semester and I should like to hope that I am not quite abundant in this world." It took me a little time to figure out that "abundant" meant superfluous.

After the papers were graded, it was a comparatively simple matter to select the 15 or 20 outstanding candidates in regard to whose superior scholastic merits there could be no question. But then came the next group, the second 25. It had been impossible to grade the papers on a strict point by point basis. The questions were too general. The fairest procedure was to use broad classifications: A, B, C. The A paper presented no problem. But how select the lucky 25 from the large batch of Bs? We sat pondering over the papers looking for omens. The lives of these young people quite literally depended on the wisdom of our decision. And the burden in these cases could not conveniently be shifted to the ratings received. Other elements had to be weighed. I had to undertake to measure need.

I sat with the papers of two young girls before me. As far as I could judge the difference in ability was slight. Both were likable and attractive. I could recommend them warmly on the score of "personality." Which one should go to America and which one should remain in a DP camp? One seemed to have somewhat more spirit and energy. I instinctively favored her—but she had a mother alive. The other girl had lost everyone in Treblinka. She had to be my choice.

Sometimes the decisive factor would have to be age. Between a boy of 21 and a man of 29, I would choose the younger. It was a cruel choice because I was adding to the already greater mass of suffering of the older student, but the boy had a better chance of adapting himself quickly to undergraduate life and to new surroundings. Besides, a college was less likely to accept an older student. Those over 30 whom the Nazis and the war had deprived of all normal opportunities for development were particularly bitter at the fate which was adding to their injuries. One of them had asked me artlessly: "What is the best age to put down?" and I, of course, had answered sternly, "The truth." Veracity was being penalized, he would have protested, had he known. I began to long for the rough justice of a mechanical measuring-rod.

After the results were announced there were those who came to inquire when they could try again. They would study in the interval. They would be better prepared. Among them was Peter. He had done only moderately well; he had a flustered, hurried manner so that I entertained grave doubts as to his "poise," and he had a mother. These had all counted against him. But Peter would not give up. He was not unpleasantly aggressive; he only wanted to know when there would be another chance. I told him of the remote possibilities. Peter was a tall, pink-cheeked boy with soft brown eyes who blushed easily. Suddenly he pointed to the large violincase he was carrying with him, and asked me hesitantly: "May I play for you?" We were in a corner of a crowded office in the Joint Distribution Committee building in Munich. Violin playing had no connection with a Hillel scholarship, but Peter looked at me so pleadingly that I agreed to listen. There was no empty room available, but Peter assured me that he didn't mind the clicking of typewriters, and the typists, on the other hand, expressed a willingness to hear Peter. He played a long Mozart concerto without notes, while people came in and out of the room attracted by the sound. I have no idea how well or badly Peter played, because the performance was too painful for ordinary aesthetic appreciation. Unless Peter had been a virtuoso of extraordinary talent, Mozart wouldn't help him. I knew that as I watched the tall, sweet-faced boy fingering the bow. When he finished he looked at me appealingly, as though the music could exorcise the need of visas, the lack of college openings, and all the other demons that imprisoned him. "Perhaps, later," I said to him, and he promised to read more and better books.

Another troubling case was that of Helen. It was all very well to determine not to be emotional but this skinny girl, with a blotched skin and no front teeth, tugged at my heart. She had done remarkably well on the examination. There could be no doubt as to her intelligence. But she was not enrolled in a German university, and she had not a single record or diploma. No college was likely to accept a student with absolutely no documents of any kind. Yet, if anyone merited a chance of the basis of ability and need, it was this lonely, scrawny girl of 23. Her command of English was so good that I asked her to write out the story of her life. She brought it to me two days later. It was the typical biography of a Jewish survivor. The story was the familiar one, yet I felt that the girl's intelligence and strength of character were revealed in the account. Some Board of Admission of some American college would, I was certain, admit her on the basis of what she had written. I had not overestimated the perception and generosity of American schoolmen. A Southern college accepted her.

Postscript

In the nearly 20 years that have elapsed since I gave the examination in Munich I lost contact with most of the students. But I know the ultimate fate of a few. Not all who were awarded scholarships were able to use them: the unfriendly American consul saw to that. A fair number, however, did reach America and entered the colleges that welcomed them. Still others, circumvented by consular red tape, reached the United States eventually as part of the regular immigrant quota. One of the girls I had placed in Group B enrolled on her own in an Eastern college where I taught. She did not prove to be a good student. She insisted on specializing in philosophy, for which she had neither aptitude nor preparation, on the theory that she had surived the Death Camps to learn about the eternal verities. When urged to study something practical, she would disarm her counselor with the statement that she had not been saved from the crematorium for that purpose. Since her graduation she has had a number of mental breakdowns.

Fortunately, not all of the tales are grim. The fair-haired girl, gifted in mathematics, who left the examination in tears eventually reached the United States. I had the joy of meeting her as a graduate student at Harvard. But the most dramatic success story was yet to come. A few years ago, in the Faculty Center of Brandeis, I greeted a newly appointed professor of physics; he was the boy whom our crude examination had placed at the top of Group I in Munich.

Helen never got to the Southern college that generously accepted her. She came to the United States eventually on the quota and went to work. I do not know what has become of her.

(June 1965)

TWO CHILDREN

Daniel is eager to talk. He is 14 years old, undersized, but pert and engaging. His blue eyes are merry, and he chatters with an assurance and facility which indicate that he must have told his story more than once. Nor has he the stolid, apathetic manner with which so many of the older survivors recount their saga. He tosses his blond wavy hair; he extends his small, childish hands dramatically. He is aware that he has something exciting, important to relate. Only he has a perverse sense of values. He is emotional at the wrong moments, or what appear to be the wrong moments to me. And he is preternaturally calm when I should expect him to be shaken. I have to orient myself in his unpredictable reactions.

The story is the usual one. It is only Daniel's vivid narrative which distinguishes it from the many others that I have heard.

Daniel could not have been more than ten years old when the slaughter of the Kovno ghetto began. Half the population was killed in the first "action." "There was more room then," Daniel recalls, "so we moved into an apartment." When a hunt of children started shortly after the new quarters had been found, children were hidden in bunkers. The Germans came with police dogs to the entrance of the bunker in which Daniel crouched. The Germans kept yelling *heraus* (get out) but Daniel did not budge. "I thought to myself, death like this, or death like that, so I stayed." He laughed remembering how he had outwitted the Germans.

Afterwards the family was deported to Dachau. The mother died in the train; the father died in Landsberg. A transport of children was sent from Dachau to Auschwitz, Daniel among them. A Pole told the children, "You are going to be burned." A few of the children became frightened and cried, but Daniel claims that the majority were calm. They said, "We have lived long enough; our time has come." Daniel shrugged his shoulders philosophically as he expressed this sentiment, and had I not seen the concentration camp number tatooed on his thin arm I would have grown skeptical of his tale. However, the main facts were accurate—as his record bore out.

At Auschwitz the children were lined up in rows. "We knew that we'd either get a bath or be gassed; and we didn't know which." The doctor examined the children and released some capable of work. Daniel was in the lucky batch. In the morning they were sent to the bath chamber; the terrifying moment came when they waited to find out if gas or water would flow from the pipes. That was "scary." Fortunately, it turned out to be water.

Though some children contracted scarlet fever, they were not exterminated, only quarantined. Afterwards, however, a "nasty" supervisor started measuring the children. If they were below a certain height, they were sent to the crematorium. Daniel was short; he was small when I saw him, and two years earlier he must have been still smaller, but he was ingenious. He managed to scurry in the direction of the taller children at the final moment. Besides, he was a good worker. He dug potatoes energetically from dawn until nightfall.

He tried to tell me how he had felt in that period. No, he had not cried. What was the use of crying? *"Men hat sich raffiniert,"* he said to me, *"men hat sich gegeben a dreh ahim, a dreh aher."* These preternaturally wise words are hard to translate literally. "One got sharp," Daniel said, "one managed to twist in this direction, or in that."

The children would regularly have to pass the huge crematorium at Auschwitz and see the smoke issuing from the belching chimneys. "There go our brothers, we would say."

"Did you ever play?" I want to know. Daniel laughed in the gay, unforced manner characteristic of him no matter what horror he was engaged in relating. "Sure," he answered. "The camp director would sometimes harness several children to a cart full of wood, and we would play horsy."

Hunger plagued the children. Sometimes they would crawl to the women's camp to *organize* potatoes. "You know what *organize* means?" Daniel wanted to know. "Yes," I said, "it means to steal." Daniel was emphatic in his denial. "No, not to steal, to organize." The distinction was not clear but we let it go at that. *Organizing* was one of the common euphemisms concocted in the concentration camps to denote the pilfering of food and other necessities.

Despite Daniel's earlier assurance that the children were not afraid of death because they had "lived enough," it was not hard to sense the constant terror in which they lived. Any visits to the bath chamber were tormenting expeditions. The way led past the crematorium and the children were always taut until they had gotten beyond the entrance. One could never be sure where an expedition would end. The problematic "bath" kept reappearing balefully throughout the story.

Because of the American advance, the children were evacuated from Auschwitz to Mathausen. There again a bath had to be faced. This time

Daniel thought *Der toit liegt shoin auf dem nos.* (Death is already on one's nose.) But again the miracle took place: water came instead of the expected gas. Nevertheless, Mathausen was dreadful—more dreadful than Auschwitz. There was much filth; as conditions grew chaotic, the rate of mortality increased. "Everywhere I had to step on dead bodies," said Daniel without blinking. Then he grew embarrassed, "It was so dirty that we became covered with. . ." He stopped, and whispered, "Excuse me, you know what a louse is?" Reassured, Daniel continued his story. The mention of lice had been the only moment in his gruesome report which seemed to disconcert him.

As the Americans came nearer, the remaining children were taken to a forest supposedly to be shot, but the SS man decided to let them scamper away. He was goodhearted.

Daniel got on famously with the American doughboys. They were always taking snapshots of him and would let him *organize* canned goods and other food for himself and his friends. "There must be pictures of me all over America," the highly photogenic Daniel announced proudly.

But Daniel's *wanderlust* had not been sated. He and his precocious comrades registered with a transport that was to go to the Ukraine—presumably to look for relatives. They stayed in a Russian camp. The Russian soldiers were jolly. They gave Daniel a big stick and said: "Do you want to beat Germans? Go ahead." Daniel grimaced and confided to me: "I said 'yes' but I didn't have the heart. Only once did I hit a German. I had been pinching apples from a German's orchard. He caught me and began beating me. Then some Russian soldiers came along. That was my chance. They let me hit the German back, and they hoisted me into the apple tree. Those apples were swell."

Daniel finally joined a transport which went to Kovno, Lithuania, his native town. There he met a cousin who had been a partisan. The cousin gave him *dem schlechten gruss* (the evil news): the whole family had been wiped out, except for one aunt. This aunt, however, was a woman of moods. Sometimes she was kind and affectionate, at other times harsh "like a stranger." Finally, she put Daniel in a children's home.

The cousin wanted to go to Palestine. So did Daniel Polish documents were secured and Daniel was brought to an *Agudah* kibbutz in Lodz. From this point on, it was a question of crossing the Czech border to reach Bratislava, one of the centers of the *Bricha* (illegal immigration across European borders, with the eventual destination of Palestine.) Daniel was caught at the Czech border. But he didn't lose his nerve. *Ich hob sich orientiert* (I got my bearings). He began to cry and talked his way out of his difficulties. At any rate, the Czech authorities let him go. In Bratislava he met a Rabbi Silver who wanted to take him to America, but Daniel was adamant. He was going to Palestine. At last he reached the children's home in Ulm, in the American Zone of Germany, and was waiting for the day when he could emigrate to Palestine.

Daniel must have had a very high IQ so I asked him if he wanted to study. "No," he said with decision. "I want to learn a trade in Palestine. I want just enough knowledge for myself. But I don't want to be a doctor or a lawyer. In the camps, it was the educated ones who were the first ones killed. None of that education for me." He shook his fair head again. Then he smiled his bright, engaging smile and asked, "Aren't you going to take a picture of me?"

S amuel, a well-built tall boy of 17 with soft, brooding dark eyes, is a perfect foil for the loquacious Daniel. He is shy and quiet, yet despite his shyness he too wants to tell his story. Only he wants privacy. The noise of the children's chatter disturbs him. He likes more silence.

The director seems to understand. He brings us to an unoccupied room and leaves me alone with Samuel. The fewer people, the easier the words come. At first he starts haltingly, scarcely lifting his eyes to meet mine, but gradually he becomes more at ease. He speaks slowly in his soft, almost toneless voice, but now and then he repeats a sentence, and looks at me inquiringly. He seems to want to make sure that I will understand how it was and what happened.

This is a very different tale—no Auschwitz, no Mathausen, no Dachau, only the woods—dark, silent, lonely. In 1941, Samuel's family fled from the Polish ghetto of Szechov and took refuge in the neighboring forest. They dug themselves a *zemlianka* (a bunker in the earth) where the family, consisting of the parents, three boys and two girls, tried to live. But there was the problem of food. The two older boys, Samuel and his brother, went to a Polish village and tried to get work, pretending to be Christians. For two weeks, the scheme was successful, then they were recognized. So they fled back into the woods. A while later they tried once more, taking their older sister with them. But the danger of exposure threatened again, and the boys went back to the *zemlianka*. The girl remained in the village. "I never found out what happened to her," Samuel told me.

Life in the *zemlianka* proved to be disastrous. The Germans began to search the woods and the family was discovered one Friday evening in late autumn. Because of the cold, they had ventured to make a bonfire. Suddenly they were surrounded by a German raiding party. Shooting began. In the melee, the thirteen-year-old Samuel and his older brother managed to escape. Afterwards, when they crept back, they found the father dead, and the little brother crying beside the body of his dead sister. The mother lay wounded, shot through the foot.

The mother was so badly hurt that the boys brought her to the barn of a friendly Pole who took her in with the small brother. A few days later when Samuel ventured to come back to find out how she fared, he was told by his benefactor that the police had discovered the Jewish refugees hiding in his home and had seized mother and child.

Now only Samuel and his older brother remained. When it was very cold, they hid in barns, and stole potatoes from the fields. In the summer life in the woods was easier, but it was on a summer day that his brother went to the village for matches and was captured and killed.

The strange solitary existence of the boy began in 1943. He was by then 15 years old and he had learned much in the two years in the forest, not only woodcraft. He had learned finally that men, *goyim*, were his enemies, and that he had to shift for himself if he was to survive. He had learned how to slink silently at night and get the potatoes which were his only food. He could melt snow into water, and he knew how to steal into a hayloft or empty barn for shelter when the *zemlianka* proved inadequate in the rigors of a Polish winter.

Once he was caught by Poles who demanded that he show them the hideouts of the Jews in the forest. They could not imagine that the boy was entirely alone. He led them back to the thick woods, and crawled away swiftly, hiding among the trees. "When they moved," he explained, "I moved. When they stood still, I stood still, so that the twigs shouldn't rustle."

I was anxious to know more about this mysterious life in the woods, but Samuel rose gently, and excused himself. It was time for prayers.

When he came back, having chanted the evening prayers as befits an orthodox Jew, he resumed his story.

Life in the woods? The worst part wasn't the loneliness. After a while he got used to that; besides he feared people. Each person that he encountered could only wish to kill him or give him over to be killed. The worst part was the rain. In the heavy rains, he was always wet. And he couldn't dry himself because the wet branches wouldn't kindle. He couldn't make a fire. But somehow he survived.

Just before liberation he met a group of Russian Jewish partisans who let him stay with their band. That gave him a breathing spell.

When the victorious Russian army arrived, he ventured into the village. He was very weak and exhausted, his clothes were in tatters, but he got work pasturing cows. At last he had food, and some clothes to replace the rags he was wearing. He started to regain his strength. However, the Russians left the village to advance further, and he had to flee, otherwise the Poles might have killed him.

He went to another town where he was not known as a Jew and managed to maintain himself until 1946. Then he learned that a Jewish community existed in Cracow. He ran away from the Pole for whom he had been working and made his way to Cracow. It was there that a Jewish committee found him and sent him with a children's group to the American Zone in Germany.

"How do you feel now?" I asked him. "Well," he said, "only my eyes and ears are strained. That's because in the forest I always had to watch and listen."

"And what do you want to do?"

"To learn—to learn a great deal—if my eyes will last; I learned nothing in the woods."

He wanted to talk more, but I had another appointment. "There was more I wanted to tell you," he said with his wistful, enigmatic smile. I expressed my regrets. He bowed his head in a gesture of farewell, and moved away delicately, noiselessly, as though he had padded feet.

A BLACK MARKETER

U ntil I reached Germany, my personal experience with the black market had been confined to dealings with the New York butcher who sold lamb chops above the current OPA ceilings. I was aware that my patronage of his establishment made me a black marketer, but I continued to buy lamb chops, and I cannot say that I lacked company, all of it apparently respectable. This I mention not in extenuation of my past sins but to place the question of the black market in the DP camps in its proper perspective. With a few exceptions, most of the loudly touted black market activities I observed proved to be about as nefarious as the housewifely expeditions in my neighborhood. The squeaks of outrage on this side of the ocean seem hardly warranted by the facts.

The mysterious black market turned out to be disconcertingly public. In the courtyard, or in the dingy corridor of a DP barracks you might come across a black marketer peddling his wares openly: small oranges, sugar, some scrawny apples, or perhaps stockings and shoe laces. More secretive black marketers kept their stock in a corner of their wretched room. A few cans of tomato juice, a piece of cheese or salami were almost certain indications that you had stumbled on a center of illicit commerce. More ambitious tradesmen managed to secure a few pounds of meat, fish, or butter which they bartered for cigarettes or other products. As the privileged owner of American cigarettes, I could, if so inclined, have bought up the stock of a dozen black marketers with a carton of Lucky Strikes, but no American was likely to patronize the meager DP black market. Americans could use their cigarettes for bigger bait. French perfume, Rosenthal china, Leicas, and luxury furs were more alluring to the well-fed and comfortably housed Allied personnel than a bunch of carrots or a can of evaporated milk. All over Europe the delights of gracious living could be tasted through the judicious expenditure of Chesterfields. This game helped make occupation less tedious and sometimes highly profitable.

The DPs however, lacked the dignity of amateur standing. They were in bitter need of a piece of meat, or a little fresh fruit to supplement the dreary subsistence diet—mostly carbohydrates—they received. Consequently, they scrounged and bartered for an orange or a bar of chocolate. They engaged in elaborate and ingenious deals culminating in the purchase of a pair of shoes that fit, or a warm sweater—perhaps the first new articles of clothing they had procured since their release from a concentration camp. Such goings-on scandalized observers whose own regular ventures into a more imposing black market could be classified as falling strictly under the heading of sport.

I would get shocked too. Just before Passover I visited the "infiltree" camp of Pocking. I had been warned that this was one of the "bad" camps, and sure enough, the housing was abysmal even according to DP standards. The crowded and grimy wooden barracks were without plumbing; the latrines had been dug some distance from the sleeping quarters, and on freezing winter nights one sank ankle-deep into the slush or snow of which the muddy paths were never free.

However, I arrived on a bright April day when preparations for Passover were in full swing. The spring sunshine had dried the roads and the air was sweet. The tawdry belongings of each family were lying in cluttered piles outside the doors, while the women scrubbed the floor and walls of the bare rooms to make sure that no leaven clung to the interior. There was an unusual air of bustle and energy, almost of expectancy, about the camp.

Special holiday fare had been furnished by the Joint Distribution Committee, and men and women could be seen trudging to the commissary for their allotment of *matzot* and other paschal provisions. Each family was given a bottle of Palestinian wine so that the *seder* would have a festive touch even though the traditional fish and chicken were lacking. I walked about the camp meditating on the thoughtfulness of American Jews who had had the grace to send Palestinian wine to destitute DPs abandoned in Bavaria. Then came the shocking scene.

A huddle of people had collected near the commissary around a bony, sharp-faced woman who was trying to sell the bottle of Carmel wine she had just received. She was doing it openly, shamelessly, with no sense of the breach of gratitude and law she was committing.

"How much do you want?" I asked her, determined to ferret out the matter.

"Eighty marks." That was approximately the equivalent of a package of cigarettes; she was not driving a hard bargain.

I dropped the pose of being a potential purchaser, and reverted to the virtuous American.

"Why don't you keep the wine for your *seder*? Why don't you drink it yourself instead of selling it?"I asked, smiling amiably to put her at ease and bring out her better nature.

She failed to melt at this approach. Her answer was curt and harsh, "Because my child doesn't need wine. She needs milk."

She was an obstinate woman. When I suggested that she could keep the wine and still get the marks or few cigarettes for black market milk, she became irritated. "If you want to buy, buy; I don't want alms." There was nothing to do but to walk away defeated amid the knowing glances of the other DPs who had watched the scene. No doubt she discovered a purchaser, and I take it Elijah has forgiven her if he found a glass of milk on her rickety table instead of a beaker of wine.

The Germans who are driven to the black market in order to satisfy their daily needs have no compunctions about their activities. They avow them in the public press as an argument against the occupation authorities. *Stars and Stripes* (March 31, 1947) carried a report by the Frankfurt Health Department to the Military Government which admitted that the actual food eaten by Germans exceeded the authorized ration by 40 percent. "If people did not obtain this excess they would die or suffer hunger edema . . . A German gets his food by violating laws." With similar candor, the report discussed "the rampant black market" and foraging of city dwellers among the farms, and explained that the only exceptions were persons who worked for the occupying authorities or received sufficient relief supplies from abroad.

Did the German Health Department blush while making these disclosures? Did it apologize for the "lawlessness" of the German population? Far from it. The German physicians concluded their report not with a sermon on morality but with a demand for a bigger food ration. The tables were turned. Not the Germans, but the authorities were at fault. The Germans, who had consumed not only their own but everybody else's cake, still wanted to eat. This desire seemed natural not only to them but to all concerned. However, when Jewish DPs whose last crumb had been devoured by the cake-eaters showed a similar inclination, the nice people were outraged.

The same edition of *Stars and Stripes* which reported the complaints of the Frankfurt Health Department carried the following by no means unusual item: "Eight senior officers of the British Control Commission and four Germans appeared before the Military Government Court on 34 charges alleging a conspiracy for the illegal export of goods from the British Zone of Germany." The charges involved sets of cutlery, rifles, rationed food-stuffs, silver, and other consumer goods.

American and British troops engaged regularly in black market currency operations involving millions of dollars. But allowance was generally made for the fact that boys will be boys. When it was revealed in the House of Commons *(Stars and Stripes,* February 19, 1947) that the black market operations of British soldiers in Germany had amounted to 80 million dollars, War Secretary Bellenger offered a qualified defense of the "underpaid troops." He stated humorously that, "Both officers and men had a hand in this merry game."

I finally found a Jewish DP for whom the black market was a game too, though not a merry one. Moehl Strasse, in Munich, is the section where most of the buildings of the new Jewish community are concentrated. It is a tiny Jewish enclave in the heart of the German city. The headquarters of the Joint Distribution Committee, the Jewish Agency, and the Central Committee of the Liberated Jews of Bavaria are all to be found within a radius of a few blocks. Jews from the nearby DP camps are constantly arriving at the various offices with requests or complaints. It is a bustling street where you are likely to hear a political harangue for or against the Revisionists, or be given a handbill in Yiddish announcing a demonstration in regard to some pressing issue. The "businessmen" thrive there, too.

I was walking along Moehl Strasse one morning, after a visit to the Jewish school recently established by the Central Committee, when I heard a whisper in Yiddish. "Chocolates, cigarettes?" Apparently I had been spotted as an American. "How much do you offer for cigarettes?" I asked.

"Sixty."

I shook my head. "It's not enough?" the trader asked. "No," I said. He raised his bid. I refused again, and then added, "Besides, I don't sell my cigarettes."

The small, middle-aged man, shabbily dressed but carrying the briefcase which was the hallmark of his occupation, caught the note of criticism in my voice.

"You have nothing better to do than to make fun of Polish Jews?" he asked me somberly.

Suddenly I was ashamed; I felt that I owed him an explanation.

"No," I said, "It's not that. But I want to understand about the black market. That's why I asked how much."

"You want to understand," he repeated bitterly. "What is there to understand? How are we going to live—on calories? *You* could live on calories?"

It was a rhetorical question, and I knew what he meant. Calories in the DP camps had ceased to be a heat or food unit but had become the symbol of the drab, squalid existence to which the DP was condemned.

Then he turned on me accusingly. "And besides who is to blame? Who sells the stuff? Where do we get it? It's the higher-ups, the big people."

"What higher-ups?" I demanded. "You really don't know?" he laughed cynically. Then his mood changed, and he added "Or perhaps I have stumbled on an innocent, a pure soul who really doesn't know."

I was prepared to agree that I was a pure soul but he didn't give me a chance, because he went on:

"But you're not really innocent. The innocent ones are the worst. Ignorance of a crime is no excuse. You are all guilty, every one of you; you are all a party to it—you with your cigarettes, and your chocolate, and your passports."

There was no answer to be made about the passport, so I shifted the ground. Besides, I had the cause of righteousness to serve.

"Couldn't you manage without the black market? Is it necessary?"

Again he answered with a question.

"Is opium necessary? What am I supposed to do with myself? I can't get work. I can't get out. This keeps me busy."

He told me something about himself. His wife and child had been killed in the extermination camp of Auschwitz. He had been in Landsberg since liberation two years before. That was a long time.

"That's why I need opium. This is like a game. It gives me something to do."

"And there's no work you can get?" I persisted. "Have you got a trade?"

"Of course I have. I am a skilled leather worker. In Poland I had a good job before the war. If I could get a machine, or a place in a factory . . ." He stopped, and looked wistfully into some past where there had been work, a wife, and a child. Then the anger returned. "What's the use; there's no machine; there's no visa. You want me to choke here with the calories— you innocent people."

I realized that the conversation on the street corner was drawing to an end. I was sorry for the bad beginning, when I had made myself his better. As I turned to go, I took the package of cigarettes out of my purse and handed it to him. "Take it," I said, "Take it as a token."

He started back. "You insult me," he said, "I wanted to buy."

"It is not an insult," I said. "It is a mark of comradeship." I walked away quickly before he could thrust the cigarettes back.

I left him standing embarrassed and puzzled, holding the cigarettes which had been neither bought nor sold, and which had not been doled out by a relief agency. I knew that he would use them in furtherance of his unmerry game, and that there were many others who were in far greater need than he—the woman who wanted the milk, for instance. But he too was in need, and so was I.

(August 1947)

MASS GRAVES AND MASS SYNAGOGUES

Driving to Regensburg we noticed a large green plot with many Stars of David not far from the main road. We stopped the jeep and walked over. Within the enclosure were neatly tended graves laid out in a circular pattern. Each grave was marked with a Star of David bearing a Hebrew inscription, "In memory of a Jewish martyr . . ." The usual gravestone information was missing. It was an obviously new memorial, a restored mass grave.

One can come across these characteristic post-war Jewish cemeteries in various parts of Germany. They have been created largely because of the grim devotion of a Dachau survivor with a peculiar history, Dr. Arkady Akabas.

The project of discovering the hidden mass graves of the Nazi victims was originally undertaken singlehandedly by Dr. Akabas shortly after his liberation. In the fall of 1945 he succeeded in enlisting the cooperation of Rabbi Rosenberg of the Joint Distribution Committee. Later he received the financial backing of the Joint, as well as contributions from the German economy through the assistance of Dr. Philip Auerbach. This was viewed as a form of restitution. Since July 1946, Dr. Akabas has enjoyed official status. His visiting card carries the title: "Officer of the AJDC for restoration of Jewish mass graves in the U.S. Zone of Germany."

Dr. Akabas's experiences in Dachau, which he described to me in Munich, afford the key to why he has set himself the task of finding and hallowing the secret pits into which the Nazis thrust Jewish dead. Born in Lithuania, he had practiced dentistry in Kovno until 1939. During the Nazi occupation, he was appointed chief of the dental department of the Slobodka ghetto by the Jewish Council. In 1943 he was deported to Dachau.

His first months in the concentration camps were spent at hard labor, carrying cement. Then the Germans decided to make use of his professional skill. His duties, however, were not confined to filling teeth. His special function was to salvage gold from the mouths of the Jewish dead. Large numbers perished daily whose corpses could not be disposed of in the crematoria. Dr. Akabas was part of a detail that had the job of collecting and transporting the corpses to a nearby field or forest for concealment. Before burial, Akabas had to remove all false or gold teeth. A sizeable amount of the precious metal was retrieved in this way. Afterwards the bodies would be thrown into a trench. Dr. Akabas winced when he described how "brutally" the dead were handled. They were not laid to rest "carefully," but were cast pell-mell into the grave. Sometimes the tightly packed bodies would be buried standing on their heads.

Dr. Akabas was forced to engage in this ghoulish labor from October 1943 until April 1945. He was the only Jew in the squad because as a rule Jews were not supposed to know the location of mass graves. The SS commander, the notorious Kirsch who was executed in 1946 as a result of the Dachau trials, used to assure him, "*Du Schweine-hund, dich knacke ich ab selber am lezten.*" (You swine, I'll take care of you myself last.) While awaiting the fulfillment of this promise, Akabas was obliged to keep the SS men in good dental repair. Plenty of gold was available for fillings, as well as for brooches and bracelets for the families of the German administrators. A Jewish goldsmith had to hammer the gold into trinkets.

The arrival of American troops kept Kirsch from making good his threat. Akabas was liberated not far from Landsberg in the village of Schwabhausen. A few months later the Central Committee of Liberated Jews urged him to start locating the graves at whose making he had assisted. He received immediate encouragement and help from an American Jewish commanding officer in Landsberg and from Rabbi Rosenberg.

Finding the graves was not an easy task. They had been dug in out of the way places and unfamiliar woods. All save the most recent were overgrown with brush and grass. Fortunately, Dr. Akabas had something besides memory to guide him. In the midst of his monstrous labor some unconscious impulse to atone to the dead in whose desecration he was an involuntary participant must have activated him. Despite the risk of detection, he had made it his business to mark the graves whenever possible.

"I used to think," he said to me, "that perhaps I'd remain alive. It was a chance. So I would put three small white stones on the grave, or a piece of wood that I could recognize. I figured if I survived, I would be able to tell the world about the graves."

This device sounds as if it were lifted from one of Grimm's fairy tales, but the macabre world of the Teutonic *marchen* was real in Nazi Germany, including the witch's oven. As a rule, a grave would contain 700-800 bodies. Seven days would usually be required to complete the extraction of gold.

This gave Dr. Akabas approximately a week in which to find an opportunity to place the stones.

Sometimes, while examining the corpses, Dr. Akabas would recognize the face of an acquaintance, generally a fellow Lithuanian from Kovno or the ghetto. On these occasions, he would secretly note the name and date of death so that the *Yahrzeit* of the victim should not go unhonored. All told, he made a record of over 100 names; not all remained legible because the paper on which he inscribed them grew moldy. Nearly 100 names can still be discerned. These, together with the *Yahrzeit*, have been made public. Surviving relatives know when to say *Kaddish.*

I was curious as to how Dr. Akabas could remember the general location of a grave. The three small white stones might designate a particular spot, but other landmarks were obviously necessary. Besides, there had been times when it had not been possible to place the three stones.

Dr. Akabas told me how he found his first grave. The ways of memory are intricate, so—to make me understand the processes by which a particular spot in the woods remained imprinted on his mind in sufficient detail to enable him to find it a year later— he narrated the following story:

Camp I, a part of Dachau, was situated near Landsberg. The prisoners would rise every morning at 5 o'clock for roll-call in the *Appelplatz* (courtyard) and stand at attention. If a prisoner fell down exhausted, no one could approach to render aid. One morning, a middle-aged man collapsed. This man's fifteen-year-old son, who was in the same group, could make no move to assist his father. When the order to march was given, the boy had to go on with his labor battalion.

The father died several hours later; in the course of the day, his body was brought to a mass grave. There happened to be a shortage of diggers; consequently a detail of men returning from work was called in to help, among them the young son. When the bodies were thrown from the truck to the ground, the boy recognized his father and began to scream "Papa." Akabas tried to quiet him but Kirsch had heard the boy's cries; he walked over and made short shrift of the boy. "Such as you have no fathers," said Kirsch, and clubbed him unconscious.

Because of his intervention, Akabas was given 25 lashes on the spot. For the flogging, Kirsch tore a branch from one of two large trees that stood near the grave. Akabas remembered the trees and the broken bough. The grave near Landsberg was the first one that was restored.

Dr. Akabas told me of another incident which further helps to explain the zeal with which he pursues his self-appointed mission. On one occasion, a Jew assigned to labor near the railroad jumped under a speeding train. He was decapitated. The economical Nazis were not going to let this circumstance deprive them of a possible source of gold. Akabas was ordered to do his usual work. But it was hard to pry open the mouth; the bodiless head rolled on the ground. When Akabas complained to the SS overseer concerning his technical difficulties, he was given a terrific clout.

Dr. Akabas stopped in his story long enough to show me a large scar on his forehead. Then he added, "I had to lie down on the ground with the head under my arm and force it open. But there was no gold. He was an eighteen-year-old boy with his own teeth."

It is these violated dead to whom Dr. Akabas now seeks to give decent Jewish burial. As the project has developed, assistance in locating the graves has been forthcoming from various sources. In addition to the graves discovered through the personal knowledge of Akabas, there are others whose existence has been reported both by Germans and Jews. Even the military government has been instrumental in bringing mass graves to light. The American commander of Landsberg led Akabas to a field some ten kilometers from Landsberg and told him that on the very day the Americans arrived, 1,300 Jews had been shut in a barracks and burned alive. The Americans came too late to stop the murder. They ordered the Germans to throw the bones into a grave. The American commander remembered the place. A memorial cemetery was made.

Despite the precautions of the Nazis, unexpected witnesses keep turning up who testify to the presence of a mass grave in their neighborhood. When such reports are received, the indicated place is opened for examination. Skeletons, bones, tatters of concentration camp uniforms are the corroborative evidence.

The bodies are generally not moved from the places in which they are found. First of all, the rabbis object to the disturbance of the dead as sacrilege. Secondly, disinterment carries with it the possibility of unpleasant incidents. When a mass grave was unearthed near Faehrenwald recently, Germans were ordered to bring the bodies to a new place of burial. In the ensuing excitement clashes between Jews and Germans took place. Jewish DPs have still not learned to view the remains of their massacred kin philosophically.

After the location of a mass grave has been definitely established, the ground is cleared and landscaped. Sometimes the plot is large and level; sometimes the earth is mounded into individual graves, depending on the particular circumstances, and on the number of individuals assumed to be commemorated. Flowers and grass are planted, and fitting monuments are placed.

Every effort is made to collect all possible information as to the identity of the dead. Through a study of the concentration camp records, and with the clues furnished by survivors, the native lands of the dead may often be determined. In Uting, for instance, one can see a grave dedicated to the memory of Jews from Shavli, Lithuania. Other burial places are known to hold the remains of Jews from Poland, or Hungary.

After the work of restoration is completed, the area is enclosed, and the cemetery consecrated according to Jewish rites and with due solemnity. In addition to the official representatives generally present at such occasions, there are delegations from nearby DP camps. The unknown dead have their particular mourners. *Landsleit*, or luckier survivors of the same concentration camp, have a special interest in the ceremony as though seeking in some measure to lift the shroud of anonymity from the corpses.

It is estimated that some 40,000 Jewish victims of the Nazis have been given burial. Many more mass graves remain to be restored. It is an ironic touch that in bombed and devastated Germany, where every stone seems to crumble, among the few fresh, whole places are these new memorial plots to the Jewish dead.

Further evidence of the stubborn Jewish refusal to abandon their sanctuaries to indignity and decay is to be seen in the restored synagogues. Perhaps the most interesting of these is the synagogue in the *Altersheim*, the Home for the Aged, on Iranische Strasse in Berlin. In the *Altersheim*, established by the new Jewish community formed in Berlin since liberation, an assembly hall has been made into a synagogue. I don't know whether a student of synagogue style would be impressed with the aesthetic harmony of the interior. The synagogue has been literally pieced together. It is composed of the parts of former Berlin synagogues destroyed in November 1938, when the Nazis burned and pillaged Jewish houses of worship throughout Germany.

The head of the *Altersheim*, Leo Fiedler, who conceived the plan of constructing this synthetic synagogue, showed me about the place. Each holy vessel and article of furniture had a different origin: the magnificent marble columns had once been part of the synagogue on Oranienburger-strasse; the candelabras came from Lindenstrasse; the ark from still another synagogue. The balustrade had been salvaged from the ancient synagogue on Heidereutergasse. In *A World Passed By*, published in 1933, Marvin Lowenthal described this synagogue: "Hidden from the street (Heidereutergasse) because when it was built in 1712 it was forbidden to face a public thoroughfare, is the old synagogue. Its tall narrow windows have a Gothic air; the women's galleries are banked in two tiers to the west; otherwise it shows the influence of the synagogues of Amsterdam. The Ark curtain was a gift of Frederick William I." Any survivor who had once worshipped on Heidereutergasse could now touch the balustrade in the *Altersheim*.

The Holy Scrolls came from all parts of Germany. They had lain buried in the great Jewish cemetery at Weissensee. Leo Fiedler opened the ark and showed me the miraculously preserved Scrolls wrapped in richly embroidered mantles of velvet and brocade. Burial had also preserved the superb gold and white *Parokhet*, the curtain that hung before the Ark.

The construction of this symbolic synagogue was begun in February 1946; it was dedicated in June 1946. A tablet on the small wall carries the inscription: *"Aus teilen unserer in Jahre 1938 von ruchloser Hand zerstörten und niedergebrannten Gotteshauser hat unser Heimleiter Leo Fiedler, in Liebe zum glauben seiner Väter, diese Synagogue wieder herstellen lassen: Sei sie gewidmet dem Andenken unserer in den Konzentrationslagern ermordeten Schwestern und Brüder."* (Of parts of our houses of worship, destroyed and burned by a ruthless hand in 1938, the leader of our Home, Leo Fiedler, reconstructed this synagogue in devotion to the faith of his fathers. May it be dedicated to the memory of our sisters and brothers murdered in concentration camps.")

T he town of Straubing now has a community of close to 500 Jews, about 85 percent of whom are Polish. Most of them are survivors of Buchenwald and Dachau who were liberated on the roads near Straubing while on the famous forced march from Flossenburg. Before the days of Hitler, several hundred well-to-do German Jews had lived in Straubing. They had built and maintained a synagogue which shared the fate of other German synagogues in 1938. A part of the synagogue that remained undemolished was used as a Hitler Youth Club. A picture of Baldur von Schirach still hung there when the Americans came. One of the first acts of the new Jewish community was to secure the restoration of the synagogue.

Thanks to the cooperation of the American Military Government, the work went quickly. Through the questioning of German civilians, the identities of some of those who had taken part in the destruction of the synagogue was ascertained. They were set to clearing away the rubble. The original plan of the synagogue, drawn by a German architect in 1905, was found, and the rebuilding began. By June 10, 1945, enough progress had been made so that the synagogue could be reconsecrated with Chaplain Lippman of the United States officiating.

The methodical nature of German vandalism made possible the recovery of the Holy Vessels. These were found in a closed case in the German police station of the town. The archives of the old Straubing *Gemeinde* were also discovered. At the time of the burning of the synagogue, prayer books and community records were tossed into the streets by the looters. The Nazis crated these for further reference and shipped them for safe-keeping to Schloss Trautnitz, where they were found.

I went over to look at the synagogue, a modest and unpretentious building with no special character or beauty. Though I did not come during services, I found a few Polish Jews there, members of the newly constituted congregation. We chatted a while, and I asked them the usual questions as to their plans and hopes, and they interviewed me as to certificates for Palestine and visas for America. Then I noticed a large tablet in the front of the synagogue, placed in memory of those who had perished in Zawierce in the massacre of October 10, 1943. I asked why a congregation in Straubing had chosen an obscure Polish town for commemoration. I was told that many of the Jews of the community had originally come from Zawierce. They had no other place in which to remember.

The restored synagogues are, in a sense, mass synagogues. Like the mass graves, they are also collectives—of former sanctuaries and of vanished congregations.

(November 1947)

REBIRTH IN SAN DOMINGO?

Until very recently the average person's knowledge of the Dominican Republic has been most casual. At best one remembered that in 1492 Columbus discovered the island in the West Indies, named by him Hispaniola and later known as Santa Domingo. But except for historic associations and the earnest tourist's assurance that ruins dating back to the white man's first settlement in the New World, as well as the grave of Columbus, could be found in Ciudad Trujillo, there has been little present awareness either of this second-largest island in the Antilles, or of its absolute ruler, Generalissimo Rafael Leonidas Trujillo Molina. A bit of undesirable publicity got bruited about a couple of years ago when some 12,000 black Haitian workers were massacred by the Dominican authorities in a border dispute, but outside of this incident the general public's concern with events in the Dominican Republic has been extremely meager. In 1938, however, Trujillo broke into the news in a big way. He offered asylum to 100,000 refugees of all religions in the Dominican Republic. This offer, alone of its kind and far larger in scope than anything proposed by other governments participating in the conference, created an immediate sensation. It was the most generous gesture made in Evian. The only country which had shown an apparent readiness to make a constructive contribution to the refugee problem had proven to be an island in the West Indies. It was time to find out something about it.

The Dominican Republic, greater in size than Belgium or Holland, occupies the Eastern two-thirds of the island of San Domingo. The Western third is occupied by the Negro republic of Haiti. Though Haiti has the lesser territory, its population is over 2,500,000 in comparison with the Dominican Republic's population of 1,500,000. Whereas Haiti is almost entirely black, the Dominicans represent a racial stock which varies from pure white of Spanish descent to mixtures of Indian and Negro blood. The population is believed to be about one-third Negro. Trujillo's desire for white settlers may in part be explained by his fear of the black republic to the West which may overflow into his less populated and more spacious boundaries. Furthermore, he has vision enough to realize how much an influx of capital and ambitious, competent human material may do to develop the latent resources of his country. In a statement which appeared in the *New York Times* of June 11, 1940, Trujillo made his position clear:

> "Our essential purpose in opening the doors of the country to immigrants is purely humanitarian. Naturally, we also saw in this policy an opportunity to contribute toward the solution of one of the fundamental problems of our country—the sparsity of population in comparison with the extent of our territory.
>
> "The natural increase of our population is quite satisfactory, but the size of our country, with a superabundance of cultivable lands, permits us to look forward to a progressive increase in population such as would place us on the same level of demographic intensity as other neighboring countries of the Antilles."

Nothing was done to implement Trujillo's offer until the formation of the non-sectarian Dominican Republic Settlement Association headed by James N. Rosenberg and Dr. Joseph Rosen who has had considerable experience with colonization problems through his work with Agro-Joint in Russia. Since January 1940, DORSA, as the association is known in brief, has been engaged in the task of laying the groundwork for a refugee settlement in the Dominican Republic. Wartime conditions, with the incident difficulties of transportation, have considerably hampered the work of the Association. Refugees selected for settlement in available European centers have frequently not been able to reach the country. Consequently, the tempo of immigration has so far been slower than anticipated. However, there are at present about 260 people in Sosua, and it is possible to form some notion of what DORSA proposes to achieve.

Sosua is a tract of land consisting of 26,000 acres on the Northern coast of the island. It has been deeded outright to DORSA by Trujillo and is rent-free and tax-free. Verdant and richly wooded, on the shore of the Caribbean, it is a place of great natural beauty. I was told by agricultural experts studying the locality that the soil is fertile and adapted to a diversity of crops. I am in no position to judge these matters, but the green fields and abundance of trees and plants of various kinds on the surrounding hills certainly give the impression of land which would generously repay cultivation. As a matter of fact a considerable variety of vegetables other than the usual tropical yucca, yams, beans and corn are already being grown there.

Settlers for Sosua are chosen in countries of Europe from which it is possible to secure emigration. The range of choice has been shrinking as the war develops. For instance, 250 prospective settlers were chosen in Amsterdam. Only 37 of the 250 were actually able to arrive. Healthy young people, of sturdy physique, and preferably with some agricultural training, are chosen. Proper selection of the prospective settler is an important element because obviously unless the individual is physically vigorous, and has an aptitude for agricultural life, his attempt to become a farmer in a subtropical climate is foredoomed to failure. Some previous agricultural training has been made possible occasionally through the agricultural training camps for the economic redistribution of Jews which have been conducted in Germany. Each settler pledges himself to become a Dominican citizen and remain as a permanent cultivator of the soil. Dominican citizenship is available after two years of residence plus the cultivation of land. This provision is an essential one as the Dominican government does not want a fluctuating population of immigrants who seek only temporary asylum.

When a group of settlers arrives in the Dominican Republic, it goes immediately to Sosua where the single men are housed in newly built barracks and the women and married couples are put up in small cottages which are on the property. The barracks and these cottages, together with some larger cottages for visitors and the administration, form a reception center. The newcomers spend between three and six months there, in the space of which they are expected to become acclimated and to receive further training in various branches of agriculture. They are organized into groups which get practice in gardening, dairying, cattle-raising, etc. The work is rotated so that it is assumed that after the initial training period, each individual will be familiar with the various departments of agricultural work, and proficient in the branches of his choice. There are a community kitchen and dining room for the men living in the barracks. The couples who have individual dwellings are expected to take in two settlers for whom the housewife cooks as well as for her own family. During this preparatory period all expenses are provided by DORSA, including ten cents a day for pocket money. When a settler feels that he is prepared to stand on his own, he is given a homestead. That is to say, he gets a bungalow with eight to ten acres of land, and whatever initial equipment of tools and livestock is required to enable him to farm his land. This represents an outlay of about $1,000 per settler—a sum which it is assumed will be repaid after 20 years. It is assumed that the homestead itself will provide the actual means of sustenance. For additional income, it is expected that settlers will join in some cooperative effort such as cheese-making, or poultry-raising. The proceeds from the sale of these products will provide capital for those engaged in the work. The ambition of DORSA is to settle people on homesteads as rapidly as possible and keep the main grounds as a constantly functioning reception and training center for new arrivals.

The Association also hopes that industries will develop around the agricultural project, so as to make feasible the integration of 100,000 people, Jews and non-Jews, into the economy of the Dominican Republic. The growing of bamboo for tropical furniture, large-scale cheese manufacture, and boat-building are some of the allied occupations which have been mentioned as growing naturally around the nucleus of the first settlement in Sosua, which represents only one colonization point in the island. Eventually to absorb the suggested 100,000 settlers, colonization will have to take place in land adjacent to Sosua, or in other sections of the Dominican Republic. Trujillo has just announced the grant of an additional 500,000 acres for settlement. Whatever else may be lacking, there will apparently be no scarcity of land.

At present, all this is in embryo. So far there are fewer than 300 settlers in Sosua, of whom one-fifth are women, and it would be presumptuous to pass judgment. One can only give impressions. When I arrived at Sosua in the middle of January, I was startled like everyone else at the loveliness of the place. One man connected with the Association remarked to me that DORSA could manage with a less picturesque setting, and I felt that he didn't want a visitor to be lulled into forgetting the real difficulties of pioneer colonization by the blandishments of a tropical moon over the Caribbean.

The barracks are far more attractive than the drab name would imply. They are newly built in staggered formation so as to benefit from any sea breezes that may be blowing. The windows within the barracks are also staggered so as to allow for the maximum of ventilation. Apparently, there has been intelligent planning of the details of construction. The cottages in which couples live looked cozy and comfortable—far less primitive than I expected. Each one is provided with a porch on which I saw people resting and reading after work hours.

The settlers looked young and husky; the average age is about 26. The broad-shouldered, bronzed chaps whom I saw bore no visible signs of the experiences that they had been through in Europe. The American agricultural expert—a gentile—who was also visiting Sosua for the first time, remarked with astonishment on how little like "refugees" these young men and women looked. There was no cowed nor beaten air about them.

When I was there, 12 settlers had already gone out to their own homesteads. The bungalows had been built by native labor, as the Association wishes to speed up the process of independent settlement as much as possible. Actual building construction is the only form of labor for which native workers are hired; everything else is done by the settlers.

I visited one of the homesteads occupied by a middle-aged German couple with two young sons. The husband had been a successful cattle dealer in Germany; the wife had been accustomed to a farmer's life. Their cottage was spick and span bearing every mark of a competent housewife's desire to adjust herself intelligently to circumstances whether in an apple orchard along the Rhine or under a mango tree in the West Indies. She was trying to adorn her tropical home with lace curtains and embroideries which probably had been salvaged from Germany. There was no gas or electricity, nor anything that we know as "modern conveniences," but in the kitchen hung a white jar marked *zwiebel*, and I wondered whether it had accompanied her on her flight from Hitler as a kind of talisman. She apologized that she had to keep her closet open—otherwise the humidity mildewed the clothes; then she showed me proudly the wooden chairs made by her skillful sixteen-year-old son. Her older son was working in the garden. She and her hale-looking husband seemed contented, happy to have escaped from the horrors of a concentration camp, and ready to work hard and live frugally in any friendly environment.

Another homesteader that I saw was feeding his pigs. He was engaged in pig-raising, and his stock was apparently thriving. It must be borne in mind in this connection that these 12 homesteaders represent the best equipped and most energetic of the immigrants. The fact that within a comparatively short time they were already on their own small farms is evidence of this. To what extent these 12 are representative of the remainder is a matter of conjecture.

I had a chance to get a bird's-eye view of all the settlers together at a dramatic reading given in the entertainment barrack on a Saturday evening. It was a German reading by a Viennese actor. The audience of over 100 young people listened intently to declamations of Goethe, Heine and other German classics. There was also a humorous part to the program. I heard a number of grim jokes about Hitler and less grim ones about the immigrants' status—a kind of specific brand of "refugee" humor was apparently in the process of development. One of the jokes, for instance, poked fun at the needy refugee who boasts of his former wealth and station. Finally his small poodle is asked, "And what were you in the good old days?", to which the poodle replies, "I was a St. Bernard." The audience, well-dressed, attractive, seemed to be having a good time. From the eagerness with which the young people listened, one felt that "culture" and intellectual diversion were needs for which provision would have to be made. Looking at the European group, listening to the German chatter, it was hard to believe that one would soon step into a bland, tropical night and go to sleep under a mosquito net.

As is to be expected, all is not a bed of roses. One cannot transplant

Europeans of various previous occupational origins into a tropical climate without a struggle of adaptation. Nor will a former lawyer or accountant be transformed into an agricultural worker capable of hard physical labor from early morning until nightfall without some backaches and heartaches. Consequently, I was not surprised at hearing stories of dissatisfaction with living conditions on the part of some settlers. The complaints I heard were the inevitable ones arising among people living in close quarters under trying circumstances. Some people objected to the type of work assigned—one man was "allergic" to kitchen work; several of the women had gotten into each other's hair over the pots and pans; some objected to the communal fare. As one wag put it, there were two schools of gastronomy: one had learned how to cook macaroni in an Italian concentration camp, the other, in a German one. Consequently, there were clashes. All these grumblings could be dismissed as part of the business of being human. Nor was it to be wondered that a few of the settlers wished to leave, having found the life too rigorous. A number of misfits were bound to form part of any group.

I was in no real position to judge the climate. When I was there—in January—it was pleasantly warm in the daytime if one kept out of the mid-day sun, and cool enough for a blanket at night. That, however, is the Dominican winter. Accounts vary as to the months of March to November. Some Americans have assured me that the days, provided one kept in the shade, are not intolerable, and that the nights are comfortable. Others, on the other hand, were equally emphatic in their statements that the heat was staggering. One thing, however, is certain: field work in the spring and summer months must be extremely wearing.

The health of the settlers has been good up to now. There have been some cases of malaria, but not enough to constitute a problem. At any rate, in the Dominican Republic, there are no dangerous pestilences, such as yellow fever or elephantiasis, which may be found in Haiti.

A more serious problem is the shortage of women. The proportion of single women in the settlement was something like one woman to ten men at the time of my visit. The Association is attempting to remedy this situation by securing visas for sisters, cousins, or brides of the settlers.

People have asked me, "Are the settlers happy?" There is no occasion for exuberance in the fate which drove these human beings across the ocean to an unknown island in the Caribbean, and I felt no glow in the air. In fact, I quite definitely felt the reverse. A refugee, whom I met in Ciudad Trujillo, the capital of the Dominican Republic, said to me: *"siedeln muss man mit Begeisterung."* (One must colonize with inspiration.) Experience has shown this to be more than a phrase. Colonization, like genius, may be nine-tenths perspiration but without that final one-tenth of "inspiration" the whole does not function. The comparison with Zionist pioneering cannot be waived. In Palestine I have seen living conditions in some of the settlements—outposts in the wilderness—far more primitive than anything I observed in Sosua. The barracks and bungalows of Sosua, simple as these are, would still seem luxurious to many a *chalutz*, and the rich soil and abundant vegetation would appear Utopian to one of our classic drainers of swamps and irrigators of the desert.

I could not help remembering the rapture with which a girl in a small *kvutza* in the Emek once brought me a radish, saying, "These are our first radishes," as though this radish sprung from Palestine earth were something unique and precious. This high sense of purpose, of exaltation, I felt at no moment, neither while in Sosua, nor while discussing the project with many people in the Dominican Republic. I stress this fact not because I believe that every human being must live in an idealistic fervor, but because I wonder whether a hard pioneering project is possible without such fervor. It is not enough to erect a homestead; one must build a home. Obviously, there can be no sense of home-coming now, when a settler arrives in the West Indies. It would be foolish to expect a refugee from a concentration camp to burst into a *hora*, or its equivalent, when he spots the shore of Puarto Plata of Ciudad Trujillo, as a *chalutz* does when he sees Mount Carmel in the distance. The crucial question is: can such a sense of home be created in the future? The eking out of an existence for oneself is not enough incentive for so complete a psychic and physical revolution as is implied in the transportation of a white man to the environment strange in climate, race, language, culture, of an island in the West Indies. Unless profound emotional ties are created, there is no reason for maintaining the effort of acclimatization as soon as the pressure is released. We know that when Hitler is defeated, and the world resumes a human aspect, immigration to Palestine will proceed with even greater impetus. The drive, beyond the immediate exigency, is there. The fate of such a settlement as Sosua, however, is largely conjectural.

The Sosua project should not be confused with a territorialist venture. Territorialism implies specifically Jewish colonization in such a manner that the Jewish character of the settlement will be encouraged and maintained—Zion outside of Palestine. Such is not the case in Sosua. The Dominican Republic Settlement Association is avowedly non-sectarian. Just before I left, preparations were being made to receive a group of Czechs. The Dominican Government has stressed its desire for refugees who will become in every sense an integral part of the country, in short, 100 percent Dominicans. In fact, resentment is felt towards Jews who merely wait for affidavits to enter the United States, and all immigration, save to the colony of Sosua, has been stopped. In view of the character of refugee needs, many of the settlers in Sosua will probably be Jews, but there is no question here of forming a purely Jewish settlement—let alone a Jewish territory.

The recent conversations between Trujillo and Otto of Austria in regard to settling Catholic refugees are another indication of how much expectation there may be of large-scale Jewish settlement. One cannot even be too sure that Jews will predominate, should a sizeable influx of refugees become possible. Trujillo's negotiations with Otto are a straw in the wind. The Spanish Loyalists, of whom there are 1,500 in San Domingo, are viewed with suspicion as potential revolutionaries, or at any rate possible opponents of a dictatorial regime. Presumably, Otto's Catholics are regarded as a politically more reliable element. Should it be possible for Trujillo to secure a sufficiently large number of politically irreproachable settlers of his own faith, who knows to what proportions the Jewish percentage in the refugee settlement might dwindle.

Any plan which proposes to save refugees from the hell of Hitler's Europe merits support. No reasonable prospect of rescue can be dismissed. So far, the grandiose schemes for 100,000 settlers have boiled down to fewer than 300 souls. However, DORSA with the aid of interested governments, hopes to increase the flow of immigration rapidly. There can be little question that Trujillo is at present anxious for settlers, and that his professions may now be taken in good faith. His word is law, and his administration and people will be sympathetic to the venture in the precise measure that he is. Of course, a dictator's policy is subject to caprice, but one can hardly ask for guarantees in the present world. What will be the future attitude of the ruler or the native population should a sizeable community succeed in establishing itself and prospering, is not a question of immediate concern to the man who is fleeing death or torture.

Assuming that it will be possible to increase the tempo of immigration, Sosua can in no sense be viewed as a rival of Palestine. It does not pretend to solve the Jewish problem or to build a Jewish future. If it is successful, it will give some Jewish refugees a chance to re-establish their broken lives and to become good Dominicans, far from the great current of European and American civilization. Such a prospect fails to fill me with enthusiasm, but then I live in the United States, not in Germany.

(February 1941)

JEWISH INDIANS IN MEXICO

The gods have not left Mexico. Despite the confiscation of church property, the anti-clericalist edicts, the revolutionary propaganda, Mexico is a land of believers. Anyone who has seen a peon devoutly trudging up a pyramid surmounted by a cross to bring flowers to the Virgin, feels this. Perhaps the children studying in the great modern public school "Revolution," erected by the government, have been emancipated from the grip of the cleric, but no one who has watched an Indian woman, with a child at her breast, praying to the Madonna, can doubt that here is faith at its simplest.

It is piety, pure, uncritical, completely credulous, completely resigned, more impressive in its quiet, motionless grace than the turbulent ecstasy of the Negro. The gods of miracle and compassion, of kindness and omnipotence, have not been exorcized from the poor Indian's needy heart by rationalist slogans. They are still there—the idols of the Aztec, the saints of the church; and, unexpectedly enough, Jehovah too may be found in the pantheon.

Tourist guide books make no mention of the Jewish Indians. There are only 3,000 of them scattered throughout Mexico. A poor and ignorant lot, with no shrine of gold and alabaster, of silver and obsidian, to attract the average sightseer. It was only after I had stood before countless rose-bedecked altars hallowed to the Virgin and had marvelled alike at the glory of the church and the beauty of the worshippers, that I learned of my Indian brethren. Their existence has been known for some years, but every Jewish journalist who comes to Mexico discovers them anew. The Mexican Jewish community, itself for the most part only some 20 years in the land, has been taking a protective interest in this strange branch of the tree of Israel, and now a visit to the Indian Jews has become a part of the itinerary of any visitor with specific Jewish interests.

The Jewish Indians are in part descendants of Marranos who came to Mexico with the Spaniards at the beginning of the sixteenth century. Most of the Marranos were eventually assimilated (two presidents of the

Republic, Porfirio Diaz and Francisco Madero, were of Marrano stock) but some remained Jews. The Jewish Indians date from these Marranos who intermarried with the natives and converted them to Judaism. These Indians, too, led a Marrano existence practicing their Judaism secretly and suffering the persecution of the Inquisition when discovered. The first *auto da fé* in America took place in Mexico in 1574. Not until 1910, the time of the Madero revolution, were the Indians able to avow their Judaism openly.

When they were brought to light, they were found to be observing a curious mixture of pagan, Catholic and Jewish rites. They knew no Hebrew; their children were uncircumcised. During the past few years, the Mexican Jewish community has taken them under its wing. A few volunteer teachers have been instructing them; and now some Hebrew words and prayers have been introduced into their services. They have been taught to unscramble Jewish from Catholic holidays. In short, they are being "enlightened," but, as the gentleman who took me to their synagogue put it, they are no longer as "original" as they were in their pristine state.

The barrenness of the Indian "synagogue," if such it could be called, was startling after the elaborate beauty of the Catholic churches I had been seeing. Nothing but a small, dingy hall on the outskirts of the city, with neither pomp nor grandeur to comfort the believing heart. A plain room with pale blue walls and rough wooden benches. A little table stood in the front of the room instead of a pulpit. No holy scrolls, no velvet curtains, no candelabras—none of the austere ceremonial permitted to Judaism. The sole evidence indicating that we were in a holy place was a large sign inscribed in Hebrew letters: *Shma Israel, adonai elohenu, adonai echad*, with a *Magen David* on each end. And then, in the more familiar Spanish, hung a placard: *Silencio en la casas de Dios* (Silence in the house of God). So it was the house of God!

I looked at the congregation. There were about 25 women, 15 men, and perhaps a dozen children, most of them typical Indians dressed in sarapes and shawls. Here and there one saw a face that looked Spanish, perhaps Semitic. An Indian in overalls entered and carefully unwrapped his Bible from its protective newspaper. An Indian woman courteously handed me a Bible. It was in Spanish, published by the American Bible Society for distribution by missionaries, and consequently contained both the Old and New Testaments.

The "rabbi," a streetcar conductor on weekdays, wore neither robes nor *talis*. The sole token of the dignity of his office was a purple skullcap. The service began with a Spanish hymn, *Zion bendita seas* (Zion be blessed) sung to a popular Salvation Army tune, and followed by the *Hatikvah* in Hebrew. "Our hope is not lost" chanted my Indian brothers with fervor.

The rabbi's sermon, in Spanish, was obviously addressed to the

American visitors as well as to the congregants. The rabbi offered his followers a simple task. European Jews, American Jews, he explained to his listeners, had lost their faith in God. It was the mission of the Indian Jew to give back faith to the Jew and the world.

The poor handful before him bowed reverently. The mission, always the mission, even here amid these worshippers.

Possibly in deference to the presence of strangers, the service was taken over by the most influential member of the congregation, the head of the Marranos, a successful lawyer in Mexico City, obviously a man of consequence and standing. Not knowing Spanish, I could not follow his sermon, but with the aid of my guide I managed to get the drift of his remarks. He covered considerable territory ranging from the Babylonians to "Dr. Theodor Herzl," interspersing his comments with Bible texts. We turned to Jeremiah, Ezekiel, Isaiah and Malachi. The details of the learned exegesis escaped me, but recurrently came the prophetic words all Jews could understand: *Asi dice Jehovah* (Thus spoke the Lord). And there were other words too whose meaning there was no mistaking: *Pueblo Israel*—I knew as well as the shawled Indian woman that he spoke of the "people of Israel." And "diaspora." Perhaps I understood that better. There were still other old friends running through the discourse: *anti-Semita; anti-Zionista;* "Hitler"; "Ford".

I looked again at the congregation. Simple Indians surely. They could have been bearing roses to the Virgin of Guadalupe; they could have been dancing in the dawn in the religious fiesta at Los Remedios; they could have been kneeling amid lit tapers and the smell of incense in a great vaulted church whose beauty offered the heaven their miserable lives desired; they could have had music and pageantry and the refuge of splendor, denied them otherwise. What strange power kept them here, in a bare room, accepting the Jewish destiny—*anti-Semitisma*; "Hitler"; *Dice el Senor Jehovah*.

Splendor was here too, but it was abstract, intangible—*la splendor* of Jerusalem, described in a Spanish hymn superbly sung by a youth whose voice would have been the fortune of any cantor. The service concluded with the same Salvation Army chant with which it had begun.

An old Indian woman came up to me and shook my hand; *Shabat Shalom*, she said.

I saw the Jewish Indians once again in the little village of Venta Prieta, a few hours' ride beyond Mexico City. A group of us had been invited to dinner at one of the Indian homes, thanks to the courtesy of their chief. Venta Prieta had about 12 Jewish families and a number of Catholic Indians, forming a small community. It was a wretched place. A poor and dirty Indian village, though no doubt there are some still poorer and dirtier. The homes were miserable one-room hovels in which the prolific Indian family slept, ate and dwelt. Pigs wallowed in the surrounding mud. The children were dirty, half-naked, many with sore eyes. A few huts had crosses to distinguish the Christian dwellings from those of the Jews. Except for this mark, there was no telling the Catholic and Jewish Indians apart.

Dinner was going to be served in the home of the "rich man" of the community. He actually boasted more than one room, in addition to sleeping quarters; he had a "parlor" furnished with chairs, a table and lace curtains. When we arrived the chairs were all piled in the courtyard while the floor was being freshly scrubbed for the expected company. Great preparations were obviously afoot. The man of the house had gone to the neighboring village to fetch water. The local supply was too filthy even for cooking, let alone drinking. All the women and children were hustling about, preparing the banquet.

We walked around the village to give our hosts an opportunity to finish their preparations. It was hot and dusty. I trudged about in the dirt trying to locate the "Jewishness" I had come to see. A sow and her litter guzzled filth energetically. A squalid and depressing place! Then we were shown the community *shul*. It was naturally even smaller than the one in Mexico City—just a little room with a few benches. But it was clean, a clean place amid uncleanliness. Outside the pigs grunted, but inside was sanctuary. There was a Bible on the table, a sign with a *Magen David*, as in the Mexico City synagogue, and a blackboard with a Hebrew prayer. On the wall was the painstaking handiwork of two Indian boys. One had drawn a map of Palestine, neatly coloring and lettering it, so that all could clearly see the holy coast line and the names of the sacred cities. The other boy—the artist—had created an elaborate composition with Moses, the Ten Commandments, and the Lion of Judah helping out. These were the only adornments in the room. The Law had found its way to an Indian village, and the geography of Zion was being studied by a few, semi-literate Indian peasants.

By the time we came back, dinner was ready. It was being served in the courtyard, where a table had been placed. Stone tubs of wash stood about. There were no pigs in this yard, but many dogs, scrawny cats and chickens wandered underfoot. And the flies were legion. I surveyed the feast with terror. I had met flies, God knows, but these were Mexican flies, bearing typhoid and dysentery, as every American tourist has been forewarned. However, to decline the professed hospitality was out of the question. Judaism, I felt, was about to claim another martyr.

It was a real Indian banquet, somewhat tempered for the weak stomachs of the strangers. Our party of five sat down with the men of the household. The only Indian woman at the table was an ancient dame, obviously the matriarch of the tribe. The other women and children were busy serving and baking tortillas, fresh hot batches of which kept appearing. The fare was native; chicken with *molle*, beans with pungent cheese, platters of young fresh corn, and endless heaps of tortillas which were used as spoons by our hosts. All this was washed down by large draughts of *pulke*, the national intoxicant made from the cactus. The bond of *gefilte fish* was absent. This was really alien territory, despite the *Magen David* which our host wore in his lapel.

The children came out to survey the strangers who were being dined in such style. We ate silently and industriously. Conversation came hard even for those of our party who knew Spanish. I marveled at the generosity of this family which had expended so much time, effort and money on a group of curious tourists. Or were we, so different in every way, more than tourists? Did they feel any kinship? It was hard to tell. We smiled at the women, trying to register gratitude, but communication was difficult.

The old woman who sat with us had a history. Her father had been scalded to death in boiling oil for "Judaizing." This had happened before 1910, when Judaism was still proscribed. We sat together, American Jews, Mexican Jews, the Indian woman whose father had perished for the faith, the Indian men—smiling occasionally at each other and eating tortillas.

It was time to go. Everybody came out to watch our departure. There were children of all sizes—obviously babies came every year without benefit of birth control. We wanted to say something pleasant to the young woman with the smallest baby in her arms—a black-eyed, little Indian boy. We asked through our interpreter as one asks all women: "What is the baby's name?"

And the Indian mother answered: "Israel."

(October 1940)

THE EMPTY CHAIR

D espite a few wavering attempts, I did not succeed in wangling a ticket for the opening session of the Constituent Assembly of the New State of Israel (held February 14, 1949). Perhaps it's sour grapes, but whenever the acrimonious discussion as to the worthies who did not get in, and the unworthies who did, starts in my vicinity, I take comfort in the reflection that I shared the great moment with Israel over the radio.

There were three of us listening: an established Israeli lady, practically a *sabra* whose husband had merited a ticket; my neighbor, a recent DP whose husband and two sons had been murdered by the Nazis, and myself, an American journalist. What with the exaltation of the hour plus the aggravation of not being among the happy few on the spot, we sat taut and silent, waiting for the broadcast.

I had been wondering about the one authentic Israeli in our midst. She did not see eye-to-eye with the powers that be; much in recent events displeased her: taxes, housing, hordes of immigrants. And sometimes listening to her sharp comments on the blessings of statehood, I had permitted myself to speculate as to what this consummation, which was also a victory for much she opposed, would mean to her.

My doubts had been silly. From the second the broadcast began, it was she who became its medium. Of course, we all had the suitable historical emotions. The greatness of the hour was not wasted. Hadn't I written a host of articles on the need for a Jewish state? But the lady with the wrong politics held this hour more firmly than any of us. I could only touch its fringes with abstract phrases. For me it was the first time in 2,000 years, for her it was the first time in her life.

At the strains of *Hatikvah* she rose, her eyes brimming with tears, and we followed her lead, standing solemnly around the dining room table. I envied her terribly. She hadn't done anything about which we grow lyrical in the States. She hadn't drained any marshes, or irrigated deserts, or spent one day on a kibbutz. She had merely lived in the land, and raised a family, and suffered the good times and the bad, and now she would know what it all meant much more surely than we who had dreamt on the outside.

The refugee felt even more out of it; she hadn't even written articles or made speeches. She sat as a guest. But when the broadcaster began describing the appearance of the hall, and came to the empty black chair placed to commemorate the six million, my refugee neighbor looked up. She began to weep, and I knew that she had crossed the threshold on which she had been waiting uncertainly. The chair had admitted her into the Assembly and the festival. Always there would be the chair to point to if anyone spoke disparagingly of new *olim* (immigrants) or commented on the lateness of their coming.

In the evening, my neighbor's chum came to visit. They had been born in the same Lithuanian town, only the chum had gone to Palestine as a *halutza* (pioneer) long, long before the six million. She too had heard the ceremony over the radio, and 30 years of memories had brimmed over into the listening. And again I felt how much more 30 years were than 2,000.

Now, on the day of the Constituent Assembly, she was recalling those early, crazy days in her kibbutz: how hard one had worked, how little one had slept, how bad the food had been, especially when it was her turn to cook in the communal kitchen.

Once she had made a *pflaumen tzimes* (a plum pudding) such as they used to prepare in Lithuania. Yes, my neighbor remembered the specialty. Her family used to enjoy it every Friday, but then my neighbor had been an accomplished housewife unlike the friend who had up and gone to Palestine. For a dreadful moment the sabbath table rose before our eyes, but it vanished mercifully in the kibbutznik's account of the *pflaumen tzimes* she had concocted. It had been such a flop that the kibbutz had made a *rakevet*. "What was a *rakevet*?" we wanted to know.

It was a train of dishes. When a dish was particularly vile, everybody in the dining hall made a train of the plates and propelled them in the direction of the kitchen where the hapless cook listened to the din. Besides that, they banged on the table with the cutlery. Afterwards, all, including the chastened cook, danced the *hora* late into the night.

I managed to secure a ticket for the last session of the Constituent Assembly when the President was inaugurated. We drove up to Jerusalem on a blue-green day past hills bright with anemones and the bloom of the almond tree. We made the ascent to the Holy City and the holy hour in a car which broke down once and had a puncture, but we got there and heard the *shofar* blown.

When I returned to Tel Aviv my neighbor wanted to know all about it. I told her as best I could and we drank a little sweet wine to President Weizmann. "And to Ben-Gurion," added my neighbor. "Yes," I said, "certainly to Ben-Gurion."

Then she asked: "How is the chair?" I had forgotten about the chair.

"The chair. . . ," she began, but I remembered in time. The truth was that I had no clear recollection of it, so I said: "Well, you know, just a black chair."

My neighbor was not satisfied. "Some day," she said, "I will go to Jerusalem and look at that chair."

II.
OF
ISRAEL

Historical Note for Section 2

Though political Zionism as an organized movement began at the end of the nineteenth century, Jewish association with Palestine had remained unbroken since the dispersion. The Return to Zion occupied a central role in the Jewish liturgy. In the Middle Ages Jewish communities could be found in Jerusalem, Safed, Nablus and Hebron. Religious Jews never stopped making pilgrimages to these holy cities. In Jerusalem Jews maintained an almost continuous presence. In the nineteenth century they became a majority of the city's population and have so remained.

After the Russian pogroms of 1881 the Lovers of Zion established small Jewish settlements in Palestine that failed to prosper. In 1897 Theodor Herzl launched the Zionist movement by convening the First Zionist Congress in Basle, Switzerland. The objective of the movement was the establishment of "a home for the Jewish people secured by public law." Young Jewish pioneers left their native countries to found cooperatives and villages on wasteland purchased by the Jewish National Fund from the Turkish government that then ruled Palestine and from Arab landowners.

In 1917, during World War I, the British government issued the Balfour Declaration, formally undertaking to establish a Jewish National Home in Palestine. After the defeat of Turkey, Great Britain assumed the Mandate for Palestine in 1922. Britain partitioned the country and set up Transjordan (later Jordan) on approximately three-fourths of the area originally encompassed by the Balfour Declaration. Considerable emigration into Palestine from neighboring Arab states, also established after the liberation of the Middle East from Turkish sovereignty, ensued.

During the thirties and forties Arab antagonism resulted in British edicts that effectively barred Jewish immigration, despite the desperate need of Jewish refugees from Hitler to find a haven. The end of World War II marked the beginning of the Jewish struggle against the Mandatory Power to "open the gates of Palestine" to Jewish survivors. Continued disturbances in Palestine as well as the plight of Jewish survivors led to the passage of the Partition Resolution on November 19, 1947 by the United

Nations. According to its terms Palestine was to be again partitioned between Jews and Arabs in the area West of the Jordan. The Jews accepted the compromise despite the further reduction of territory and proclaimed the State of Israel in their sector in May 1948. Six Arab states, instead of setting up a Palestinian state in their sector, attacked Israel. In the War of Liberation Israel repulsed the attack; however, Jordan captured the Old City of Jerusalem and the West Bank, while Egypt occupied Gaza. One result of the war was the flight of 600,000 Arabs from the Israeli sector to the West Bank and Jordan.

In June 1967 the Arab states again massed to destroy Israel. In a lightning pre-emptive strike Israel recaptured the West Bank and Gaza, re-united Jerusalem and occupied Sinai. During the sixties Arab demands changed from stress on Arab refugees to calls for a Palestinian state. United Nations Resolution 242, adopted at the close of the 1967 war, had specified a just solution for the problem of "Arab refugees" and the right of the states of the area to live in "secure and recognized boundaries." In a carefully drafted wording, the Resolution also called for the withdrawal of Israel from occupied territories not, it should be noted, from the occupied territories.

In the surprise attack of the Yom Kippur War in October 1973, Egyptian troops crossed the Suez Canal and Syria moved into the Golan. After heavy fighting the Egyptian advance was stopped; Israeli troops succeeded in crossing to the West bank of the canal and in encircling the Egyptian Third Army; the Syrians were driven back toward Damascus. At this point the Security Council intervened to impose a cease-fire. In subsequent negotiations Israel agreed to withdraw her forces from the West bank of the canal and from the strategic Mitla and Gidi passes in the Sinai. A buffer zone under UN supervision was established. A disengagement agreement was also signed with Syria. Jordan, as well as Iraq, Morocco and Libya were among the belligerents.

In May 1977, the Labor Coalition, first headed by David Ben-Gurion, was after 30 years of rule replaced by the Likud Bloc with Menachem Begin as Prime Minister. In the same year Egyptian President Sadat began the peace initiative that culminated in the Camp David agreements. These re-affirmed the principles of United Nations Resolution 242.

WHY PARTITION?

There is a strong likelihood that the coming twenty-second Zionist Congress (held in Basle in December 1946) will be another "Partition Congress." That is to say the question of a Jewish state in a part of Palestine will probably be among the acute issues before the delegates. This has resulted in a re-alignment of forces; parties are going on record in their official platforms as to whether they oppose or accept partition; Zionist leaders are committing themselves *pro* and *con,* and Zionist meetings are being prodded to make their sentiments known so that the "entrenched bureaucracy" will not be able to betray the will of the Jewish masses.

In view of the charged atmosphere it is therefore not premature to discuss the question of partition, despite the fact that no formal British offer envisaging the establishment of any kind of Jewish state has been made. In the present deadlock, the Jewish Agency has openly advanced the compromise formula of a "viable Jewish State in an adequate portion of Palestine" as a basis for discussion. It is this formula which has precipitated the familiar charges of "treason" and "timidity," raised by both the ideological opponents of partition and the political adversaries of the Jewish Agency. Though we have no assurance that partition will actually serve as a springboard for further negotiations with Great Britain, the fact that Zionist bodies are being urged to define their position and to pledge their representatives to definite stands before the Congress indicates the need for re-examining this question.

It should be superfluous to state that every member of the Agency Executive in Paris who voted for the partition formula did so with a full sense of the immense and bitter sacrifice of Jewish rights implicit in the proposal. The legitimate claims of Zionism can only be fulfilled through the establishment of a Jewish commonwealth in the Palestine of the Balfour Declaration. Those who clamor that partition is unjust, that it is a patent betrayal of Jewish rights, that it is contrary to international covenants, are knocking down a straw man. It is all that and more. None know this as well as the political representatives entrusted with the burden of defending Jewish interests before the Mandatory Power. The only relevant question is whether better terms than partition can be secured in the present crisis. The situation both of the *Yishuv* and of the Jews of Europe is too grave to admit of a rhetorical maximalism which has no prospect of realization within the predictable future.

It may be salutary to review the partition debate of nine years ago in the light of subsequent development. In July 1937, the Royal Commission, dispatched to Palestine as a result of the Arab riots, recommended that the Mandate should terminate and that Palestine should be divided into three parts, in which there would be set up Arab and Jewish states and a British enclave to protect the Christian holy places. The report expressly excluded a Palestinian State. "In these circumstances to maintain that Palestinian citizenship has any moral meaning is a mischievous pretense ... Manifestly the problem cannot be solved by giving either the Arabs or the Jews all they want . . . But while neither race can justly rule all Palestine, we see no reason why, if it were practicable, each race should not rule part of it."

The report then proceeded to point out the advantages accruing to all parties if this plan were adopted. The Arabs would be delivered from the fear of being "swamped" by the Jews. The sanctity of places dear to Christian sentiment would be inviolate. And Jews would be enabled in the fullest sense to call their National Home their own. "For it converts it into a Jewish State. Its citizens will be able to admit as many Jews into it as they themselves believe can be absorbed. They will attain the primary objective of Zionism — a Jewish nation, planted in Palestine, giving nationals the same status in the world as other nations give theirs. They will cease at last to lead a 'minority' life."

The proposal of the Royal Commission met with a general hue and cry. Jews protested; Arabs protested. The best the British press could say for the plan was to characterize it bleakly as a "counsel of despair." It must be indicated, however, that Arab clamor was largely for the record. Such a notorious philo-Arab as the Honorable St. J. Philby, head of the British Political Mission to Central Arabia, hailed the report as a "substantial verdict in their (Arab) favors." And an equally ardent champion of the Arab cause, Major Harold Temperley, urged "the execution to the letter" of the Royal Commission's report. So that it was amply demonstrated that it was chiefly Jews who had good reason to protest the further amputation and fragmentation of their already truncated Homeland.

And yet, even in the, comparatively speaking, halcyon days of 1937, the immediate rejection of partition did not appear a simple or clear-cut move to the Zionist world. Despite the tragedy of further despoiling the already despoiled area of the Jewish National Home, despite the proposal's obvious violation of Britain's international commitments, the Zionist Congress which met that summer did not permit itself the luxury of an outright rejection of partition. Every Zionist remembers the passionate and solemn debate which shook the entire movement in 1937. The outcome of the discussions was the resolution adopted by the Congress in one of the most crucial votes taken by any Zionist Congress since the historic rejection of Uganda. The Congress declared the particular partition scheme presented as unacceptable, but empowered the Executive to enter into negotiations with Great Britain in regard to the establishment of a Jewish state under other terms. The result of such negotiations was then to be brought before a newly elected Congress for consideration and decision.

We e know what happened before that next Congress could convene. The world situation deteriorated so rapidly that Chamberlain, as part of the "appeasement" strategy of the period, issued the White Paper of May 1939. Within two years the "counsel of despair" of the British had been transformed into the "counsel *to* despair" to the Jews—the despair this time to be exclusively Jewish. The talk of a Jewish state was abandoned. Instead there was to be an Arab state with a permanent Jewish minority, amounting to not more than one-third of the population. The 1939 Zionist Congress was no longer in a position to discuss any type of Jewish state. It had to content itself with denouncing the annihilation of Zionism begun by the British in the panic engendered by Hitler's designs in Europe and the Middle East.

The war stopped the formal process of liquidation, though the British insistence on barring Palestine against Jewish refugees continued. It is unnecessary to rehearse the all too familiar details of this terrible and infamous chapter. But even the Allied victory brought no abatement in the British effort to repudiate the responsibilities of the Mandate.

The Bevin government impudently rejected the unanimous recommendations of the recent Anglo-American Commission of Inquiry. Though the Commission had failed to come forward with a satisfactory political solution for Palestine and instead envisaged a weird tri-national hybrid, it did urge the immediate immigration of a substantial number of refugees from the DP camps. The British Labor government did not hesitate to repudiate even this modest recommendation. Instead it hatched the outrageous Morrison cantonization plan, which has been aptly described as having all the disadvantages of partition with none of its advantages.

The cantonization plan is of sufficiently recent vintage so that it is unnecessary to review its salient features. It is well to bear in mind, however, that according to its provisions the Zionist district would include

1,500 square miles instead of the 2,600 recommended in the partition proposal of a decade earlier, and that this so-called "province" would be deprived of virtually all political autonomy. Compare this travesty with the 45,000 square miles of Palestine when it was originally promised a Jewish "national home," and you get the measure of the deterioration of the Zionist and Jewish position, through a variety of international factors which it would be beside the point to review now.

What is the purpose of indulging in this dreary recital of the whittling down of the covenant, this familiar catalogue of broken pledges? A blast at Albion's perfidy and American passivity is, unfortunately, always in order, but that is not the object of this analysis. It is essential for us to appreciate the full significance of an objective fact (whatever we may think of the motives or the reasoning involved), namely, that British policy has been following an increasingly unfavorable line in regard to Palestine. The line has been going steadily downhill, heading toward rock bottom in the ghetto-canton of the Morrison plan. In 1946, the fear of Russia has been producing an even acuter case of the jitters in the British Labor government than the threat of Nazi Germany did in the Chamberlain government. At any rate, there is little to choose between the White Paper and the cantonization plan. If anything, the prognosis today is worse because the canton is being offered in all seriousness as part of the post-war world order, whereas the White Paper was part of pre-war strategy. The Morrison plan was the formal gravestone designed to be set upon Jewish hopes.

In view of this progressively swift decline, it became the first task of the Zionist movement to arrest the descent. The Morrison proposal required a quick countermove before the United States would accede in the plan. It was obvious that to do no more than echo the Biltmore Program and to remind the respective governments of the promises and resolutions binding them would not achieve the desired goal. Such reminders have their obvious merit and serve sound tactical ends, but they are not magic incantations. Probably not even the rosiest optimist believes that in the present political constellation—national and international—we could secure the immediate establishment of a Jewish state in all of Palestine, despite the several declarations in favor of such a Commonwealth passed by the American Congress and by leading political parties in the United States and Great Britain, including the parties in power.

The counterproposal of partition advanced by the Jewish Agency checked the calamitous descent to "crystallization" by dramatically providing a basis for negotiation which the United States could advance as a serious attempt at a compromise solution, and which England could not brush aside.

Painful though this may be, we must realize that insistence on the immediate establishment of a Jewish Commonwealth in the whole of Palestine, to which we are entitled, furnishes a green light for Britain's course. It even accelerates its speed, because it encourages the British contention that further talk is useless. The partition proposal is a red light which calls a halt. The British cannot continue to claim that Jews are unwilling to negotiate on a compromise basis. The world is informed that we are prepared to sacrifice a great deal, provided a fundamental solution for the Palestine *impasse* is found at once. Britain's cynical *Realpolitik* cannot be wholly impervious to the force of this argument, especially since the notion of partition has been a recurrent aspect of British thinking on the subject of Palestine.

Of course, partition must have more to recommend it than a hypothetical acceptability to the British. It has to offer Zionism definite immediate advantages to compensate for the losses we incur. Perhaps such advantages become clearer if we venture to look back upon the past decade. Let us suppose that partition had been accepted in 1937 and a Jewish state had been established in a part of Palestine. It is not easy to be wise even after the event, because we have no *post facto* knowledge of what other concomitant developments might have taken place had such a state been established. But it seems reasonable to assume that even a small Jewish state would have meant the salvation of hundreds of thousands of Jews destined to perish in the crematoria and gas chambers. A Jewish state would have had the right to determine the rate of immigration into its boundaries. And we may also assume that even a small Jewish state would have been represented at the San Francisco Conference, and would have enjoyed membershp in the United Nations, just as Lebanon does. For reasons which appeared valid to us then, our decision on partition was deferred. No one could foresee the catastrophe that would engulf the Jewish people. Similarly, the flexibility of the Biltmore Program was reasonable and statesman-like under the conditions that prevailed at the time of its adoption. Just as we could not foresee the ferocity and extent of the Nazi assault upon the civilized world, so we could not foresee the spiritual bankruptcy of the victors. Jews were not unique among peoples in their inability to perceive the shape of the future. They were, if anything, more sensitive than others in their apprehensions, but even their awareness was inadequate.

We cannot blame ourselves for not having been seers. But if we may be forgiven for lacking foresight, we cannot afford to neglect the indications provided by hindsight. That too is a form of vision. We now know that a status in Palestine which will create possibilities for immediate immigration and which will offer Jewish independence is the primary need of the Jewish people. It might be sensible to seek to delay a final political solution if there were any likelihood that an interim period would provide for such immigration and would improve Zionist prospects for better ultimate terms. But all the evidence points to the contrary. The British and the Arabs are pressing for the crystallization of the present Jewish minority. A viable Jewish state in a part of Palestine, on the other hand, would allow the absorption of hundreds of thousands of immigrants and would at once secure political independence, with all that that implies for the Jewish people. A viable state would naturally have to include the undeveloped Negev and the untapped water sources of Northern Galilee.

The objection has been raised by some American Zionists that it was bad tactics for the Jewish Agency to make its partition offer. Shrewd bargainers hold out for the maximum and then they scale down their terms, if they have to. Those who advance this curious argument seem willfully to forget that the Zionist movement has been engaged in endless heartrending negotiations with the British. The commissions and conferences before which our spokesmen have stated the Zionist case cannot be ignored in an evaluation of the situation. It is ludicrous to pretend that the Jewish Agency pulled a compromise out of a blue, unclouded sky. The discussions had been proceeding rapidly to a disastrous conclusion when the Executive made its supreme effort to stay the collapse.

Those who are already seeking to hamstring the deliberations of the forthcoming Congress by binding their members to *a priori* positions belong to various camps. They are the political doctrinaires who hold to the purity of their faith with theological fervor. The undiscouraged proponents of a binational state, who still expect to dwell in connubial affection with the Arabs despite the negative response their suit receives, oppose partition. On the other hand, the "maximalists" of long standing, who will surrender no jot of their claim to a Jewish state on both sides of the Jordan, are equally adamant. Religious Zionists, who feel that they cannot barter with the Lord's promise, are split on the issue of partition. These factions are theoretically committed to the particular solutions they have been advocating since their inception. They are intellectually and spiritually obstinate—the modern Zealots.

However, the real danger that the Congress may be stratified into anti- and pro-partition blocs which will paralyze its functioning stems from another source. It is not the ideological doctrinaires who represent the real threat. One may as well say it plainly. There are sectors of the Zionist movement who are not averse to making political capital for their own partisan ends out of the present crisis. Partition is popular with no one. To seek to transfer the indignation engendered by the necessity for considering such a sacrifice to those who labored under the bitter obligation of making the proposal is a discreditable maneuver.

Partition must not become a stick with which to attack the Zionist Executive or the Jewish Agency. Personal antagonisms and party rivalries can no more be avoided in the Zionist movement than in other movements. But there are moments in history which impose their responsibilities and restraints. This is one of them. Every Zionist aware of the desperate plight of the Jews of Europe and of Palestine must bear in mind that partition may represent the only immediate, realistic means of preventing the British from carrying out their unconcealed effort to liquidate Zionism. In 1937 partition was called a Solomon's judgment. Today we must perhaps consider that the child is a Siamese twin whose life can only be saved by a drastic operation.

(November 1946)

HONEYMOON WITH HISTORY

Since my arrival in Israel in July 1948, I have heard many attempts to characterize this period. Even the seasoned veterans of the struggle are groping for words to express their sense of wonder at what has come to pass. Indeed, the word *ness* (miracle) is the one heard most frequently. A current joke divides the population into three classes: pessimists, optimists, and *nessimists*, and the latter seem to have won the day.

There is a touching modesty about this readiness to explain the extra-ordinary achievements of the young state in terms of the miraculous. The *Yishuv* (the Jewish community of Palestine), aware of the tremendous odds it faced on every front, political, economic, military, seems reluctant to give the credit to its own prowess.

"We were so few; we had so little arms," people tell me, "and the Arab armies stood on every border with tanks, real tanks. It was a *ness.*"

Still another remark is repeated over and over: "When the whole story can be told, nobody will believe it." Men and women make this announcement dogmatically: the miracle will never be believed by a skeptical, brutal world. Consequently, there is no use even in telling the tale, and so inviting the sacrilege of doubt.

The phrase which rang truest to me was one I heard casually in a conversation with a young soldier. He had been giving me an unvarnished account of the difficulties besetting the present and future. Then, he added; "But it doesn't matter. Whatever happens, now Israel has its honeymoon with history."

I can't think of a better way of putting it. Amid the variety of conflicting emotions which one senses here, the dominant mood is still that of the honeymoon. Grief for the many dead, uncertainty as to the future, weariness, even disillusionment; all are present, but the strongest feeling is that of exultation. The long hunger for historic recognition, for status, is being appeased. This explains the almost childlike enchantment with form and the paraphernalia of statehood. It is an active delight to salute Jewish government officials. It is exciting rather than burdensome to submit to various controls and examinations along the road. "Ours, *shelanu*, not the British," my companions say rejoicing. And the simple Hebrew possessive pronoun, *shelanu*, begins to sound like a thanksgiving prayer.

No doubt the time will shortly come when a rigorous examination by customs officials, or even an army parade, will seem less entrancing than they do today, but now every sign of independence, or nationhood, no matter how trivial, has a symbolic value still unexpended.

From the moment my plane landed at the Haifa airport, and we saw the Israeli flag waving over it, the jubilee was on. Though many of the passengers had been in Palestine on previous occasions, it was our first entry into Israel. At every step of the inevitable formalities, which are generally endured with a minimum of enthusiasm by the badgered traveller, I could hear the admiring comments of my companions: "An Israeli entry permit! An Israeli stamp! How smartly the boys do their job."

Even the unlucky passenger whose baggage was scanned with a thoroughness never observed by me on previous trips paid a stiff duty for such items as medicinal cognac and pungent sausage with less bitterness than might have been expected. He did venture to point out that he had brought the stuff to help his hungry brethren, but that was his sole protest. His companions cheered him with the reflection that it was all for the *medinah* (the state). And besides, he was having a unique opportunity. How many men in modern times had been blessed with the chance to pay duty to a Jewish state? He finally packed up his costly historic sausage with a smile.

Perhaps the climax of the "honeymoon with history" mood came three days after my arrival on July 27, the anniversary of Herzl's death, which has been designated as Nation Day.

It would be idle to pretend that anyone accustomed to military demonstrations on the American scale would be overwhelmed by the parade as such. Watching this cross-section of the forces that had repulsed the Syrians, the Arab Legion, the Iraqis, the Lebanese and the Egyptians, I kept thinking that never had so many been overcome by so few. And when one remembered under what conditions the Israeli army had to be forged, in the teeth of the British Empire's determination to keep the Jews disarmed and defenseless, the effect of the spectacle went far beyond the visible. The people lining the streets, filling every window, were intoxicated not only by the accomplishment, but by the fact of the army itself. Israel had a force, no longer underground, but an army with banners—a symbol of strength and renascence. When two tanks captured from the Egyptians rolled past, there was an outcry, but perhaps the greatest ovation was reserved for the planes that circled overhead. Tel Aviv remembered the bombings it had endured, day after day.

One old Yemenite, standing on the sidewalk with his son, whispered to the boy: "I must be a saint; if I were not, I could not have lived to see this day."

If you had not known that this small group marching by had held Jerusalem, and the other came straight from the Negev, you might have permitted yourself a wry smile at the human weakness for martial pomp, whatever its size. But here was no smiling matter. *Shelanu!*

In every parade of soldiers, the dead march too. I have seen them march in the United States after World War I and World War II. For all save the immediate relatives, they are the anonymous, unknown dead. Here, because of the smallness of the population and its consequent intimacy, the dead could be called by name, even as the living. Two of the men near me had each lost a son. I watched them applaud the marchers. And when one woman, unable to contain herself, exclaimed mournfully: "What a price this has cost!", the only obvious reaction from the bereaved fathers was more determined applause.

The military punctilio and fanfare worried one of the older comrades. Such had not been the dream of the early pioneers. Would the people's militia remain a democratic force of workers devoted to the goal of a cooperative society or would baser values seep in? These were problems sharpened by the success of Israel arms.

It takes a little time for the newcomer to get used to the idea that the Jewish state is a concrete fact, and that authority from the highest to the lowest levels is entirely in Jewish hands. The first day or two I found myself looking unconsciously for a British official or an Arab assistant. Finally the tremendous reality penetrates: the British are gone. The only Englishman I have seen since my arrival is one with a Jewish wife who has chosen to cast his lot with Israel.

The only visible signs of 30 years of British rule and misrule are English notices which have been overlooked on some office wall. They may be dated 1947, but the yellowing paper already seems pre-historic.

There had been one worry in connection with the going of the British. The legacy of calculated chaos which the British had planned to leave had filled the *Yishuv* with apprehension. The people had faith in the state; however, they didn't know how it would be able to operate under wartime conditions since there had been no gradual, organized transfer of authority. When the population discovered that the departure of the British was a rose with no thorn, that the whole apparatus of daily life started functioning smoothly except for war emergencies, the people were as startled as by the exploits of the army. Heroism has long been no novelty in Palestine. But nobody knew what would happen when the whole machinery of government and all its services would devolve suddenly on a young state beset by enemies.

I have heard people delight in the swift, uneventful establishment of telephone service, transport and post, and then confess shamefacedly: "We did not know our boys and girls would be so polite, so efficient." People long inured to wrestling with political and physical problems of the first magnitude evince this poignant surprise at the conquest of the comparatively trivial. This does not prevent them from griping at a thousand things. If you point out the paradox they answer cheerfully: "What do you want? At last we are a normal people!"

THE SIEGE OF JERUSALEM

When the British left Palestine, the new State of Israel faced invasion by seven Arab armies. The extraordinary heroism of Jewish Jerusalem during nearly two months of total siege—from April 22, 1948, when the last convoy and reinforcements reached the beleaguered city, until June 2, the beginning of the first truce—was all the more astonishing because of the unique character of the city. Its 100,000 Jewish inhabitants included scholars, religious zealots, civil servants, and a conglomerate of the various tribes of Israel who had gathered from the old Jewries of Europe and the Orient to pray, study, or simply dwell in the city of peace. This population, ranging from the academic elite of Mt. Scopus to illiterate stone hewers, was singularly unprepared for the demands of the coming war. The pioneer settlements and young towns of Jewish Palestine had developed a sturdy tradition of self-defense. But over Jerusalem hung the Holy City's peculiar aura, fashioned of its ancient stones and more ancient dreams. Aesthetically, spiritually, the city cast its quiet spell, pervasive as its radiant starlight.

The native youth of Jerusalem, except for the students at the Hebrew University on Mt. Scopus, tended to drift away. Robust, idealistic young men and women went to the settlements; more worldly spirits preferred Tel Aviv. Consequently, Jerusalem was psychologically less prepared for battle than many small pioneer villages. Besides, the population stubbornly believed that Jerusalem would be inviolate.

Despite Arab riots and disturbances, which broke out immediately after the passage of the UN Partition Resolution in November 1947, the city was sustained by the faith that its sacred character would safeguard it from outright attack. As elsewhere in Palestine, the youth of Jerusalem enlisted for secret military training with the Haganah[1], but because of the paralyzing conviction that the international community would protect Jerusalem the boys of Jerusalem were stationed on the borders and in the heart of the imperiled new state.

Consequently, the Jews of Jerusalem found themselves unarmed, untrained, and, except for a small Haganah unit, virtually helpless in the face of mounting Arab outrages which began in December 1947. The British police, instead of protecting Jews, dismembered Jewish Jerusalem through the creation of so-called "security zones" and kept arresting any members of the Haganah they could discover. They also systematically sought to disarm the Jews. While the Arabs accumulated huge stocks of arms in the Mosque of Omar, safe from British search as a sanctuary, the "neutral" British police would confiscate any pocket knife longer than four inches a Jew might possess.

The policy of the Mandatory Power obviously called for the surrender of Jerusalem to Abdullah;[2] secret steps for defense had to be taken. Though the Jewish community still nursed the illusion that an international force would intervene in the event of a full-scale Arab invasion, the citizenry began to create a home guard which in time would involve every man, woman, and child. Colonel David Shaltiel, Haganah commander of Jerusalem from February to August, and his small staff had the tough task of welding the city's baffling aggregate of Israel's tribes, each resolutely clinging to its particular pieties, into a secret fighting force which would voluntarily accept the stern discipline and shadowy authority of the Haganah. But the miracle took place.

At first, all males between the ages of 17 and 45 had to give 24 hours of service a week. This was quickly changed to 48 hours. When a general mobilization was declared in the beginning of May, everybody, men and women, old and young, was on full-time duty.

Industriously and ingeniously, the home guard strove to barricade the Jewish quarter with a barbed-wire network, particularly after the Ben Yehuda Street bombing. Though a little of the scarce barbed wire had been bought from British soldiers willing to drive a good bargain, most had to be gotten by other means. In March all available wire around private homes and factories was confiscated. Even after barriers had been erected, there was always the likelihood that British tanks would roll in to destroy the protection the Jews had devised. Only as the British withdrew to their bristling "Bevingrad"[3] in the center of the city, did Haganah defensive measures have a chance to stand.

Even more difficult to endure than the deliberate destruction of the improvised barriers was the Mandatory regime's relentless hunt for weapons. At a time when Jewish homes were being bombed, Jewish traffic ambushed, and Jewish civilians attacked without the benefit of government protection or redress, the British still maintained the fiction that they were responsible for the maintenance of order, and that any Jewish attempt at self-defense was lawless.

The morale of every inhabitant of Jerusalem was subjected to a prolonged test. For months before the shelling of the city started on May

15 there was no respite from the terror of violent death. Every day brought fresh casualties. The incidents were of a monotonous regularity: a grenade hurled into the Zion cinema, a bomb thrown at a bus or through a window in Rehavia, a passer-by stabbed or shot.

The attack on Jerusalem was directed primarily against the civilian population. Arab snipers, entrenched in the heights overlooking the Jewish quarters, imperiled the movements of every pedestrian. Women and children were not exempt. Not only were they victims of random explosions, but no silhouette was too small for the Arab sharpshooter who was troubled neither by the size nor sex of his target. The home guard drew sacking across the open spaces between houses to foil the aim of Arab sharpshooters, but every day the snipers claimed new victims among housewives who had ventured out to get their food ration, or children who had run out to play.

This indiscriminate, unceasing sniping was periodically punctuated by equally indiscriminate bombings. In addition to constant attacks throughout the city, three major disasters followed each other in swift succession: the dynamiting of *The Palestine Post*[4] on February 2, 1948; of Ben Yehuda Street on February 23; and of the Jewish Agency on March 12. Of these, the Ben Yehuda Street explosion, with 54 dead and over 100 wounded, was the most frightful. The blast wrecked Ben Yehuda Street from Zion Circus to King George Street, brought down three- and four-story buildings, and maimed and killed entire families asleep in their homes. The assault was carried out by men in British uniform driving British army lorries.

Still another major Arab terrorist outrage was to strike the community: the slaughter of the Hadassah Convoy[5] on April 13, when 67 doctors and nurses were massacred. The mass murder of Palestine's leading physicians and scientists was perhaps the most monstrous result of the vacuum caused by the British abdication of responsibliity while denying its assumption by the Jews.

But the Arab attack on the civilian population was to assume an even more ruthless form. The Arabs had a cheap formula for victory: the reduction of the city through famine and thirst. Jerusalem was in a particularly vulnerable situation. Surrounded by thickly populated Arab villages, the 100,000 Jews of Jerusalem were completely isolated from the rest of Jewish Palestine. Their sole link to the coast ran almost entirely through Arab-held territory; Arab strategy concentrated on breaking this link. Neither water, food, arms, nor men could reach Jerusalem if the road to Tel Aviv were cut and the pipeline from Ras El-Ein severed.

The Battle of the Roads began early in December, even though the Mandatory Power had promised to maintain freedom of traffic on the Tel Aviv-Jerusalem highway. The British gave their customary interpretation to this undertaking. Jewish buses would be painstakingly searched for arms while Arab attackers enjoyed a minimum of interference. The disarmed Jews then had the privilege of fighting it out.

This concept of "neutrality" resulted in the repeated massacre of unarmed civilians, forced to ride the gauntlet of Arab bands crouching in the hills. The skeletons of overturned buses, which could long be seen all along the winding Jerusalem highway, testified to the ambushed convoys whose passengers were murdered by Arabs. It was in one such convoy that Hans Beyth, the head of Youth Aliyah,[6] was shot down in cold blood on December 28, 1947.

Nevertheless, the contact with Jerusalem had to be maintained. The inadequately protected convoys of Egged buses set out regularly on their perilous journey accompanied by Palmach[7] girls with Sten guns hidden under their skirts. As a rule British soldiers did not search women.

Primitive devices to reinforce the buses came into being. Since Jews had no armored plate, they used metal sheets so thin that the buses were derisively called "sardine tins." To make matters worse, the thin sheet would be wedged between layers of wood to save precious metal. This economy made the buses cumbersome as well as readily penetrable.

Between December and February, these lumbering convoys continued to crawl through the deep gorges and up the steep hills. The effort to reach Jerusalem at whatever cost went on doggedly. In February, however, the Arabs blew up a mountainside between Babel-Wad and Castel, covering a stretch of the road with debris.

This huge natural roadblock meant the virtual isolation of Jerusalem. Neither supplies nor reinforcements could reach the city. The desperate situation of Jerusalem prompted "Operation Nachshon"[8] (named after the Biblical hero who plunged in first when Moses divided the Red Sea) for the purpose of opening the road.

The question of water for Jerusalem was perhaps the most crucial of all. No measure of valor could avail if the Arabs succeeded in their scheme to cut off the water supply. Water had always been a serious problem. Even in the best of times, the Jerusalem householder had to husband water.

As late as 1919 Jerusalem had depended on rain water, stored, as in Biblical times, in cisterns and pools. King Solomon had constructed huge reservoirs for collecting the water of several springs in addition to rain water from the hills, and had built an aqueduct which the Romans later improved. The Turks also laid a pipeline. These had been adequate as long as the population of the city was small and its hygienic standards primitive. With the spurt in population and a rise in its hygienic requirements, modern methods had to be introduced. Since 1880, the city had grown from 20,000 to 100,000; a large proportion of the increase consisted of Westernized householders who insisted on modern plumbing and refused to promenade to the well with pitchers gracefully poised on their heads.

During the Mandate, pipelines were laid which greatly increased Jerusalem's water supply. In 1947, when hostilities broke out, Jerusalem was serviced by three sources, chief of which was Ras El-Ein, near Latrun, 70 kilometers West of Jerusalem. From the east flowed spring water from Ein Farah, and to the South near Bethlehem was the pumping station at Solomon's Pools which had been used as a storage supply since the days of Herod. These three sources supplied Jerusalem with its normal requirement of two-and-one-half to three million gallons of water daily. During the dry summer months, temporary shortages might be experienced but these were not serious. There was only one drawback. All three pipelines ran through Arab territory and could be readily cut.

After the outbreak of Arab disturbances, Dr. Zwi Leibowitch, the Jewish Manager of the Water Department of the Jerusalem Municipality, realized under what grave threat the Jewish community labored. The attitude of his British and Arab colleagues in the municipality left no room for the illusion that he could expect cooperation in protecting Jerusalem's water supply. The memory of the 1936 riots, when Arab gangs had tried to sabotage the water plant, was still fresh. As Dr. Leibowitch put it, the knowledge that all three pipelines could be readily tampered with gave him "one big headache." He knew that there was no point in discussing the problem with the British representatives, and even less with the Arab members of the Municipal Council.

The only practical solution was to store an emergency ration within the city itself. Water, like arms, would have to be stored secretly. Fortunately, Jerusalem was a city of cisterns and wells. But while almost all Arab homes had cisterns, in Jewish Jerusalem only old houses were so equipped. New buildings were blessed with modern plumbing. The first step, therefore, was to locate cisterns, most of them long abandoned, wherever they might be, and determine the amount of water they could hold.

A clandestine survey was made in the houses and courtyards of the city. Two thousand old cisterns, with a total capacity of 22 million gallons, were discovered in the Jewish area. On the basis of ten quarts daily per individual the supply could last three months.

The cisterns could not be used in their present condition. Dirty, neglected, they first had to be cleaned and repaired. A volunteer force, working secretly, managed to restore them with great rapidity. The next problem was to fill the cisterns without arousing British or Arab suspicions and precipitating hostile action. By February, Dr. Leibowitch and his volunteers had scored a great coup. The cisterns, some in private homes and others in public institutions had been filled and sealed. An emergency ration of water was now at hand, which could be tapped in the hour of need.

It was obvious that when such an extremity arose, the population would not be able to move about freely. Since the cisterns were located in various parts of the city, some of them not readily accessible, a system had to be devised which would bring water to the consumer. The town was, therefore, divided into districts according to the number of cisterns within the area, so that the water would be equitably apportioned. Each district had its own supervisor who was responsible for the distribution of water. Ration cards for water were drawn up and printed to insure fair distribution. Special carts to transport water were allocated by the Emergency Committee, under the chairmanship of Dr. Dov Joseph, despite the already desperate shortage of transport and gasoline. Fortunately, everyone understood that preparations for the supply and distribution of water rated top priority.

Nothing was left to chance or to last-minute improvisations. Designated individuals knew that they would have the task of transporting the water from street to street. A driver and two attendants were assigned to each cart. Provision was even made for delivering the water inside the dwelling. Each cart was provided with a long rubber hose so that water could be piped from the curb into the hallway in case exceptionally heavy shelling made it impossible for a woman to step out on the sidewalk with her pail.

Another problem was to keep the water in the cisterns from stagnating, and a staff of technicians and bacteriologists, recruited from the Hebrew University, inspected and chlorinated the water to keep it potable.

The plan, worked out in every detail, was ready to go into effect at 24 hour's notice. It was soon to be tested.

On May 8, 1948, the Iraqis cut the pipeline from Ras El-Ein; the other two pipelines were also quickly sabotaged. Despite the critical situation in which 100,000 helpless civilians now found themselves, the British authorities neither repaired the pipe themselves, nor offered protection to Jewish engineers willing to do so. The emergency ration, which if carefully hoarded in the summer heat could last a maximum of 90 days, now had to be tapped.

The first time that the inhabitants of Jerusalem opened their faucets and no water flowed was terrifying despite the fact that the population had been carefully coached in the procedures to be followed. For weeks the citizens had been preparing for just such an eventuality, but now the children had to be told that there was no water for a bath, or even for a drink. On the first day there were a few scattered attempts to break the sealed cisterns. The primitive terror of death by thirst in the desert broke out hysterically in some sections of the city but the panic was rapidly stilled.

By May 9, within the scheduled 24 hours, the water carts began their service to the reassurance of the population, and the bafflement of those who had anticipated swift capitulation. From that day until the end of the siege, the water carts appeared regularly even in the midst of the heaviest shelling. Not a day was missed even though drivers and householders were often struck by flying shells, and more than one life was lost in the effort to give and get water. The citizens of Jerusalem could well add another verse to their prayers: "Blessed are they who bring water.."

Siege conditions had prevailed in Jerusalem for months before the actual Arab invasion. Already in February the food supply was precariously low. At the beginning of March the city had food for only three weeks, and the intervals between the supply convoys which succeeded in battling their way through to Jerusalem kept growing longer. As the situation continued to deteriorate, the provisioning of Jerusalem was entrusted to Dov Joseph, Chairman of the Emergency Committee, set up to prepare specifically for a siege. The spare stocks of barley, beans, and flour husbanded in this period were to prove the mainstay of Jerusalem when the city was completely cut off. "Joseph, the Provider," as he came to be known, commandeered trucks and lorries throughout the country, despite the acute need for transport in all parts of the country. Tel Aviv stores denuded their shelves of non-perishable foods to send to Jerusalem. The result of this swift action was that on the morning of March 26 a huge convoy with food reached the city. Each of the trucks bore the Biblical pledge: "If I forget thee, oh Jerusalem." The last convoy to reach Jerusalem arrived on April 20, the eve of Passover, after the Nachshon operation had temporarily opened the road. It carried *matzot* and arms.

There were 2,000 infants in Jerusalem who would have perished without milk powder. In the beginning of April, a primitive air field was constructed in the Jewish quarter of Rehavia. A small moth plane, known as "primus," flew regularly between Tel Aviv and Jerusalem, bringing milk powder, drugs, and desperately needed ammunition. There were ten weeks when this tiny plane, shuttling back and forth under constant shelling, was the sole contact between Jerusalem and the rest of Palestine. It was Israel's air lift.

Hand in hand with the efforts to provide water and food for the threatened siege, measures were being taken to create a military force capable of repelling an invasion. For the reasons already mentioned, the Haganah was particularly weak in Jerusalem.

The number of rifles and grenades on hand was absurdly small. Of heavy arms there were none. In the whole Jerusalem area there were some 500 rifles, 400 Sten guns, 28 machine guns, three heavy machine guns, five three-inch mortars, and 20 two-inch mortars. There was a growing pile of "homemade" ammunition. Only a fraction of the required ammunition could be spared by the central authorities in Tel Aviv, and of that only a small percentage managed to reach Jerusalem before the siege. Nevertheless, secret preparation proceeded within the tightening ring of the Arab armies converging upon the city.

As the day of the Mandate's close approached, British military interference with Jewish defense efforts slackened. It was obvious that they expected the city to fall easy prey to the Arab armies. To protests against the lawlessness engulfing the city still under their tutelage, they had a stock answer: the bland counsel to "evacuate" or surrender. When, on April 30, *Palmach* and Haganah units succeeded in storming the Arab quarter of Katamon, from which Iraqis had been firing incessantly, the British did not at first intervene. Two days later, in the face of continuing Jewish victories, British military barred further advance.

On May 1, as the British retreated to their "security zones," Colonel Shaltiel ordered a general mobilization of all citizens. This meant the shutting down of schools, shops, offices, factories and laundries. Only bakeries and food stores remained open for stated intervals daily. Such all-inclusive mobilization had been hotly debated because the measure meant the total paralysis of the city, but the Jewish authorities knew that all available fuel and electric current had to be conserved for the essentials of life and for defense. Every person had to be available for service in the home guard.

The full-scale invasion of the Arab states on May 15 completed the encirclement of Jerusalem. Enemy armies lay entrenched on the hills surrounding the city, and a large Arab force held Latrun, midway between Tel Aviv and Jerusalem, and the seat of the pumping station of the Jerusalem water pipeline.

The agony of Jerusalem had begun. The plan to starve the city into submission and reduce it by thirst appeared to be diabolically easy of execution. All the sections of the young state were reeling under the impact of invaders on every border. Tel Aviv was being bombed by Egyptian planes. Syrian and Iraqi tanks were battering at the settlements in Galilee. Egyptian battalions were marching up the dusty roads of the Negev. The scant arms and men available had to be divided among many fronts, each of which was in a desperate position, each of which was vital to the defense of the country. The same brigades of Jewish youth had to answer the call for help which came from Northern settlements in Galilee, from the Southern outposts in the Negev, or from the heart of the Sharon. And over the whole land lay the shadow of the besieged citadel.

Two battalions of *Palmach*, a total of 1,200 men, got through to Jerusalem in the last weeks before May 15, and their presence heartened the population. Together with the locally mobilized Haganah and the home guard capable of bearing arms, Jerusalem now had a force of about 6,000 men of whom 35 percent had arms. Success in building up this makeshift army under the very nose of the British had been considerable.

It was essential to prevent the British "security zones," including "Bevingrad," from falling into the hands of the Arabs. These zones cut

Jerusalem into islands which had to be linked up without delay. The British positions, as well as their large camp, the Allenby Barracks, were seized by the Haganah as soon as the British withdrew. Since most of the New City was already in Jewish hands by May 15, this meant that the Haganah had to concentrate on preventing the juncture of Arab forces coming from the North and the South. In addition, the Haganah was trying desperately to re-establish contact with Mt. Scopus and to break through to the Old City. It failed in the last two objectives but the main thrust against Jerusalem was checked.

On May 15, the columns of the Arab Legion started advancing against the city. Smoke and fire could be seen at the Dead Sea: the cottages of *Beth Ha-Aarava* (the House in the Desert), directly in the Legion's path, were burning.

Mine fields had been laid on the road to stop the tanks of the Legion. To the surprise of the watchers, the Arab columns, instead of continuing to march against Jerusalem, turned at Jericho and went toward Nablus and Ramallah.

On May 19, however, the Legion made a determined attempt to capture Jerusalem from the North. It succeeded in taking the Sheikh Jarrah quarter, whose defense had been entrusted to the Irgun;[9] this meant the continued isolation of Mt. Scopus.

The whole population rallied to stop the further advance of the Legion. At the first rumble of the tanks on the outskirts of the city, there had been momentary panic. But it was short-lived. Even the old Jews of Orthodox *Mea Shearim* joined in improvising tank traps. Before dawn, a crier had awakened them, calling: "Arise and save Jerusalem." Half-dressed, they had rushed out into the dark to dig up their streets and pile stones across the roads.

When light broke, the Haganah majestically drove three armored cars (acquired from departing British soldiers for a price) through the streets to encourage the people. The sight of "Jewish tanks" raised drooping spirits.

On May 20, the Arab attacks started. Characteristically, the Arab columns led with tanks instead of infantry. After several Arab tanks had been put out of commission, and two others had been captured, the Arab columns retreated. No further direct onslaught was attempted. To enter a built-up area with mechanized armor was costly, and apparently the Arab command was not prepared to storm the city with infantry.

However, what the attackers failed to achieve on the field of battle they hoped to encompass by terrorizing the population at long distance. The bombardment of Jerusalem started at once. The British-led Arab Legion pounded the Holy City unremittingly with heavy mortars. Day and night shells hailed down on the streets, struck the improvised shelters, or exploded in homes. The shelling was wanton and savage, directed at no military objective, but striking at random through the city.

The Jewish defense units had no heavy artillery with which to silence the Arab guns, but wherever they encountered the invaders in combat, they drove them back. Though the Arab Legion and the Egyptians had ravaged the outlying Jewish settlements of *Kfar Etzion* and *Ramat Rahel*, they could not advance into the heart of the city. Instead, the Haganah kept progressively clearing the New City of the enemy. The fortitude of the citizenry was its chief ally.

Between May 15 and June 11, every person who ventured out into the street did so at the peril of his life. The heavy stone houses of Jerusalem afforded some protection, but outside of their walls death struck wantonly. But because the people understood the intent of the enemy, they refused to be cowed. A proud code developed, according to which housewives went at stated hours to collect their ration of bread and beans, and over-age men went to their posts or to work in such institutions as were kept open. *The Palestine Post* was issued daily. Doctors and nurses made their way on foot to the makeshift Hadassah Hospital in the city, no matter how thickly the shells fell. Individuals developed a technique for figuring out the number of minutes between shells in the course of which one could advance along the street. Within one fortnight the civilian casualties exceeded 1,000, a heavier proportion than in the fiercest times of the London blitz.

The shells were not only killing men, women, and children; they were destroying the city. No shrine in Jerusalem was safe from the havoc unleashed by Glubb Pasha's[10] Arab Legion.

At Lake Success, the representatives of Israel kept requesting that action be taken to protect Jerusalem. On May 22, the Truce Commission transmitted to the Security Council an appeal signed by the President of the National Jewish Council, the Mayor of the Jewish area of Jerusalem, and the Chairman of the Jewish Community Council of Jerusalem. The cable read:

> *For past 5 days. . . . Jerusalem, including old city, subjected indiscriminate attacks and nightly shelling by mortars of Arab Legion. Among attacked are hospitals, religious and social institutions including Hadassah Medical Center on Mount Scopus and mainly non-combatant citizens. Does world intend remaining silent? Will United Nations who expressed fears for peace Holy City permit this to continue? In name Jewish Jerusalem we demand immediate action to patrol Holy City.*

The appeal was disregarded. Nevertheless, when the Security Council called for an immediate cease-fire without demanding the withdrawal of the aggressors, the government of Israel immediately agreed to order a cease-fire on all fronts. The Israeli order to its commanders called for "particularly scrupulous observance" of the cease-fire in Jerusalem.

The Arab states, however, still dreaming of conquering Jerusalem and placing it under Arab rule—a dream openly abetted by the former Mandatory Power—rejected the cease-fire order. Abba Eban warned the members of the Security Council of the imminent danger of destruction to which Jerusalem was now exposed because of the violent attacks of the forces of Egypt and Transjordan:

> *The State of Israel does not shrink from its own defense, and now that its offer of cease-fire has been rejected, it sees its duty shining clearly before it. But it did yield Jerusalem to the International community upon which now devolves the responsibility for protecting that City.*
>
> *We cannot forbear to ask ourselves again whether the United Nations, even at this late hour, will not take cognizance of the effects on its own authority and prestige if within the next 48 hours, or thereafter, the Arab Legion manages to complete the devastation which it hoped to achieve in the last 48 hours.*

In the New City, the Haganah was holding off the tanks of the invaders and clearing out the Syrians and Iraqis. But within the Old City a handful of old men, women and children were waging a brave but losing struggle. Some 2,000 Orthodox Jews, living beleaguered among 30,000 Arabs, had been cut off from the New City since February when the Arabs blocked Zion Gate. The British had declined to remove the barrier or let the Haganah do so. As usual they offered to assist in "evacuation." But the venerable inhabitants, their wives and children, clung to the crooked alleys of the ancient city. For 2,000 years Jews had prayed near the Wailing Wall and studied the Law within its precincts. The old men and their families refused to abandon their sanctuaries.

The Mandatory Power finally agreed to permit the passage of food convoys which were carefully checked for arms and "non-residents." No such checks were exercised to curtail the activities of 30,000 Palestinian Arabs as well as Syrians and Iraqis who were openly buying arms and brandishing weapons in the Arab quarter adjoining the Jewish section. Within this armed camp the Jews of the Old City continued their traditional unworldly existence. The broom-maker and the sandal-maker plied their crafts as long as they could. Prayers could no longer be said at the Wailing Wall itself, but the great Hurva Synagogue was still filled with worshippers.

A small Haganah force managed to smuggle its way behind the thick walls to defend the Jewish quarter but it was wholly inadequate. Without ammunition and manpower, the Jewish quarter held out for two weeks against the Arab onslaught unleashed May 15.

The inhabitants of the Old City were actually besieged from February until their surrender May 28, 1949. I heard many strictures about the morale of the "old men" from professional soldiers. The old men, they complained, were not eager to fight. They kept babbling that the outcome was in God's hands. Some even protested that the Messiah would come in his own good time and that secular efforts to hasten his arrival were impious. A few had cared so little as to which national flag hung over the walls that they had been ready to raise the white flag. All that mattered to them was the Torah, which they were willing to study under any Caesar.

"A real ghetto mentality gripped some of these Jews. They said they wanted to live for God, not die for a Jewish state," complained an Israeli commander.

No doubt the charges were partly justified. In the New City, as well as in the Old, there existed clerical extremists who saw in all earthly measures to affect the course of events opposition to God's will. In the darkest days of the siege, a small fanatical sect known as the "Neturei Karta" (Watchers of the City) had demonstrated in the streets of Jerusalem with placards calling for food, modesty in dress, and surrender. The Haganah broke up the procession without establishing the comparative value of the three demands. The more mundane citizens of Jerusalem, despite their troubles, had a chance to smile at the infinite variety of their fellows. As one woman, still haggard from the months of semi-famine, put it to me:

"That's all they had to worry about, modesty in dress! It would have been funny if not for that talk of surrender."

Though it is not hard to understand the vexation of the Haganah commanders or the more worldly civilians, one cannot readily agree with the contemptuous charge of cowardice frequently whispered. On the contrary, anyone who has seen the winding streets, the huddled courtyards, the narrow passages of the Old City, intertwined like a beehive and compressed by the Arab quarter directly adjoining, must marvel that any group could have held out in such unlikely surroundings. The age distribution and special mentality of the inhabitants made their endurance even more startling.

In normal times the tumult of the world did not reach the Old City. Even the revolution in speech, which transformed Hebrew, a sacred tongue reserved for prayers and religious study, into a secular language, had not affected many of the inhabitants. One could find children born in Jerusalem who spoke Yiddish to their parents and knew Hebrew only as a holy script. The young people, for the most part, would leave for the pagan world outside the great walls as soon as they were able. The old folks and children remained behind, reinforced periodically by a residue of their own youth or by zealots from the outside. That such a population whose "quaint" manners and exteriors were a standard tourist attraction before 1948, should have displayed the physical stamina to withstand the siege for any period of time is cause for more surprise than reproof.

As early as December, Arabs began to block the gate leading to the Jewish quarter. When they succeeded in blocking Zion Gate completely, the population found itself encircled and cut off from Jewish Jerusalem, which in turn was encircled and cut off from Israel. Permission to leave the Old City and safe convoy were offered by the British but only with a one-way ticket. Those who had affairs to transact in the New City could not get out except on the understanding that they would make no attempt to return home. On the other hand, inhabitants of the Old City who had been caught outside the walls on the day when the gate was blocked could not get back. Mothers separated from small children, who were left helpless and untended in the Old City, begged in vain for permission to re-enter. Finally, after lengthy negotiations with the Haganah, the British allowed special cases to return with the food convoys.

The problem of defense was more crucial than that of food. Before May 14, the Haganah succeeded in smuggling in about 100 men. In addition, one local platoon (consisting of 40 men) had been mobilized. This was the sum total of those who could be expected to fight. All one could ask of the rest was that they endure patiently. As Zion Harush, aged 20, born in the Old City, said charitably when recounting the details of the struggle after his return from imprisonment in Transjordan: "Old people, what did they understand about war?"

Between December and May 14, the aim of the Haganah was to keep the people occupied and to prepare for the attack. Food was rationed and distributed. Work details were organized to prevent demoralization in the virtual imprisonment of the tight Jewish quarter. Some of the men cleaned the narrow streets daily; others baked bread with the available flour. Occasionally it was possible to purchase arms from an Arab acquaintance who came secretly from the nearby Arab market whose stalls were now full of guns as well as the usual knives. The chief defense measure was the digging of underground cellars to unite the houses whose courtyards were in full view of the Arab snipers.

Whenever the British spotted Haganah soldiers they would expel them from the Old City. The Palestine government which had declined to remove the Arab roadblock from Zion Gate kept pressing for the disarmament of the Old City and branding the presence of the Haganah as a "menace to peace." The British professed to believe that the Arabs would not assail unarmed Orthodox Jews, a belief which the Jewish Agency in Jerusalem termed as "dangerous nonsense" taking occasion to remind the Mandatory Government of the Arab massacres of Orthodox communities in the Old City, Safed, and Hebron in the years before the Haganah had undertaken their defense.

The British capture of several Haganah commanders added to the terror of the increasingly terrorized population. One must understand in what a palpable sense the Old City was isolated to appreciate the feelings of the inhabitants. All Israel was an encircled pinpoint in an Arab world, but the individual Israeli saw the world not from the point of view of a map but from within his Jewish environment. Around him, or in back of him, were Jewish villages. Even in besieged Jerusalem, cut off from the rest of the land, there were friendly streets and avenues which stretched around his house for blocks. In the Old City, however, the enemy was on the other side of the wall. One could hear him breathe and move. One could only escape by retreating further back along the alleys to the last Jewish house of a dead end street.

On April 27, a Hadassah team under the charge of Dr. Abraham Laufer, consisting of three doctors, a nurse, and an orderly, entered the Old City. Medical headquarters were set up in the two-story building of the old Misgav Ladach Hospital, which adjoined a synagogue. Preparations were made, but, as Dr. Laufer put it later, the prognosis was bad and the staff was doing its duty automatically, without real hope that a successful defense could be waged.

Measures to prevent epidemics were taken. Flies were beginning to breed and it was urgent to spread DDT. The water in the cisterns was chlorinated. A list of blood donors was compiled. Clean linens were stored, and by May 14, 50 white beds and a frigidaire with plasma stood in readiness.

The Arab attack started promptly. On May 15, the Arab Legion in the Old City began shelling the Jewish quarter. By May 16, the Haganah radioed to the command in the New City: "Our position is desperate; they break through from every side." And another message, sent several hours later read: "Send help—Arabs are attacking Misgav Ladach" (the hospital whose name meant "Help to the Destitute").

From May 16 to May 28, the agonized messages were received sometimes at intervals of 20 minutes. And to the plea for help would come the stern injunction: "Hold out." The exchanges of May 16 were typical of the next ten days. At 4 pm the message read: "Arabs have broken into the houses, some want to surrender." At 6 pm of the same day: "No munitions whatsoever; send help; we cannot hold out; how long are you going to wait." And the answer came: "Hold out one more hour; help will come."

On May 17, at 11:30 am, the message from within the Old City announced: "Arabs inform us that if we don't surrender by 12 pm they'll repeat massacre of *Kfar Etzion*." To which came the calm rejoinder: "The

Arabs see our preparations and know that you are not alone. Don't lose your nerve and think of the seriousness of the situation."

The appeals for help included directions as to specific localities to be shelled so as to stem the Arab advance. But the Haganah command outside the Old City was unable to take advantage of the information for fear that their shells would strike a shrine or church. This failure added to the torment of the besieged who could not sympathize with a regard for religious edifices when their lives were at stake.

Despite the threats of surrender, the Old City continued to hold out, but the messages grew more desperate and peremptory: On May 17, at 5:30 pm they radioed: "The one hour for which you asked yesterday is over. If you want to find fewer people massacred, let us know when help comes."

And 20 minutes later: "There is no sense repeating 'hold out a little while.' Help should come at once. Where are our forces? The messages from the town are ridiculous. Thirty-six hours have passed since this hour yesterday. Bomb and shell [names position]."

In the meantime, the Haganah in the New City was trying desperately to break through Zion Gate and effect a juncture with the Jewish quarter. Not only were the Jewish forces handicapped by a lack of arms and men at a time when all Jerusalem was under Arab attack, but, in addition, the Arabs knew that the only possible place for a breakthrough was at Zion Gate. The mighty walls of the Old City were too thick to be stormed. This meant that the Jews lost the advantage of surprise. Nightly the Harel Brigade of the *Palmach*, which had fought its way to Jerusalem, strove to breach the gate, while the Arabs, entrenched behind the shelter of the thick walls, shot at them through loopholes.

As the Arabs captured house after house in the Old City, the Jews converged to the small cluster of buildings formed by the hospital and the synagogue. They overflowed the courtyard, the rooms, and the shelter. Though the courtyard was not safe, they hoped that the Red Cross flag raised over a hospital would protect them. The hope was ill-founded; the Red Cross flag was shot to ribbons almost immediately by snipers from the Haram esh Sharif Mosque.

The burial of the dead presented a special problem. According to religious tradition there may be no interment within the walls of the Holy City. At first bodies were stored in the hospital's mortuary, but this soon overflowed. Neither was cremation permitted. Finally, to avert an epidemic, the religious injunction was waived and a common grave was dug in an open square. To the rigorously observant Jews of the Old City this was profanation.

The children were as brave and lively a lot as elsewhere in Israel. Boys of ten and eleven maintained communication between posts of the defenders. Little boys with earlocks and skullcaps carried messages under fire as efficiently as their shortcropped counterparts in the collective settlements.

But whatever the morale of the young and active, the endurance of the old people was being strained to the breaking point. They huddled in the last refuge of the ancient Yohanan Ben Zakai Synagogue, where wards for the wounded and dying had been set up after the second story of the hospital proved unsafe. The operating room was lined with holy books; medicines and dressings had to be placed in closets reserved for the scrolls. The medical staff had the unenviable task of ejecting unwounded women and children from the comparative safety of the wards because medical treatment became impossible in the congestion.

The latrines were in the courtyard. When the shelling reached a point where people either had the choice of practically certain death by venturing into the midst of falling shells or defiling the precincts of the synagogue, the limit had been reached. (As always in such conditions, dysentery was rampant.)

Outside the synagogue the hundred-odd fighters tried to push back the Arabs swarming into the streets. They shot from the rooftops in a manner reminiscent of the Warsaw ghetto battles of 1943. The Arabs then began to dynamite the houses, one by one. Like the Jews, the Arabs knew each square foot and hole of the Old City; the few streets of the Jewish quarter were familiar territory.

On the midnight of May 19, the awaited "miracle" took place: the *Palmach* broke through Zion Gate and brought in reinforcements and munitions.

The *Palmach* operation had been in the charge of the legendary Uzi, the twenty-five-year-old youth who had commanded the forces that captured Castel. His order to the troops had a special ring:

"You stand before the walls of Jerusalem. For 1,870 years no Jew has climbed them. Tonight you will mount them."

It had taken the Legions of Titus three years to break through one of the massive ramparts. Now the commandos of *Palmach* were trying to blast Zion Gate, through which the main drive had to be made. *The Palestine Post* of May 20 described the operation:

> *At exactly 3:15 two young Palmach sappers crawled across the faintly moonlit field to Zion Gate itself, planted their charge, and crawled back under cover of the heavy fire their comrades maintained. This operation is laconically referred to as "withdrawing" but was, in this case at least, a full military operation demanding the utmost training and steel nerves if it is to be carried out without exposing oneself to the enemy's return fire.*
>
> *Within five minutes, when the smoke had cleared enough for the men to see that the Arabs' sandbags and towering curtain of barbed*

wire blocking the gate had been properly blasted away, members of the Palmach, the Portzim (those who break through), stormed into the walled area, and within 15 minutes had tossed their grenades into the ring of Arab defense posts opposite them and cleared the path to the Jewish Quarter, 150 meters away. Seconds later, when the wireless operator shouted to us "they're inside," we heard the rumble of an armored car as it toiled up Mt. Zion road, bringing supplies.

At 4:15 am the radio from the Old City flashed the joyous news: "We have met."

But the joy was short-lived. Tanks and cannon were rolling against Jerusalem from Jericho. The *Palmach* could not be spared. The Portzim had to return after storming the gate. The men they had brought with them were members of the civil guard, brave and willing but with little training and experience. Not many hours later, a radio complained: "The men you sent are inadequate. Send the *Palmach*; the whole quarter has to be stormed."

At 8:15 pm of May 20 came the despairing message: "The Arabs have taken the Nissim Bek Synagogue. We cannot drive them out." And again from the outside came the insistent: "Hold out; reinforcements will arrive in time; be strong."

On the morning of May 21, more arms reached the defenders by parachute but also the news that reinforcements had not succeeded in breaking through again.

On the same day an Arab broadcast was picked up which boasted:

The Jews have renewed their desperate attempts to save the encircled Jews in the Old City by attacking churches . . . all these attacks have been repulsed with heavy casualties. The great synagogue of the Jews has been stormed after clearing out the evil Jew.

The rabbis within the Old City asked for a cease-fire to evacuate the wounded, women and children. But the question had to be brought before the representatives of UNO who had to negotiate the terms of a truce. This meant further delay.

The monotonous drama continued. At 2 am of the 25th, the news came from the outside: "Our men have broken through," but at 4:15 am it was followed by the announcement, "They did not succeed in establishing a link and we are returning."

The commander in the Old City radioed back at 10 am: "Last night's failure has broken people's spirit altogether. At least parachute munitions." And at 11:30 am, came the terse tidings: "No commanders left."

On the morning of May 26, a plane circled the quarter four times and dropped munitions by parachute, but apparently nothing reached the defenders. They radioed: "We have not received anything; send plane again."

At 10 pm the Arabs tried an old trick. Through loudspeakers and amplifiers—the words could be heard even in Yemin Moshe, in the orthodox quarter outside the walls—they threatened: "Surrender within seven hours because all the Jews of Jerusalem are about to surrender." To the dispirited population, the false information that all Jerusalem was on the verge of surrender was the last blow.

A cease-fire could not be negotiated because one of the Arab demands was that the Haganah abandon Mt. Zion, a position vital to the defense of Jerusalem. Messages from the outside kept heartening the population: "We prepare a large operation for your rescue. Fire only at targets (to save ammunition)."

At 10:20 pm the Old City sent out the news: "The Hurva Synagogue has been destroyed; there is no bread."

At 6 am on the 28th, the outside commander was still urging: "Hold out for a day; we shall try again at night," but at 1:30 pm he agreed to a cease-fire. The situation was hopeless. The Yohanan Ben Zakai Synagogue was completely encircled, and the munitionless defenders knew that they would be unable to prevent a wholesale massacre of the wounded and civilians once the Arabs broke into this last retreat.

Permission to surrender had been given reluctantly; preparations for the long-promised "large operation" were actually being made for that night because the first onslaught of the Arab armies on New Jerusalem had already been withstood. But from Mt. Zion, the Haganah commanders could see the hopeless case of the surrounded synagogue. The risk of waiting another 24 hours was too great.

When the Legion commanders entered, after the surrender terms which called for the imprisonment of all those of military age and release of women and children had been signed, they found it hard to believe that this pathetic handful had withstood the Legion for two weeks. Even for the Arabs it was not a glorious victory.

Long lines of women, children and old men staggered through Zion Gate to the Haganah lines: 294 men of military age, a group which included the surviving soldiers and all civilian males except the very aged, were led into captivity to Amman.

The medical staff remained behind with 120 seriously wounded who were to be evacuated the next day to the Armenian Convent. A guard of the Arab Legion had been provided. Nevertheless, Arab mobs surrounded the hospital, striving to break in and savor the triumph to the full. The rabble could be seen through the windows armed with rifles, daggers, and hand grenades. While looting the surrounding houses, they had set fire to the buildings. Fire began to sweep toward the hospital and the choice seemed to be that of burning to death or being massacred by the mob.

An Arab officer went out to the mob and fired into the air. The mob recoiled and held back until more soldiers of the Arab Legion arrived. According to witnesses, the Arab soldiers bravely carried out the wounded, saving them from being burned to death and protecting them from the excited mob.

The Legion had also protected the sad-eyed lines of civilians who had filed through Zion Gate. "It was quite a job protecting these Jews from the thousands of Arabs, but the Legion saw to it that not a single Jew was harmed on the way out," proudly said the Legion commander to the correspondents who watched the surrender.

The same could not be said for the Jewish quarter. The 27 synagogues had been systematically dynamited by the Arabs and the Jewish homes reduced to rubble. "Like Stalingrad or Berlin" reported the neutral correspondents who had been permitted to roam among the shell-torn remains of houses and of rubbish which were all that was left of homes, religious schools, and ancient sanctuaries.

The devastation was total. It should be noted again that while Arab shells exploded in the narrow streets, close to the holiest shrines of Christendom, no move was made to stop the destruction. For the first time in centuries the site of Solomon's Temple was without Jewish worshippers, but the old Jews who departed bearing whatever Holy Scrolls they could rescue, vowed to return to the "City of David, the Tower of Zion."

In the meantime, within the New City, the military success of the Haganah in holding off the invaders was accompanied by a progressive deterioration in the condition of the civilian population. The water carts delivered water under the heaviest shelling, but the woman who waited for her pail of water never knew if she would leave the doorway alive. Great ingenuity was displayed in regard to the use of the meager daily ration. Charts were distributed to every household indicating how the ten quarts should be utilized. Only two quarts—for drinking and cooking—could be "wasted." The other eight had to be used successively for washing, laundry, and finally for flushing the toilets. Naturally, there was no water for baths or showers in the summer heat, but the supply could be stretched out for 90 days provided that no cisterns were demolished by Arab shells.

The distribution of food had to be controlled with equal rigor. During the last weeks of the siege the population was subsisting on 600 calories daily. Toward the end, the food ration consisted of three slices of bread; by then families had long used up whatever stock of cans or biscuits they might have had at hand at the beginning of the siege. The only fresh greens were dandelion leaves which venturesome women and children picked in the empty lots.

There was no fuel with which to cook the dry beans or the occasional potatoes. Bonfires would have to be made in backyards or gardens with whatever wood could be found; furniture was being burned. But the people scraped together whatever they could and shared.

There was no light. Electric power could be used only for vital necessities such as the public bakeries concentrated in one section of the city so as to simplify the provision of current. To make certain that the population would at least have its bread ration of three slices, the electricians' team, organized by Dov Joseph, developed a special technique for repairing electric lines damaged by the shelling. During the day, they would cruise about the city in an armored truck, looking for broken wires through a peephole and memorizing their exact location. At night they would return and make repairs in the dark.

This combination of courage and ingenuity was practiced in every department of life. All kinds of devices were used to eke out the waning food supply. A diary kept by the young inmates of a children's home at Motza, a few miles outside Jerusalem, gives a vivid glimpse of life in the besieged city. The children had been evacuated from the exposed suburb where the institution was located in February. As early as April 4, an entry reads:

> *We are always hungry soon after meals. We must be very careful with water and use every bit over and over again. We write letters to our friends but get no answers. Every day we go out into the fields and pick wild leaves and thistles which our cook prepares for meals.*

After an attack on April 11, the diary notes:

> *Today we went out to gather the shrapnel and spent bullets of last night's attack. We have quite a collection of many kinds by now. The mortars and cannon shells are made in England; it says so on them.*

And they add: *"Women go about gleaning everywhere like Ruth in the Bible."*

The day after the invasion, on May 16, we read:

> *Heavy shelling, day and night. From the room of our house we can see the smoke of the cannon at Nebi Samuel. We went out to glean wood again today, for we have nothing to eat but beans and we must cook them . . . . Every day we ask our teachers who has advanced, and, thank God, it is usually us. We can no longer play freely outside as shells might strike at any moment and we must be ready to dash into shelter quickly at all times. For the past days we have had hardly any classes because so much time is taken up getting water, fuel, food, So we too feel as though we are full-time soldiers.*

The teachers were apparently doing a good job. There is only one break in the resolutely optimistic tone. On May 30 came bad news: "We have just heard of the fall of the Old City! How terrible! How very terrible! The children are all crying."

Happier notes were to be struck later: On June 1, the children rejoice: *"Oh what good news! We have just heard of the Burma Road."*[11]

Many more shells were to fall before the children could write on September 15, 1948 (after the second truce):

> *Our new year of studies has begun again. We go to school in town and we all have new school bags and pencils and notebooks and books. This is the first time we are studying outside our own home because so many teachers are in the army and classes have to double up. We keep thinking about this year which was both hard and great.*

Older civilian survivors of the siege relate similar experiences, except that for them the crux of existence revolved around the efforts to get to their place of work or service no matter how heavy the rain of shells. After the general mobilization, when all except services essential to life stopped, it became a matter of honor not to sit cowed in the shelters but to move about. Those engaged in vital service had no choice. Bakers were obliged to report daily to the central bakery no matter what the chance of getting through alive or unmaimed might be. The city had to have its minimal bread ration; if a baker were afflicted with a nervous wife who urged him to skip a day, he was likely to be reminded that he was "mobilized."

And there were less obviously vital activities for which death was risked daily. The editor of *The Palestine Post* and the Jewish manager of Barclay's Bank walked daily from Rehavia to their offices in the center of the city. So did their staffs. Each person knew that fear was progressive and contagious and that the fight against panic had to be won by each individual daily.

A technique reminiscent of battlefields was worked out by those who made their way along the streets. People learned to distinguish the sounds of the shells and to estimate the intervals between their falls. In the intervals of a minute or two they would dart along the street and rush into a hallway just before the next shell. By this process a distance normally covered in ten minutes might take over an hour, depending on the intensity of the bombardment, but usually the destination would be reached, though a number of casualties were inevitable.

The housewife going for her bread ration; the Yemenite charwoman going to help her mistress; the fourteen-year-old boys reporting for work on fortifications alike become expert students of the traffic signals provided by the shells.

Every survivor of the siege has his favorite "miraculous escape" story: the shell that missed by a hair's breadth as one lay in bed, or sat near a window, or darted into a hallway "just in time." And each has his favorite tale of civilian valor.

A professor's wife, herself not Orthodox, told me how heartened she would be on Saturdays to see her pious old neighbor, dressed up in his Sabbath best, setting out for synagogue as usual, walking unhurriedly to the morning service no matter how fierce the bombardment. But nerves grew tauter and bodies thinner.

The dead could not be buried save at the risk of further death. Religious law forbade cremation (the dead must rise whole on Mt. Zion at the trumpet call of the Last Judgment). In obedience to the religious injunction that graveyards must not be located within the city, funeral processions had to brave Arab attack on the way to the cemetery on Mt. Zion. Amid the mounting casualties the question of the unburied dead became as oppressive as that of the living.

The Arabs waited for the moment when thirst, hunger, and unremitting shelling would force the population to surrender; but the unspectacular heroism of plain men and women proved as unpredictable as the spectacular feats of the Haganah. However, the Jewish military authorities knew that the flour had been used up, and that there were no more munitions for the homemade "Davidkas," the improvised mortars of the army.

There was a period when the men and women of Jerusalem believed that they had been forgotten by the rest of embattled Israel. As the weeks drew on and neither food, water, nor reinforcements, reached the city, the sense of abandonment grew. But it was in these weeks that the attempt to break through to Jerusalem was assuming its most dramatic form. A way to Jerusalem was being hewn through the rocky hills. The Burma Road was a neat chart. It was born, foot by foot, and remained to the last a living thing.

Through "Operation Nachshon" much of the Tel Aviv-Jerusalem highway had already been cleared. Only Latrun remained in the center blocking traffic; or waiting to be by-passed.

On the night of May 5, three *Palmach* scouts set out on foot from Jerusalem to discover whether they could link up with the nearest Jewish outpost from the Tel Aviv side. They threaded their way through the Judaean hills following ancient foot-tracks and camel paths which usually followed natural contours and utilized easier grades.

The scouts returned with the message that a road suitable for jeeps might be made along the wadis and camel paths. The very next night a small convoy of jeeps carrying desperately needed flour and munitions began to make its way up the dirt track traced by the scouts. On some stretches the jeeps had to be carried. One incline was too steep to be negotiated by any type of vehicle, and even the small jeeps had to be hauled up by means of a windlass. Since the road was within plain view of Latrun and within easy range of Arab shells, all construction had to take place at night. In the meantime, heavy engagements, under whose cover the building of the alternative road could proceed, were fought.

The construction of this road and its use proceeded simultaneously. From both the Jerusalem and Tel Aviv ends the work went on, and while the gap narrowed, the jeeps continued to clammer around the hairpin turns and up the steep rock mountainside. Where jeeps could not go, donkeys went. On one precipitous incline soldiers and civilian volunteers would trudge up the three-quarter-mile stretch carrying sacks of flour and guns on their backs. At the foot of the hill, the sacks would be piled into trucks which had been sent from Jerusalem.

The road grew like a living organism advancing tenaciously forward in the wake of the men, mules and jeeps. Finally, by the beginning of June, the 16 kilometers of this so-called "Burma Road" were completed. A truck from Tel Aviv could reach Jerusalem.

While the road was being built, a new pipeline was being laid alongside it. Those jolting for the first time on this road had the added thrill of seeing the new pipeline which drew its water from Hulda. Soon water would again flow from the taps of Jerusalem.

With the coming of the first truce, the worst was over.

There are moments whose significance becomes apparent only in retrospect. During the siege of Jerusalem each individual knew that he stood at a climactic point in Jewish history. Each was prepared to concede that he, the individual, might be struck by a splinter, or that his son would be killed in battle, but the City would live. Men have died for cities before, but this was far beyond patriotism. For many, Jerusalem was not the city of their birth or childhood. A large percentage of the population consisted of immigrants. Yet for both the girl recently arrived from Yemen and for the veteran it was equally the meeting point of the prophetic past and the Messianic future—the city holy and beloved.

For centuries, the name *Yerushalaim* had been pronounced by Jews with a special reverence. Since the siege both a new awe and intimacy had been added.

"Those were great days," the survivors said, and one got the impression that to have been in Jerusalem during the dreadful time had been the crown of life. In Israel's aristocracy of valor, the highest rank was awarded to those who held Zion itself.

NOTES

1. ("Defense") Palestinian Jewry's underground defense organization, founded in 1920, which functioned, under the Jewish Agency's jurisdiction, until the creation of the Israeli Army on May 25, 1948.

2. King of Transjordan and grandfather of King Hussein.

3. One of a number of British "security zones" to which the Mandatory authority's forces retreated while engaged in liquidating the Mandatory administration prior to their departure from Palestine. Palestinian Jews called these zones "Bevingrads" in ironic reference to the role of British Foreign Secretary Ernest Bevin.

4. Jerusalem's English language daily, today called *The Jerusalem Post*.

5. On their way to the Hadassah Medical Center on Mt. Scopus.

6. Child Rescue Program, sponsored by the Jewish Agency.

7. *Plugot Mahatz* ("shock companies")—the commando units of Haganah.

8. Launched by the Haganah during the first two weeks of April.

9. Irgun Tz'vai L'umi—an independent military underground Palestinian Jewish extremist organization created in 1931.

10. Brigadier John Glubb, the British Commander of the Arab Legion.

11. Reminiscent of the road constructed by the retreating British in Burma during World War II.

THE DOG AND THE DEER

I must admit to a measure of skepticism when in August 1948 I was first invited to visit several friendly Arab villages. The existence of acquiescent Arabs, in villages which had surrendered or been conquered, was well-known, but "friendly" sounded a bit too much. However, after having drunk innumerable small cups of powerful black coffee, reclined on cushions, squatted on low stools, sat on plain Western chairs in various Arab homes, I am prepared to testify that "friendly" Arabs are not an invention of wishful thinkers.

My first conversation with an Arab was not precisely amiable. We had been walking through an Arab quarter of Haifa which had not been abandoned by its inhabitants. Many Arabs had remained and the stirrings of returning life could be seen. We chatted with the burly owner of an Arab cafe where Jews and Arabs were playing chess, and stepped into a bakery to see *pittah* being baked. The round, flat pancakes were fashioned from dough brought by the customers and baked to suit each family's taste.

A mattress-maker wandered down the narrow street carrying a curious wooden instrument for carding wool. A melon vendor chanted his wares. The scene called for snapshots.

While I adjusted my camera, a disgruntled, unpicturesque Arab, dressed in Western clothes, walked over and remonstrated in fluent English:

"Why do you take pictures of a slum section? Why don't you go where the better class lives? Before the troubles you should have seen how elegant our people were—like New York or Paris."

We explained that we were interested in "life"—poor or rich, what was the difference? The Arab was not mollified. Obviously unconcerned about providing us with sociological or exotic data, he insisted: "You should have seen how our better people lived before they left."

I wanted to say: "Don't be such a snob," but instead inquired politely: "Why did they leave?"

"Because they were fools," was the surly answer.

The reply encouraged me to ask: "Did the Jews drive them out?"

His answer was emphatic: "No."

"Who drove them out?"

The Arab was silent a moment, and then he said guardedly: "You know."

"The Mufti?"

My interlocutor edged away, allowing himself a final word: "If you know, why do you ask?"

The conversation having ended like a Yiddish joke, I went back to my camera. But by this time the mattress-maker was out of sight.

This debut in Arab-Jewish contacts proved to be untypical. My subsequent encounters with Arabs, whether in townhouses or clay hovels, were marked with the oriental punctilio which is as stylized as a decoration in a Mosque. The grace with which we were welcomed had its charm, though I was prepared to interpret it as the famous Eastern hospitality which supposedly bound the host only as far as his threshold. However, the children convinced me that there was more to it.

As soon as our car would stop in an Arab village, we would be surrounded by a swarm of curious children, obviously not the least bit afraid of the Jewish "conquerors." Smiling, anxious to give directions, they would climb up on the running board and start chattering with those members of the party who knew Arabic. Such cordiality could not be simulated; it was plain that in their homes talk about the "Yehudi" was probably not hostile. Occasionally, one of the elders of the village would utter the Arab equivalent for "scat," but in a moment the youngsters would be back, entranced by the car and the visitors.

Of course, we were visiting villages which had not fallen prey to Arab League propaganda about the "Jewish terror," and whose inhabitants had refused to flee despite the pressure of the Arab commanders. The fact that they had remained indicated an *a priori* readiness to come to terms with their Jewish neighbors.

Not only the children displayed an unsolicited warmth. As we would trudge along narrow dirt roads, past clay hovels or low stone houses, Arab women standing in the doorways and modestly averting their faces (veiled or unveiled according to the tribe) from the gaze of strange men, would call out to me: *"Saida"* (the Arab greeting). More than one ventured: *"Shalom."* *"Saida,"* I would answer, and they would smile shyly.

In one village which had steadfastly refused to participate in the hostilities against the Jews, our appearance assumed the character of "old home week." Arabs don't slap their guests on the back, but the welcome was as hearty as the more delicate gestures of the East permit. Acquaintances in our party were embraced like returning buddies, and the air was thick with *Saidas* and *Shaloms.*

Other villages were less exuberant, but the willingness to sit down and talk things over was notable. After the ceremonial coffee drinking, long conversations would be held in a setting which varied with the economic status of our host. No matter how poor the village, the Sheikh would generally have a stone house, often the only one amid the clay hovels, set high on the mountain slope. We would be received in a cool, bright room with a freshly scrubbed stone floor and light blue walls—an unexpected oasis in the squalor of the village. The furnishings might be cushions and small stools, or wicker chairs according to the degree of Westernization, but the talk would run the same course. The Sheikh would bide his time until a few of the leading men of the village had joined the company. I could not figure out whether they had been summoned or whether the mere arrival of guests was reason enough for their appearance.

Though I had to follow the conversations through an interpreter, it was impossible to miss the amazing articulateness of these untutored Arab villagers. Some of the men to whom we spoke were illiterate but their discussions of local politics and the war sounded about as reasoned and informed as that of the average literate citizen of the U.S.A. I heard men who could neither read nor write discourse on the respective roles of Great Britain, the United States, and Russia in the Middle East. This display of political acumen, as distinct from folklore and marketplace gossip, was something of a revelation. To a sedulous reader of four daily newspapers and several weekly journals of opinion, it was even disconcerting.

One old Druse Sheikh, who weighed his words carefully before answering questions, gave an exposé of international rivalries which could have appeared in a letter signed "Pro Bono Publico." He pointed out that the United States was unduly influenced by Great Britain, suggested what might be expected from Russia, and analyzed the strength of the Jews.

He had always liked the Jews, he told us, because they had bought the land, not conquered it by force. Furthermore, as a Druse he too belonged to a minority and appreciated minority problems.

So far this sounded like a speech I might have delivered in Poughkeepsie; then, of his own accord—the theme was too delicate to raise—he began discussing the reason for Arab defeats. He summed up his explanation with the tale of the dog and the deer:

The dog's master had bidden him to catch the deer. The dog ran fast but the deer was fleeter. Finally, the dog gave up. When peace was made between the two, the dog asked the deer:

"Why are you swifter than I? Why do you always outrun me?"

The deer answered: "I can run better than you because you run at your master's bidding, only to do me hurt, whereas I run for my life."

That is why, said the old Sheikh, the "Yehudi" had scored such victories despite the fact that they were so greatly outnumbered.

The Sheikh's tale, I decided, was better than anything I had produced in Poughkeepsie.

In a Bedouin village consisting of the typical black tents of the tribe, we were received under a canopy stretched between several trees. The Sheikh, a lusty old fellow, had dyed his graying moustache a fierce black, and I suspect had touched up his eyes. His costume was a hybrid common in Palestine—a tightly fitting khaki military jacket worn over a long striped robe, and of course, a flowing *keffyah*.

The tribesmen squatted around a small fire in the open, over which coffee was already being prepared; the guests enjoyed a wooden table and chairs. Large platters of rice, bowls of sour *leben*, lamb, and tomato were served by the Sheikh's sons. Forks were mysteriously produced, but the better schooled among us scooped up the food with *pittah*. The women, as usual, had withdrawn; we saw them peeping from behind the flap of a tent or out of a doorway. The children, male and female, ran freely about.

After having industriously dipped many pieces of *pittah* into the common bowls, and later having loudly sipped the coffee in the approved style, we got down to serious talk. Palestinian Arabs, said the Sheikh, wanted peace and prosperity. He personally wasn't going to be terrorized by foreign Arabs. Nobody was going to tell him what to do.

A small boy ran by noisily.

"You Syrian," one of the tribesmen shouted to quiet him. Apparently Syrians were not popular in the vicinity.

The Sheikh peppered his discourse with proverbs, one of which I had already heard from other Arabs: "Whoever marries my aunt is my uncle."

The peasant candor of this bit of folk wisdom seemed to me an honest expression of Arab sentiment at the time when not artificially stimulated. It was hardly a flaming slogan and no doubt would have been repudiated by Arab extremists, just as its simple-hearted opportunism would have offended some Jews. But by and large it stated the case. The average farmer wanted to till his soil and live peaceably. He had learned from bitter experience that the war precipitated by the Mufti and the "foreigners" had proved disastrous to his house, his sons, his harvest. Now he would like to come to terms with the Jewish "uncle." Of course, there was always the chance that if uncle lost auntie, the allegiance might shift.

(December 1948)

FROM YEMEN

A Yemenite legend tells of a pious old widow named Saada who feared greatly that the Messiah might come while she slept and that she would fail to hear the blast of his trumpet. This danger was particularly acute on Passover, the time when the Messiah was most likely to arrive. For at the Passover feast one had to drink four glasses of ritual wine, after which one slept soundly. To forestall the danger of being left behind in the exile of Yemen, Saada went to sleep in the doorway of her house, first tying her donkey to her foot. Everyone knew that the Messiah, as foretold, would arrive riding on a donkey, whom her beast would no doubt seek to welcome. This would awaken Saada.

Comforted by this precaution, Saada fell asleep. During the night, the donkey grew restless and trotted out into the village dragging his mistress behind him. The happy Saada, confident that the Messiah had finally appeared, kept imploring the donkey who was dragging her along the streets: "Not so fast, dear Mr. Messiah, not so fast!"

The 30,000 Yemenite Jews flown to Israel since the establishment of the Jewish state in the fabulous Operation Magic Carpet might well have echoed the old lady's cry. Within the course of one year the most ancient Jewish community in existence was being thrust headlong into the twentieth century. The Yemenites were probably the "purest" Jews extant; they had lived isolated on the tip of the Arabian peninsula since Biblical times. Untouched by the development of the Western world and by the global course of Jewish wanderings for nearly 2,000 years, they had been preserved in their pristine state, picturesque and not quite credible, like an animated Old Testament illustration. Rebecca at the well must have looked like one of these lithe, sloe-eyed Yemenite girls walking barefooted in her long robes.

Yet despite their remoteness from the currents of medieval and modern civilization, the Yemenite Jews not only clung to their faith in the face of savage Moslem persecution, but even kept alive a mystical expectation of the "Return." Throughout the centuries Jewish scholars occasionally visited them, bringing books and commentaries whose origin the Yemenite could no longer recall. They only knew that "wise men" had come as messengers from the world outside. Rumors of the various Messianic movements which periodically stirred Jewry would mysteriously reach them, and a few sturdy spirits would try to make the long trek across the desert to Zion, defying the Imam's edict against emigration, particularly to Palestine.

There is a tradition to the effect that the Yemenite Jews originally migrated from Palestine to Yemen before the destruction of the First Temple in 586 B.C. The prophet Jeremiah is supposed to have warned them to escape in time from doomed Jerusalem. Even when the Temple was rebuilt, the cautious Yemenites refused to heed the call to return to Zion for they knew that the Second Temple, too, would be destroyed. Now the unhappy Yemenites believe that the wretchedness which has been their lot for centuries is the punishment for this excessive ancestral prudence.

Whether or not Jews lived in Yemen as early as the sixth century B.C., there is solid evidence that a Jewish community existed in Yemen by the second century A.D. Since that period their economic status appears always to have been depressed, but active Moslem persecution did not start until the twelfth century. Until that time they enjoyed the protection of a letter from Mohammed which enjoined the Moslems from molesting the "Children of Israel" and from disturbing their "reading of the Torah which was revealed through Moses, peace be with him, who spoke with God on Mount Sinai." Mohammed's tolerance, unfortunately, proved to be of limited influence. From the twelfth century on, Moslem fanaticism could no longer be contained. Word of their sufferings reached Maimonides who, in 1182, sent them his famous *Epistle* urging them to remain steadfast.

The condition of the Yemenites continued to deteriorate until it reached a pariah status. Though the attempt to escape was punishable by death and entailed confiscation of all property, individual Yemenites would flee into the desert and wander for weeks trying to reach a port on the Red Sea from which they might embark to Palestine. Often they would be captured by bandits who would return those unable to pay a ransom to Yemen for execution.

However, these sporadic, unorganized attempts to reach Palestine did not assume the character of a movement until the beginnings of the twentieth century. The first Zionist stirrings in the 1880s, when the *Bilu* wave of emigration started from Eastern Europe apparently reached remote Yemen. But the nucleus of what could be called a genuine Zionist movement did not take shape until 1910, when Shmuel Yavnieli, a young Palestinian pioneer, decided to explore the *terra incognita* of Yemen and bring the message of Zion to his fellow Jews.

The self-appointed mission of Yavnieli is one of the peaks of Zionist romanticism though little is known of it outside of Israel. Today you can still see Yavnieli sitting at conferences of the *Histadruth,* and those in the know will point out the rugged old man who in his youth tried to lead the Jews out of unknown Yemen.

Forty years before the flight of the Skymasters of Operation Magic Carpet, Yavnieli, who had come to Palestine from Russia with the group of Socialist idealists known as the Second *aliyah* (Second Wave of Immigration), made his way to Yemen. Dressed in native garb, he spent a year going from village to village in Yemen and Aden.

In the account of his journey, Yavnieli relates how the Yemenites would gather around him to ask ecstatically: "What of the Wailing Wall? What about Rachel's Tomb? And the tomb of Rabbi Shimon Ben Yochai?"

The young pioneer would answer: "Why ask about tombs and dead stones? Ask about Zion coming to life and its children returning from dispersion."

The Yemenites, among whom religious ecstatics and pseudo-Messiahs had more than once appeared, were not easily discouraged. They kept asking: "Do you know any tidings? Is the time drawing nigh? Are there signs?"

The young pioneer would make a good Socialist-Zionist speech trying to conceal his vexation: "I am not the Messiah nor the messenger of the Messiah. Nevertheless I do have tidings . . . I have come to tell you that soon our land will be free. Every part of the land of Israel that is worked by Jewish hands is liberated. The land has begun to return fruit to its children who work it, and this is a sign that redemption is near."

The Yemenites wanted trumpet blasts, miracles—the Messiah. Instead, here was a young fellow who, rather than promising them paradise, was picturing a realistic life of hard physical labor with no Messianic fanfare. Besides, most of the Yemenites had imagined a dreamland—Zion, whose dust one came to kiss rather than irrigate. "He who lives in the Land of Israel, all his sins are forgiven."

Some objected that the hour of redemption was not yet at hand: "There have been no signs. We will not go. You are only trying to force the end." Others announced passively: "If a ship will come to take us, we will go."

Yavnieli had a hard job. He had to transform the abstract religious rapture, which impelled them vaguely "to die in the Holy Land" into a desire for a concrete Palestine of fields and farms rather than holy cities and tombs.

Because life in Yemen was so wretched they dreamt of release in Zion. When Yavnieli stressed the importance of agricultural work, they would counter with hopeful sayings such as : "If one is found deserving, others will do his work," or "There is no easier and cleaner trade than tailoring."

Sometimes they would become unexpectedly practical, and demand: "Is it true that as soon as we get there we will be taken into the army?" or "Is it true that you are an agent of the Sultan in Constantinople and were sent here to take us for military service? What about the desecration of the Sabbath while in the army? And the non-kosher food?"

Yavnieli did his best to dispose of these doubts: "I tried to make them see their own pitiful state in Yemen, far from their ancestral land, subject to an alien people, so poor that they could barely afford a piece of corn bread twice a day and a garment to cover but half a man's body, living in hovels without floors and with but small holes in the walls for windows.

"Yet these people were addicted to jewelry. I would address the small pitiful Jewish women and tell them: 'Throw away these trinkets; sell them and give the money to your husbands so that you can go to Palestine. Wouldn't it be better if you were to buy clothes for yourself and your children, or blankets and pillows instead of these pieces of silver?' They eyed me in wonder, these people who drank liquor made of dates to forget their sorrows, studied mystical works without understanding them, yet were satisfied with their lot.

"All these things I pointed out to them and called their attention to the abandoned villages and the overflowing cemeteries where the victims of the last famine were buried."

But Yavnieli's most telling argument was the failure of the Yemenite community to multiply: "You have been in Yemen for many generations, yet you have not increased. Our forefathers went down to Egypt numbering seventy souls, yet after two hundred ten years they departed from Egypt numbering six hundred thousand. You have been here for centuries and you are not even forty thousand. Is not the curse of God upon you in this land?" The men nodded assent.

Yavnieli suffered all kinds of difficulties in his efforts to organize small transports of Jews out of Yemen into Aden, and from Aden to Palestine. The worst blow came in 1911, after a year of labor which included imprisonment by the Arab authorities.

In the course of the winter two old men who left for Palestine, though Yavnieli had advised them not to go because of their age, succeeded in returning to Yemen with reports of the hard life in pioneer Palestine:

"They were a living protest against Palestine. When their fellow citizens saw them they wept and cursed me and my work . . . Whereas formerly the popular imagination and dreams combined to help the movement, these now worked against me. 'This man is merely an agent of the Sultan sent here to take the Jews into the army and lead them to war.' Others declared, 'This man came here to enslave us to work in his fields and vineyards in *Eretz Yisrael*. He escorts the people to the ship and there he brands each one with a special sign to show that they are his slaves.'"

But despite these setbacks, Yavnieli's journey through Yemen bore fruit. Before he left Aden, a group of six hundred Jews from Yemen were preparing to embark for Palestine.

Since the days of Yavnieli, the situation of the Yemenite Jews became, if anything worse. According to the Imam's decrees, all Jews are Satans and consequently may not pass to the right of a Moslem since their shadow is evil. They may not ride on a horse or donkey. This restriction effectively deprives Jews of all means of transportation since Yemen does not abound in subways, streetcars or buses. Jews may not carry arms, and in law their testimony is invalid. Though Yemenite Jews have been skilled craftsmen for centuries—silversmiths, blacksmiths, potters, embroiderers—they are compelled to clean privies and dig ditches.

Socially and politically, they are degraded "untouchables" with no hope of emancipation save through conversion. To the extremely religious Yemenite Jew the danger of forcible conversion to Islam is perhaps the most fearful aspect of his oppression. According to Yemen's law every Jewish orphan under the age of 13 must embrace the Moslem faith.

To save their children from forcible induction into the Mohammedan fold more and more Jews began to escape to Palestine. The flight gathered momentum with the growth of the Jewish National Home.

In 1934 the Mufti of Jerusalem visited Yemen and demanded that the ban against emigration to Palestine be strictly enforced by the Imam. Nevertheless, the Yemenite Jews kept fleeing into the desert. By the time of the establishment of the Jewish state there were 15,000 Yemenite Jews in Israel. Another 40,000 still remained behind in Yemen.

The Arab-Israeli war added the danger of massacre to the previous oppressions. The situation of the Yemenites became so desperate that they kept fleeing by the thousands to the British Protectorate of Aden where they sought shelter in a refugee camp maintained by the Jewish Distribution Committee. This frantic flight prompted the JDC to start Operation Magic Carpet in 1948. Many of the Yemenites had trudged as long as six weeks across the rough Arabian desert to reach the camp in Aden. Their physical condition was so poor that the pilot of one plane decided to take twice the number he had originally intended. The frail emaciated Yemenites weighed less than 90 pounds each; he could double his passenger load safely.

The Yemenites are industrious, patient, pious. The *Yishuv* has always taken kindly to them. But before the establishment of the state, because of their low cultural level in modern terms, they were largely a menial class. Now Israel has the obligation to transport the Yemenites not only geographically but culturally into the life of a modern state. The Yemenites have many advantages over other immigrants. They speak a Biblical Hebrew, as well as Arabic. They are at home in the climate; the landscape is familiar to them, and they are familiar to it. The hills and valleys of Israel know their slight, graceful figures and their pure Semitic profiles. The most ancient diaspora has come home.

THE ARAB REFUGEES

If there is anything that can be said to trouble Americans sympathetic to Israel, Jewish and non-Jewish alike, it is the problem of Arab refugees. This problem, according to Mr. Laurence Michelmore, Commissioner-General for the UN Relief and Works Agency (UNRWA), has not grown "any less complex or less dangerous to the peace and stability of the region," nor has the desire of the refugees to return to their homes grown any less intense. "From their standpoint," Mr. Michelmore recently told the current session of the General Assembly, "a nation has been obliterated and a population arbitrarily deprived of its birthright. This injustice still festers in their minds."

Though it is obvious that the Arab refugees are being used by the Arab states as pawns in a political game, such exploitation does not necessarily invalidate claims put forward on their behalf. The Arabs continue to call for "repatriation," Israel continues to refuse, and people whose scruples can only be those of conscience and not of *Realpolitik*, continue to wonder how Jews, themselves such recent refugees, can bear to add to the sum of human suffering by declining to admit Arab refugees into Israel. Even committed Zionists are disturbed by this question. Exile and longing for return—key words in Jewish national experience—carry powerful echoes. Am I as a Zionist insensitive to these echoes? Do I ignore them, hoping solely for the success of Israeli arms? Despite the hazard of self-righteous protestations by a partisan, let me address myself here to the ethical issue.

I write, of course, on the premise that the establishment of Israel was an act of historic justice and that its continued existence is to be desired. On the Arab postulate that Israel must be obliterated and its inhabitants driven into the sea, there is no room for discussion. On the assumption, however, of Israel's right to survival, is the Jewish state facing in the Arab refugees a reverse Zionism whose impulse it should be the first to meet with sympathy? The comparison, superficially intriguing, is essentially false. Jews were driven to the "national home" granted by the Balfour Declaration by homelessness, necessity, a centuries-old historic attachment, and a search for national identity. They purchased and reclaimed its deserts and swamps, acre by acre, and finally defended a shrunken area of it against the attack of the combined Arab armies. None of these elements, physical or emotional, lies behind the Arab will to return.

The very origin of the Arab refugee problem indicates the difference. The tragedy of the Jewish refugee lay in his absence of choice. He was driven out by force or by decree and he fled from a real, not a mythical, terror. His only refuge was the remote "homeland" which the Arab refugee left of his own will; the Arab was free to remain. There is a crucial distinction between fleeing *to* a land because of desperate need, and fleeing *from* the same land without need. But perhaps the simple historical record makes the point best.

I arrived in Palestine in June 1948, when the Arab exodus was in full swing. One of my tasks was to draw up a report on the subject for the newly formed Israeli Bureau of Information. There were no documents and no studies. All that was available in those days were the fresh reactions of Jews and Arabs—as yet undoctored by policy. From my interviews with Arabs in villages which had accepted the authority of the State of Israel instead of fleeing to the enemy, and from my discussions with clergy of various denominations who had helplessly watched the departure of their flocks, the chief impression I got was one of astonished dismay on all sides. The Arabs agreed that the villagers who had fled could have stayed as they themselves stayed, but the refugees had "listened to Mufti;" and the Christian clergy described scenes of ungovernable fear which no reassurance had been able to stem. One sturdy Mother Superior told me, "I said to them, 'Don't be afraid; I'll protect you,' but they ran." The Jews to whom I spoke were still bewildered by the spectacle of tens of thousands of Arabs leaving their homes and possessions and rushing in wild panic toward the sea or the mountains. The deserted Arab villages, the abandoned Arab quarters of Jaffa and Haifa, presented the same baffling picture. I heard many conflicting explanations: the Arab leaders had ordered the exodus; the British had instigated it; the Mufti's "atrocity-propaganda" had backfired; the Irgun massacre at Deir Yassin had terrified the Arabs.

The two schools of thought—that the exodus was a deliberate part of Arab military strategy, or that it was an uncontrollable stampede which the Arab leadership strove unsuccessfully to check—were not contradictory. Apparently, what began as a calculated move degenerated into irrational frenzy. The development of the exodus as well as Arab statements indicate that the flight was at first stimulated by the Arab leadership to inflame the populace (since the Palestinian Arabs had shown little stomach for battle), to create an artificial Arab "refugee" problem which would elicit world sympathy to counterbalance the claims of Jewish refugees, and to prepare the ground for invasion by the Arab states who could then appear as the saviors of their brethen. An additional reason was no doubt the desire to evacuate Arab civilians from territory which the Arab states expected to bomb. But the smooth functioning of this scheme was impaired by the very completeness of its success. A considered evacuation turned into a hysterical stampede.

Wealthy Arabs began to leave Palestine shortly after the passage of the UN Partition Resolution and the outbreak of disturbances in December 1947, planning to return after the Jews had been liquidated by the Arab states. As early as January 30, 1948, a Palestinian Arab newspaper (*As Shaab*) took occasion to chastise the first wave of refugees:

> *The first group of our fifth column consists of those who abandon their houses and business premises to go live elsewhere. Many of these lived in great comfort and luxury. At the first sign of trouble they took to their heels in order to escape sharing the burden of the struggle, whether directly or indirectly.*

The departure of individual wealthy Arabs could, however, hardly be described as flight. The condition in which these Arabs left their homes, without bothering to remove even readily transportable valuables, indicated that they had complete confidence in the rapid success of the Arab invasion and were merely absenting themselves temporarily. They left neither in haste nor in fear; they merely locked the front door, and drove off for what was to be a vacation at some distance from the local unpleasantness. And their departure was observed with understandable alarm by less-moneyed Arabs unable to make similar travelling arrangements.

The first signs of a large-scale exodus were noted in March 1948 (though several hundred Arab children had been evacuated previously from Haifa to Syria as a routine safety measure). In the last week of March and the first week of April thousands of Arabs started to trek from the Sharon coastal plain to the Arab-controlled hill regions. Many sold their poultry and flocks to Jewish friends before leaving.

This first wave of departure was viewed with a mixture of fear and regret by their Jewish neighbors, who wondered uneasily what evil it might signify. The obvious explanation seemed to be the imminence of a full-scale Arab attack with heavy aerial bombardment. In those instances where Arab and Jewish farmers had been on friendly terms, there was a genuine desire to maintain relationships which boded well for the future. But the Arabs would not stay. Later it was learned that the Arab Higher Committee had ordered the evacuation of the coastal plain after the picking of the citrus crop. So calm and well-organized was this phase of the exodus that the cooperation of Jewish settlement guards was enlisted to provide transportation for women, children, and the aged through Jewish areas. The evacuation of the Sharon is notable because it disposes of the Arab charge that the flight started as a result of the massacre at Deir Yassin by Jewish terrorists. The massacre (April 9) took place *after* the evacuation of the Sharon.

Another example of evacuation by Arab command was provided by Tiberias. Since March, there had been sporadic clashes in this sleepy, idyllic little town on the shores of the Lake of Galilee. After Arab gangs infiltrated the Arab quarter and transformed it into a base against the Jewish residents, serious fighting broke out. On April 18, when the battle turned in favor of the small Jewish community of 2,000 souls, the 6,000 Arabs, obviously in obedience to a directive, suddenly began leaving in long convoys. The British, instead of aiding in the pacification of the town, provided transport.

The Jews of Tiberias were so startled by the unexpected departure of the Arabs that the Jewish Community Council of Tiberias issued a statement declaring: "We did not dispossess them; they themselves chose this course. But the day will come when the Arabs will return to their homes and property in this town. In the meantime, let no citizen touch their property." The months of savage warfare ahead were to change these kindly sentiments, but they are important historically as evidence of the original Jewish reaction to the Arab exodus.

Perhaps the clearest indication of why the Arabs fled is afforded by the events in Haifa. On April 22, after the breakdown of Arab resistance in Haifa, truce terms were offered by the Haganah which specifically guaranteed the right of Arabs to continue living in Haifa as equal citizens under the then-existing bi-national municipal council. The British let it be known that they considered the terms "reasonable." The Arabs at first agreed, but changed their minds later in the day, explaining that they could not accept the terms for reasons beyond their control. The "reasons" were not far to seek. The Arab radio was broadcasting directives from the Arab Higher Executive ordering all Arabs to leave Haifa.

The reports of the Haifa British Chief of Police, A. J. Bridmead, suggest how earnestly the Jews tried to persuade the Arabs to stay. On April 26, Bridmead wrote: "The situation in Haifa remains unchanged. Every effort is being made by the Jews to persuade the Arab populace to stay and carry on with their normal lives, to get their shops and businesses open and to be assured that their lives and interests will be safe." In a supplementary report issued the same day, Bridmead repeated: "An appeal has been made to the Arabs by the Jews to reopen their shops and businesses in order to relieve the difficulties of feeding the Arab population. Evacuation was still going on yesterday and several trips were made by Z craft to Acre. Roads, too, were crowded. Arab leaders reiterated their determination to evacuate the entire Arab population, and they have been given the loan of 10 three-ton military trucks as from this morning to assist the evacuation." And on April 28, Superintendent Bridmead was still writing: "The Jews are still making every effort to persuade the Arab population to remain and settle back into their normal lives in the town."

However, no assurances could stop the flight. Very quickly, the proposed strategic evacuation turned into a panic, as the 70,000 Haifa Arabs began to flock wildly toward the port, seeking to "escape" by any craft available. Families crouched for days on the docks, refusing to move until some vessel took them to Acre. Unlike the quiet departure of the Arab gentry months earlier, this was a headlong stampede in which people seem to have jumped suddenly from the dinner table, from bed, or from their work, driven by an impulse to flee. Neighbor followed blindly after neighbor until the port was filled with terrified, squatting figures and every road was clogged.

An article in the London *Economist* (October 2, 1948) quoted a British eyewitness account:

> *During the subsequent days the Israeli authorities who were now in complete control of Haifa . . . urged all Arabs to remain in Haifa, and guaranteed them protection and security. So far as I know, most of the British civilian residents whose advice was asked by Arab friends told the latter that they would be wise to stay. Various factors influenced their decision to seek safety in flight. There is but little doubt that by far the most potent of these factors was the announcements made over the air by the Arab Higher Executive urging all Arabs in Haifa to quit. The reason given was that upon the final withdrawal of the British the combined armies of the Arab States would invade Palestine and drive the Jews into the sea, and it was clearly intimated that those Arabs who remained in Haifa and accepted Israeli protection would be regarded as renegades. At that time the Palestinian Arabs still had some confidence in the ability of the Arab League to implement the promises of its spokesmen.*

The startling example of Haifa was bound to have a profoundly disquieting effect on the whole Arab population of Palestine. The subsequent flight from Jaffa can be viewed as a natural corollary of the exodus organized by the Arab leadership in Haifa. The mass hysteria which developed resulted in the abandonment of many Arab villages even before these were threatened by the progress of the war. After May 15, the process was accelerated. The extraordinary resistance displayed by Israel to the invasion of the Arab states added fuel to the "terror" propaganda of the

Arab League. There are repeated instances of thousands of Arabs fleeing before a handful of Jewish troops.

In Safed, for instance, some 14,000 Arabs picked themselves up one night and fled from the 1,500 Orthodox Jews who lived in the winding, cobbled streets of the ancient town. One must see Safed to appreciate what this means, for the Arabs not only outnumbered the Jews but had every strategic advantage. They occupied all the strongholds of the town, as well as dominant positions on the surrounding hills. The Jews were caught in a kind of narrow trough.

I came to Safed on a late Friday afternoon. Amid the debris of recent battle, the Jews of the town were dressing up for the Sabbath. In the twilight, walking along the streets, one could already hear the chanting of prayers. Old men in round, furred hats and long cloaks were going to the synagogue. Women with lace shawls over their *sheitels* (wigs) sat in the doorways of their shelled homes. Up above, in the main streets, soldiers were strolling along with their girls; Jewish refugees, just a week from the British detention camp of Cyprus, were seeking lodging in the abandoned houses; but below the old Jewish quarter, nothing had changed. "It is all in God's hands," the Orthodox Jews of Safed had declared in refusing to evacuate the town despite the urging of the British.

The Hotel Merkazit, where I stayed during my visit, had been completely riddled with bullets. Most of the windows were broken and many of the walls were damaged. The place had obviously received a thorough shelling. But the aging, bearded innkeeper and his wife had stayed, despite their apparently hopeless position, exposed to the heavy fire of Arab citadels on three sides.

I asked the innkeeper why the Arabs had suddenly decamped. His explanation, which I heard repeated by others, was that it had rained unseasonably on May 9. Because of this, the Arabs decided that the Jews had dropped an atomic bomb—they had heard of heavy rains in Hiroshima. The son of the innkeeper, a member of the small Haganah force which had come to Safed, pooh-poohed the atomic bomb theory. His explanation was simple: "We were few, but our aim was good. Our King Davids [mortars] hit the right spots."

Whatever the reason, the Arabs fled from Safed, as they had from Haifa, in the wake of their leaders.

It should be added that while it was not Haganah policy to encourage the exodus, some hostile villages threatening the road to Jerusalem were evacuated by individual Haganah commanders. The relief of Jerusalem, besieged by the Arab Legion (which had cut off the city's water supply), constituted one of the major struggles of the war. Consequently, a number of villages which served as bases for the enemy camped in the surrounding hills were forcibly cleared, and their inhabitants joined the exodus. But these were isolated instances, occurring late in the fighting, and involving numbers too small to affect the scope of the mass flight or to explain it.*

To compound the confusion surrounding the flights from different towns and villages, the various Arab factions were not agreed as to the tactics pursued by the Arab Higher Committee, the tool of the Mufti. In Baghdad, on July 25, 1948, a radio commentator criticized refugees who complained of the treatment they were receiving in the Arab states and who wished they had stayed in Palestine with the Jews. Such people should be shot as spies, he said, and he added: "The Jews will make you their slaves if you return to them; they will feed you only on bread and water; they will force you to sleep in the open, five on one blanket; they will take your wives and daughters from you. Prefer death to the Jews."

But dissident voices could also be heard from the outset; and as the strategy turned to a calamitous defeat and the manufactured refugee problem became a genuine one, the chorus of dissatisfaction grew progressively louder. As early as March 30, 1948, a Palestinian Arab paper (*As Sarih*) wrote:

> *The inhabitants of the large village of Sheikh Munis and of several other Arab villages in the neighborhood of Tel Aviv have brought a terrible disgrace on us all by quitting their villages bag and baggage. We cannot help comparing this disgraceful exodus with the firm stand of the Haganah in all localities situated in Arab territory or bordering on it. But what is the use of making comparisons; everyone knows that the Haganah gladly enters the battle while we always flee from it.*

King Farouk of Egypt, in a broadcast to the Arab world on July 9, 1948, also expressed his dissatisfaction with "the Palestinian Arabs who ran away leaving their houses and lands behind, giving a chance for a large Jewish immigration and putting Palestine in danger of a Jewish majority."

In Damascus, too, the Arabic radio (August 3, 1948) had occasion to find fault with the refugees: "The Arabs of Palestine are responsible for the heavy losses of the armies in Palestine and the present unfavorable situation. They ran away in the face of a threat by a small minority and spent more time talking over their own affairs than fighting for their country."

But perhaps the most telling comment was made by the Near East Arabic radio broadcast on May 15, 1949, a year after the establishment of the Jewish state:

> *If the Arab leaders had not spread the most horrible and frightening stories of Deir Yassin, the inhabitants of the Arab areas of Palestine would never have fled their homes and would not today be living in*

> *misery. The Arab leaders and the Arab press and radio announced on May 15 that the Jews were scared to death and would soon be thrown into the sea by the advancing Arab armies, but it wasn't long before opinions had to be changed as the Jews scored nothing but victories and the Arabs suffered nothing but defeats.*

A curter summation was offered five years later by the Jordan daily, *Al-Difaá*: "The Arab governments told us, 'Get out so that we can get in.' So we got out, but they did not get in." (September 6, 1954).

This is neither ancient nor irrelevant history. That the Arab refugee chose to cast his lot with the Arab invaders of Israel is a matter of record. The aggression in which he joined in defiance of the Partition Resolution of the United Nations created new circumstances, and by no rational, legal or moral standard could the fledgling state, unexpectedly victorious, be asked to welcome its enemies.

Such champions of the Arabs as Soviet Russia and Communist China have been somewhat less than cordial to those of their citizens who sided with opponents, and the emigrés from those countries are somewhat less than eager to return, knowing the reception that would await them. It is even more instructive to recall the attitude of the American revolutionaries toward the Tories who fled the Thirteen Colonies and made cause with the British. The Founding Fathers, notably Benjamin Franklin, objected not only to their return but to the granting of compensation for their confiscated estates. So long as the young republic was in danger, Franklin, who conducted negotiations with the British in regard to the Tory refugees, refused to countenance their return. In 1789, he wrote of a group of Loyalists who had settled in what was then British territory: "They have left us to live under the government of their King in England and Nova Scotia. We do not miss them nor wish their return." Though the Loyalists were of the same stock as the revolutionists and there was no scarcity of land for them to return to, the Americans were not disposed to trust their good faith: "I believe the opposition given by many to their reestablishing among us is owing to a firm persuasion that there could be no reliance on their oaths" (Benjamin Franklin, in a letter dated June 25, 1785).

I will not deny that after the war was over I heard few expressions of regret from Israelis for the departed Arabs. The months of bitter fighting in which 600,000 Jews repelled the onslaught of five Arab states had changed original attitudes. Now the flight of the Arabs was viewed by many Israelis as another in the series of "miracles" which had made possible the emergence of Israel, for the tiny state had been obliged to offer refuge not only to the survivors of Hitler's death camps but to Oriental Jews fleeing from persecution in Moslem lands. An unofficial population transfer took place. Somewhere between 500,000 and 600,000 Palestinian Arabs left; approximately the same number of destitute Oriental Jews came in from Arab countries in the Middle East and North Africa.

The exact number of *bona fide* refugees has become a matter of contention, with the numbers varying according to who is doing the counting. In answer to the present Arab claim of over a million refugees, Israel cites the figures supplied in December 1946 by the government of Palestine (the British) to UNSCOP. According to these figures, the total number of Arabs in unpartitioned Palestine was 1,288,000; of these 500,000 resided in mandated territory later annexed by Jordan; 100,000 lived in the Gaza Strip, later annexed by Egypt; and 140,000 Arabs remained in what became Israel. The total number of Arab refugees, then, could not have exceeded 550,000. That there are today more than a million on UNRWA's relief rolls can be explained by a combination of factors: a high birth rate; a low death rate (achieved by good sanitary conditions, along with the failure to report deaths so as not to lose ration cards); the padding of relief rolls; and the registration of local Arabs eager to enjoy free lodging and better diet than are available to the indigent in the Middle East.

An even more striking conclusion emerges from the figures supplied in 1946 by the government of Palestine. Most of the refugees now reside in Jordan and Gaza in territory which was formerly Palestine. Thus it is clear that the majority has merely moved from one area of what was mandatory Palestine to another. They left their native villages, not their native land. This, too, must be borne in mind when an attempt is made to picture the Arab refugee as dwelling in an alien *galut* and passionately fixed upon his Palestine Zion.

In 1946 I visited DP camps in the American Zone of Germany. There I saw Jewish children poring over homemade maps of Palestine labelled simply, *Artzenu* (Our Land), pretty much as I am told Arab children study the geography of a country they have never seen. But with this difference: in Jordan the Arab children are in an Arab land among brothers who are concerned for their destiny (even if this concern is subordinated to political considerations). In no fundamental sense are they homeless. They are not the few accidental survivors of a terror which pursued them wherever they sought to escape. If they continue to live in UNRWA camps, it is not because of necessity but because they are being held hostage by Arab belligerence which refuses to permit their absorption in Arab host countries.

Were it possible for one wild moment to imagine that the Jewish children I saw in 1946 had not been on German soil but in a Jewish land surrounded by large, independent Jewish states, every significant element in the comparison would crumble. Let me continue the fantasy: suppose the talk I heard in the bleak barracks had been not of quotas barring survivors from every country except the one remote, besieged "homeland"; suppose, instead, the survivors had been informed that huge international funds were available for their immediate resettlement, without perilous journeys, in their familiar environment, Hebrew in speech, Jewish in tradition and religion, and governed by the Jews. So nonsensical a speculation points up the hollowness of attempted parallels between the status of the Jewish survivors of the war and that of the Palestine refugees. Every detail of the fable, consisting as it does of impossibles which do violence to the whole course of Jewish history, highlights the difference between the Arab and Jewish plight. What the Jews would have hailed as Utopia, the Arab can afford to reject as injustice.

Certainly it is true that the Palestine Arabs left homes and villages dear to them, and no supporter of Jewish nationalism like myself has the right to minimize the intensity or equivalent dignity of Arab nationalism. What may legitimately be questioned, however, is the existence of a genuine *Palestinian* nationalism as distinguished from an attachment to the home town. While Palestine has for Jews been the two-thousand-year-old Zion of history and religious tradition, for Arabs it was a geographical locality, a small sector among huge Arab lands whose independent sovereignty was secured by the Allied powers after two world wars. The most extreme of the Arab spokesmen, Ahmed Shukairy, head of the Palestine Liberation Organization, while developing his case for the UN Security Council (May 31, 1956), categorically stated: "It is common knowledge that Palestine is nothing but southern Syria." Historically, Shukairy is right, just as he was right when he recently included several prominent Jordanians in the executive of his organization on the theory that there was no difference between a Jordanian and a Palestinian and that both sides of the Jordan might as well be called Palestine. More astute Arab propagandists, notably the editor of the Amman weekly, *Amman al Masa*, warned that this thesis was bound to make resettlement in the underpopulated Arab territories up to the border of Iraq more "respectable," since the advocates of resettlement would be able to claim with justice that the Palestinian Arabs were merely being urged to move to another part of their country. On this point Zionists agree with Shukairy.

Insofar as the Arab refugees case rests on the satisfaction of a unique Palestinian nationalism which can be gratified only in the particular town or village that was abandoned in the exodus, it breaks down on the basis of what Shukairy admits is "common knowledge." For the Arab, Palestine is a geographic fact, not an historic concept—and a very recently created geographic fact, at that. According to the 1922 census taken by the British government, at the beginning of the British Mandate, only 186,000 Arabs lived in the area which is now Israel. The present State of Israel represents a second partition of the original area designated by the Balfour Declaration as the Jewish homeland. In 1922, the two-thirds of Palestine East of the Jordan was set up as the independent Arab state of Transjordan, and the UN Partition Resolution of 1947 further divided an already truncated country.

It is hard for Israelis to understand what violence is done to the national ego of the Palestinian Arab if he is resettled in Jordan (only 40 years ago the major part of Palestine) or another underpopulated Arab land. The change from Louisiana to New York or from New York to Nebraska is more dramatic than a move across the borders of the neighboring Arab lands. The same landscape, the same climate, the same ethnic community remain to the Palestinian refugee.

Does the loss of a particular village or courtyard constitute exile as the term is normally understood? In the course of the construction of the Aswan Dam in Egypt, thousands of villagers were relocated by government decree. In preparation for filling the Bratsk reservoir in Siberia, more than 100 villages and towns, including the 300-year-old settlement of Bratsk, were moved to other sites. Nasser and the Soviet authorities acted in the name of progress, whatever the sentiments of the villagers. This is not a frivolous comparison written in disregard of the deep passions generated by the Arab-Israeli conflict, or of the suffering and dislocation that followed in its wake for both sides—in this connection the half-million Jewish refugees from Arab lands should not be forgotten. But most of the subsequent suffering of the Arab refugees has been deliberately provoked for reasons bearing little relation to the needs of the individuals involved.

No one in his right mind would expect Nasser to equate the viability of Israel and the answer it provides to unprecedented human suffering with progress or with any positive achievement. But is it far-fetched to suggest that if relocation may be accepted matter-of-factly for a dam or a reservoir, it can be countenanced where large historic issues are at stake? In the narrow confines of Israel, twice whittled down from the original boundaries of the Promised Land of the Balfour Declaration, there is no room for an uncontrolled Arab influx—not unless the objective of an independent Jewish state be abandoned after the brave resurgence of hardly two decades. Were Israel to be swamped by an Arab tide, its inhabitants lost in an Arab sea or, as is daily threatened, driven into the sea, would justice be served?

Admittedly, the lot of the Arab refugee is miserable. Even though physical conditions in the camps maintained by UNRWA compare favorably with the standard of living of the local population, no one will pretend that camp existence is normal. However, the refusal of the Arab countries to permit the liquidation of the Arab refugee problem, their artificial maintenance of the refugees as a rallying cry against Israel, is motivated by purely political considerations. Arabs make no secret of the fact that they view the refugees as "the cornerstone of the Arabs' struggle against Israel . . . the refugees are the armament of the Arabs and Arab nationalism" (Egyptian government radio, Cairo, July 19, 1957).

From the point of view of Arab belligerence, this makes good sense; it keeps the pot boiling and prevents a peaceful accommodation to contemporary realities. Nasser put it succinctly when he told an interviewer in *Zuercher Woche* (September 1, 1961) that "If the Arabs return to Israel, Israel will cease to exist." It is pointless to multiply quotations from Arab statesmen—Iraqi, Saudi Arabian, or Syrian—since none pretends to any other purpose. A resolution adopted at a Conference of Refugees in Syria in July 1957 makes Arab past and current policy crystal clear: "Any discussion aimed at a solution of the Palestine problem which will not be based on ensuring the refugees' right to annihilate Israel will be regarded as a desecration of the Arab people and an act of treason."

Those who share the Arab conviction that Israel should be destroyed have good reason to applaud such declarations. I find it hard, however, to understand those who on the one hand accept the existence of the Jewish state as a fact of contemporary history, and at the same time urge the "repatriation" of what has to all intents become an invading army. Israel, a country the size of New Jersey, with a population of two-and-a-quarter million, already has an Arab minority of 286,000 (ten percent) within its borders. The original group of Arabs who chose to remain in the Jewish state has doubled through natural increase and the return of members of families whose admission was permitted by the Israeli government. An exercise in arithmetic readily indicates what would happen were a million hostile—or, for that matter, hypothetically friendly—Arabs to enter the country. Israel would cease to exist as a Jewish state even if we assume that the threatened physical obliteration of its inhabitants would not take place. That Israel should decline to collaborate in its own destruction is at least as reasonable as the Arab zeal to destroy it.

Were the same criteria applied to the Palestinian Arabs as to other victims of post-war dislocation, resettlement would be viewed as a satisfactory solution. Vast exchanges of population have taken place in the post-war world. As the result of territorial partitions, there has been an exchange of 15 million refugees in India and Pakistan; 400,000 Karelians in Finland have been absorbed by the Finns without appeal to the outside world, and 350,000 *Volksdeutsche* by Austria; the West German government has successfully integrated nearly nine million refugees from Eastern Germany; the UN Agency for Relief to Korean Refugees, established in 1951 on the pattern of UNRWA, was dissolved in 1956, by which time at least four million Korean refugees had been absorbed. Only the Arab refugees, constantly increasing in number, remain—as a monument to Arab intransigence.

Neutral students of the refugee problem have reached the same conclusions:

> *I hold the view that, political issues aside, the Arab refugee problem is by far the easiest postwar refugee problem to solve by integration. By faith, by language, by race and by social organization, they are indistinguishable from their fellows of their host countries. There is room for them, in Syria and Iraq. There is a developing demand for the kind of manpower they represent. More unusually still, there is the money to make this integration possible. The United Nations General Assembly, five years ago, voted a sum of 200 million dollars to provide, and here I quote the phrase, "homes and jobs" for the Arab refugees. That money remains unspent, not because these tragic people are strangers in a strange land, because they are not, not because there is no room for them to be established, because there is, but simply for political reasons which, I re-emphasize it is not my business to discuss.* (From the report of Dr. Elfan Rees, Commission of the Churches on International Affairs and World Council of Churches' Adviser on Refugees, Geneva, 1957.)

In the years since Dr. Rees rendered his report, the Arabs have continued for "political reasons" to oppose the implementation of all constructive proposals for resettlement. Only on the assumption that Israel must be destroyed does the Arab tactic acquire cogency. Otherwise, the resettlement of Palestinian Arabs among their kith and kin with full international assistance and Israeli compensation for abandoned properties outrages neither the heart nor the imagination. Unless, of course, totally different standards of rectitude are applied to Arabs than obtain for any other group, particularly Jews.

In this discrepancy lies the glaring injustice. Jews can live as an independent national entity only in the minuscule area of the State of Israel. If their longing for national independence is dismissed as a chauvinistic throwback, then the overnice regard for the full appetite of Arab nationalism, including the manufactured one of Palestinian Arab nationalism, is hard to justify on moral grounds. Nationalism cannot be revered in one and condemned in the other. To the primitive argument of ownership—this is ours and we want it back, and your need and our abundance have nothing to do with the case—one would have to counter with the history of Zionist colonization. Israel did not appear as a conquering invader. The state represents the culmination of decades of peaceful settlement sanctioned by international agreements, just as the sovereign Arab states liberated from the Turks are the result of such agreements. It would be pointless at this stage to rehearse such familiar events.

When Mrs. Golda Meir, Foreign Minister of Israel, was asked by a correspondent how the Arab refugee problem would be solved, she answered, "When the Arabs love their children more than they hate us." She might just as well have said grandchildren, for in this current General Assembly debate on the Arab refugee problem the question of UNRWA support for the grandchildren of refugees has arisen. For how many generations is a refugee a refugee? By now UNRWA has spent $450 million without being allowed by the Arab states to utilize these enormous funds to implement any of the constructive proposals for resettlement which have repeatedly been made. Another curiosity of the UN relief program is the maintenance on its rolls of members of the Ahmed Shukairy's Palestine Liberation Organization, a frankly revanchist army sworn to the destruction of a member state of the United Nations, and held temporarily in check only by Nasser's declared unreadiness for hostilities in Israel. The debate at the Special Political Committee of the General Assembly has been enlivened by the pressure of 13 Arab states for the recognition of the Shukairy battalions; in the same breath they interpolate into these demands equally impassioned ones for repatriation—basing themselves on Paragraph 11 of a UN resolution of 1948 which recommends that "refugees *wishing to live at peace with their neighbors* should be permitted to do so at the earliest practicable date" (my emphasis).

None of this makes sense except from the point of view of Arab war aims. But I am concerned here not with the rationale of Arab hatred nor with the reasons governments of East and West may have for wooing oil-rich Arabs rather than a handful of Israelis. In each instance the motivations for belligerence or compromise are self-evident. But I do remain troubled by the moralists, Jewish and non-Jewish, who blandly, and I think sanctimoniously, fail to weigh the Arab and Israeli case in the same scale.

(January 1966)

*NOTE

In 1979 former Prime Minister Rabin wrote an account of the expulsion of 50,000 Arabs from Lydda and Ramle during the Israeli War of Independence in 1948. Rabin, at the time the commander of a brigade assigned to eliminate Arab Legion bases on the strategic Tel Aviv-Jerusalem road and to capture the Lydda airport, describes a "troublesome problem for whose solution we could not draw upon any previous experience. . . . We could not leave Lydda's hostile and armed populace in our rear" during the battle with the Arab Legion. According to Rabin, Lydda's population was forced to march 10 to 15 miles to the protection of the Legion. Ramle's inhabitants agreed to voluntary evacuation and were transported by bus.

Rabin comments on the effect of this action on the Israeli soldiers: "Great suffering was inflicted upon the men taking part in the eviction action. Soldiers of the *Yiftach* Brigade included youth movement graduates who had been inculcated with such values as international brotherhood and humaneness. The eviction action went beyond the concepts they were used to. There were some fellows who refused to take part in the expulsion action. Prolonged activities were required after the action to remove the bitterness of the youth movement groups and explain why we were obliged to take such a harsh and cruel action."

Yigal Allon, then Rabin's superior officer, denied that there was a forced evacuation. According to Allon, the Arab civilians sought to escape the fighting and were assisted in their flight by the Israeli Army. In any case, Rabin's version reinforces rather than invalidates the Israeli contention that most of the Arab refugees fled of their own volition. The battle for Ramle and Lydda took place in July 12, after the first truce. By then the overwhelming majority of the 600,000 who joined the Arab exodus had already left. It is obvious from Rabin's account that the "action" was unprecedented. Had the Israeli pattern of warfare included expulsion the soldiers would not have suffered the shock described. As Rabin put it, the army had no "previous experience" on which to draw.

THE PALESTINIANS

In the current Middle East scenario the pathetic Arab refugee has been replaced by the husky Palestinian commando; during the recent United Nations debate on refugees Arab spokesmen made no secret of the change of emphasis. Instead of refugees maintained in constantly swelling numbers in UNRRA camps, the scene is dominated by organized guerrillas, well-stocked with the ubiquitous Russian arms, and supported by oil royalties from Saudi Arabia and Kuwait as well as UNRRA rations. The rallying cry has changed from "repatriation" to "liberation." Not bound by tenuous considerations of cease-fire lines, the terrorist groups can maintain tension along the Northern and Eastern borders, while Egypt wages its war of attrition across the Suez Canal. In addition to whatever military advantage may be gained from such harassment of Israel in anticipation of the promised Fourth Round, the guerrillas play a significant part in the continuing political struggle against Israel. As a movement of "national liberation" they have captured the imagination of much of the Left, who hail them as the Vietcong of the Middle East; their slogans and acts of terror arouse instant sympathy among disciples of Fanon and devotees of the Third World. Even those not automatically turned on by revolutionary jargon are troubled by the vision the commandos raise of a lost Palestinian homeland temporarily obscured by Zionist chicanery but now emerging into the light of day. The focus of the ideological debate has shifted. For the Palestinian refugee whose problems could eventually be solved by compensation, resettlement and partial repatriation has been substituted a dispossessed Palestinian people whose aim is restoration.

Arab strategy may prove inimical to the best interests of the Middle East in terms of the welfare of its peoples, but it has shown itself unfailingly resourceful in keeping the pot boiling. The Arab states' political exploitation of the refugees by preventing their resettlement and absorption is too familiar to require comment. With the pretense to refugee status of a second and third generation born in the UNRRA camps growing thin, a new tactic has been devised. The substitution of the burly Palestinian exile for the frail refugee has changed the terms of the argument and disposed of any solution save through the elimination of Israel. Even the withdrawal of Israel to the 1967 borders would not lessen the force of the Palestinian's demand for his homeland. While the Arab states re-occupied the territories they lost in 1967, the guerrillas would remain free to undo the evils of the Partition Resolution of 1947. Nasser has made no secret of this strategy.

Though the immediate military success of this scheme may be limited, the emergence of the commandos has undoubtedly borne fruit on the propaganda front. A reappraisal of the Zionist idea appears to be taking place *post facto*. Judging from articles and letters to the editor whose composers increasingly bolster their positions by references to the history of the Mandate, confidence in the moral validity of Israel's case has been shaken among people who formerly accepted the rise of Israel as the rectification of an historic wrong. Some are now disturbed not only by the endless warfare and its grim aftermath of human suffering but by the very existence of Israel itself. Despite all its wonders and achievements should it be there? In this context the wrongs of the Arab refugees of 1948 merge with the fresh problems generated by the Six Day War of 1967, particularly that of Palestinian nationalism.

The suffering of the Arabs who abandoned their homes and villages in 1948, and in lesser measure in 1967, is incontestable, and I do not propose to argue against whether they were the victims of Israel or of the failure of the Arab design to liquidate Israel. Whether they fled or were driven, whether the Israelis were savage or generous victors, is no longer of the essence of the debate. A refugee problem, given the will, can be settled in the Middle East as elsewhere in the world; an irredenta with all the profound passions it arouses is another matter. Hence the continuing debate on the rights and wrongs of the Arab-Israeli conflict particularly insofar as it presumes to question the continued existence of the Jewish state must frankly face the new problem posed by the Palestinians.

Are we witnessing the synthetic creation of a Palestinian identity as a weapon in the anti-Israel arsenal? In the total evaluation of Arab and Jewish rights this question looms large. The Palestinian nationalist, whether in costume or true guise, is a new factor in the Arab-Jewish conflict; and one treated respectfully by Israeli commentators many of whom argue that the origin of Palestinian nationalism is irrelevant to the issue. Supposing it did spring belatedly out of the head of Arab nationalism merely as a hostile response to Israel? The lad is alive, and kicking and calling him bastard will not exorcise him. But by the same token Israel is also there; if its ouster is demanded on the grounds of illegitimacy then the counterclaims must be examined. Can the newcomer be fed only at the expense of the Jewish state or is there room elsewhere in the family domain for his natural developments?

The question of origins is not merely academic. The El Fatah terrorist who attacks an El Al plane in Zurich justifies his act on the grounds that the first Zionist Congress took place in Switzerland in 1897 so ushering in the "horror" of Zionism to the world scene. Commentators of all shades of the political spectrum seek to determine future policy according to their view of what actually took place in the last 50 years. Obviously, if the British sponsorship of the Zionist endeavor was a bad business to begin with, at best an error of judgment as Dean Acheson discreetly indicates in his recent memoirs, or at worst, a gross injustice as Toynbee would have it, then the possible accommodations of the present must be made with such history in mind. Even those who believe that truth is best served by granting the clash of two wrongs or two rights will fit their prescription to their diagnosis of the cause of the trouble. Any view of what should be done now to achieve a peaceful settlement between Arab and Jew is bound to be practically affected by a determination of the extent of the injury. A dispossessed Palestinian people, able to flourish only within the area of the Jewish state, would require compromises from Israel other than those to be made for the same number of dislocated refugees. For this reason a discussion of Palestinian nationalism is not a futile semantic exercise. There is little hope of devising a satisfactory territorial solution if the existence of Israel is really predicated on the ruthless dispossession of a people from its homeland—something radically different from the dislocation or resettlement of individuals as an aftermath of war, a familiar process in the Europe and Asia of the twentieth century.

The first point to be made is that the characterization of Palestinian nationalism as "artificial" does not come from Zionist adversaries but from classic Arab sources. In the period before and after the issuance of the Balfour Declaration Arab nationalists consistently protested the use of the name "Palestine" or the adjective "Palestinian" to demark them from other Arabs in the region. All the declarations of the nascent Arab nationalist movement from 1880 on concentrated on "the unity of Syria" with no references to Palestine as other than "south Syria." Nothing could be more explicit than the statement of the General Syrian Congress in 1919: "We ask that there should be no separation of the southern part of Syria, known as Palestine, nor of the littoral western zone which includes Lebanon, from the Syrian country. We desire that the unity of the country should be guaranteed against partition under whatever circumstances."

The Arab Congress meeting in Jerusalem in 1919 formulated an Arab Covenant whose first clause read: "The Arab lands are a complete and indivisible whole, and the divisions of whatever nature to which they have been subjected are not approved nor recognized by the Arab nation." George Antonius, the Arab historian, makes sure that there will be no misunderstanding on this score. In *The Arab Awakening* (1939) he writes: "Except where otherwise specified the term Syria will be used to denote the whole of the country of that name which is now split up into mandate territories of (French) Syria and the Lebanon, and (British) Palestine and Transjordan."

The extremist Mufti of Jerusalem originally opposed the Palestine Mandate on the grounds that it separated Palestine from Syria; he emphasized that there was no difference between Palestinian and Syrian Arabs in national characteristics or group life. As late as May 1947, Arab representatives reminded the United Nations in a formal statement that "Palestine was . . . part of the Province of Syria . . . Politically, the Arabs of Palestine were not independent in the sense of forming a separate political entity."

Before the creation of the Jewish state the whole thrust of Arab nationalism was directed against what its proponents viewed as the dismemberment of an ideal unitary Arab state. Even the setting up of several independent Arab states was viewed as a subtle thwarting of Arab nationalism not its fulfillment. Nor was there a change after the establishment of Israel. In 1952, Charles Malik, the well-known Arab scholar and statesman, described the process dourly (*Foreign Affairs*): "greater Syria was dismembered, the southern and northern parts being put under different administrations." And his demonstrative comment on the settlement "of countless Jews on Syrian soil" (not "Palestinian") should be noted.

With an eye to the future, the Arab *Ba'ath* Party, which describes itself as a "national, popular revolutionary movement fighting for Arab Unity, Freedom and Socialism" declared in its constitution (1951): "The Arabs form one nation. This nation has the natural right to live in a single state and to be free to direct its own destiny," and equated the battle against colonialism with the "struggle to gather all the Arabs in a single, independent Arab state." No mention of Palestine, except as usurped Syrian territory, tainted any of these formulations. So rabid a figure as Ahmed Shukairy had no hesitation, while head of the Palestine Liberation Organization, in announcing to the Security Council that "it is common knowledge that Palestine is nothing but southern Syria." (May 31, 1956)

F rom the foregoing it is obvious that for Arabs "Palestine" was merely an inaccurate name for a sector of the Middle East whose separate designation was the result of imperialist plotting against Arab independence. Unlike its role in Jewish history and tradition, in Arab eyes Palestine was neither the cradle of a nation nor a holy land. It aroused none of the memories or special attachments given a homeland. Arab national passion was engaged by the concept of a greater Syria or an even larger united Arab state, not by this tiny segment which had become detached through the *force majeure* of foreign colonialism. In the lexicon of Arab nationalism the independent existence of a Palestine state, like the existence of an independent Lebanon, represented a violation of the Arab national will.

Historians have repeatedly pointed out that Palestine as a political unit ceased after the Roman conquest of the Jewish commonwealth, and that it was restored centuries later as a distinct political entity by the British Mandate for the specific purpose of establishing a Jewish National Home. Admittedly this fact of ancient history would have little relevance to the present if up to the Balfour Declaration there had ever developed an Arab diaspora, which like the Jewish diaspora, had an emotional fixation on Palestine. Nothing of the kind took place. Even when the desert Arabs revolted against Turkish rule during World War I, the Arabs in Palestine were so little concerned with independence that they continued to fight alongside the Turks until liberated by the Allies.

The concept of Palestine as a separate national entity arose among Arabs as a purely negative reaction to Zionism after the Balfour Declaration. It is worth noting in this connection that those Arab spokesmen who originally welcomed the setting up of a Jewish homeland in a small portion of the territories freed from Ottoman rule made no pretense that they viewed the abstraction of Palestine from the total area assigned to the Arabs other than the loss of a given number of square kilometers. Emir Feisal signed his celebrated agreement with Dr. Weizmann (January 1919) in behalf of the "Arab Kingdom of Hedjaz," and in his letter to Felix Frankfurter, then a member of the Zionist Delegation to the Peace Conference, the Emir wrote a few months later (March 1, 1919) "We are working together for a revived Near East, and our two movements complete one another. The Jewish movement is national and not imperialist. Our movement is national and not imperialist, and there is room in Syria for us both."

The Arab guerrillas who justify their demand for bases in Lebanon as in Jordan and Syria with the argument that the Arabs are one nation and therefore have the right to use each other's territories interchangeably, operate completely within the tradition of orthodox Arab nationalism. Some sophisticated Arab spokesmen have become aware of the pitfalls presented by Arab avowals that they are all one people with no difference between Jordanian, Palestinian or Syrian. The editor of the Amman weekly, *Amman al Masa* has warned that such reasoning might make the notion of the resettlement of Arab refugees "respectable," since its advocates could justly claim that the refugees were merely being moved to another part of their Arab fatherland, whatever its name. Such considerations, however, trouble neither the guerrillas who move freely across the borders of the Arab states as citizens of the Arab nation, nor their sponsors. The same Syrian *Ba'ath* leaders whose program calls for one Arab state are the most zealous supporters of the terrorists whose purpose is to recover the "Palestine Homeland."

The youth born in Lebanon or Jordan who is taught on the one hand that the Arabs are one people whose land was cut up by the imperialists, and on the other that his family was thrust out of a Palestinian Eden whose allurements increase with each decade of Israeli achievement is not likely to be worried by logical niceties. Whatever the contradictions, current Arab strategy is not likely to renounce a successful technique. Nevertheless, in the face of the evidence no proponent of Arab nationalism would deny that the Palestinian variant is a very recent mutation.

E qually to the purpose is the fact that the absence of such a distinct Palestinian nationalism provided a rationale for the Balfour Declaration. In their various negotiations with the Arabs in regard to the territory liberated from the Turks the British were faced with demands for a greater Syria, a kingdom of Hedjaz, an Arab state, never for an independent Arab Palestine for the reasons already indicated. The Arabs who opposed the Balfour Declaration and the Mandate objected to a foreign intruder in their midst and to the diminution in any measure of their vast holdings. All this is human and understandable. Just as understandable on another level is the not ignoble calculation which allotted one percent of the huge area freed by the Allies for the establishment of a Jewish National Home. Lord Balfour expressed the hope that the Arabs would recall that the Great Powers had liberated them from the "tyranny of a bestial conqueror" and had given them independent states. He trusted that "remembering all that, they will not grudge that small notch—for it is no more geographically whatever it may be historically—that small notch in what are now Arab territories being given to the people who for all these hundreds of years have been separated from it."

It is necessary to repeat this statement because contemporary anti-Israel polemics maintain the fiction that the British and the Jews proceeded with a total disregard of an Arab presence in Palestine. In support of this accusation all kinds of stray bits from Herzl and lesser luminaries have been exhumed, though their bearing on the actual political deliberations which culminated in the Balfour Declaration was nil. The many pages devoted to analyzing the Sykes-Picot Agreement, the McMahon Letter or the recommendations of the King-Crane Commission—all pre-Mandate documents—indicate that however proponents varied in the solutions or interpretations they offered, every aspect of the Arab case was weighed and considered; it did not go by default as re-writers of history like to pretend.

The King-Crane Commission, appointed by President Wilson to study the question of the Palestine Mandate, brought in an outspokenly hostile report; it urged the abandonment of a Jewish National Home and proposed instead that Palestine be included "in a united Syrian state" for which the United States should hold the Mandate. The very nature of the anti-Zionist opposition—American, British and Arab—its indifference to Palestine except as part of an Arab whole, made the reasoning of pro-Zionists like Lord Balfour plausible. Their psychology may have been faulty; the Arabs did and do "grudge" the "little notch," but nothing could be more irresponsible than to foster the myth that Arab national feelings were ignored by the promulgators of the Balfour Declaration.

The same holds true for the Zionists. Those who lived to graduate from Utopian visions to the hard bargaining tables of diplomacy were foolhardy innocents only in the extent of their hopes for Jewish-Arab cooperation in the Middle East. They were thoroughly aware that Palestine, though denuded and sparsely inhabited, had a native population. They came prepared with agricultural studies and demographic charts demonstrating that soil reclamation in Palestine would make room for more Arabs as well as Jews and would provide a better life for both. They were certain that the Arabs would prosper materially as the result of Jewish settlement, nor did they disregard the more delicate matter of Arab national feelings. Weizmann, a more reliable authority on this subject than romantic predecessors like Herzl whose idyllic vision of co-existence of Arab and Jew in *Altneuland* bore no relation to the facts of life, declared unequivocally that the Zionists assumed that the "national sentiments of the Palestinian Arabs would center in Bagdad, Mecca and Damascus, and find their natural and complete satisfaction in the Arab kingdoms which resulted from the Peace Treaty settlements in the Near East."

The Zionists proved poor prophets with one vital exception. Paradoxically, their coming did make more habitable room in Palestine. I refer of course to the period of Jewish settlement until the establishment of the state—the period in which the Jews strove unsuccessfully to live in peace with their Arab fellow citizens. If peaceful Jewish colonization beginning at the turn of the century had resulted in the dispossession of the local population this would have been a more serious indictment of Zionist policy than the subsequent flight of refugees in later wars. No such dispossession took place. Since the current indictments of Israel include not only the urgent troubles of the present, but the "historic wrong" done the Arabs through their dispossession by Jewish settlers, this must be clearly established. Instead of diminishing, the Arab population increased spectacularly in the three decades after the Balfour Declaration. It grew from 565,000 in 1922 to 1,200,000 in 1947—an increase of 100 percent and striking evidence of the stimulus provided by the agricultural development. During the same period Egypt showed an increase of 25 percent, while Transjordan, lopped off from Palestine in 1922, and also under a British Mandate but closed to Jewish immigration, remained static.

Not only the local Arabs prospered because of the better sanitary and economic conditions created by Jewish labor. After the Balfour Declaration Palestine changed from a country of Arab emigration to one of Arab immigration. Arabs from the Hauran in Syria as well as other neighboring lands poured into Palestine to profit from the higher standard of living and fresh opportunities provided by the Zionist development.

All reports agree that prior to the Jewish return Palestine was a dying land. Throughout the nineteenth century the favorite adjectives of travellers describing the Holy Land, beginning with the French Volney who visited the country in 1785, are "ruined" and "desolate." Each successive writer mourns the further decline of the country. A. Keith (*The Land of Israel*) writing some decades after Volney, comments: "In his (Volney's) day the land had not fully reached its last degree of desolation and depopulation" and he estimates that the population had shrunk by half. By 1883, Colonel Condor (*Heath and Moab*) calls Palestine bluntly "a ruined land." And, of course, Americans are familiar with Mark Twain's shocked account of the Holy Land's total "desolation" which introduces a somber note into *Innocents Abroad.*

U p to World War I the picture of Palestine is one of a wasteland inhabited by impoverished, disease-ridden peasants in debt to absentee landlords residing in Beirut, Damascus, Cairo or Kuwait. The transformation of the country comes when the sand dunes and marshes purchased by the Jewish National Fund from absentee landowners at fancy prices are reclaimed at an even greater expenditure of Jewish lives and labor. The Valley of Esdraelon, today one of the most fertile regions of Israel, the location of flourishing kibbutzim, was described by the High Commissioner of Palestine for 1920-1925 in the following words: "When I first saw it in 1920, it was a desolation. Four or five small, squalid villages, long distances apart from one another, could be seen on the summits of the low hills here and there. For the rest the country was uninhabitable. There was not a house or tree."

Not to exculpate the Jews but to defend British policy, the not overfriendly British Secretary of State for the Colonies declared in the House of Commons (November 24, 1938): "The Arabs cannot say that the Jews are driving them out of the country. If not a single Jew had come to Palestine after 1918, I believe the Arab population of Palestine would still have been around 600,000 at which it had been stable under Turkish rule. . . . It is not only the Jews who have benefited from the Balfour Declaration. They can deny it as much as they like, but materially the Arabs have benefited very greatly from the Balfour Declaration."

In the light of the grim present, a recital of former benefits rings hollow if not downright offensive. But this much emerges from the record. In 1948, the Jewish state created through partition in one-sixth of the territory originally envisaged by the Balfour Declaration emerged without dispossessing a single Arab. Pre-state Zionist settlement had brought Arabs into the country instead of driving them out, uninhabited land had been made habitable, and the abstraction from Arab sovereignty of the territory on which the Jewish state arose represented no blow to the goals of Arab nationalism as until then expressed. Had the account between Arabs and Jews been closed in 1948 with the acceptance by the Arabs of the compromise represented by the Partition Resolution, it would have been difficult to place the Arabs in the loser's column. The Jews had their minuscule, much amputated state. The original area envisaged by the Balfour Declaration in 1917 had been approximately three percent of the former Turkish Provinces. But by the time of the Mandate in 1922, the Promised Land had been whittled down to less than one percent (.8 percent) through the truncation of the territory East of the Jordan for the purpose of establishing Transjordan. The Jewish state that emerged after the Partition Resolution shrunk further to one-half of one percent. In other words while six independent Arab states had emerged to enjoy sovereignty over a million and a quarter square miles, the Jewish state was ready to dwell in peace with its neighbors within its 8,000 square miles. But this balance could not be struck. Arab calculations were different and the attack of the Arab states on newly declared Israel, with all that followed in its wake, changed the bookkeeping.

Now there were to be dispossessed Arabs who would continue to multiply but without flourishing, while the Jewish state would expend on war and defense the energy and tenacity that had formerly been expended on the desert. From this point on the drama unfolds with the fatality of a self-fulfilling prophecy. The Arabs, who in the thirties had raised the false specter of dispossessed Arabs, created the reality of the Arab refugees. I have written elsewhere about the refugees and will not rehearse the familiar arguments as to Arab and Jewish responsibility. However, one element of relevance to the present discussion should be noted particularly as it has escaped the attention it merits.

All kinds of reasons have been offered for the wild flight of the Arabs from Israel in 1948 when hostilities started: they were driven, they were terrified, they acted in obedience to the orders of the Arab High Command, etc. Whichever of these explanations is believed or dismissed, none makes adequate allowance for the swiftness and readiness with which the flight took place. People picked themselves up as though they were going from the Bronx to Brooklyn, not as though they were abandoning a homeland. Part of the speed was due to irrational panic, part to the assurance of return after the victory, but it was undoubtedly abetted by the subconscious or conscious feeling that flight to a village on the West Bank or across the Jordan was no exile. The Arab who moved a few miles was in the land he had always known though not in the same house. He arrived as no stranger and any differences between himself and his neighbors were due to local antagonisms not national alienation. The West Bank which had been Palestine until its seizure by Abdullah in 1948, Jordan which had been Palestine until 1922, offered the familiar landscape, language and kin of the abandoned village. No tragic uprooting such as befell the Jews in Europe lucky enough to survive, or the countless millions shuffled around in World War II by the victors, particularly by the Soviet Union, took place.

TV interviews have familiarized us with the Arab refugee pointing from his hillside barracks toward his native village in Israel. Sometimes a well-dressed young Arab student indignantly claims to behold the house his family left behind. His anger is understandable. Nobody enjoys seeing his property used by others even if compensation is available. But the very proximity of the abandoned neighborhood, while tantalizing, is the true measure of how little national loss the Arab from Palestine suffered. Even for so slight a cause as a new subway or urban relocation people are shifted larger distances and to stranger surroundings than the changes endured by the majority of the Arab refugees.

Arab refugees left so readily not because of cowardice, but because departure represented no fundamental wrench; they had a choice. I refer to the aftermath of the 1948 fighting. Even in June 1967 the comparatively small number who crossed into Jordan did so in the inner assurance that both banks of the Jordan were home regardless of the physical privations endured as a result of the war. The mobility of the Arabs as refugees or guerrillas, within Jordan, Lebanon and Syria indicates strikingly the strength of Arab nationalism and the tenuous character of the Palestinian attachment except as a political tactic against Israel.

What bearing has all this on the present? Guerrillas will not be disarmed by documents irrefutably demonstrating that they are really Southern Syrians, nor by British census figures which prove just as convincingly that Jewish settlers did not displace their Arab neighbors. The refugee camps, with their potential for violence, continue to exist and the furies fed by a humiliating defeat show no sign of abating. Under these circumstances is any accommodation short of the destruction of Israel possible? A Fourth Round, whatever its outcome, won't provide a solution. Should the Arab states with the active aid of Russia succeed in destroying Israel, a harvest of horror will be reaped for generations, as after the "final solution" of the Germans. Should Israel win again—the probable result unless the Soviet Union openly intervenes in behalf of its clients—Arab rage will not be lessened. The prospect of Fortress Israel, besieged by hostile millions, will become a bitter parody of the vision of the Jewish state which animated its founders.

The answer to the apparent impasse is not a Palestine state in which Jews—if we take at face value the assurances given—will be relegated to the status of a steadily dwindling minority. And anyone who has read the fine print of such Arab proposals knows how even the promise that the Jews will be allowed to live is amplified by references to "Zionists," "foreigners" and "imperialist criminals" to whom the amnesty would not extend. A small number of Arabic-speaking Oriental Jews might qualify for citizenship under these generous provisions. (It should be clear that no bi-national state is intended. The latter, though advocated by some Israeli groups before the declaration of the state, never found a response among Arabs.) That the Jews of Israel remain skeptical of El Fatah soothing syrup may be taken for granted. In any case, even if they believed that they would be neither exterminated nor deported, Israelis would be hard to persuade that some moral imperative demands the snuffing out of their country. They cannot understand the tenderness to every variant of Arab nationalism allied to a brutal disregard of the sole national hope of the Jews.

As they see it, no development in the contemporary world has weakened the ideological argument for a Jewish state. On the contrary, the wave of romantic internationalism which threatened to swamp Zionism as a form of parochial nationalism has long receded. Emergent nationalisms are burgeoning all over the globe with the full blessing of the anti-colonial Left whose latest discovery is Palestinian nationalism. In the midst of this ardor for movements of national liberation it is difficult to convince survivors of the Hitler era that Jewish nationalism is the only heretical specimen. Remembering not only active persecution but the barred doors and closed immigration quotas of every land during the Holocaust, Israelis are unlikely to agree that the only people with no national need are the Jews. Surveying the globe from European Poland to Asian Iraq, they would reverse the order: no people is still in such desperate need of national independence if only to ensure physical, let alone cultural, survival. "They killed us because we had no country," Jewish refugees in Israel repeated over and over again. And they view indifference to the fate of Israel as simply another manifestation of an ineradicable anti-Semitism which interchangeably exploits the slogans bequeathed by Hitler and Stalin, be it the Elders of

Zion of medieval legend or the "Zionist imperialist" of Communist doxology.

Ideology aside, no Israeli of the pioneer generation will take seriously charges that his coming displaced the Arabs. His personal experience in the process of rebuilding the country testifies otherwise. That is why more concern on this score is to be found among some *sabras*—not because the young are perverse or more ethically aware than their ruggedly idealistic parents but because they have no memory of the country to which their elders came. Golda Meir knows that her toil in malaria-ridden Merhavia made an uninhabited spot livable, just as she knows that her grandchildren in Revivim, a Negev kibbutz, are creating another oasis in the desert. In human terms is this good or bad? Every farmer and kibbutznik will indignantly echo the question. A scientist at the Weizmann Institute may less rhetorically point out that only a dozen Arabs lived on the waste on which Rehovoth was founded in 1891. Even a city dweller in Tel Aviv will remind you that Jews built this bustling city on a sand dune; the only ones displaced were the camels who used to parade slowly along the beach. All are united in the conviction that their coming enlarged the habitable area for both Arab and Jew.

The post-1948 inhabitant of a former Arab house in Jaffa or Jerusalem must resort to a more modest rationale. He cannot speak grandly of his creative role as a remaker of land and bringer of light. If he is an Oriental Jew he may call to witness the house and possessions of which the Arab despoiled him when he fled from Iraq, Yemen or another of the Arab countries from which half a million destitute Oriental Jews escaped to Israel in an informal population exchange. A Western Jew will use the mundane terminology of *Realpolitik:* what morality demands that foiled aggressors escape scot-free? Besides, Israel is prepared to discuss compensation for abandoned Arab property any time the Arabs want to negotiate a peace settlement.

The Israeli government has repeatedly announced its readiness to negotiate "secure and agreed" borders whenever the Arabs were ready to discuss peace. Though there are differences of opinion with regard to what should be retained or returned, for the overwhelming majority of Israelis the conquered territories with the exception of Jerusalem have no value in themselves; barring peace, their occupation makes defense against attack easier. The Sinai desert which three times served as the staging ground for Nasser's armies, the fortified ridge of the Golan Heights from which Syrians shelled the Israeli settlements at will, the enclave of *fedayeen* in Gaza, are cases in point. Neither the empty Sinai nor the Golan Heights present a human problem. Gaza and the West Bank are another matter. There live the bulk of the Arabs displaced by the fighting of 1948.

The most reasonable solution among the many informally discussed, the one which does least violence to the vital interests of the parties concerned, is the proposal to set up a Palestine entity on the West Bank and the East Bank of the Jordan. To begin with, the actual territory was part of historic Palestine, until 1948 and 1922 respectively. The area represents five-sixths of the territory originally set aside for the Jewish home by the Balfour Declaration. It is the place where most Arab refugees already live for the reasons of consanguinity and proximity already indicated. The dominant role of the Palestinians in Jordan is an open secret. Such a Palestinian state could serve to satisfy newborn Palestinian nationalism and in conditions of peace prosper economically in partnership with Israel. The emergence of such a state would mean compromises for both parties to the conflict. Israel, regardless of victory, would have to accept the narrow confines of its much amputated state, and the Arabs would have to come to terms with the reality of Israel.

(1969)

AFTER THE YOM KIPPUR WAR

T he realization that despite the remarkable accomplishments of Israel, or perhaps because of them, the present situation of Israel, and consequently of Zionism, is troubled, has become increasingly disquieting, particularly since the Yom Kippur War. Within Israel the causes for discontent are acute and concrete; specific targets for the people's displeasure are readily available from Mrs. Meir and Dayan to a host of petty bureaucrats. In the diaspora concern is more diffused. Zionists are baffled and worried. Though their allegiance to Israel is as sturdy as ever they have lost the facile optimism of recent years.

The surface reasons for the current state of mind are obvious. Despite a military victory against formidable obstacles Israel's situation politically is more precarious than before October. This paradox leads to the breast-beating and recriminations now tormenting Israel, with inevitable repercussions in the diaspora. Disenchantment which vents itself as rage in Israel may in the diaspora be transformed into a paralyzing sense of impotence if uncritically prolonged. It bears examination.

The state of mind in Israel may best be likened to battle fatigue. Four wars since 1948 have left their toll. In too many cases a grandfather, father and son have successively given their lives for the Jewish state, and where such sacrifices have not been exacted the awareness of loss pervades the extended family which is Israel. The effect has been cumulative. During the War of Independence the fighting lasted much longer and the casualties were far heavier than in the Yom Kippur War—6,000 in a population of 650,000. Yet those who were in Israel in 1948 recall the exaltation with which the 650,000 Jews of the *Yishuv* threw themselves into the struggle for Jewish independence; no price was too great. In 1956, the quick defeat of the Egyptian army during the Sinai Campaign brought immediate results in relief from *fedayeen* terrorist incursions; and the euphoria following the dazzling triumph over the massed Arab armies in June 1967 was self-explanatory. But in October 1973, there was no instant victory. Israel was fighting for its life. True, the Arab invasion was halted on both fronts in less than three weeks; at the time of the cease-fire Israeli forces were within 20 miles of Damascus, and had crossed the Suez Canal into Africa. However, in recent years the country had become conditioned to an expectation of swift, magical victory whatever the odds or the objective situation. Faith in an invincible Israel was the heady brew that the small state swallowed and of which the world cheerily partook. Just before the surprise Arab attack in October, military commentators in the West were smugly describing tiny Israel as the "strongest military power in the Middle East."

The gap between illusion and reality has resulted, naturally enough, in a search for scapegoats. Admittedly, the Israeli army was caught unprepared by the Arab attack. Grave charges of arms that did not fire, of tanks that were inoperative, of a lack of essential equipment for soldiers and reservists, have been circumstantial and numerous. These are under investigation. Further charges that the soldiers manning the Bar Lev line were not informed of the imminence of Egyptian attack even after military headquarters had already announced an alert, indicate a major failure in communication. Every soldier returning on leave after the cease-fire has contributed his quota to the grim tales of chaos, surprise—and heroism. A Commission of Inquiry now piecing together the record of the Yom Kippur War is studying the evidence to allot blame in regard to specific derelictions.

In the areas mentioned guilt can be assigned. Presumably it will be possible to determine who in the chain of command was responsible for defective armor or the incredible failure to alert soldiers on the Bar Lev line. According to first-hand reports, the comparatively few Israeli troops—many had Yom Kippur leave—were overrun as they prayed or rested. These are formidable accusations and if sustained will require appropriate disciplinary measures. The fury of Israelis at needless deaths because of wanton inefficiency will not easily be assuaged or deflected. But the crux of the difficulty lies not in what—without seeking to minimize their impact—may be considered failures in technique rather than policy. In the last analysis, lack of preparedness in detail stemmed from a basic policy formulated on the assumption that the Arabs were not about to or able to launch a full-scale attack. Is an honest error in judgment culpable? Who is to blame?

In their search for answers serious Israeli commentators tend to distinguish between failures in the execution of policy and the soundness of the policy itself. There is a world of difference between fiery protests against Dayan's alleged failure to keep the Israeli armed forces adequately prepared against possible attack and the kind of fundamental soul-searching to be found in the Israeli press since the Yom Kippur War.

General Meir Amit, for instance, Chief of Military Intelligence and Head of Israel's Security Services in the 1960s, refuses to hold an oversight in Intelligence primarily responsible for the fact that Israel was surprised by the Arab attack:

> *It is no accident that we appeared as we did on the sixth of October. It is a process which we all created; no one is innocent, including myself. Everyone contributed to the process in his own field. The responsibility, though, does not fall equally on everyone. There are things for which leaders are responsible and for which the common people are not, or at least are much less responsible. All of us among ourselves took the stance of exaggerated self-confidence, a sense of power, of "there is me and nobody else." We lived in this state and enjoyed ourselves and permitted ourselves to act the way we did. This mentality rested on two cornerstones: our enormous strength and an underestimation of the power of the enemy. This led us in the course of six and a half years to that feeling of security which is expressed in these words: "It cannot happen! It simply cannot happen!" The point being, of course, that the war cannot happen because the Arabs simply would not dare commit suicide. This sense of confidence, that it simply "cannot happen," gave birth to a series of beliefs that affected the conception of warfare, the organization of the Israel Defence Forces, and tactical questions within the army. All the oversights and mistakes in these areas derived from the basic assumption that "it cannot happen." (In an interview in* Ma'ariv, *November 16, 1973.)*

The doves and hawks as might be expected have, respectively, no doubts as to where the blame lies. Naftali Ben Moshe of Mapam has no hesitation in placing responsibility for the tragedy that befell Israel on the "hawks and other extremists" whose "delusions" led to a "short-sighted, arrogant, inflexible and illusory policy."

> *We* [Mapam] *did not have the delusion that time is on our side, and that we could wring territorial concessions from the Arabs later, which we were unable to get from them now, after it had become clear to them that their chances of receiving their territories back were getting smaller every day. We did not claim their stubbornness would bring them losses and no gains.*
> *We did not suffer from the delusion (prototype of all the delusions) that the military gap between us and the Arab countries was continually widening in our favor, because of the quality of our soldiers and our technological superiority, and because Arab society*

Marie Syrkin

> *was so backward and primitive that it could not possibly catch up with us. . . . We were not the ones who deluded ourselves into believing that the best way to guarantee their territorial ambitions in the administered areas was to establish physical facts in the field: to establish settlements, to consolidate them and to present the Arabs with a* fait accompli *. . . We were not the ones who deluded ourselves with the thought that, in the absence of far-reaching and bold political initiatives, command of the new borders would, of itself, forestall the possibility of a successful large-scale Arab attack and would, in the final analysis, force our neighbors to accept our peace conditions.*

He concludes that mistakes in security had political origins and should lead to a new political orientation in which the concept of borders for "strategic depth" must be abandoned. Yet when in a subsequent article, the writer describes the minimal conditions Mapam considers acceptable, he makes demands which despite their moderation, no Arab state has been ready to accept:

> *These minimal conditions should contain several elements: border corrections on the West Bank, a border in the Golan Heights, minor rearrangements of border in Sinai, our presence in Sharm-el Sheikh, demilitarization of the returned areas, inspection arrangements, international guarantees, free navigation in the Suez Canal, and of course: a peace treaty duly and properly signed. (Al Hamishmar,* November 23, 1973.)

Moshe Shamir, the Israeli playwright, a leading spokesman of the Greater Israel Movement, expresses a contrary view. He believes that the Arabs attacked because the Israeli government was unduly conciliatory:

> *Once again, the illusion is being cultivated among us that concessions on our part (our enfeeblement militarily and territorially) are likely to bring peace closer. . . . The truth is —that cruel truth we must know without being dismayed before it—the truth is that Egypt and Syria, under the management and direction of the Russian Empire, opened hostilities against a state that had declared over and over again its acceptance of Security Council Resolution 242. They assaulted lines the government had announced readiness to vacate given peace negotiations. They prepared for war, planned it and launched it at the very time that the ruling party was going before the electorate once more under the slogan of concessions through negotiations for the sake of peace. They did this after years of refusing any contact, after years of repeatedly reiterating that only flowing rivers of blood would bring about the solution. An Israel*

*government more willing to make concessions, more amenable to
negotiation—they will never have. They knew this then and they
know it now.* Therefore *they hurried to attack. (Ma'ariv,* November
16, 1973.)

The debate as to whether Israel's security will best be secured by
withdrawal to points not yet determined or by "strategic depths"
continues. Nor have the recent elections provided a clear answer as is
indicated by the Labor Party's need to form a minority government for the
first time in Israel's history. Apart from discussion as to the political
constellation to emerge or the political program to be adopted, the ongoing ferment has brought to the fore a kind of questioning from which
Israel thought itself finally immune. Fears that Jewish destiny is inevitably
tragic and that even Israel, the Zionist solution, can provide no escape have
been voiced by those who contrast the mentality of the conflict *sabra,*
certain that "there will be no Auschwitz in Israel" with the state of mind of
the eternally apprehensive survivor of the death camps. One such survivor,
the poet Ittamar Yaoz-Kest, underlines the differences between what he
calls the "Israeli" and the "ghetto Jew":

> *During times of tension and crisis these two elements amongst us
> arise (the "Israeli" and the "Jew"), pulling in opposite directions.
> After the Six Day War, it was the former, the "Israeli" element that
> was uppermost, filling us with the feeling of victory and courage;
> whilst now, the "Jewish" element is gaining the upper hand. It may
> be because the second element raised its head without warning,
> without a transitory period, that the spiritual damage caused to many
> was so severe at the sight of Israeli POWs sitting in rows on the
> ground, as in a concentration camp.*
>
> *In fact, our dejection is the result of the breakdown of basic
> concepts concerning our lives (and not of the failure of one or
> another security matter, which is likely to recur under the leadership
> of any government or regime, with no guarantee that it won't recur).
> That is to say, it is a question of the breakdown of the "Israeli" or
> "sabra" image which, because of education and ideology, has to be
> different from the "Jewish" or "ghetto" image which is prey to
> irrational or mystic delusions of fate, as it were. Suddenly it turns out
> that the Israeli citizen is by no means more secure physically than a
> Jew living abroad. (Yediot Ahronot, November 23, 1973.)*

The theme of an inexorable Jewish fate is taken up from a different angle
by the Israeli writer, A.B. Yehoshua.

> *Zionism worked toward an independent, normal existence, with*

all the patterns and signs of a normal society, a real producers' society, with a political framework, and exercising national and international responsibility. . . . And today, some hundred years later, with aircraft and tanks, the aviation industry and super-modern agriculture, with ambassadors and laborers, in a state which we and others have called a medium-sized power, we are still struggling over the question of our legitimization in a total conflict. This sense of our legitimization and normal relationship with the world seems to be deteriorating. . . . And the only question to be asked is not whether we will be able to stand up to this (which we almost certainly will), but was all this necessary? Is this our inexorable Jewish fate which we cannot escape from, even here? . . . If in fact it becomes undoubtedly clear that this really is the fate imposed upon us, then we shall know at least that this conclusion will cause unparalleled despair, despair first and foremost, of Zionism and the great hope it gave us. The conclusions are extremely grave regarding both ourselves and the Jewish nation whom we want to concentrate here. And what is worse than to hear nowadays "this is not a country into which to bear children."

I think we must absolutely refuse (not out of naivete but from sober reasoning and faith in man wherever he is) to accept the edict of an imposed fate. This would be a betrayal of Zionism. (Ha'aretz, November 11, 1973.)

Finally, to indicate the range of sentiment and perhaps as a corrective to the above, one should quote Hanoch Bartov, who in a biting article, "Without Charisma, Please" equally excoriates the former blind faith in charismatic leaders and the present depression, the "group hysteria that shifts from irrational faith to irrational despair." He asks: "Is there really nothing in the middle? Is there no path away from the messianic talk and big-power conceit except one leading to this complete collapse, this 'haplessness?' " He concludes on a note of Zionist realism:

Politics is the art of the possible. This view formed the practice of the central elements in the Zionist movement, and this was their strength. Not to wait for a telephone call. To do something. Everything within the limits of the possible—and even a bit more, but always to know where the mine-fields begin.

From the trauma of the Yom Kippur War it's possible to extract a silver lining too, if only we realize that though we're no more than a middle-sized power we're also not about to collapse. Precisely in these days we've been able to see what powers are concealed in this people, how courageous and how noble was the conduct of the recruits in those first evil days. Not without cause were the songs of the War of Liberation revived. We relived the experience of the great Jewish family defending its home. .

We need a political path and fortitude on the part of a team that believes in this path, that can go to this wise people and say: we've only started. Even now we can point to great achievements such as our fathers never dreamed of. Let's return to temperance, forbearance, and faith in the future. Perhaps we're not able to promise ideal peace, but neither is the prospect of war forever before us. Our right to this land is a complete right, but there are political bounds to this right. Within these, the Jewish people will renew itself; it will not give up for one moment its hopes for peace and its efforts to attain it (Ma'ariv, November 16, 1973.)

The foregoing excerpts are all taken from statements made in the weeks immediately following the war. Though with the passage of time the mood has lightened the basic questions remain. The country is still rent by political strife as to what should be conceded for the sake of peace or a *modus vivendi* with the Arabs. There are very few votaries of expansionism or occupation *per se* in Israel. But when the Moslem states in their recent conclave at Lahore announce categorically that Jerusalem must be wholly Arab or that Israel must leave the ridge of the Golan Heights whose scaling by Israel in 1967 at last relieved Jewish settlements in the valley below from being shelled at will by the Syrians, even the doviest doves bristle. Like the previously quoted Mapam spokesman each citizen of Israel has "minimal demands" for which he is prepared to make a stand. The situation is further complicated by the internal debate on Who Is a Jew—a debate curious at the best of times but maddening at the present moment when Israel's future must be determined by a united people. The inner turmoil has far from subsided though people are picking up the pieces and going about their business. Outwardly life resumes its normal flow but a deep unease remains.

It is bound to remain—in Israel and the diaspora—as long as the immediate, let alone long-range, problems facing Israel are being argued in Geneva and the capitals of the world. The Jewish state is again an object of international bargaining and concern as it was in 1947; however, fortunately, with this enormous difference: the successful existence of Israel for a quarter of a century creates a reality which may be threatened but not obliterated. This reality is the antidote to loss of nerve among Israelis and diaspora Zionists alike.

Admittedly, a number of illusions were punctured in the Yom Kippur War, chief of these the notion that the Israeli army could easily overcome any combination of Arab states. Since this view was based on solid experience, it was not a "delusion." Nevertheless it was an illusion because it assumed an indefinite continuation of the fabulous, for it was fabulous for two-and-a-half million to fight back assorted foes armed by Soviet Russia and numbering between 60 and 100 million, depending on which new Arab or Third World state joined the fray. Even in the Biblical tale David overcame only one Goliath, not a conglomerate.

The indignation of Israelis at leaders who beguiled them into unwarranted faith in the power of the Israeli army has little justification. Past events spoke for themselves; Israeli generals could be forgiven their confidence and elation. Besides, hardheaded officials at the Pentagon and supposed military experts throughout the world united in their plaudits for Israel's fighting force and in denigration of Arab troops. (Incidentally, this made it easier to answer Israeli requests for arms with the assurance that one Phantom in the hands of an Israeli pilot was worth a dozen Migs or sophisticated arms operated by Arabs. This dubious compliment further increased the gap between the Israeli and Arab military potential in the latter's favor.) If anything, the events of October confirmed the legend of Israeli valor and resourcefulness, otherwise the thousand Syrian tanks would not have been turned back on the Golan Heights and the Egyptians would not have been stopped in the desert. But October also drove home the obvious: that there was a human limit to the extent by which an immense disparity in arms and manpower could be made good once the Arab hosts were united and better trained for technological warfare than in the past.

This sobering realization would not have been so traumatic if not for the preceding illusions. Yet surely the ultimate illusion would be to assume that Israel's altered position has resulted primarily from a given error by a given commander, or that any shift in leadership could recreate a supposedly "invulnerable" Israel. Undeniably much precious blood might not have been shed if the level of preparedness had been higher, but there is no retreating from the hard truth that Arab performance, military and political, has brought about a new situation in which Israel is not the controlling factor. This is what Israel must face with as much political wisdom and stamina as the country can summon. It is idle to blame the gods of yesterday for having been fallible in not foreseeing what is all too clear *post facto*. While exhaustion and bitterness are all too understandable, the kind of masochistic flaying of the government, rival parties and institutions taking place verges on self-indulgence rather than productive criticism.

(April 1974)

THE REVISIONIST IN POWER

Recently a number of commentators, friendly and otherwise, have been urging American Jews to express their dissatisfaction with the policies of the Begin government. Ideological and political debate flourishes in democratic Israel, so why is the "Jewish establishment" in the United States less vocal, in fact supinely acquiescent? I.F. Stone, though hardly lacking forums for expressing his views, disingenuously mourns the failure of American rabbis to invite him to expound his familiar pro-Arab stance to their congregations. Counsel to speak up comes from those whose concern for Israel is credible as well as from those whose motives are suspect.

Old Labor Zionists like myself cannot pretend to enthusiasm for either the domestic or the foreign policies of Begin. At the same time I am repelled by the cynical pro-Arab tilt of the Carter administration and the readiness of Israel's active foes to shed crocodile tears over her intransigence. I find the hosannas that greeted Sadat as a messenger of peace excessive, especially since the frequent repeated public offers by Israeli leaders to travel to Cairo or Damascus for face-to-face negotiations evoked no such genuflections. Admittedly, Sadat's dramatic gesture, the right of Israel to exist, was from the Arab point of view substantive. But Israel could hardly be overwhelmed with gratitude for this sole, if significant, contribution to the peacemaking process. What mattered were the terms of this existence and in this regard Sadat presented the total roster of Arab demands. When the smoke cleared, a polite, adamant Sadat had encountered a soulful, rigid Begin; on some points Begin actually proved unexpectedly flexible. Sadat rapidly grew less polite at the failure of instant capitulation.

All this acts as a powerful inhibition to those who disagree with Begin yet do not wish to signify agreement with the similarly intractable Sadat. Furthermore there is the danger that any Zionist opposition to the present government will be exploited by the anti-Israel cabal to undermine Israel's position with the American administration. Despite this dilemma, I venture some observations.

In the past the Zionist and Jewish consensus in support of Israel rested, first, on deeply felt belief in the absolute justice of Israel's cause; and, secondly, on confidence in the relative justice and good sense of Israel's proposed solutions for the Arab-Israeli conflict, even though the Arabs vehemently rejected the compromises offered by the moderate Labor government. Now this consensus is being shaken regarding one issue—Begin's obdurate stand on the future of the West Bank. Anyone present at the recent Zionist Congress in Jerusalem would have discovered that delegates from all parts of the world were far from giving blanket approval to Begin's settlement policies. Diaspora Jews were as vocal as Israeli citizens in challenging the government position. Almost half the Zionists present—including a large representation of Americans drawn from such various Zionist parties in the United States as Hadassah and *Arzah* (Reform rabbis) as well as Labor and Mapam—supported a demand for a settlement policy that would preserve "the Jewish and democratic character" of the state and take the peace negotiations into account. This meant that a large sector of organized American Jewry went publicly on record against the incorporation of the West Bank with its million Arabs into the Jewish state, and in favor of territorial compromises for the sake of peace.

It should be noted that the months since Labor's defeat in the Israeli elections have proven instructive. At first even some liberal Zionists, normally opposed to the rightist Likud, tended to view the change of governments as therapeutic. Disenchanted with Labor's long tenure and recent demerits, many hailed change itself as a positive achievement. Begin's social and political views were well-known, but comfort was sought in contradictory truisms: a strong leader can afford to be yielding; while pseudo-doves flutter helplessly, an unequivocal hawk will make adversaries talk turkey; a fresh broom sweeps clean; give a man a chance. In a climate skeptical of all professions of faith, public opinion found it hard to take Begin at his word or to respect him for what he was: an individual with simple, stubborn beliefs and a fanatical readiness for their execution. Integrity was mistaken for opportunism—so creating a situation baffling to the *Realpolitikers*. The brief warmth created by Sadat's visit also impelled a suspension of disbelief; perhaps the unlikely Begin would net the peace that had eluded Ben-Gurion and Golda Meir.

By now the warm mist has dissipated enough for American Zionists to report what they see. Whether Sadat will accept any proposal short of total withdrawal is questionable. But if there is to be any hope for peace, then Begin's fixation on the sacred historic right of the Jewish people to Judea and Samaria, the biblical names for the West Bank, should be removed. Paradoxically, Begin is much readier for territorial concessions in other areas. All previous Israeli peace plans stressed the need for security zones in unpopulated or barely populated border regions.

To blur his tough image, Begin has tried to create the impression that his settlement policy was merely a continuation of that of the former government: he was straightforwardly enacting what the Labor government had deviously planned with a bit of dovish camouflage. This is hardly accurate. Moshe Dayan, who was Minister of Defense in Mrs. Meir's government and surprisingly emerged as Begin's foreign minister, has plainly stated the difference: "For ten years, between 1967 and 1977, the government of Israel was committed to territorial concessions in return for genuine peace and this implied redivision of the area. Now our view is that redivision is not the answer." Here is certainly an authoritative assessment of a difference in ultimate goals. A resolution passed by the Labor government on July 21, 1974 underlines the distinction: "The peace will be founded on the existence of two independent states—Israel with united Jerusalem as its capital, and a Jordanian-Palestinian Arab state east of Israel, within borders to be determined between Israel and Jordan." Granted the terminology is vague. An Arab state "east" of Israel allows considerable latitude for negotiation. But while exluding a PLO state, the wording concedes substantial withdrawal from the West Bank, possibly along the lines of the Allon Plan, which called for Israeli withdrawal from heavily populated areas while retaining military supervision of strategic points along the Jordan. At any rate this program is a far cry from the current insistence on Judea and Samaria as an inalienable part of the Jewish national heritage.

The irritating sophistry of Begin's dictum that Resolution 242 does not apply to the West Bank represents another sharp divergence from previous Israeli interpretations of this much-debated resolution. Despite the deliberate omission of the crucial *the*—the resolution calls for Israeli withdrawal from occupied territories, not from *the* territories—the Labor government never pretended that its interpretation completely excluded the West Bank. But here again complications appear. Once Resolution 242 becomes an issue, its other features should be stressed—such as the assurance of "secure and recognized borders." It also should be noted that the resolution calls for a "just settlement of the refugee problem," with no mention of Palestinians or a Palestinian state. On these grounds it is rejected by the PLO. The phrasing of the resolution reminds us that as recently as 1967, when the Security Council adopted the resolution, its members failed to specify Palestinians, not out of regard for Israeli wishes but because there were no Palestinians to mention. The 1967 debate centered on the Arab refugee problem. There were 600,000 refugees (and their descendants) who had joined the exodus from Israel in the wake of the Arab attack on the new state in 1948. How the Arab states systematically prevented the absorption of the refugees so as to turn their plight into the "dynamite" with which to destroy Israel is an old story. Arab leaders originally opposed the establishment of a Jewish state in the Middle East on the grounds that there was no such country as Palestine. In 1956 Ahmed Shukairy, subsequently head of the PLO, declared to the UN Security Council, "It is common knowledge that Palestine is nothing but southern Syria." But then, in a further refinement of their strategy, these same leaders transformed the refugee problem into one of a newly hatched Palestinian nationalism. The strategic nature of this move in an era of emergent nationalisms in no way detracts from the present military reality of the passions so fomented, but it does suggest that Israel's refusal to countenance a PLO state on its borders does not arise from an unimaginative disregard of the national longings of a disinherited people.

Still another aspect of the Begin settlement policy gives cause for concern. Spokesmen of the kibbutz movement have charged that because of Begin's infatuation with Greater Israel, funds and manpower are being diverted for settlements in Judea and Samaria in preference to establishing new agricultural settlements within Israel in Galilee, the Negev or the Dead Sea region. In Galilee, for example, there has been a dramatic increase in Arab population due to a high birth rate, and simultaneous Jewish drift toward the towns. To preserve the original Zionist vision of a cooperative society built by Jewish labor, pioneering idealism should be expended on new kibbutzim in Galilee or the Negev. Yet Musa Harif, secretary of the largest kibbutz federation in the country, has charged that Minister of Agriculture Sharon discriminates against cooperative settlements inside the "Green Line" (the pre-1967 borders) in favor of those being established in the occupied territories.

Q uite apart from the folly of jeopardizing fragile peace negotiations by the demonstrative establishment of new settlements during a sensitive period, this change in priorities poses a threat to the character of Israel. Because the Israeli Arabs are multiplying much faster than Israeli Jews, demographic projections envisage the possiblity of Jews becoming a minority in vital parts of the small Jewish state. The settlement policy of the Likud party seems bent on increasing this risk. The precarious demographic balance should be rectified through emphasis on under-populated areas within Israel. And there is an ethical consideration as well. The redemption of the Jewish homeland through the toil of Jewish workers has been a central tenet of Zionism since earliest pioneering days. Under present circumstances I doubt whether a large reservoir of Arab labor from the Gaza Strip and the West Bank has been an unmixed boon for Israel, whatever the economic advantages enjoyed by the Arab workers. A greater dependence on Arab labor lessens the participation of Jewish labor in all phases of national reconstruction. This is a treacherous argument. Reluctance to employ Arab labor will be damned as Jewish exclusiveness (I am not referring to Israeli Arabs); hiring non-Israeli Arabs, on the other hand, even at the same wage rates as Jewish labor, is strictured as colonial exploitation. If the West Bank were to become part of Israel, no equitable controls could be devised to prevent participation of its population in the Israeli work force or against the temptation of the Jewish sector to depend upon it. Such a development, like a demographic shift, would fundamentally compromise the moral assumptions of the Jewish state.

That the Begin government challenges these assumptions is no accident of personality. Begin, a disciple of Jabotinski, founder of the rightist Zionist revisionists, has not wavered in his allegiance to the original doctrine, though he has become more circumspect in expressing it. Now that he's in the saddle, both the policies Begin advocates and his *modus operandi* reflect, less flamboyantly than in the past, the fundamental revisionist credo. From the outset, Revisionism was characterized by an enchantment with maximalist slogans, dramatic gestures and an amazing disregard for the realistic consequences of what they advocated. When Great Britain began whittling away at the substance of the Mandate, revisionist response was to clamor for "a Jewish state on both sides of the Jordan." In 1930, the revisionist leadership soberly proposed a "pause" in settlement and in the raising of Zionist funds. The "pause"—which would have meant the voluntary demise of Zionism—presumably was supposed to force an intimidated Great Britain to capitulate. This naive faith in the magic properties of declamation and demonstrations was viewed by its proponents as *political* Zionism, in contrast to the less spectacular day-by-day work of purchasing and reclaiming tracts of barren land. The revisionist record is studded with such self-deluding proposals offered in fulfillment of what Jabotinski described as the greatest principle of political struggle: "Never take no for an answer."

But the differences between Labor Zionism and Revisionism never were merely tactical; they sprang from antithetical ideologies. Socialist pioneers came to Palestine inspired by the dream of creating a cooperative society through peaceful settlement. Revisionism fought the concept of a worker society and the "gradualism" of the settlers. Proclaiming themselves as nationalists opposed to "the class struggle while a state is being built" and to costly "utopian experiments," revisionists set themselves the task of "breaking" organized labor. In a notorious 1932 article, Jabotinski magniloquently sanctioned strike-breaking. "I removed the stigma attached to the expression 'strike-breaking' in Palestine." His followers did their utmost to destroy the developing labor movement and their failure did not diminish their zeal. Yet *kibbush ha-avodah*—the determination that Jewish labor should build the Jewish homeland, so that no charge that Jewish independence had been achieved by proxy could ever be raised—was one of the sanctities of pioneer Palestine. Also, the settlers as Socialists believed that the peaceful reclamation of uninhabited marsh and desert within the area designated as the Jewish homeland constituted an even firmer moral title than international agreements. They proved to be right, for the eventual partition resolution, though further reducing the scope of the already amputated Jewish state, by and large followed the area of actual Jewish settlement. But in the critical pre-state period, revisionists made no secret of their disdain for "practical" work. Of 231 agricultural settlements established by various Zionist groups before the state, only one was revisionist. While unmartial farmers plowed fields in Palestine, revisionist youth groups strutted in uniforms and military regalia in Poland.

On the question of resistance, too, there was a wide cleavage between the authorities of the *Yishuv*, the Jewish community of Palestine, and the revisionists. During Arab attacks on the settlements in the 1930s, the Haganah, the peoples army largely recruited from the kibbutzim, adopted the policy of *havlagah* (self-restraint). This called for self-defense but not indiscriminate reprisal, a policy adopted on moral grounds and in the stubborn hope of peaceful coexistence. Naturally the Irgun, the smaller underground of the revisionists, excoriated *havlagah* as pusillanimous. In the 1940s, during the struggle against the British, the ideological clash between the Haganah and the Irgun intensified. The Haganah opposed wanton terror. Its military encounters with the British specifically involved attempts to bring in "illegal" refugees from the Nazis, and to establish new settlements on land purchased by the Jewish national fund. Again the reasons for this course were ethical as well as tactical.

The metamorphosis of the romantic enthusiasts of *havlagah* into a formidable Israeli army is one of the ironies of history, resulting from the invasion of Israel by the Arab states. On the other hand, after the creation of the state, the revisionist *Herut* as a party in opposition became more temperate. But since Begin has come to power, it is obvious that the original intoxication with maximalist rhetoric remains. So does the ideological antagonism to organized labor and the kibbutzim. So does the readiness to indulge in provocative acts—such as General Sharon's new outposts in the Sinai, just approved by Begin and his cabinet.

In Israel, opposition to Begin, at first muted, is becoming louder. Labor spokesmen, long disciplined by the responsibility of power, uneasy in the unaccustomed role of loyal opposition, showed themselves less forthright and challenging than anticipated, though Allon and Eban voiced criticism. Now the reluctance is ending. In a debate in the Knesset on Begin's policy,

Shimon Peres focused on the sticking point: "Without a readiness to compromise on Judea and Samaria there will be no peace." Opposition is likely to intensify. Recent demonstrations by army veterans, rallying to the slogan, "peace is more important than Greater Israel," testify to this.

At the same time a caveat is in order. Sentiment in Israel is for reasonable compromise, not suicidal retreat. Few would favor total withdrawal to the vulnerable 1967 borders which invited Arab aggression in the past. The same applies for those American Zionists who distrust Begin's course. Any attempt by the Carter administration to sacrifice Israel to oil and petrobillions would swiftly rally the "establishment" around the government of Israel.

This means that distinctions must be drawn between border settlements in Sinai and the Golan Heights, and those on the populated West Bank. It is hard to oppose settlements in the Rafia sector—a strip along the Mediterranean in the Sinai—developed by the Labor government as a buffer zone on the classic invasion route along which Egyptian armies have periodically marched to attack Israel. The fortified ridge of the Golan Heights also presents an acute security problem. Until its capture in 1967, this series of military bunkers was used by the Syrians exclusively for the shelling of kibbutzim directly below. The kibbutzim understandably decline again to be sitting ducks for Syrian artillery. After the town of Kuneitra was returned to Syria, the problem became one of sparsely inhabited territory whose primary function was to facilitate Syrian harassment of cooperative settlements in Galilee. Meaningful peace negotiations can no more ignore the experience of 1948, 1967 and 1973 than they can ignore the existence of an Arab population on the West Bank. No mechanical formula asserting the righteousness of total withdrawal makes sense either politically or morally. Begin can bolster his romantic assertion of divine right to Judea and Samaria with cold secular documentation of a legal claim on the grounds that the West Bank was originally designated as part of the Jewish homeland by the terms of the Balfour Declaration and the Mandate. But such claims turn hollow in the light of present demographic realities. So do Arab demands for sovereignty over every grain of Sinai sand and every Golan stone. History more recent than the era of Biblical glory imposes its lessons on Arab as well as Jew.

Zionists who oppose Begin do so for both pragmatic and high-minded reasons. Concern for the rectitude as well as viability of Israel is integral to Zionism. Nevertheless, the world's insistence on judging the Jewish state by criteria applied to no other country adds a disturbing rather·than flattering complication. Millions of refugees, sheltered in no UNRA housing among sympathetic brethren, still wander over Asia and Africa. Soviet Russia, spearhead of the anti-Israel coalition, displays no qualms about its swallowing of large slices of conquered Eastern Europe. Fratricidal and tribal wars rend the Third World. Yet if a visitor from Mars were to wander into the United Nations or scan the world press, he would learn little about Cambodia, Uganda, Bangladesh, Biafra or Czechoslovakia—to mention a few relevant spots. On the basis of the exhortations and vituperation of which Israel is the object, he might well conclude that a mighty empire, Israel, seemed to be the source of most earthly ills. How else could he account for a terrorist internationale of Japanese, Cubans and Germans, armed by Communists, financed by oil potentates and dedicated to the eradication of this "cancer of humanity"? Is it paranoia to interpret this concentration on the tiny Jewish state and its three million Jews as the massive rallying of anti-Semitism in modern guise? At any rate, when the terms of a viable peace are finally hammered out, Israel should be spared the dubious compliment of alone being required to serve as the world's conscience.

(April 1978)

REMEMBERING GOLDA

T he United States Presidential Delegation to the funeral of Golda Meir in its composition reflected essential aspects of her life; the dignity of our transport—United States aircraft known as Air Force One when the President is aboard—indicated the honor accorded by the American government to a national figure who had died when no longer in office. The act went beyond the requirements of protocol. It was a genuine tribute to an Israeli head of state who, despite her toughness, had commanded the affection and respect of every American President with whom she had dealt. Her legend persisted beyond the period of her ministry, so that Mrs. Lillian Carter, head of the delegation, could sincerely voice her admiration of a contemporary she had never met. Senators Javits, Moynihan, and Ribicoff, as well as several congressmen, were obviously suitable representatives in view of their activities in behalf of Israel. Henry Kissinger, though without official obligation, had made a point of being in the party despite his ambivalent relationship with Golda—their disagreements tempered by mutual admiration were well-known. Important labor leaders were making the journey in deference to Golda's life-long involvement with the trade union movement and the cause of labor. And, of course, Jewish community leaders, as well as a couple of old personal friends like myself, had been thoughtfully invited. Considering the limitations of space—only some 40 delegates could be selected from among numerous eager candidates—the State Department had shown tact as well as propriety in its choices.

Consequently I was on my way to Jerusalem as a member of a prestigious delegation—and not oblivious of its glamor—to attend the funeral of the woman I had held in love and honor for over 40 years. I had known for some weeks that Golda was dying, so that the news, when it came, had only the shock of finality, not surprise. Now in the midst of State Department officials, political notables, and the distractions of this particular flight, she kept eluding me. Even in the throng on Mount Herzl, where we stood in a driving rain huddled under umbrellas, she was remote. The prayers at the

---

Golda Meir, former Prime Minister of Israel, died in December 1978.

Marie Syrkin

grave site could not be heard by most of us, nor could we see the ceremony. Only the immediate family and the chief dignitaries stood close enough to view the austere proceedings. I wondered if Golda would have wanted this huge state funeral from which, because of the number of foreign delegations and government officials, the plain folk of Jerusalem had to be excluded. In endless processions the men and women of Israel had circled around the bier where the body lay in state, and they lined the streets as the cortege wound its way up to Mount Herzl. But the ordinary citizens were neither in the limited hall of the Knesset at the services nor at the burial, for compelling reasons of space and security. Nevertheless I could not help thinking that just as Golda had forbidden the reading of eulogies at her funeral, had she known how large and distinguished an array of personages from all parts of the world would pre-empt the ranks of the mourners she would have left word that room be found for the kibbutzniks and comrades she had cherished. But her simple instructions had been written before she became Prime Minister and she had failed to anticipate the pomp that would attend her passing. Not that she would have been indifferent to the magnitude of the tribute; she was human enough to appreciate recognition, but an even stronger impulse of her nature was an abiding loyalty to those who had shared her struggle and had been her fellows for over half a century. I had witnessed too many poignant meetings between her and comrades from the distant days of Merhavia to the present to doubt that such would have been her feeling.

I have often had occasion to write about Golda, even a biography at a time when the publisher to whom I offered it asked me politely, "This sounds very interesting, but who is Mrs. Myerson?" (She had as yet not changed her name.) Since that editorial query the course of her life has become general knowledge—the whole spectacular drama beginning with a persecuted childhood in Czarist Russia and culminating in the premiership of an independent Jewish state. There is little point in dwelling again on the familiar great events of her extraordinary career. Nor have I any inclination for repeating the hackneyed though merited superlatives employed to describe her achievements: "the greatest woman in modern Jewish history," "the founding mother of the Jewish state," and the like. They are true and need no demonstration, so I shall permit myself to write more personally.

I first met Golda in the thirties when she returned from Palestine to serve as an emissary to the Pioneer Women. Her audience in those days was limited to the small circle of the faithful—Labor Zionists like herself whom she addressed in Yiddish and English. American Jewry as a whole was as yet largely untouched by the Zionist idea and amazingly ignorant of the small pioneer settlement of the *Yishuv*. The kibbutz was a barely

164

known, exotic concept. But if she had no multitudes to captivate, Golda's effect on the members of her movement was immediate. Labor Palestine could have had no more impassioned and persuasive exponent than Golda. All that subsequently became the trite rhetoric of Zionist oratory—making the desert bloom, renewing an oppressed people in a just, cooperative society—was both challenge and revelation when she spoke. Though an unknown young woman, she required no panoply of office to reveal her unique force, and I, like others, came under her spell.

In the forties, at the close of World War II, when the revolt against the restrictions of the Mandatory Power and the drive to bring Jewish survivors to their only haven was in full swing, I was in Palestine. By now Golda was an acknowledged political leader, head of the Political Department of the Jewish Agency when Sharett was imprisoned by the British. Her major role in the underground operations of the Haganah and in open confrontations with the High Commissioner, who confessed that Mrs. Myerson was a formidable lady, is part of Israel's history. However, slight revealing moments, which no historian would bother with, tell something of her particular stamina.

She lived in a modest apartment in a cooperative apartment house (owned by the *Histadrut*) near the seashore in sparsely settled Northern Tel Aviv. I had a room in the same complex. This made it possible to visit without breaking the total curfew which the British frequently imposed. Curfew was a day of obligatory rest when Golda could catch up on household chores and even bake cookies and cakes in preparation for the streams of visitors who unceremoniously dropped in on the Sabbath. Telephones were a rare luxury, though Golda had one because of her special responsibilities. Once during curfew I watched her carefully turning a skirt—to me a novel process. The badly worn skirt was turned inside out and meticulously resown. This feat was an indication of how sparingly Golda still had to live though her economic circumstances were far better than in the Jerusalem days of the twenties, when her small children sometimes lacked bread and milk and she had scrubbed the laundry of the school they attended to pay the tuition. As she sewed, the telephone would ring periodically, and I would gather that she was being consulted in regard to some "action." She would resume her sewing without explanation; secrecy had to be maintained even with intimates.

The encounters with the British took their toll. At the simple funerals for fallen comrades I for the first time heard what was to be her characteristic utterance, *Ein lanu derech acheret*, "We have no alternative." This constituted almost the first Hebrew sentence I learned because I heard the words spoken so often in moments of anguish and crisis. They were to reverberate throughout Israel's turbulent future. In their slogan-like simplicity they crystallized Golda's conviction and commitment at each stage of Zionist development: there was no other way for the Jewish people to be emancipated except through their own labor in an Emek marsh or a Negev desert. There was no other way to national independence and salvation for Hitler's victims save through the willingness of Jewish Palestine to risk its precious youth—boys and girls over each of whom Golda mourned, as she would in the future larger wars that would be waged. And yet each time that she made her stern, unhesitating declaration, she did so with a tragic sense of the other glorious alternative of which she and Israel were being deprived. She had, perhaps naively, come to Merhavia to make a wasteland blossom. She never ceased rejoicing in the transformation of her daughter's forbidding Negev kibbutz of Revivim into an oasis famous for its flowers and fruit. It was with an authentic sense of personal loss that even as a seasoned stateswoman she turned so often to Israel's foes with the vision of the harvest of plenty that peace might bring. This tantalizing prospect of a bountiful Middle East shared by Arab and Jew haunted her not as a diplomatic phrase but as a generous human possibility in whose achievement she had believed from the outset of her life as a Palestinian pioneer.

It was completely in character for her to begin an address in Madison Square Garden immediately after the Six Day War not on a note of triumph, but of solemnity. The huge ecstatic audience, which only a week earlier had feared for the existence of Israel as the Arab armies massed for her destruction, had been celebrating jubilantly as they awaited Golda's arrival. Golda's first words, grave, almost sorrowful, "Again we have won a war; we do not want to win wars; we want peace," will not be forgotten by those who crowded the huge auditorium. She had made the same declaration at a kibbutz funeral decades earlier; she repeated it with the same emotion and longing 20 years later to a worldwide audience.

Yet her deeply personal suffering for the consequences endured never lessened her resolution. Of the many striking instances of her courage with which I am familiar, one of the most impressive is an incident she mentioned only in passing. She was one of the few in the country who knew the date set for the Suez strike in 1956. Reminiscing about that period she remarked casually, "Since I did not know what would happen I thought I had better visit Sarale at Revivim the day before." She went to the Negev kibbutz, chatted with her daughter and grandchild as though she had no particular reason for dropping in, and kissed them goodbye without a word of warning. I asked her why she had not made some excuse to take them back with her to the greater safety of Jerusalem; Revivim was in the immediate path of the Egyptian army. She answered, "There are many daughters." This scene in which a mother, aware that on the next morning the kibbutz might be under attack, lets no word slip for fear of prejudicing the impact of the next day's campaign, and who resists the temptation to find some easy reason to take her grandchild back with her is almost intolerably stoic. A woman maternal enough to steel herself for the hard journey to Revivim in those final hours, and strong enough to make small talk and sip tea during what might have proved to be an ultimate farewell, obviously belongs to a special breed. Her life abounded in dramatic adventures; the perilous journey, when disguised as an Arab woman she went to plead with Abdullah in 1948, was only one of many. Yet this unpublicized domestic moment seems to me to be among the most revealing of that combination of sensibility and fortitude which was one key to Golda's greatness.

Facile journalists sometimes picture Golda as Israel's Jewish Mother, dispensing a sublimated Hebraic chicken soup. In her unflinching demands on herself and her people she was the reverse of the cliché. She had small sympathy for fellow believers who were not prepared to be fellow workers in the building of a Jewish homeland. In 1921, shortly after she arrived in Palestine, she wrote a circumstantial letter to a relative in which she described the hardships of her new life without illusion. But she concluded with typical directness: "If one wants one's own land, and if one wants it with one's whole heart, one must be ready for this. . . . Get ready. There is nothing to wait for." Decades later, after all that had been endured and achieved, she could still say in full sincerity that she pitied her old comrades in the United States who had failed to join her on the Pocahontas, the decrepit ship on which she had left America. At a time of extreme danger to Israel she expressed a paradoxical concern: "My friends worry about their grandchildren; I do not have to worry about mine." She meant, of course, that despite the hazards to which her children were exposed, their Jewish future was assured, whereas in the comfortable suburbia of the United States Jewish identity was being extinguished. Of the two perils the latter seemed to her infinitely greater. Because she believed this without wavering she was able not only to act without faltering but to demand action from others. Many an inferiority complex flourished in her presence, particularly among Labor Zionists who had sung pioneer songs with her in Milwaukee but had never become pioneers.

Some years before her death she declared her life had been blessed. She enumerated the blessings; they were not the conventional ones of prosperity, high office, or good health. She stressed instead the fulfillment of the two dreams that for her constituted a single vision: the child who had cowered in fear of a pogrom had lived to become a free citizen of an independent Jewish state. And her daughter worked in a cooperative society in which respect for equality and human dignity prevailed.

Not that she was unaware of how much still was lacking. The ideal kibbutz society was an enclave whose moral influence had to be treasured and extended. And Israel's dearly acquired independence had still to be protected without compromise. The trauma of the Yom Kippur War, when she had to make crucial military decisions while her generals were at odds, had left her wounded but unchanged in determination. And she never stopped hoping for a just peace with the Arabs. There is no need to review the detailed peace proposals of her government or to comment on her frequently expressed readiness to go to Cairo long before Sadat came to Jerusalem. These are matters of record. But with her genius for simple yet profound formulations she made two statements which while not political in the usual sense are humanly memorable. Once she said, "Peace will come when the Arabs will love their children more than they hate us." Some years later she made a declaration which has often been misquoted: "When peace comes we will in time perhaps be able to forgive the Arabs for killing our sons; but it will be harder for us to forgive them for having forced us to kill their sons." These words, sublimely moral and deeply Jewish in their ethic, are a gloss on her violated credo, "We wanted to be good farmers not good soldiers."

The disclosure of the cancer from which she suffered for the last 12 years adds another dimension to her valor. During those years I was often a guest in her home in Jerusalem. Hearing her steps on the stairs to her bedroom I would know how late she had been working. And I would hear how early she would rise. There were many nights in succession when she could not have had more than three hours' sleep before leaving for a meeting of her cabinet. Neither age nor illness overcame her will. She always lived as though the spirit were stronger than the flesh. That is why, though she was a shrewd tactician and realistic enough to measure how much material reinforcement the spirit needed, she had the power to lead and inspire her people in their hours of victory and adversity.

(February 1979)

III.
THE
ARGUMENT

Note for Section 3

The polemical articles in this section are self-explanatory. Volume 8 of Arnold Toynbee's A Study of History *appeared in 1954.*

Adolf Eichmann, a key figure in the Nazi extermination program, was tracked down by Israelis in his hiding place in Argentina on May 11, 1960, and was brought to stand trial in Jerusalem. Hannah Arendt attended the trial as a correspondent for The New Yorker. *Her report appeared in February and March 1963, in five successive issues. In May 1963, these articles were published in book form as* Eichmann in Jerusalem: A Report on the Banality of Evil. *Arendt's conclusions and charges aroused heated discussion and precipitated the debate about "Jewish complicity" and the role of the "little man" in the Nazi extermination scheme. It is a debate that still continues.*

I.F. Stone's essay "Holy War" appeared in The New York Review of Books *immediately after Israel's victory in the June 1967 war. The essay, though mild by contemporary standards, marked the beginning of a sustained attack on Israel by spokesmen of the Left. It attracted particular attention because Stone had previously been a supporter of Israel.*

In view of the repetitive nature of the accusations, some repetition in the answers was unavoidable if the thread of the argument was to be held.

TOYNBEE AND THE JEWS

In Volume 8 of Arnold Toynbee's *Study of History* is to be found a chapter entitled "The Modern West and the Jews." I make no pretense to the scholarship required for an evaluation of Mr. Toynbee's monumental work as a whole, and I approach the Toynbean sweep and erudition as humbly as most of his fascinated readers. But in the chapter on the Jews the author is not discussing Hindu, Babylonic or Andean societies. Here he is on familiar territory and his statements are no longer obscured by the aura of his formidable and mysterious learning. When one has finished this chapter the vision of Toynbee, half-mystic, half-historian, pointing to God's web on the loom of time, becomes a bit shaky. The robes of the prophet drag all too plainly in the dust of human bias and error.

Toynbee's conception of the Jews as a fossilized relic of an extinct civilization was given to the world in his earlier volumes. No matter how unattractive the role assigned appeared to the energetic fossils, Toynbee, sketching the fall and rise of civilizations on his great canvas, could only do so according to his own, not infallible, lights. Whether or not one agreed with his slighting evaluation of Judaism he was within the province of the philosopher of history who must make his judgments in the terms of his subjective illuminations and prejudices. No serious historian with an animating world view is objective, and it would be the height of stupidity to complain that Toynbee is not "objective." But there is a point where the distortion and suppression of available evidence transforms what purports to be history into unabashed journalistic propaganda no matter how elegantly expressed. It is this point which Mr. Toynbee reaches in his discussion of the Jews in the modern world.

In his customary formidable manner Toynbee starts out by tracing the tensions between "the peculiar Jewish millet" and the homogeneous Christian society in which the millet found itself. By the sixth and seventh centuries after Christ this tension was registered "in a series of anti-Jewish enactments of a Judaically fanatical ferocity." While deploring the savagery of the anti-Jewish persecutions, Toynbee is careful to point out that the ferocity of the Christian persecutors was really "Judaic." There is a tragic irony in Visigoth bigotry because the Visigoths were not the first bigots. "The earliest known instance of bigotry is the compulsory conversion of the conquered gentiles of Galilee to Judaism by their Maccabean Jewish conqueror, Alexander Jannaeus, in the first quarter of the last century B. C., and the Maccabean temper was inherited by Christendom from a Jewry that came to be the principal victim of this Jewish vein in the Christian religion." Mr. Toynbee magnanimously goes on to indicate that Maccabeanism was not "the sole source" of Christian anti-Semitism but by this time the villain is pretty well localized—that Jewish vein. One cannot help being puzzled by the "earliest known instance of bigotry" so categorically cited. Even a layman seems to remember relevant episodes considerably prior to the Maccabees. How would Mr. Toynbee characterize persecutions of the Jews by Pharaoh? Of course, Mr. Toynbee might question the historicity of the Old Testament account but then much of the evidence he adduces from the same source would become equally questionable.

However this might be, anti-Semitism, according to Toynbee, is something "into which Christianity was betrayed by the Judaic not the Hellenic element in its ethos." Presumably the Greeks who made Socrates drink the hemlock some centuries before the Crucifixion were under Judaic influence, and the acts of savagery recorded in some of Thucydides' most eloquent pages were inspired by a sea voyage to Palestine. Mr. Toynbee's rigorous regard for truth makes him face squarely the unpleasant fact that Christians persecuted Jews through the ages but the truth becomes more palatable when the country of origin, "Judea," is stamped on each fresh massacre. So single-minded is Mr. Toynbee in his fealty to the notion that fanaticism is a Jewish growth wherever it occurs, that even when describing the growing indifference to religious issues among Christian sects he writes of the "damping of a Judaic flame of religious fanaticism in the relations between Christian and Christian."

The Moslems, however, uninfected by the Judaic flame, were according to Mr. Toynbee notably tolerant in their treatment of minorities. True, the Koran enjoined tolerance but anyone familiar with the experience of Jewish communities in Moslem lands must marvel at Toynbee's encomium. Moslems persecuted Jews centuries before the arrival of the wicked Zionists on the scene of history. Has Mr. Toynbee never heard of the Jews of Yemen who from the twelfth century on suffered so cruelly from Moslem fanaticism that in 1182 Maimonides sent them his famous epistle urging them to remain steadfast? It would be pointless to multiply the instances.

Mr. Toynbee's anti-Jewish and pro-Arab bias appears most spectacularly in a section of his chapter significantly headed, "The Fate of the European Jews and the Palestinian Arabs, A.D., 1933-48." The equation is all the more shocking since Toynbee himself describes the fate of European Jewry in these terms: "Within a period of no more than twelve years, they [the Nazis] reduced the Jewish population of Continental Europe, west of the Soviet Union, from about six and a half million to one and a half million by the process of mass-extermination which was so unprecedently coldblooded and systematic that the new word *Genocide* had to be coined." Toynbee seems to be adequately appalled by the "maniacal sadism" of the Nazis. However, after deploring the moral nadir to which the Germans sank, Toynbee permits himself the following sentiments: "But the Nazi Gentiles' fall from grace was less tragic than the Zionist Jews'. On the morrow of a persecution in Europe in which they had been the victims of the worst atrocities ever known suffered by Jews or indeed by any other human beings, the Jews' immediate reaction to their experience was to become persecutors in their turn for the first time since A.D. 135—and this at the first opportunity that had since arisen for them to inflict on other human beings who had done the Jews no injury, but who happened to be weaker than they were, some of the wrongs and sufferings that had been inflicted on the Jews." And Mr. Toynbee sanctimoniously concludes the indictment with the blasphemous statement that, "On the Day of Judgment the gravest crime to the German Nationalists' account might not be that they had exterminated a majority of Western Jews but that they had caused the surviving remnant of Jewry to stumble." Such sensitiveness to Jewish virtue can only be explained by a wholehearted indifference to Jewish survival.

On the basis of Mr. Toynbee's chapter, readers without a special knowledge of events in Palestine in 1948, and that means the overwhelming majority of present and potential students of this history, must assume that the Jews in a bloodthirsty frenzy murdered or expelled peaceable Arabs in the Nazi fashion. This is of course the daily staple of Arab propaganda and would hardly merit rejoinder if it appeared through the usual channels. But Toynbee is a revered thinker whose idealism and Christian dedication are touted on every page. One would assume, therefore, that whatever subsequent interpretation the historian might choose to make, a number of simple facts would be mentioned. Mr. Toynbee surely knows that from the first moment of hostilities until the invasion of Israel by six Arab armies it was the Arabs who were the aggressors in defiance of the United Nations Resolution. A man with so much curious information about vanished civilizations is surely aware of the fact that the Palestinian Arab exodus was deliberately stimulated by Arab strategists to create an artificial Arab refugee problem and to evacuate Arab civilians from territory which the Arab States expected to bomb. Contrary to Arab plans, the considered evacuation turned into an uncontrollable stampede. Arab incitement had backfired. The evidence exists in readily available texts of Arab radio broadcasts and accounts in the Arab press of Syria, Jordan and Egypt. Let me remind Mr. Toynbee of events in Haifa in April 1948 (not 1400 B.C.).

After the defeat of the Arabs at the hands of a force of 200 Jewish soldiers, the British High Commissioner, who could hardly be suspected of pro-Jewish bias, issued the following statement: "The Jewish attack on Haifa was a direct consequence of continuous attack of Arabs on Jewish Haifa over the previous four days. The attack was carried out by the Haganah and there was no massacre. Arabs in Haifa were thus themselves responsible for the outbreak despite our repeated warnings."

The flight of 70,000 Arabs from Haifa proved contagious. One can cite instance after instance of Arabs abandoning their villages as the result of the terror propaganda of the Arab League. After the Arab invasion it was inevitable that the Jews, who at first had been perplexed and even troubled by the Arab exodus, should have welcomed the departure of professed enemies or tools of enemies.

Undeniably the condition of the Arab refugees is an unhappy one. They live and multiply in camps maintained by the United Nations in the Arab lands adjacent to Israel. The Arab states responsible for their plight decline to permit their rehabilitation and resettlement among their kin. Being pledged to the sacred cause of the destruction of Israel, they must exploit rather than alleviate the sufferings of their Palestinian brethren. All this is understandable from the point of view of political tensions and hostilities. But from the point of view of that other-worldly justice in human affairs which Mr. Toynbee propounds, is the notion that the Palestinian Arabs be resettled in the neighbor Arab lands so outrageous? They would be among people of their own race, religion and language. They would enjoy a familiar landscape and climate. The Arabs speak of themselves as one people and one land. The Palestinians would be part of it. Tiny Israel is crowded with refugees from Europe and the Moslem lands. The Arab states are large and underpopulated. Population transfers have been made repeatedly under far less favorable circumstances in order to solve less vital issues. The Greek-Turkish exchange in 1923 or the more recent resettlement of Hindus in India and Moslems in Pakistan involved a more fundamental uprooting than would the settlement of Palestinian Arabs in Syria or Jordan. After all, Jordan was part of Palestine as recently as 1921. Then two-thirds of the original territory set aside for the Jewish National Home was lopped off and set up as the Emirate (later "Kingdom") of

Transjordan. Nor is it irrelevant to mention that until World War I Arabs called Palestine "Southern Syria." There is even no specific Palestinian Arab nationalism to which violence would be done through resettlement. Admittedly the pain of leaving one's home town and home is genuine. I have no wish to slight this pain even after adequate financial compensation has been made. The Palestinian Arabs have suffered, and whether those responsible were the Jews, or the Arab States, or their own folly in joining the enemy instead of remaining with the thousands of Arabs who made their peace with Israel and became Israeli citizens, is not the immediate issue in this discussion.

I am concerned with the moral perversity which views as equal the systematic murder of six million men, women and children and the resettlement of 800,000 Arabs.

Another of Toynbee's pontifical statements is of a piece with the foregoing: "The calamities which inexorably overtook the Jews in continental Europe and the Arabs in Palestine in the twentieth century of the Christian Era were indeed implicit in the decision taken in the nineteenth century by a section of the Jewish diaspora in the West when they adopted a program of collective Westernization on the lines of the archaistically oriented Modern Western ideal of Nationalism." In other words, Zionism was responsible. One can see the application to the Arabs but how do the European Jews get into the act? Hitler arose in Germany, where the Jews were well on the road to complete assimilation. It is hardly necessary to belabor this point. But Toynbee does not like the Zionists and he is not likely to relinquish a thesis in favor of the evidence. Instead of perceiving that the Jewish homeland was the direct response to the challenge of Jewish martyrdom and the refugee ships driven from port to port, Toynbee reverses the process. He is so bereft of any compassionate understanding of that great agony that he permits himself to refer to the help of American Jews at this period in terms all too reminiscent of the shoddiest Arab spokesman: "The American Jews may have been moved partly by a self-regarding consideration that even a moderate further increase in their own numbers might prejudice their already delicate relations with their Gentile fellow-neighbors." Just a vestige of research would have indicated to Toynbee that American Jews were as active in their efforts to increase immigrant quotas into the United States as they were in behalf of the Jewish state.

Zionism is an archaism which inverts Jewish values. And what is the distinctively Jewish ethos according to Toynbee? "A meticulous devotion to the Mosaic Law and a consummate virtuosity in commerce and finance." It is these precious values that Zionism has the imprudence to change. When

Marie Syrkin

one reads Toynbee one would never suspect that Jews had made great contributions to the thought and science of the West. The fossil quickens into a shrewd Rothschild.

Though deploring "archaic" Jewish nationalism Toynbee has a tender regard for Arab nationalism. He wonders pensively whether the Palestinian Arabs would have the spirit to maintain their identity. Mr. Toynbee's pro-Arab activities in the British Foreign Office help to explain many of his contradictions and omissions. Mr. Toynbee has every right to be an Arab propagandist, but then one wishes that he would doff his hieratic vestments.

When he finishes "The Modern West and the Jews," the reader is left with an impious question: If this is how the great historian treats a local and contemporary moment, just how erudite is the rest of the vast erudition?

Reply from Arnold Toynbee

January 10, 1955

To the Editor,
Jewish Frontier,

Dear Sir:

A copy of Miss Syrkin's article "Professor Toynbee and the Jews" has been sent to me by Professor Ernest Samuels of Northwestern University. After reading the article and thinking it over, I do not find myself convinced by its criticisms of the section on "The Modern West and the Jews" in vol. 8 of my book *A Study of History*. I should like to explain briefly why I think as I do.

Miss Syrkin is mistaken in supposing that "Mr. Toynbee's pro-Arab activities in the British Foreign Office" help to explain this. Though in both world wars I have served as "a temporary Foreign Office clerk," I have never been employed in pro-Arab activities and have always been person- ally opposed to British policy regarding Palestine. Miss Syrkin does not mention the piece in my chapter headed "Great Britain's Responsibility," in which I maintain that Great Britain bears the heaviest share of the responsibility for the Jewish-Arab conflict. Being myself an Englishman, I feel this responsibility personally. Being neither an Arab nor a Jew, I have no personal reason for being prejudiced either for or against either of these

176

two parties. I do believe that, in the issue between the Palestinian Arabs and the Zionists, the Palestinian Arabs are in the right and the Zionists in the wrong. My opinion on this issue is, like Miss Syrkin's, open to challenge; but, for what it is worth, it is based on nothing but the facts as I see them.

I see the whole story as a tragedy, and I do not see the tragedy as beginning with the outbreak of fighting in Palestine in April 1948. Much of the responsibility for the actions of both the Zionists in Palestine and the Palestinian Arabs in 1948 falls, as I believe and have said, upon Great Britain, because, as mandatory, she used her power to make possible an immigration of Jews into Palestine on a scale that would never have been accepted voluntarily by the Arab inhabitants of the country, and because, at the same time, Great Britain always refused to face the truths that she was pursuing simultaneously two incompatible policies and that, in refusing to choose between them, she was steering Palestine toward a disaster by creating a situation in which it was becoming more and more difficult for Jews and Arabs to live together in Palestine side by side. But the tragedy, as I see it, goes back far further than the date of the Balfour Declaration. I see earlier stages of it in the conversion of both the Zionists and the Arabs to a Western secular ideology, Nationalism. The fanatical spirit in Nationalism comes, as I see it, from Christianity; and Christian and Muslim fanaticism, as well as Christian and Muslim charity, comes, I believe, from Judaism.

I think Judaism is like every other human institution in being a tragic mixture of good and evil. What is peculiar about Judaism is not this; it is the potency, in Judaism, of both the two conflicting elements and the conversion of half the human race—the Christian-Muslim half—to the Jewish spirit, so that the extremes of good and evil in Judaism have been reproduced in Christianity and Islam. All three religions have two incompatible visions of God. They see God both as Love and as Jealousy. When we Christians, Muslims, and Jews think of God as being jealous and of ourselves as being a chosen people, we are tempted to despise other religions and to suppress them when we can, and the first "bigots" in history that I know of are, as I have said, not my barbarous Teuton kinsmen and Christian co-religionists the Visigoths (from whose name the word is derived), but the Maccabees, if "bigot" means, as I believe it does, not just any persecutor, but one who persecutes people of another religion on account of his difference from them in religious practice and belief. The Maccabees forcibly converted Idumaea and Galilee to Judaism and thereby brought it about that Herod and Jesus were Jews, not gentiles. The effects of fanaticism are often tragically ironical.

It is, in fact, tragic to be either guilty of fanaticism or to be the victim of it, and the Jews have been alternately guilty of it and victims of it since the second century B.C. The irony of Jewish history surely is that the Jews have been the chief sufferers from a spirit which they themselves originally kindled. The tragedy of recent Jewish history is that, instead of learning through suffering, the Jews should have done to others, the Arabs, what had been done to them by others, the Nazis. Though I was careful to bring out the Zionists' innocence of the Nazis' cold-blooded, systematic "genocide," and the disparity in numbers between the Jewish victims of the Nazis and the Arab victims of the Zionists, I am sure I am right in holding that degrees of sin and tragedy are not determined by the numbers of the souls concerned. Sin and tragedy are done and suffered by each of us individually; they are not, and cannot be, collective. Nor is the tragedy of the Palestinian Arabs' sufferings at the hands of the Israelis a peculiarly Jewish tragedy; it is a common human tragedy, like the Jews' own sufferings at the hands of the Nazis. To fail to learn by suffering, and to inflict on others some of the wrongs that have been inflicted on oneself, are sins into which all human beings are prone to fall. This is one of the most odious and most desperate characteristics of our common human nature.

Everything has its price as well as its compensation. The compensation for the tragic position of being a member of a persecuted diaspora is that, as such, one has the beau role. The price of the tragic position of being a citizen of a sovereign independent state of Israel, carved out, by force, first of British and then of Israeli, arms from a country previously inhabited by other people, is that, as such, one has exchanged roles with one's former persecutors. Today Israel is politically like all the nations (a formidable fate). But the Jews are still spiritually a peculiar people in having had a greater experience of suffering than any of the rest of us and in having learnt from their sufferings those deep spiritual lessons that they have communicated to the Christian-Muslim half of Mankind. And that is why I feel that the tragedy of Zionist Israel's sins is greater than the tragedy of Nazi Germany's. The measure of tragedy is not statistical but spiritual, and my German fellow-gentiles, when they sinned as they sinned against the Jews, had not had either the intense experience of suffering or the intense spiritual enlightenment that the Jews have had. "Unto whomsoever much is given, of him shall be much required." I am sure that this piece of insight is Jewish, because it is attributed to Jesus; I am sure it is true; and I am sure it is preeminently true when what has been given is suffering and enlightenment and what is required is mercy and charity.

Israel's spiritual, as well as her political, future is bound up with the future of the Palestinian Arab refugees. The righting of the wrongs that these refugees have suffered is, I believe, Israel's supreme duty and interest. Being human, one is always tempted to minimize the wrong that one has done and the suffering that one has inflicted. But, of all Man's spiritual infirmities, this is one that brings the surest nemesis. The only way of ending a tragedy is to break the fatal chain of sin and suffering; and the only way of breaking this is to recognize one's sin and to do everything possible to atone for it. This is the only way for Israel, as well as for Britain and for Germany, because it is the only way for any of us.

Yours very truly,
Arnold Toynbee

Marie Syrkin's Response

In his reply Professor Toynbee repeats his charge that fanaticism is Jewish in origin; as evidence he again designates the Maccabees as the first religious persecutors in history. There is a great temptation to dismiss this bit of debatable information with an impatient "so what." Supposing the first instance of bigotry in mankind's bloodstained annals were the one cited by Professor Toynbee, just what would that prove? We would have some data about the second century B.C. which students of the period might find more or less significant. But Professor Toynbee is not content to leave this episode as part of his vast mosaic of antiquity. It does not remain one "fact" among the countless thousands in his scholarly treasure. He transforms an incident of 2,000 years ago into a cosmic drama of guilt and atonement: "The irony of Jewish history surely is that the Jews have been the chief sufferers from a spirit which they themselves originally kindled." Nothing could be more explicit.

What is implicit in this statement? At the bar of history the Jewish sufferer is not innocent. He may have perished on the pyres of the Inquisition or in the gas chambers of the Nazis, but the guilt is as much his as that of his persecutors. The bloody hand of a Hitler appears as the instrument of retributive justice—Professor Toynbee's "German fellow-gentiles" sinned because they had been infected by a Jewish virus, air- or blood-borne through the centuries since that fatal moment when the Maccabeans "forcibly converted" the Idumeans to Judaism. Jews are accustomed to a venerable bill of particulars. Much Jewish blood has spurted through the ages to the cry of "Christ-killer." But the drunken reasoning of a Russian peasant inflamed to pogrom retribution is intellectually less offensive than Professor Toynbee's virtuous pedantry. The peasant is explaining his own act and Professor Toynbee is explaining the peasant's act. Viewed purely as exposition there is little to choose.

However, since Professor Toynbee constructs a formidable rationale of Christian-Muslim fanaticism on the basis of the misdeeds of the

Maccabees, it might be well to consider the incident in question. The only historical source for the episode which looms so large in Professor Toynbee's thesis is a statement in Josephus (Antiquities of the Jews, chapter 9): "Hyrcanus . . . subdued all the Idumeans; and permitted them to stay in the country if they would circumcize their genitals, and make use of the laws of the Jews; and they were so desirous of living in the country of their forefathers that they submitted to circumcision and of the rest of the Jewish ways of living; at which time therefore this befell them, that they were hereafter no other than Jews." In the absence of confirmatory documents many serious historians question the unqualified acceptance of Josephus as a source. Similarly, students of the period are by no means agreed that the population of Galilee at the time of the Maccabees was exclusively gentile. It is held that the population was probably mixed with an element of Jewish natives who had never been carried off into captivity and an influx of Jewish citizens after the re-establishment of the Jewish state. I do not pretend to be in a position to evaluate the scholarly debate, but it is abundantly evident that dogmatic generalizations such as Professor Toynbee permits himself rest on insecure historical structure.

Another point should be mentioned in this connection. Professor Toynbee insists on the primacy of the Maccabeans in the field of religious persecution, but what about the original cause of the Maccabean revolt— the religious persecution of the Jews by Antiochus? In the Annex to Volume 5 of his *Study of History*, Toynbee himself refers to the Maccabees as the "champions of Jewish religion against forcible Hellenization." Of course, he promptly and characteristically adds, "These violent-handed opponents of the persecuting Power immediately became persecutors in their turn." Nevertheless, no matter how "immediately" the Maccabees got to work, the first place, even according to Toynbee, appears to go to Antiochus Epiphanes. Hyper-subtle distinctions as to the exact nature of the religious persecution, in order to ensure the laurel for the Maccabees, are too fine-spun even for a metaphysician. Professor Toynbee also seems to have overlooked the religious persecutions attendant upon the reforms of Ikhnaton and of the corresponding religious persecutions when his successors overthrew what Ikhnaton had attempted to establish in the fourteenth century B.C. in Eygpt, a long time before the Maccabees.

Another point stressed by Professor Toynbee is that Jesus was of gentile descent. The Maccabees brought it about "that Herod and Jesus were Jews, not gentiles." Once the New Testament genealogy which traces the descent of Jesus from the House of David is rejected, the veriest layman can safely assert that no one knows anything about the family tree of the Jewish teacher whose figure is so hauntingly etched by his disciples. The introduction of a racist motif in regard to Jesus is not new. Such fanatical racist publicists as Houston Stewart Chamberlain have long familiarized us with the thesis, but of what relevance is an Aryan Jesus to the thought of Professor Toynbee?

Professor Toynbee observes: "It is, in fact, tragic to be either guilty of fanaticism or to be the victim of it, and the Jews have been alternately guilty of it and victims of it since the second century B.C." It would be interesting to know what instances Professor Toynbee could adduce to justify his mystifying "alternately." In his chapter on "The Modern West and the Jews" in which he discusses the Arab-Jewish war, Professor Toynbee writes that the Jews became "persecutors in turn for the first time since A.D. 135." Even this date and interpretation allow the Jews over 1,800 years in which they were exclusively at the receiving end. Is it unfair to detect in this "alternately," a curious adverb for so monotonous a history of martyrdom, further evidence of Professor Toynbee's readiness to transmute the victim into the sinner when Jews are concerned?

Nowhere is this acrobatic reversal of moral values more nimble than in Professor Toynbee's discussion of the fate of European Jewry and the situation of the Palestinian Arabs. Professor Toynbee returns to his accusation that the Jews did to the Arabs "what had been done to them by others, the Nazis" and he adds that "degrees of sin and tragedy are not determined by the number of souls concerned." Nothing could be truer than that the "measure of tragedy is not statistical but spiritual." I am in complete agreement with that. One gassed Jewish baby should weigh as heavily on the world's conscience as the whole murdered six million. But the sense of outrage aroused by Professor Toynbee's comparison is not caused by the disparity in the numbers of the sufferers. We are concerned here with quality in the absolute sense quite apart from the changes in quality which are introduced by quantity. What happened to the Arabs was different in *kind*; the Jews did *not* do to them what the Nazis did to the Jews. Arabs are refugees because they joined the losing side in a war which the Arabs started. They were not driven out. Their plight is being deliberately and artificially aggravated by the states of the Arab League which made political capital of their situation. It would be pointless for me to repeat the arguments which I made in my original article. And I cannot understand the ethical yardstick which measures as equal the gas chambers of the Nazis and the refusal of Israel to re-admit its avowed enemies. May I remind Professor Toynbee that Israel itself consists largely of refugees, and that European Jews who survived to the status of refugees considered themselves strangely fortunate. Perhaps that is why a Jewish refugee cannot understand why it is so infamous to suggest that an Arab in Jordan settle down among his kin and make a new life for himself instead of multiplying idly in camps maintained by the United Nations.

Professor Toynbee writes movingly of the need to break "the fatal chain of sin and suffering." I should like to address myself to these words not polemically, not as a journalist somewhat nervously challenging a great scholar, but simply, on the level where there is no distance. Part of Jewish suffering during the Nazi years consisted in the realization of the apathy of the Christian world in the face of a horror unique in kind and magnitude in the history of mankind. Today, when a Christian thinker, engaged in the solemn task of compiling and judging the record, equates a crime so fearful that only the charred ash of the crematoria make it credible, with an experience which, unhappy though it be, is one of the commonplaces of our imperfect world, the sense of outrage and bitterness is heightened. It is tragic that our post-war world swarms with millions of refugees in Korea, in Formosa, in India, in every country of Europe, in Africa . . . It is tragic that there are Arab refugees and it is tragic that I must rejoice in the existence of Jewish refugees. All this is suffering, but it is suffering which the mind comprehends, for which remedies can be found, for which solutions are sought. Surely even on the altitude where the fall of a sparrow is as the destruction of cities, Professor Toynbee's comparison of the German murderers and the Zionists must ring as blasphemy. Professor Toynbee writes that the only way to end a tragedy is to recognize one's sin; if so, should not then a serious Christian historian stop qualifying the awfulness of the crime against the Jews by the introduction of ancient Maccabeans and contemporary Arabs into the Nazi charnel-house?

As to the sufferings of the Palestinian Arabs which are real, however caused, what is to be done to break the "fatal chain" in which their plight is a link? I do not propose to reargue the Zionist case or again review the events which led to the creation of Arab refugees. This I did in my article (Professor Toynbee is strangely silent about these events) and nothing will be gained by repetition of familiar facts. But I should like to ask Professor Toynbee how is the chain to be broken at this point? Little Israel has within its borders, in addition to European refugees, 500,000 refugees from Arab lands—Oriental Jews who fled from persecution in Yemen, Iraq and North Africa. A chaotic population transfer took place in the course of the Arab attack on Israel. What purpose would be served by introducing a large hostile Arab segment into the desperately burdened tiny Jewish state other than the destruction of that state? And what then? The million and a half Israelis will not become refugees; there are no lands, no quotas for their resettlement. Does Professor Toynbee believe that the chain of evil will be broken if another million Jewish dead burden the conscience of the world? Is not the resettlement of Arabs among Arabs in the huge underpopulated Arab territories more likely to be productive of ultimate good for Arab and Jew?

To answer in the affirmative one must be prepared to grant one thing:

the right of Jews to live. But for Professor Toynbee Jews are a fossil whose very existence is an anachronism. A fossil that bleeds, thinks and desires is an object of alarming curiosity rather than fellow sympathy. That is why Professor Toynbee can understand every shade of Arab nationalism, even the heretofore unknown variety of *Palestinian* Arab nationalism, but not the Jewish longing for peoplehood in a desert spot they revived. That is why, above all, a sensitive Christian scholar can philosophically equate the systematic murder of six million Jews with the *flight* of the Palestinian Arabs.

In God's name let the chain be broken. Perhaps the first step is to discontinue that double system of ethical bookkeeping in which sin and suffering, life and death, assume such different meanings when applied to Jew and non-Jew.

HANNAH ARENDT
SURVEYS THE HOLOCAUST

It looked like a foolproof choice. Who better qualified to report on the trial in depth than Hannah Arendt, scholar, student of totalitarianism and of the human condition, and herself a German Jewish refugee who came to the United States after the rise of Hitler? Consequently, it was with more than ordinary anticipation that many readers approached *The New Yorker* issue in which the first of her articles finally appeared. As one plodded through five successive issues this initial expectation was quickly and thoroughly disappointed. I write this regretfully because of my long admiration for Miss Arendt's great intellectual gifts. But the reader soon discovered that in her alternate roles of Clio, muse of history, and Dike, spirit of Justice, Miss Arendt was as fallible as any mortal. Her air of Olympian detachment only served to make her preconceptions and tendentious reporting the more distasteful. All-too-human bias and brash manipulation of the evidence are more tolerable when offered less ostentatiously as oracular pronouncements.

In her lengthy chronicle of the destruction of European Jewry Miss Arendt adds nothing new to the vast literature on the subject. Basing herself largely on Raul Hilberg's impressive study (*The Destruction of the European Jews*) she goes over familiar territory. The recapitulation of known material for the purpose of fresh interpretation or new conclusions is, of course, completely legitimate, as legitimate as the question: what new light does Miss Arendt throw on the dreadful past? The author's considerable reputation and that of the magazine in which the articles were published unfortunately make it impossible to dismiss her account out-of-hand as a prime example of arrogance and intellectual irresponsibility.

The author's apparent first concern is Justice, whose nature she has no diffidence in defining and expounding; her second, the psychology of Eichmann, the over-conscientious "little man" caught by the "Zionists" (one of her prime aversions); and, finally, the guilt of Jewish leaders and Jewish organizations in what befell European Jewry. Her account of the trial of Eichmann, the Nazi henchman, is transformed in its emotional impact, implicitly throughout and explicitly, into an indictment of the victims. The crux of Miss Arendt's charge—which appears midway in the report—should be given in her own words. Granting that the Jewish people had no land, no government, no arms, she writes: "But the whole truth was that there existed Jewish community organizations and Jewish party and welfare associations on both the local and the international level. Wherever Jews lived, there were recognized Jewish leaders, and these leaders, almost without exception, cooperated in one way or another, for one reason or another, with the Nazis. The whole truth was that if the Jewish people had really been unorganized and leaderless there would have been chaos and plenty of misery but the total number of victims would hardly have been between five and six million."

As usual, Miss Arendt has no difficulty in determining "the whole truth." Nor is her charge limited to the Jewish Councils which functioned in the ghettos. It extends to all Jewish organized life on the national and international level—Europe, America, Palestine; in other words, practically to all Jewry. This is the thesis which Miss Arendt hammers home. One need hardly expatiate on the gravity of the accusation. How does the presumably responsible drawer of such a total indictment proceed to construct her case?

We are early introduced to "Justice" threatened by this "show trial" whose "invisible stage manager" is Ben-Gurion; the latter speaks through his Attorney General who "does his best—his very best—to serve his master." Miss Arendt continues charitably: "And if his best often turns out not to be good enough, the reason is that the trial is presided over by some one who serves Justice as faithfully as Mr. Hausner serves the State of Israel." The antithesis is clear: Justice versus the State of Israel.

We are treated to further disquisitions on Justice compromised by the prosecution's case: "For this case was built on what the Jews had suffered not on what Eichmann had done." Miss Arendt reminds us a number of times that Justice demands that the accused suffer "for what he has done not for what he has caused others to suffer." The many survivors who testified in regard to the fate of European Jewry indulged in irrelevant, unseemly emotional outbursts which shocked Miss Arendt. Since Miss Arendt never disputes Eichmann's role in rounding up and transporting the Jews of Europe to the gas chambers her distinction becomes elusively fine, and the witnesses may be forgiven if they failed to see the difference between Eichmann's "deeds" and the results of those deeds. Is an arsonist who sets fire to a house with the deliberate intent of killing all within to be judged only by the wood he burned? Are the charred corpses incidental to his deed or are they the deed? If Miss Arendt writes as a lawyer I shall not venture to dispute these distinctions. But if Justice is the issue, as she claims, then perhaps one may marvel at the super-subtle niceties she sees fit to invoke, particularly as on other occasions she permits herself the widest latitude in further dissertations on Justice.

Yet despite the author's insistence that Eichmann's "deeds" be firmly demarked and all other questions be "left in abeyance," she finds herself immediately involved in the supposedly irrelevant question: the tragedy of European Jewry and its architects. The doors from Eichmann's transports lead to the gas chambers, and it is impossible even for Miss Arendt, despite her strict recommendation, to disentangle the dutiful bureaucrat issuing travel orders from the destination of the death trains he despatches.

In describing Hitler's master plan of destruction, Miss Arendt examines the various stages of its evolution and Eichmann's part in the several phases. Before the Nazis decided to implement the Final Solution (extermination) they considered the possibility of making Europe *Judenrein* through expulsion or concentration in some remote territory such as the island of Madagascar; Eichmann was involved in this plan. Miss Arendt explains his motivation: the reading of Herzl's *Judenstaat*, "the famous Zionist classic," had "converted Eichmann immediately and forever to Zionism." These are Miss Arendt's, not Eichmann's words. From this point on, Miss Arendt's equation of Nazi expulsion schemes and Zionism is unabated and unabashed. Eichmann's "dreams" are "inspired" by Herzl. When some Austrian Jews who had been deported to a "god-forsaken place" in the East, a place without houses or water, rife with "cholera, typhoid and dysentery," managed to escape back to Vienna they were registered by Nazi police as "returning from vocational training." This Miss Arendt describes as "a curious relapse into the pro-Zionist stage of the movement." One can understand the Nazi nomenclature—they consistently called the journey to the gas chambers "resettlement"—but Miss Arendt's use of terms is more than curious.

In the pre-extermination stage (what Miss Arendt describes as the "Zionist" stage), the Nazi high command, among them Eichmann, debated the possibility of concentrating expelled Jews in some region of Eastern Europe instead of killing them outright: they would perish more slowly and work for the Nazis in the meantime. With the exception of Hitler, the Nazi hierarchy was as yet afraid to begin the systematic mass murder of a people in the heart of Europe: the effect on public opinion was unpredictable no matter how secret the operation remained. In that period "Eichmann's solution was a police state." Miss Arendt quotes Eichmann's request to Heydrich: "Give enough room [in Czechoslovakia] to transfer the Jews who now live dispersed." In parentheses Miss Arendt mocks: "(A Jewish homeland, a gathering in of the exiles of the Diaspora.)"

One hesitates to characterize this kind of thing. Miss Arendt is entitled to her views on Zionism, the State of Israel, Ben-Gurion or the justice (without a capital "J") of trying Eichmann. But there are limits to which polemical vulgarity should not descend, particularly when trailing moralistic clouds. Opponents of Zionism may attack it for any number of reasons which seem good to them—as illusory, narrowly parochial, contrary to the long-range interests of the Jews—but the persistent parallel between Eichmann's "dream" of a Devil's Island and Herzl's vision of a Jewish state, of the Nazi expulsions and concentrations of their captives for their destruction with the hope, even if mistaken, of Jewish revival, is out of the realm of decent argument. The smearing of a concept by repeatedly confounding it with something admittedly evil is a technique with which the student of Nazi practices is not unacquainted. It is hard to believe that Miss Arendt does not know what she is doing.

The smear technique works both ways. Not only are Nazi concentration schemes labeled as "Zionist" by the author but all the agonizing efforts of the Zionists to save whomever they could from Germany before it was too late are described by Miss Arendt as a cheery collaboration with the Nazis. Referring to the Transfer Agreement arranged by the Jewish Agency with the Nazis in the thirties, according to which an emigrant to Palestine could transfer his money in German goods instead of arriving completely destitute, Miss Arendt sees fit to describe this desperate attempt to wrest something from the devil as a "mutually highly satisfactory agreement between the Nazi authorities and the Jewish Agency for Palestine." That "highly" seems a shade intense to describe the Jewish Agency's delight. In recounting the activities of the emissaries of the kibbutzim who entered Germany to organize illegal immigration into Palestine and negotiated with Eichmann in the process, she writes: "These Jews from Palestine spoke a language not totally different from Eichmann himself." So much for the distinction between the kidnapper and those who selflessly seek to ransom his victims.

In recounting this phase of the Palestinian effort to save Jews before the war, Miss Arendt bases herself on Jon and David Kimche's, *The Secret Roads: The Illegal Migration of a People, 1938-1948.* A glance at the book shows how selective is Miss Arendt's use of its information. Kimche points out correctly that originally the Palestinians had come to Germany to find would-be pioneers. According to Kimche, "They were looking for young men and women who wanted to go to Palestine because they wanted a national home of their own, and were prepared to pioneer, struggle and, if necessary, fight for it." Before 1938, the Palestinians limited themselves to this objective, not the general rescue of German Jews. "That was not their job," writes Kimche. Sure enough, Miss Arendt picks this up and announces, "They were not interested in rescue operations," and she quotes, "That was not their job."

Miss Arendt does not bother to quote a passage which appears only two paragraphs further down. After November 9, 1938, the night of the first physical excesses against German Jews, the limited program of the Palestinians was jettisoned. Kimche writes: "They [the Palestinians] now had to change their focus. The aim was no longer the need of the Jewish community in Palestine, but to save what they could of the Jews in German hands."

By conveniently failing to include this quotation, Miss Arendt is in a position to moralize about the inevitable process of selection (since, whatever the criterion, only hundreds out of thousands could be chosen for the small, illegal ships): "They, like Eichmann, somehow believed that if it was a question of selecting Jews for survival, the Jews should do the selecting themselves. It was this fundamental error in judgment that eventually led to a situation in which the non-selected majority of Jews found themselves confronted with two enemies—the Nazi authorities and the Jewish authorities." What does Miss Arendt suggest as an alternative to "selection"? Should the Palestinians merely have announced: "Run pell-mell to the ships and let the fastest board!"?

Another instance of Miss Arendt's high-handed manipulation of material to suit her purpose is her quotation from Raul Hilberg in regard to Rabbi Leo Baeck, the internationally known Jewish scholar who despite all pleas to leave Germany refused to abandon his flock. As late as 1939, when it was still possible for him to emigrate, the Rockdale Temple of Cincinnati implored him to come as associate rabbi. He chose to remain in the concentration camps of Germany so as to hearten his people. It is this man whom Miss Arendt describes as follows: "Dr. Leo Baeck, Chief Rabbi of Berlin, who in the eyes of both Jews and Gentiles was the 'Jewish Führer'." The sentence in Raul Hilberg's work on which this statement is based reads: "The Jewish 'Führer' in Berlin, as one of Eichmann's people called Rabbi Leo Baeck. . . ."

The fact that Zionist emissaries, in and out of Europe, were engaged in a constant, chiefly abortive but heroic, effort to save Jews from Hitler by illegal immigration or ransom—since there were no other means—is not presented by Miss Arendt as something positive (this would invalidate her thesis about Jewish organizations). On the contrary, the suggestion of something sinister pervades her account. On the one hand, Miss Arendt writes, "Whatever else the Zionist leaders might have been, they knew they were outlaws and they behaved accordingly." But, in the same paragraph, in an account of Joel Brand's unlucky negotiations with Eichmann in regard to the ransom of a million Jews for 10,000 trucks to be used on the Eastern Front, we discover that Eichmann and company turn "to the Zionists as a matter of course." We are further told that the Zionists enjoyed all kinds of privileges: "The Zionists were free to come and go practically as they pleased; they were exempt from wearing the yellow star; they received permits to visit concentration camps in Hungary. . . ." The same buddies of the Nazis apparently whom we had met earlier in her script! Not one word is vouchsafed to explain that only a few Zionist leaders, such as Brand, for the brief period during which the hopeless negotiations were conducted were permitted to circulate freely for *that specific purpose*. Miss Arendt manages to imply that "Zionists" as such were a privileged group enjoying Nazi favor, instead of being the spearheads of whatever resistance to the extermination program was offered.

This ability to disregard whatever does not suit her thesis does not desert the author when she comes to her analysis of Eichmann—only here we get the opposite side of the coin. In the dissection of Eichmann the more favorable of possible interpretations is invariably offered—perhaps because then his trial at the hand of the "Zionists" becomes all the more culpable. Miss Arendt sees Eichmann as a cog in a machine, a little man with a respect for the law of his master, who performs his job with meticulous care and without any hate of Jews. He was not "a monster" even though his deeds were monstrous. This image of the law-abiding automaton was the one Eichmann himself strove to project. Miss Arendt not only accepts it *in toto* but in this regard she is more pious than the pope. She rejects even Eichmann's own testimony in regard to his enthusiasm for killing Jews.

How does Miss Arendt explain the most damaging admission Eichmann made, an admission which destroyed the skillfully contrived picture projected by the defendant at the trial? "Bragging was the vice that was Eichmann's undoing. It was sheer rodomontade when he told men working under him in the last days of the war, 'I will jump into my grave laughing, because the fact that I have the death of five million Jews [or, 'enemies of the Reich,' as he always claimed to have said] on my conscience gives me extraordinary satisfaction.'" (It is interesting to note with what pedantic accuracy Miss Arendt makes the correction in Eichmann's statement though it is hard to see what it achieves. Hitler, too, spoke of the Jews as enemies.)

Miss Arendt goes on with her study of Eichmann's psyche. He was "boasting" when he "pretended" to have invented the ghetto system or to have originated the idea of shipping all the Jews to Madagascar. His chief and most preposterous boast, however, was his claim of responsibility for the death of five million Jews. "He had kept repeating the damning sentence *ad nauseam* to everyone who would listen, even long after the war, when he was in Argentina." Miss Arendt declines to believe these protestations. She has a formula which effectively disposes of the damning sentence repeated *ad nauseam*. "Bragging is a common vice," writes Miss Arendt.

As to the testimony of Rudolf Höss, Commandant of Auschwitz, concerning Eichmann's ingenuity in introducing Cyclon B, an economical gas which facilitated the killing of thousands of human beings daily in the extermination centers, Miss Arendt remarks *en passant*, "And with the use of gas Eichmann probably had nothing to do whatever." Why only "probably"?

There remain the uncontested examples of Eichmann's disobedience, the occasions when the good soldier deliberately disregarded the orders of his superiors. Throughout the war, as described by Miss Arendt, he had punctiliously followed directives, a faithful servant of the Reich. When German defeat approached and Himmler, considering the benefits of a more "moderate" policy, ordered Eichmann to stop the transport of Jews to the death camps, Eichmann, instead of passively obeying, speeded up the transports on his own initiative. The judges in Jerusalem viewed these examples of Eichmann's enterprise as incompatible with the picture of the little bureaucrat who wrote travel orders. How does Miss Arendt account for Eichmann's "crisis of conscience" when he was in "open conflict with his superiors"? We discover that in Germany "to be law-abiding means not merely to obey the laws but to act as though one were the legislator of the laws that one obeys. This accounts for the conviction that nothing less than going beyond the call of duty will do." So again the thesis remains unshaken. All evidence of Eichmann's murderous initiative is merely a further instance, not of anti-Semitism or of relish in the Final Solution as he had "boasted," but of his high sense of duty to the law of Hitler.

Miss Arendt, surveying Eichmann in his enclosure in the Jerusalem courtroom, understands him better than he understands himself or than his associates do. The testimony of Nazi accomplices like Höss is disregarded because these may be interested in throwing the blame on someone else. On the other hand when a "good" German, one of the few who tried to help the Jews, a Lutheran minister, Heinrich Grüber, testifies about his negotiations with Eichmann, Miss Arendt complains that Grüber was full of "pat judgments" because he characterized the defendant as a "block of ice" and like "marble." The image of the Eichmann who in April 1944, tells Joel Brand, "I am ready for business; goods for blood: blood for goods" (*Ware für Blut; Blut für Ware*); who when Horthy in Hungary orders the stoppage of deportations contravenes the "old fool's" orders, who shows energy and authority in every phase of the implementation of the extermination program, is cavalierly ignored by Miss Arendt. She knows better than Eichmann, Höss, Grüber, Brand or the host of victims. She makes no "pat judgments" as to what motivated Eichmann. She merely pronounces: "For the uncomfortable truth of the matter probably is that not Eichmann's fanaticism but his very conscience had prompted him to adopt his uncompromising attitude during the last year of the war. . ."

There is little point at this stage in rehashing the rights and wrongs of the Eichmann trial. What is of interest, however, is the evidence her manner of argument affords of the way Miss Arendt summarily marshals or dismisses relevant data. When she comes to her central accusation—that of "Jewish organizations" and "Jewish leaders"—this method must be borne in mind to determine how much credence her generalizations merit.

Her indictment, as has already been indicated, extends to all Jewish organized activity—Zionist, non-Zionist, in Europe, outside of Europe— not only to the Jewish Councils and Jewish police who functioned in the ghettos. Let us start with the ghettos.

In regard to the evil role of the Jewish police there can be no dispute. When in 1945 I interviewed Jewish survivors, Palestinian parachutists, ghetto fighters, partisans, and, incidentally, Joel Brand, for my account of Jewish resistance to the Nazis (*Blessed Is The Match*), there was general agreement that the Jewish police had been recruited by the Germans from the scum of ghettos to serve their purpose. In no sense can they be viewed as representatives of Jewish organizations or of their leadership, and they have been consistently repudiated in every account of the survivors. The role of the Jewish Councils is more ambiguous and more difficult to evaluate.

The Jewish Councils (*Judenräte*) were established by Nazi decree in 1939. Just as every Jew had to wear an armband with a star so in every Jewish community a Council was appointed. For the most part, pre-war community leaders were chosen whose function now was to deal with the Germans in regard to all questions affecting the ghettos—the distribution of the starvation rations, sanitation, and compliance with German demands for Jewish labor. In the final stage of the ghettos, they determined the order in which Jews were rounded up for the death camps. When Adam Czerniakow, head of the Warsaw Jewish Council, at last understood where his labor battalions were going, he committed suicide "to arouse the world." Some members of the Jewish Councils admittedly abused their brief authority and collaborated with the Germans not to alleviate the plight of their people but in the mistaken hope of saving themselves and their families. In most cases, the Councils viewed themselves honestly as a buffer between German savagery and the helpless ghetto. Someone had to be responsible for the distribution of rations such as they were; some type of organization had to exist among the thousands—500,000 in Warsaw—immured within the ghetto walls if chaos were not to be complete and immediate; and, grimmest of all, any disobedience meant the entrance of stormtroopers shooting and seizing indiscriminately.

When Prosecutor Hausner asked witnesses why they had boarded the death trains without resistance, Miss Arendt characterized the question as "cruel and silly," and she described the immediate destruction of any group who ventured to oppose the Germans. In regard to the Jewish Councils, however, she raises the question: "Why did you cooperate in the destruction of your own people and, eventually, in your own ruin?" One fails to see how this query is kinder or more intelligent than Hausner's. Not to fulfill German orders would have been resistance with all the instantaneous consequences that such resistance entailed—consequences visited not only on the venturesome individual but on the ghetto as a whole. For just as the masses within the ghettos, unwilling and unable to believe in the reality of the extermination plan (the Germans used every device to keep the truth from their victims), hoped that some part of the people would survive until liberation and sought ways of living until that time, so many of the Jewish Councils genuinely viewed themselves as shields to temper Nazi brutality and make the survival of a fraction of the people possible. It was only when all hope was abandoned that the youth groups could persuade the Warsaw ghetto to make the last stand in which it perished. Had the Jews of Europe been able to foresee their fate they would perhaps have chosen immediate death through opposition, one by one, family by family, rather than the prolonged agony that was to be theirs. But it must be remembered that the Jews of Europe were not a host of six million facing the Germans, but individual groups of unarmed, helpless men, women and children, herded by stormtroopers to their destinations. One need merely look at the photographs of ghetto round-ups, at the baffled, frightened faces of the children, to understand the impossibility of resistance. And if, as sometimes happened, a young man sprang at a German it meant a volley of shots in which a hundred fell at once. Fear of punitive actions inflicted on all—as the Germans intended—held back the strong and bold.

Whatever the heavy sins of the Jewish Councils, let those certain that they would have first chosen death for themselves and their families judge them. In every process of "selection," life for one meant death for another. In a sense everyone who escaped from Hitler, as in all escapes from disaster where the possibilities of rescue are limited, took the place of another, if only by being one of an immigration quota. The implications of guilt and innocence become incalculable and few are morally entitled to pass judgment.

Attacks on the vulnerable Jewish Councils have frequently been made, and it is not this aspect which is worth noting in Miss Arendt's account. One must return to her original statement that Jewish organizations, parties, welfare associations, locally and internationally, collaborated in the destruction of their people. This is Miss Arendt's original contribution to the history of the Holocaust. All else we have often heard before: the details of the extermination plan; the role of the Jewish Councils; the "little man" extenuation of Eichmann. Even the discrediting of particular individuals (Kastner, for instance) or internecine struggles between various groups as to whose role in the rescue was greater (the claims of the Revisionists versus Mapai might serve as an example) are an unhappy and familiar part of the tragic aftermath. It is the wholesale nature of Miss Arendt's accusation which is so striking and, if not sustained, so scandalous. What is the record? Let us summarize briefly.

"On the international level" rescue attempts proceeded legally and illegally. Miss Arendt herself refers to *Aliyah Bet*, the illegal immigration into Palestine for which the Zionists were responsible. Before, during and after the war, the "emissaries" strove to bore their way into the Hitler fortress from their footholds on the continent to reach the entombed Jewries. The slogan of the Palestinian community was Golda Meir's plain formulation: "There is no Zionism save the rescue of Jews" (April 1943). On the legal level, the "miserable" Jewish Agency struggled with Great Britain for larger quotas and more certificates. All this is history—both the successes and the failures. Through illegal immigration and Youth Aliyah thousands were saved—a tragically small proportion despite the heroism and devotion of the effort.

American Jewry, far more passive despite its power and wealth than the 600,000 Jews of Palestine, protested, agitated and raised money. It could admittedly have done more financially and politically, though its welfare organizations raised millions of dollars.

On the "local level"—which presumably means Nazi-held Europe—the "organizations" and "parties" struggled through cultural and educational activities to maintain spiritual resistance within the ghettos, to establish contact with the "emissaries" for rescue missions, and finally to organize resistance. Heroes and heroines of the ghettos (whose names are known to every student of the period) who travelled disguised as "Aryans" between the ghettos to bring information, who smuggled arms for the last stands, were members of organized movements with particular ideologies. Miss Arendt might have interviewed some who survived the Warsaw Ghetto's battle (Zivia Lubetkin for one) in the kibbutzim of Israel. In Miss Arendt's desire that Zionists take no undue credit for resistance or rescue, she momentarily forgets her indictment of parties and organizations and writes: "The witnesses told the court, truthfully, that all Jewish organizations and parties had played their role so the true distinction was not between Zionists and non-Zionists but between organized and unorganized people, and even more important between the young and the middle-aged." (In the last phrase Miss Arendt scrambles back to her original position.)

One can understand and share the feeling that whatever was done was inadequate. Had the Jews of Europe understood the nature of their doom, had the self-sacrificial heroes been more numerous, had the world not assumed the infamous role of bystander, perhaps the juggernaut would have been stopped. In retrospect the tormenting "ifs" are numerous. But Miss Arendt's charge is that all the brave, heartrending efforts, slight as they were against the Nazi machine, added to the disaster. Things would have been better had there been no organized illegal immigration, no Youth Aliyah, no organized ghetto teachers and fighters, no pouring in by "welfare associations" of millions for ransom and rescue, no political negotations for immigration quotas and certificates, no Jewish leaders from Henrietta Szold to David Ben-Gurion. Such a charge by a serious thinker cannot be explained in rational terms. Is the answer Jewish self-hatred or possibly the assimilated Jew's aversion to all manifestations of organized Jewish life?

Miss Arendt finds singular ways of making hay where no sun shines. In her animus she takes extraordinary liberties with record. Commenting on the situation in Belgium she writes: "Moreover, among those who had fled were all the more important Jewish leaders (most of whom had been foreigners) and this meant that there was no Jewish Council to register the Jews—one of the vital prerequisites for their seizure. With this 'lack of understanding' on all sides, it is not surprising that not a single Belgian Jew was deported." What are the facts? There was a *Judenrat*, the *Association des Juifs en Belgique* formed by the Germans in 1941. The real difference lay in the fact that the Belgian population lacked "understanding of the Jewish question" according to the German administrators. Therefore, foreign Jews were rounded up first; deportations and seizures from Belgium went on until 1944 by which time a total of 25,000 Jews had been deported. Most Belgian Jews were hidden by the population or managed to flee. This was possible because the Germans did not venture to establish a ghetto in Belgium, thus sealing off the Jews from all human contact with the outside world. There was no Jewish Council in the Polish sense because there was no ghetto. Miss Arendt has arbitrarily confused cause and effect.

Miss Arendt further cites the truly noble example of the Danish refusal to collaborate in the destruction of their Jewry. Danish resistance to the Nazi decree is one of the few bright spots in the martyrdom of European Jewry. The Jews in Denmark, some 8,000, were saved because the Danes were not anti-Semitic, because the Germans had a grudging respect for their fellow "Aryans" and did not venture to set up a ghetto, and because Denmark was on a coast opposite Sweden. This element of geography in no way lessens Danish valor and goodness. The Danes, despite their non-violent resistance, knew that they would be unable to protect their Jews and so ferried the Jews of Denmark nightly to Sweden (which had agreed to give them sanctuary). One horror of the ghettos of Eastern Europe was that they were established in the midst of hostile, anti-Semitic populations who collaborated willingly with the Germans in the extermination of the Jews, and that they were located in the heart of Europe far from the coasts where an illegal ship might lie waiting. If the Poles had sought to save their Jews as did the Danes, if the facts of geography had been otherwise, there might have been another outcome. But the fault was not that of "the Jewish leaders."

H aving established to her satisfaction the guilt of the Jews and the minor role of Eichmann, the bureaucrat suffering from an excessive sense of duty, Miss Arendt returns to the subject of justice. Here she appears to switch tracks. At the outset of her long report, she had disapproved of the "Ben-Gurion trial" because it stressed "general issues to the detriment of legal niceties," and she had protested as irrelevant any introduction of evidence not directly related to Eichmann's "deeds." When she at last reaches the court's judgment her objections veer in the opposite direction—the judgment is too narrow, too limited. And again we are involved with Miss Arendt's view of Jews.

Her examination of the various legal questions (Israel's jurisdiction, a retroactive law, etc.) goes over well-worn ground. But she is quite *sui generis* when she reports on the spirit of the trial. The trouble with the trial, according to Miss Arendt, was that it demonstrated that Israel and the Jewish people had failed to realize that Eichmann was accused of an "unprecedented" crime: "In the eyes of the Jews, thinking exclusively in terms of their own history, the catastrophe that had befallen them under Hitler, in which a third of their people perished, appeared not as the most recent of crimes, the unprecedented crime of genocide, but on the contrary, as the oldest crime they could remember. This misunderstanding, which seems almost inevitable if we consider not only the facts of Jewish history but also, and more important, the view Jews commonly have of their own history, is actually at the root of all the failures and shortcomings of the Jerusalem trial. None of the participants in the trial ever arrived at the clear understanding of the actual horror of Auschwitz—which is of a different nature from other atrocities—because it appeared to prosecution and judges alike as not much more than the most horrible pogrom in Jewish history." Nor did the court ever "rise" to "the challenge of the unprecedented." (Here Miss Arendt wants to have it both ways: the court must be strict in its demarkation of the admissible but it must also "rise" beyond it.)

However, Miss Arendt's verdict on Israel's and the Jewish people's view of the nature of the crime is—to say the least—puzzling. The recurrent adjective describing the Nazi crime in almost every important Jewish statement on the subject has been precisely "unprecedented" or "unique" or "unparalleled." The term "genocide" was introduced into the language by a Jew (R. Lemkin). The purpose of the trial, as stated by Ben-Gurion and others, was to arouse the conscience of mankind because its moral order had been violated. The many witnesses, whose irrelevant harangues Miss Arendt deplores, cried out against the sin against mankind. Eight of the counts against Eichmann dealt with "crimes against humanity." Even here Miss Arendt wags an accusing finger: "At no point however, either in the proceedings or in the judgment, did the Jerusalem trial ever mention even the possibility that the extermination of whole ethnic groups, like the Jews or the Poles or the Gypsies might be more than a crime against the Jewish or the Polish or the Gypsy people—that the international order, and mankind in its entirety, might have been grievously hurt and endangered." To this one can only say: the trial dealt with nothing else. Surely Miss Arendt did not require more "cheap rhetoric" to point out the connection between genocide and crimes against mankind.

With unfailing assurance Miss Arendt composes the speech the judges should have made at the conclusion of the trial, just as she never hesitates to reshuffle facts to fit them into the vise of her pre-determined ideas about Zionists, Jews, Eichmann or justice in Israel. Since she is a very gifted writer, there are many brilliant perceptions in the account, particularly when she writes of the totalitarian mind, but the overwhelming effect of her report is of a blinding animus and of a vast ignorance—ignorance not in the sense of lack of knowledge (who would question Miss Arendt's erudition?) but a willful ignoring of the obviously pertinent which would invalidate her basic position.

What is at the root of the shortcomings of Miss Arendt's trial of the trial is *her* view of Jewish history, a view commonly held by assimilationists of the Council for Judaism stripe, on the one hand, and "radicals" of the old school on the other. In this view every affirmation of Jewish national awareness is culpable and to be strictured either as multiple loyalty or treason to a larger international ideal. That is why a Jewish intellectual of Miss Arendt's caliber is able not only to distort the facts but—more important—to fail so signally in sympathy and imagination.

Her much-acclaimed formulation, "the banality of evil," is the corollary of her contention that the Nazi executioners were small ordinary men. In many ways they were. However, in one respect they were extraordinary. In their single-minded dedication to the extermination of the Jews, Hitler and his accomplices were anything but banal; they were zealots. Their historic distinction is that they succeeded in making unprecedented evil banal—a different matter. Through them the gas chamber and the death factory invaded the human mind. The tenacity and special character of the Nazi purpose cannot be glossed over by the partial extenuation implicit in Arendt's facile phrase.

(May 1963)

I. F. STONE:
THE BARRAGE FROM THE LEFT

In a lengthy review of "*Le conflit israelo-arabe*," the special issue of Jean-Paul Sartre's *Les Temps Modernes* devoted to the Arab-Israeli conflict, I. F. Stone re-examines the Zionist case (the *New York Review of Books*, August 3, 1967). Mr. Stone explains that "as a Jew, closely bound emotionally with the birth of Israel" he felt "honor-bound to report the Arab side, especially since the U.S. press is so overwhelmingly pro-Zionist." Whatever the reasons for his posture, his conclusions and arguments must stand on their own. It is unfortunate that his declared stance as the man of "rationalist and universalist ideals" offers a protective shade to the weighted scale in which he judges Arab and Jewish claims. Familiar misstatements dismissed as the usual anti-Israel line when coming from Arab propagandists, the American Council for Judaism or Mr. Fedorenko, are admittedly more distressing when repeated by a respected writer of intellectual independence. Mr. Stone concludes: "If God as some now say is dead, He no doubt died of trying to find an equitable solution to the Arab-Jewish problem." I am more inclined to attribute the demise to despair at the willful casuistry of some of the high-minded disputants.

In reviewing the Arab and Israeli contributions to *Les Temps Modernes*, Mr. Stone complains that both sides "have put their better foot forward." The Arabs fail to include their "bloodcurdling broadcasts" demanding the extermination of Israel; the Israeli section offers no contribution from "right-wing Zionists" with expansionist dreams, also "no voice on the Arab side preaches a Holy War in which all Israel would be massacred, while no voice on the Israeli side expresses the cheerfully cynical view one may hear in private that Israel has no realistic alternative but to hand the Arabs a bloody nose every five or ten years until they accept the loss of Palestine as irreversible."

This plea for honesty disguises a dishonest equation. The cries for the extermination of Israel, as every reader of the daily press knows, emanate, beginning with Nasser, from the presidents, prime ministers and foreign ministers of the Arab states; the expansionist visions of "the right-wing

Zionists" are limited to a small group of extremists who at no time since the creation of Israel have controlled its government or have made its policy. On what basis does Mr. Stone equate the openly declared official policy of all the Arab states with the views of minority groups in Israel whose programs have been consistently repudiated by the Israeli people and government? And by what yardstick are the Arab will for a "Holy War in which all Israel would be massacred" and the Israeli will to oppose this ambition given a common measure? Mr. Stone describes the Israeli determination as "cheerfully cynical." Neither the adverb nor the adjective seems appropriate. I, too, have heard in many not-so-private conversations in Israel the view that as long as Arabs were bent on the destruction of the country, Israelis would be obliged to demonstrate, at whatever sacrifice, that it cannot be done; but to detect cheer or cynicism in this resolution is, to say the least, far-fetched.

The burden of Mr. Stone's analysis is the dispossessed Arab, and no matter where his argument strays he returns to this central question. Of the Arab refugees, Mr. Stone writes: "The argument that the refugees ran away 'voluntarily' or because their leaders urged them to do so until after the fighting was over not only rests on a myth but is irrelevant. Have refugees no right to return? Have German Jews no right to recover their properties because they too fled?" And he continues: "Jewish terrorism, not only by the Irgun, in such savage massacres as Deir Yassin, but in milder form by the Haganah itself, 'encouraged' Arabs to leave areas the Jews wished to take over."

First as to the "myth." It is hard to understand why Mr. Stone finds it necessary to quote a notorious pro-Arab advocate like Erskine Childers or any other commentator to make his point. Mr. Stone was in Israel in 1948 and gave an enthusiastic account of the Israel struggle. In *This Is Israel*, published in 1948, Mr. Stone wrote: "Ill-armed, outnumbered, however desperate their circumstances, the Jews stood fast. The Arabs very early began to run away. First the wealthiest families went; it was estimated that 20,000 of them left the country in the first two months of internal hostilities. By the end of January, the exodus was already so alarming that the Palestine Arab Higher Committee in alarm asked neighboring Arab countries to refuse visas to these refugees and to seal the borders against them. *While the Arab guerrillas were moving in, the Arab civilian population was moving out.*" (my emphasis).

Mr. Stone goes on to describe the "phenomenon" of the "sudden flight" of Arabs from Tiberias and Haifa. Not one word in Mr. Stone's first-hand, on-the-spot report suggests the "milder" terrorism of the Haganah which he now discovered in retrospect. On the contrary, his own account fully supports the "myth." Admittedly, Mr. Stone is entitled to change his mind about the rights of the Zionist case in the course of 20 years—there have been changes of heart in regard to Israel from Soviet Russia to De Gaulle—but he should not revise history. Either what he himself saw in 1948 or what he reads now about 1948 is accurate. Which is the myth and who is being mythopoic?

The Arabs fled; they were not driven out. Equally true is that the Jews of Palestine, at first baffled and alarmed by something they could not understand, subsequently shed no tears for defectors who had cast their lot with the Arab invaders. The Arab onslaught transformed the situation physically and psychologically.

So much for the "myth." How about Mr. Stone's argument that it is in any case "irrelevant"? When Mr. Stone asks, "Have German Jews no right to recover their properties because they too fled?" his implied comparison of the Palestinian Arabs with the Nazi victims and consequently of the Israelis and the Nazis is disquietingly reminiscent of the crudest Arab propaganda and of the diatribes of the representatives of the Soviet Union at the General Assembly. It is shocking to hear this line from Mr. Stone. What choice except the gas chamber remained for German Jews who did not manage to escape? Mr. Stone can hardly pretend that the Arabs ran from systematic extermination. This "too" thrown in so casually to associate the fate of German Jewry with that of the Palestinian Arabs in the reader's mind is a sample of Mr. Stone's fair play. If Mr. Stone is convinced of the unqualified right of all refugees to return, why does he not raise his voice for the return of millions of German refugees to East Prussia, Pomerania and Silesia? In the context of war and its aftermaths, such a demand would be as absurd as in the case of the Arab refugees. However, reparation for abandoned Arab property is another matter and subject to negotiation as the Israeli government has repeatedly stated.

The Arab states have made no secret of the objective of an Arab "return"—the liquidation of Israel. Nasser put it simply and candidly: "If the Arabs return to Israel, Israel will cease to exist." (*Zuercher Woche,* September 1, 1961.) The numerous official Arab pronouncements on "the refugees' right to annihilate Israel" are not the statements of extremist groups but official Arab policy enunciated by Arab statesmen. Consequently when Mr. Stone asks, "Have refugees no right to return?" and conjures up the image of despoiled and persecuted German Jews, he should consider Shukairy's Palestine Liberation Organization, an army of 300,000 refugees concentrated in the Gaza strip. That a would-be invading army fails of its purpose does not make it innocent or innocuous.

A good example of the complexities of the situation is provided by the new refugee problems resulting from the Israeli victory of June 1967. Some 150,000 Arabs fled from the West Bank of Jordan to the East Bank. They fled for a variety of reasons chief among them the conviction that Israeli soldiers would massacre them; they had been promised that the victorious Arabs would slaughter every Israeli "man, woman and child." Hussein's broadcast to his people gave full instructions as to how to treat a conquered enemy: "Kill the Jews wherever you find them. Kill them with your hands, your nails and teeth." It is hardly surprising that Arabs so commanded expected no better from the soldiers of Israel. As in 1948, Arab atrocity propaganda backfired. But unlike 1948 the Israelis were neither bewildered nor alarmed. If Arabs preferred the East Bank of the Jordan to life on the West Bank under Israeli occupation, Israelis could readily make peace with this predilection. They remembered how savagely Jordan had shelled Jerusalem despite all urging by Israel that Hussein not join the Arab attack. They knew that had Israel been defeated there would have been no Jewish equivalent of the East Bank and no Jewish refugees. Nevertheless, after the cessation of hostilities, Israel agreed to repatriate all *bona fide* residents of the West Bank who had fled. Yet after this decision, in the course of the negotiations, the Jordanian Finance Minister, Abdul Wahab Majali, publicly urged the refugees to return "to help your brothers continue their political action and remain a thorn in the flesh of the aggressor until the crisis has been solved." It is hardly surprising that after this pronouncement some members of the Israeli Cabinet, meeting on August 13, several days after the Jordanian Finance Minister's counsel, raised the question of the advisability of the return of these "thorns." Though the Cabinet reaffirmed its previous decision despite this blatant provocation, no government can be expected to welcome a returning Fifth Column, even the Israeli.

No doubt just as Mr. Stone, despite his own testimony of 1948, now finds it possible to write of "the expulsion of the Arabs from Palestine" so the contemporary reports of correspondents who watched the trek of Arabs across the Allenby Bridge from the West Bank to the East Bank will weigh little with the scribes of the future or, for that matter, of the present. Already the whole anti-Semitic, anti-Israel cabal from Fascist to Communist, from Black Power to White Power, is in full swing, as Soviet cartoons *à la* Streicher and accounts of Israeli "massacres" of Arabs in the publications of SNCC and of the white supremacist National States Rights party, indicate. The notion that TV, radio and instant reporting have made the distortion of events taking place under our eyes more troublesome than in the past appears to be increasingly naive. The Arab who on the Israeli side of the Allenby Bridge testifies in the presence of the Red Cross and neutral observers that he is leaving voluntarily, and signs a document to that effect, may tell an opposite tale to the Jordanians on the other side of the bridge. That the Jordanian government urges refugees to return and even ventures to recommend insurrection merely confirms the statement of the UNRWA chief representative in West Jordan who stated on July 4 that not one of the 20 refugee camps in West Jordan was affected by the hostilities during the war, nor one resident killed. (Reporting by Martha Gellhorn in *The Guardian*.)

In a sense Mr. Stone is right when he declares that the discussion as to whether Arab refugees fled voluntarily or were driven out is "irrelevant." It is irrelevant because his objection to the resettlement of Arab refugees or to any reasonable accommodation with reality is based on his rejection of the right of Israel to exist as a Jewish state. He believes that General Dayan's statement, "We want a Jewish state like the French have a French state" must "deeply disturb the thoughtful Jewish reader." He is equally shocked by a reported conversation with Ben-Gurion in which the latter said: "You must know that Israel is the country of the Jews and only of the Jews. Every Arab who lives here has the same rights as any minority citizen in any country of the world, but he must admit the fact that he lives in a Jewish country." Mr. Stone observes, "The implications must chill Jews in the outside world."

$\mathbf{P}$ resumably he accepts the existence of France, or Soviet Russia, or China, or the United States without frostbite. While we judge the democratic character of these states by the rights enjoyed by their ethnic or religious minorities, each of these states has a dominant majority culture. Why is a Jewish state which, while giving full political rights to all its citizens and prepared to respect their cultural and religious differences, more disturbing than any other democratic national state? Israeli Arabs speak Arabic and are Moslems or Christians; the Jewish majority speaks Hebrew and is Jewish, and the Arabs would be the first to protest linguistic or religious "integration." Their minority rights are precious just as are the rights of minorities in the United States or, hopefully, in Soviet Russia. But Mr. Stone, thoroughly congealed, is only able to compare a Jewish state with Spain of the Inquisition and, in an indecent innuendo, with "more recent parallels."

If Mr. Stone were advocating the abolition of all national states and raising the vision of the Federation of the World and the Parliament of Man, his ideological horror of a "Jewish country" would be comprehensible. But he is not unfurling a belated internationalist banner under whose folds the tribes will merge. On the contrary, he is sympathetic to national claims, and particularly sensitive to the claims of Arab nationalism. It is only Jewish nationalism that by definition becomes "narrow," "tribal," "exclusive," or "racist." For Israel to call itself a Jewish state is "supra-nationalist," unlike the other countries of the earth whose national character leaves thoughtful Jews and non-Jews unchilled. In the vocabulary of Jewish leftists as of Jewish bourgeois assimilationists (*vide* the Council of Judaism's espousal of Mr. Stone), Jewish nationalism is always "chauvinism"; it is never "emergent," "renascent," "progressive," "revolutionary." No matter how many national "liberation movements" may burgeon with radical and liberal approval in Asia or Africa, Jewish nationalism is a suspect growth to be eradicated as energetically by the hammer and sickle as by the Fascist axe. A totalitarian Egypt, where former Nazi henchmen not only receive refuge but are influential in government, is acclaimed in preference to socially advanced Israel. The Left has long abandoned its old-fashioned Utopian enchantment with internationalism and has developed a sturdy regard for the national identity of all the tribes of the globe—yellow, black, red—with the one exception already noted. I am certain that the same Russian Communists who proscribe the study of Hebrew in the Soviet Union as reactionary will, without batting an eyelash, endorse SNCC's suggestion that Swahili be taught in American public schools.

Mr. Stone finds nothing reprehensible in love of country if Arabs do the loving. Writing in *Ramparts* (July 1967) he writes: "The refugees lost their farms, their villages, their offices, their cities, their country." In the mounting crescendo of this listing, the climactic "their country" is worth noting. And in the *New York Review of Books* he comments on the longing of the Arab refugees for Palestine. " 'Homelessness' is the major theme of Zionism but this pathetic passion is denied to Arab refugees." The homelessness in question here is, of course, national homelessness.

Mr. Stone stresses not only the Arab refugee who—whatever the explanation—left his home and his home town but the Palestinian who lost his country. And he charges the Zionists with a "moral imbecility" which enabled them to ignore the existence of a native Palestinian population when they began the return to the ancient homeland. Through the Jewish return to Palestine a Palestinian people was ruthlessly dispossessed. Here Mr. Stone echoes the theme song of Arab belligerence.

Though it seems late in the day to re-argue the ABCs of the Zionist case, the current barrage from both the extreme Right and Left makes a few reminders mandatory, particularly as many well-intentioned people are troubled by such charges. Did Jewish aggressors set up their homeland in total disregard of a native people with prior claims?

Now for the ABCs: to make his point Mr. Stone comes up with all kinds of nuggets from his mining of *Les Temps Modernes*. Herzl never mentioned the Arabs in *The Jewish State* (1896); Nordau wept when he learned of the existence of Arabs; Mr. Stone fails to mention the fact that by the time Herzl wrote *Old-New Land*, he was well aware of the Arabs and dreamed of happy co-existence. But whatever were the deficiencies of early Zionist fantasies, the Balfour Declaration issued in 1917 took full cognizance of the 600,000 local Arabs. The underlying assumption of the Declaration was that while over 97 percent of the huge territories liberated by the Allies from the Turks would be devoted to the setting up of independent Arab states, the "small notch" of Palestine would be reserved for the creation of a Jewish state. This "small notch" (Lord Balfour's term) was in 1922 further reduced by two-thirds through the amputation of the East Bank of Palestine for the establishment of Transjordan, later Jordan.

But the Arabs and their supporters reject this comparison as irrelevant. That the Arabs received much and the Jews little has nothing to do with the case. Arab nationalism cannot be sated by less than 100 percent gratification; 99 percent plus won't do. What about the Palestinian Arabs? Why should they surrender their Palestinian identity to become Syrians or Jordanians as the Jews irrationally suggest? True, all Arabs are brothers when the Pan-Arab dream beckons but it is criminal imperialist aggression to suggest that the Arabs, particularly the Palestinians, relinquish one jot of their national claim because of Jewish need, Hitler's victims and the rest. Such is the Arab argument.

Simpleminded though the pioneers may have been in believing that their physical reclamation of desolate wastes would win them affection or gratitude, they were right in their estimate of the economic and demographic results of their labor. Far from dispossessing Arabs Zionist colonization resulted in their numerical increase.

According to the 1922 census taken by the British government only 186,000 Arabs lived in the area which later became Israel. The increase in the Arab population of Palestine took place not only because of a very high rate of natural increase due to improved health conditions and standards of living but also because Palestine became a country of Arab *immigration* from adjacent Arab countries. Arabs were attracted, mainly from Syria and Egypt, to the Jewish areas of Mandated Palestine by the swift industrial and agricultural growth which the Jews had started and were constantly enlarging and diversifying. This is confirmed by the testimony in an UNRWA bulletin of 1962:

> *A considerable movement of people is known to have occurred, particularly during the Second World War years when new opportunities of employment opened up in the towns and on military works in Palestine. These wartime prospects and, generally, the higher rate of industrialization in Palestine than in neighboring countries attracted many immigrants from those countries, and many of them entered Palestine without their presence being officially recorded.* (UNRWA Review, Information Paper No. 6, Beirut, September 1962.)

In the whole of Palestine the Arab population doubled between 1920 and 1940, growing from 600,000 to well over a million. In Jordan, closed to Jewish immigration, the population remained static. Paradoxically, in the period between the issuance of the Balfour Declaration and the establishment of Israel, Palestine changed from a country of Arab emigration to one of Arab immigration—a phenomenon observable in none of the adjacent Arab countries.

Perhaps the most telling demonstration of what had actually taken place has ironically been provided by Israel's June victory. When publicity focused on the Arab refugees, the overwhelming bulk were discovered dwelling on the West Bank, the part of Palestine annexed in 1948 by Jordan, and in Gaza, the Palestinian city, occupied by Egypt. The refugees, maintained by UNRWA in camps whose standard of living was higher than that of many an Arab village, had never left Palestine.

In addition to dwelling on the "expulsion" of the Arabs, Mr. Stone finds much wrong with Israel. He complains that Israel is creating a kind of "moral schizophrenia in world Jewry." Outside Israel, Jewish welfare depends on the existence of "secular, non-racial, pluralistic societies"; yet Jews defend a society in Israel in which "the ideal is racial and exclusionist." Israel is a theocratic state, with second-class Arab citizens and with ingrained prejudice against Oriental Jews. Mr. Stone makes these charges categorically without offering a shred of evidence of their truth. Blanket denunciations, if false, can only be answered with a blanket denial. The one specific point Mr. Stone makes ("In Israel Jewry finds itself defending a society in which mixed marriages cannot be legalized") is patently untrue. Both in Israel and outside of Israel the requirements of rigid orthodoxy instead of being defended, are constantly under attack. If Mr. Stone read the Hebrew press he would appreciate the vigor of its self-criticism in this and other respects. Israel has many imperfections but to pretend that any of its inadequacies are its "ideal" rather than the result of human failure or of the economic and political pressures to which the small beleaguered land has been subject since its establishment is again to judge Israel by an invidious criterion applied to no other people. No country in the world has so bold a social vision or has tried so bravely to integrate the excluded of the earth who came to it—were they survivors of the gas chambers or despoiled Oriental Jews. Born in great travail to find an answer for Jewish need and to achieve Jewish national independence, it is not called upon to answer non-existent needs or desires which have ample scope for their satisfaction elsewhere.

Mr. Stone perceives a growing divergence between Jew and Israeli: "the former with a sense of mission as a Witness in the human wilderness, the latter concerned only with his own tribe's welfare." The reverse, of course, is true. It is the Israelis whose concerns are global, whose emissaries penetrated Hitler's Europe, who brought Eichmann to justice, whose instructors teach new and advanced social techniques to emergent countries in Africa, whose kibbutzim serve as laboratories for Africans and Indians and Burmese and Europeans, whose social dynamism and accomplishments inspire all poor and undeveloped countries. The world sympathy for Israel last June was not a tribute to tribal egoism but to courage and vision on an unprecedented scale.

Mr. Stone makes another nasty charge. Since Zionism "grows on Jewish catastrophe," it now "casts longing eyes on Russian Jewry." Mr. Stone wants to know if it would not be better if the Soviet Union wiped out anti-Semitism and gave equal rights to its Jewish citizens. Better than what? Better than another large-scale Jewish catastrophe which Israel apparently desires? This is a disgraceful accusation. Israel is in the foreground of Jewish agitation for unrestricted cultural rights for Russian Jews. Among the rights sought is the right of emigration for those Russian Jews who have families in Israel or elsewhere. Were there to be free emigration from Russia, Israel would be delighted if Russian Jews came. But that is a very different matter from desiring another "catastrophe" which would supply "another flow of desperate refugees to an Israel already short of Jews if it is to expand as the Zionist militants hope to expand it." Here we get a double dig; not only is Israel lusting for Jewish tragedy but it is expansionist. Let me tell Mr. Stone a secret: not only Zionist "militants" want Jewish immigration; all Israel does. The call for *aliyah* (immigration) has gone out not to "expand" but further to develop the country. Ben-Gurion's great dream is to "expand" into the Negev, the desert that constitutes two-thirds of Israel. This creative vision—to regenerate sand and stone as the Emek was reclaimed—is Israel's "hope." Mr. Stone who so eloquently expounds universal values and universal visions should be warier of lending his authority to vicious anti-Israel smears.

Finally Mr. Stone suggests: "The ideal solution would allow the Jews to make their contributions as citizens in the diverse societies and nations which are their homes while Israel finds acceptance as a Jewish state in a renascent Arab civilization. This would end Arab fears of a huge inflow to Israel." At first reading, most Zionists would enthusiastically embrace such a solution; that's what they have been wanting all along—a renascent Jewish state to be accepted by a renascent Arab civilization. Stone might be quoting Herzl. But a second reading is less reassuring. To calm Arab fears of a "huge inflow," Jewish immigration to Israel would presumably be restricted (though Mr. Stone appreciates that the prospect of an inundation is slight). If, despite his cautious phrasing, I read Mr. Stone correctly, the one group that the "exclusionist" Jewish state could rightly exclude would be Jews. Such is the *reductio ad absurdum* of Mr. Stone's universalism.

Given a will to peace on the part of the Arabs all the problems of the Arab-Israeli conflict can be settled reasonably and to the advantage of Jew and Arab. This includes the definition of boundaries and the integration of refugees into a productive life, but the elementary recognition of Israel's right to exist is the precondition of any settlement. And the emergence of Israel as a Jewish country with the same rights for self-defense and normal development as other democratic countries should scar no psyche able to envision "renascent" civilizations all over the globe.

A word of warning should be added. The Zionist visionaries who came with the Bible and Socialist tracts to a build a "just society" in the desert have lost many illusions. They have learned the stern lessons of recent history. I have watched this transformation. In 1936, on my first visit to Palestine I attended a *seder* in Ein Harod, a kibbutz in the Emek. In addition to the traditional questions—why is this night different?—the children asked *Kashes* of their own. One of the questions was, "Why do the Arabs live on the hills and we in the valley?" The answer, understandable only to those aware of the exposed position of the kibbutzim was, "Because we want peace and friendship."

The children who heard this answer grew up to fight for hills in three wars since 1948. Last July, three weeks after the end of the 1967 battles, I was in Galilee in a kibbutz shelled for months from the Syrian ridges. I saw the destroyed cottages and the underground shelters where the children routinely slept. The next morning I visited the Golan Heights, the fortified Syrian hills bristling with Russian armor from which Syrian soldiers equally routinely attacked the kibbutz. The ridge was scaled by Israeli soldiers on the last day of the fighting and the bunkers dismantled in one of the toughest fights of the war. Perhaps the most illuminating circumstance of this battle was that the kibbutzim, not the Israeli military, insisted on the capture of the ridge: "Our children must sleep in bed not in shelters." Anyone standing among the masses of Russian armor on the ridge and seeing the guns pointed at the settlements would probably find it difficult to continue prating about Israeli expansionism. Until the Arabs make peace, Israel is under attack by Arabs who outnumber her twenty to one; it will perforce be militant. If instead of indulging in strictly one-sided pieties, the self-declared humanists and universalists would unequivocally grant the rights of the farmer in the valley rather than of the gunner on the hill, peace might come sooner. Otherwise the enemies of Israel may be caught in the vise of a self-fulfilling prophecy to the detriment of all.

(October 1967)

REDWASHING TERRORISM

An effective bit in *The Palestinian*, Vanessa Redgrave's film about the PLO, is the scene in which she dances her equivalent of the carmagnole made notable in the French Revolution. With gun lifted erect or cradled horizontally, she gyrates gracefully inside the circle of her PLO admirers. Lithe, pretty, she gives the weapon she brandishes its full significance. It will be used and the dancer invites its use.

I went to see the film on the third night of its showing in Beverly Hills. Though the theater had been bombed at 4 am on the day of the opening the only visible damage was one boarded window. There were no demonstrators or those whom Miss Redgrave called "Zionist hoodlums" on the sidewalk; the Jewish Defense League, which had paraded against an award for the actress, perhaps had realized that their tactics were counterproductive. Nevertheless my handbag was searched as I went in: the first time this has happened to me at a movie since I went to a theater in Jerusalem. The audience was sparse, mostly Arab. I was probably one of the very few "Zionists" present. As the showing was sponsored by the Workers League there was a large display of Trotskyite literature in the lobby. The youth in charge explained that his organization was engaged in exposing "Zionist lies," and a pamphlet proudly announced that "Comrade Redgrave is a member of the Central Committee of the Workers Revolutionary Party, British section of the International Committee, with which the Workers League is in political solidarity."

Curiously enough, in view of its objective, the film devoted considerable time to an account of the siege of Tal Zaatar, the refugee camp and PLO stronghold which held out for nearly two months during the Lebanese civil war. By the time the Lebanese Christians conquered this camp of 30,000 the death toll was high. A personable doctor who directed the camp hospital gave a moving account of the suffering of the defenders. Survivors of the battles contributed their tales. One old Arab chanted a newly fashioned epic of Tel Zaatar: "On this day the bombs came, on this day. . . ." It was evident that Tel Zaatar had entered into Arab folklore as a tale of exemplary valor. Miss Redgrave, who conducted the interviews, regrettably distracted the viewer by periodic close-ups of her blazing blue eyes and undeniably lovely face, which registered a monotonous intensity of emotion guaranteed to lose an Oscar.

A recurrent theme in the story was the lack of water during the final two weeks. Women ran to get water under shellfire; children perished from dehydration. "A second Leningrad," said one narrator. I thought of another comparison: the siege of Jersalem in 1948 when Arab attackers tried to conquer 100,000 Jewish men, women and children by cutting the pipeline to the only source of water. Despite thirst, famine, blockage and shelling, the city held out for two months before its deliverance; the heroic endurance of its population has become legendary. But Miss Redgrave has probably never heard of the siege of Jerusalem and the prolonged agony of its Jewish inhabitants, so she failed to suggest a parallel more apt than Leningrad.

In the songs and stories of Tel Zaatar, Falangists and Christian Lebanese figured as the assailants. But the true villain of Miss Redgrave's tale soon emerged: the Zionists, the Zionist-Imperialist-Fascists. This triad kept surfacing as the explanation of the Lebanese civil war. Obviously Comrade Redgrave would disdain a more complex analysis of sectarian rifts, religious antagonism between Christian and Moslem, Syria's ambiguous role or conflicting national ambitions of Arab states interested in the possible dismemberment of Lebanon. A simplistic slogan was there to be brandished like a gun: the Zionists, the Elders of Zion. Not the Jews, to be sure; the English subtitles were never sullied by references to Jews. But there was no missing the Arabic *Yahud* which somehow became transformed into "Zionist" in the English translation.

The film gives a revealing picture of a PLO camp. The children, a very attractive lot, are shown in classrooms and in drill formations. Husky young men are shown undergoing arduous military training. Older women sew in workshops; younger women train as nurses. It is a close-knit community with an overriding purpose: to "liberate the homeland," to drive the " Zionists" out of Israel. Kindergarten children, elders and armed youths with whose exploits we are familiar, reiterate this endlessly.

Miss Redgrave tenderly asks a little boy, "Where is your home?" "Safed," he replies. "Do you remember it?" "No, but my grandfather told me." Then follows a description of the six-room house from which grandfather had been driven.

Too bad that Miss Redgrave is so ignorant of the actual history of the conflict; otherwise she might not have chosen Safed. In this town the British, expecting an imminent Arab invasion, advised the 1,500 orthodox Jews who lived there to evacuate the ancient city, sacred in Jewish tradition. The Jews refused to leave but the more numerous Arabs joined in a mass exodus at the bidding of their leaders. I was in Safed in 1948 and remember the bewilderment of the small Jewish population at the Arab flight. But the little boy has been thoroughly indoctrinated. His family was "expelled." And the myth takes root, all documentary evidence to the contrary.

A charming little girl is asked, "What would you do if you saw a wounded Israeli soldier?" The child answers virtuously, "I would take care of him and explain our cause to him." Then Miss Redgrave inquires disingenuously, "What would you do if he tried to kill you?" At this point my mind wandered to the prioress of the Canterbury Tales who devoutly recounts a medieval tale of a Christian child murdered by the Jews. The killing of children: the hoariest of anti-Semitic libels. As to the child's touching altruism, those who have examined Arab textbooks know that their inspiration comes more from Nazi pedagogue Streicher than from the Sermon on the Mount.

T he children appear healthy, well-fed and well-dressed. So do the young men and their counsellors. In general, conditions in the camp shown seem better than those of an average Arab village in Jordan or Lebanon. And we may be sure that Miss Redgrave has no interest in creating a Potemkin village of economic well-being. This situation is not surprising. For 30 years the camps have been maintained by UNRRA, to which the United States makes a substantial annual contribution. Because of the provision of basic housing, food, schooling and other necessities the camp rolls from the first have been swelled by local Arabs who sought the advantages provided to the original 600,000 Arabs who had left the part of Palestine that became Israel. Subsidies from the oil states and the Communist bloc have succeeded in transforming many of the camps into relatively comfortable military settlements. Nothing makes this clearer than an account of the last days of Tal Zaatar as reported by a correspondent of *The Los Angeles Times* two years ago. The reporter described looting by the victorious Falangists: "Many looters were joined by whole families driving into the camp to see what they could retrieve for their own homes. Their booty included living-room suites, television sets, air conditioning units, refrigerators, carpets, clothing—and even a Chinese lacquered table." Very few Arab villagers without "refugee" status could boast of such possessions.

To emphasize the theme of class struggle the scene shifts to various specimens of the Lebanese bourgeoisie. A portly Lebanese cleric with a large cross descants on the need to fight international Communism and to protect Lebanese "banks" and homes against the hungry hordes. An equally gross Lebanese capitalist in luxurious surroundings states matter-of-factly that he is prepared "to kill" Palestinian children because they will grow up into enemies. Shots of a Lebanese riviera and elegant lollers in beach chairs provide further desired contrasts between Fascist oppressor and revolutionary ardor.

The outrageous statements of the capitalist heavies shocked a young Arab woman whom I heard expostulating in English to a companion in the ladies' room after the showing: "I don't get it. He says that he wants to kill children." Miss Redgrave has the killing of children on her mind. But they are not the children of Maalot and Kiryat Shmoneh deliberately massacred by the PLO revolutionaries she celebrates, or the children murdered last March by terrorists who landed on the Israeli coast.

An eloquent, eminently photogenic PLO spokesman explains why the PLO concentrates in Southern Lebanon and why the warriors must return: they have to be close to the Israeli border to facilitate raids into that country. Besides Lebanon is only an extension of Northern Galilee. Borders are artificial, he tells us. Such candor must be respected. It may also account for Israel's refusal to have this force of would-be liberators on her Northern frontier. Terrorist incursions and shelling of kibbutzim make too long a list for complacency. Furthermore, the Arabs seem to be getting their nomenclature mixed. Until the 1960s, when Arab refugees were transformed into Palestinians, Arab leaders bolstered their anti-Zionist arguments with the assertion that there was no such entity as Palestine; the locale was really Southern Syria. Only Jewish pioneers proclaimed themselves as Palestinians. Now the process had been reversed; Lebanon is part of Palestine. How well does this sit with the proponents of a Greater Syria? In either case the definitions bode ill for the independence of Lebanon.

In the finale a rapt Vanessa questions a patriarchal Arafat, who smiles benevolently at his enthusiastic auditor. He oozes goodwill for the Jews who will be allowed to live in a "democratic Palestine." Neither speaker bothers to mention that all "Zionists"—that is to say the overwhelming majority—will be thrust out of this non-racist Utopia. This interview apparently has been doctored for the American showing. Theodore Bikel, president of Actors Equity in the United States, who had read a transcript of the film, reported that the original script contained the following exchange: Arafat, "The only solution of the Middle East problem is the liquidation of the state of Israel." Miss Redgrave agrees, "Certainly." This bit of harmony has been diplomatically omitted.

It is not surprising that so much of the film is devoted to an episode in the Lebanese civil war. Little mileage would be gotten out of a straightforward report of actual PLO achievements: the gunning down of civilians at airports, the slaughter of Puerto Rican nuns at Lydda or of Israeli athletes at the Olympic games—the whole monstrous roster. The terrorists have been redwashed into highminded revolutionaries, and it would be naive to carp at the producer's scandalous ignorance of the history

Marie Syrkin

of Zionist settlement or at her primitive manipulation of facts. A fanatical believer is not likely to confuse an issue with relevant truths. In its dogmatic ferocity, its fixation on the destruction of the small Jewish state, the film is a vivid exhibit of the mentality of the extreme Right and Left.

The chief value of the film is the way it reveals how justified is Israel's opposition to a massive PLO presence in Southern Lebanon. Any viewer who toyed with the notion that a PLO state on the West Bank might be anything but a first move toward the attempted dismantling of the Jewish state would be swiftly disabused.

(July 1978)

IV
THE
AMERICAN
SCENE

NOAH, ARARAT, U.S.A.

F ew know that the Jewish state was "revived, renewed and re-established under the auspices of the United States government" at Grand Island near Buffalo, as recently as 1825. In that year, "the ancient but wealthy" people of Israel was urged to find asylum in the verdant territory selected, and build up an independent Jewish nation in the State of New York. The moving spirit behind this exuberant enterprise was no harmless crackpot with Messianic delusions, but a leading politician, diplomat and journalist of his period—Mordecai Manuel Noah. That the gentleman was no anaemic visionary but a man of parts, may be gathered from the encomium of a contemporary: Noah was "learned not only in the Jewish and civil law, but in the ways of the world at large, and particularly in the faith and politics of 'Saint Tammany'." With such a patron saint, a man may wander but cannot go far astray.

George Washington is supposed to have danced at the wedding of Mordecai Noah's parents, possibly as a delicate tribute to Noah senior's services in the general's army. At any rate, Noah came of good revolutionary stock, his father being Manuel Noah of Charleston, S.C., and his mother Zipporah Phillips of Philadelphia. Noah's ancestors, originally refugees from the Spanish Inquisition, settled in Georgia in 1733. Only by reserving a cabin on the Mayflower could his forebears have ensured a more impeccable American background for the Noah who was born in Philadelphia in 1785. Yet despite the irreproachable character of his connections, and his own eminently successful career, Noah worried about the Jews. He worried himself, he worried several American presidents, and, above all, he worried his fellow Hebrews, who viewed his philo-Semitic preoccupations with more misgivings than gratitude.

Noah early displayed the versatility and energy which was to make him not only the founder and editor of a number of important Democratic newspapers, but Consul, Judge, High Sheriff of New York County, playwright, essayist—not to mention his periodic excursions into the dizzier altitudes of prophecy and Jewish state-building. By 1811, his reputation as editor and sound partyman was sufficiently well established to secure for him the appointment of American Consul to Riga-Russia, an appointment which he rejected because it afforded too limited a scope for his talents. In 1813, however, President Madison appointed him Consul for the city and kingdom of Tunis. This diplomatic post he accepted, presumably with alacrity, particularly because he wished to secure authentic information about the Jews in Barbary. The specific mission of the twenty-eight-year-old consul was to negotiate the release of an American crew from Salem which had been captured by Algiers.

In Tunis, Noah despatched his official duties with such zeal that he became leader of the foreign consuls stationed there. In fact so high did he haul the honor of the stars and stripes that an Italian merchant sought protection with him from the Bey. When the outraged ruler threatened to send 20 mamelukes to cut the Christian to pieces unless surrendered by the American Consul, Noah so successfully defied the Bey and his janizaries that the potentate retracted all sentiments injurious to both Noah and the Italian. As Noah modestly puts it: "Having confirmed the rights and privileges due to the American consulate, and defeated the intrigues of these rogues, I returned to Tunis triumphant."

Besides keeping the escutcheon of the American consulate unstained, Noah found time to study the habits of the local Jewish population. The fruits of these researches he embodied in *Travels in England, France, Spain and the Barbary States*, published in 1819, and supposedly the first travel book by an American. On the 700,000 Barbary Jews he had occasion to comment that despite all their handicaps, "yet with all this apparent oppression, the Jews are the leading men."

His special task of freeing enslaved Americans he apparently executed with more enthusiasm than discretion. He was accused of having exceeded instructions by spending more funds for the redemption of the crew than his budget warranted. In the midst of his triumphs over the Bey and his mamelukes, he was suddenly recalled by a letter which bears quotation:

April 25, 1815

"At the time of your appointment as Consul at Tunis, it was not known that the religion which you profess would form any obstacle to the exercise of your consular functions. Recent information, however, on which entire reliance may be placed, proves that it would produce a very unfavorable effect. In consequence of which the President has deemed it expedient to revoke your commission.
(Signed) James Monroe"

In the course of his travels, Noah had had occasion to observe the disabilities under which foreign Jews labored. That a 100 percent Yankee Jew whose father had served with Washington should have his "religion" offered as a reason for recall was a blow to which he gave expression in many indignant and eloquent pages. He returned to the United States, secured a complete vindication of his excess expenditures in the noble cause of freeing American seamen, and began to ponder more subjectively on the peculiar status of Jewry.

The completeness of Noah's political vindication may be gauged from the number of political offices he subsequently held. Yet, somehow, most of his achievements ended on a note of misadventure. When he was elected High Sheriff of New York County—an occasion which elicited the inevitable lament from the local patriots—"pretty pass for a Jew to hang a Christian" and to which he retorted neatly enough, "pretty Christian, forsooth, who deserves hanging"—imprisonment for debt was still permitted. An epidemic of yellow fever was raging in New York. When it broke out in the Debtor's Jail, Noah threw open the doors and generously urged the debtors to save themselves. This they proceeded to do, leaving Noah responsible for a grand total of $200,000 in debt which he paid out. The loss was never made good to him. But Noah's quixotic act did not prevent some clergymen from considering the Yellow Plague a just visitation from heaven because New York had chosen a Jew for Sheriff.

The citizens of New York gave him a benefit, producing one of his patriotic dramas, "The Siege of Tripoli". The house was packed, netting the beneficiary several thousand dollars, but the theatre promptly took fire as the curtain rang down on the first performance, and Noah, characteristically enough felt duty-bound to give the entire proceeds to the cast who had lost all their costumes in the blaze.

Though Noah had several dramatic hits to his credit—"The Grecian Captive" and "She Would Be a Soldier" were well thought of in their day— he did not attach undue weight to his career as a playwright. Writing to Dunlop, a leading dramatist of the period, he admitted, in a passage which offers a fair example of his epistolary style, "my line, as you well know, has been in the more rugged paths of politics, a line in which there is more fact than poetry, more feeling than fiction."

Noah's most telling dramatic moments were those in which he was the chief protagonist. It would take a good comedian to better Noah's famous encounter with his father. Noah had left home in early boyhood. One day he spotted a vaguely familiar face in a crowd. Inquiring after the stranger's name, he was told, "Mordecai Noah." "Then you are my father," cried the happy son in belated filial recognition. And it would take a very reckless melodramatist to improve on the following occurrence. Noah, walking

Marie Syrkin

about town on a winter day, saw a little girl alone in the cold. He took the child into a neighboring store, fed her, warmed her, and upbraided the hard hearted public. A crowd gathered, among whom stood a notorious gambler known to Noah. The gambler was so affected by Noah's behavior that he forthwith adopted the child. Noah kept surveillance over her fate and in time the maiden married with a $40,000 dowry.

After he was appointed Judge of the Court Sessions, his alarmingly active conscience made him resign because he could not bear to judge a member of Congress, a former acquaintance, who was up for forgery.

How with these singularities and niceties of behavior, Major Noah managed to prosper as well as he did is testimony to the essential good sense of his character. He had his moments of being Don Quixote. He could climb on Rosinante and sally forth on strange adventures, but he knew when to dismount. He might get a little battered but he was never irretrievably lost among windmills.

Probably no aspect of his career afforded richer opportunities for the display of his peculiar gifts of temperament than his classic venture to solve the Jewish problem. Perhaps President Madison's little note in the Tunis days had set him thinking. Apparently he imparted his difficulties to the brighter lights of the Republic. A letter from Thomas Jefferson, which he received in 1818, deplores religious intolerance as it affects "your sect." John Adams was even more helpful. Some of his best friends were Jews, or as he put it: "I have had occasion to be acquainted with several gentlemen of your nation and transact business with some of them, whom I found to be men of as liberal minds as much honor, probity, generosity and good breeding as any I have known in any sect of religion or philosophy."

Nor was John Adams content with this blanket approval. He nurtured prouder hopes for Jewry than even Noah dared dream. "I really wish the Jews again in Judea an independent nation . . . once restored to an independent government and no longer persecuted they will soon wear away some of the asperities and peculiarities of their character, possibly in time, become liberal Unitarian Christians." Noah's reply to the kindly suggestion that the Jews return to Judea for the purpose of becoming "liberal Unitarian Christians" has unfortunately not been preserved for posterity.

But before shipping the Jews to Judea, whether to fulfill John Adams' ingenuous Messianic fancies or more traditional Jewish visions, Mordecai Noah conceived the notion of establishing a Jewish state in New York, which would serve as a training ground for the eventual return to Palestine. For his project he chose Grand Island, a beautifully wooded island on the Niagra River, equally distant from Lake Erie and the Falls. He was actuated in his choice by the most practical considerations. He foresaw commercial development for his site due to its strategic location near the

218

Great Lakes, the Erie Canal and Niagara Falls. He did not hesitate to assure the world that Grand Island "is preeminently calculated to become in time the greatest trading and commercial depot in the new and better world." Being no idle dreamer, he persuaded a friend, Samuel Leggett, to purchase 2,555 acres which would form the nucleus of the city of Ararat to be founded by Noah on Grand Island. He began to herald his intentions through his own paper, the *National Advocate*, inviting world Jewry to establish the Jewish state under the protection of the American flag. Undaunted by either ridicule or apathy, he and his friend, A.B Seixas, set forth for Buffalo, than a village of 2,500 souls, to solemnize so historic an occasion. A cornerstone with the following inscription was prepared:

> *A city of refuge for the Ararat Jews, founded by Mordecai Manuel Noah, in the month of Tishri, September 1825, in the 50th year of American Independence.*

The ceremony struck a few unexpected snags. As no boats could be procured to transport the celebrants to Grand Island, the laying of the cornerstone of the Jewish city of Ararat had to take place in an Episcopal Church in Buffalo, which generously offered its hospitality. There on September 2, 1825, the foundation ceremony was held. *The Buffalo Patriot Extra* published an account of these singular proceedings, penned by none other than Noah himself. "The revival of Jewish government under the protection of the United States, after the dispersion of that ancient and wealthy people for nearly 2,000 years" was not lacking in pomp and circumstance. There was a procession consisting of military, citizens, civil officers, State officers in uniform, stewards, apprentices, Masons, Senior and Junior Deacons, corn, wine, oil, globes, a plumb, a compass—all finally culminating in the Judge of Israel, in black, wearing Judicial robes of crimson silk—none other than Noah himself. So accoutred, Noah announced that "I, Mordecai Emanuel Noah, citizen of the United States of America, late Consul of the said states to the city and kingdom of Tunis, High Sheriff of New York, Counsellor at Law, and by the grace of God, Governor and Judge of Israel, have issued this my proclamation announcing to the Jews throughout the world that an asylum is prepared and hereby offered to them where they can enjoy that peace, comfort and happiness which have been denied them through ignorance and misgovernment of former ages." Nor did Noah confine himself to an invitation. In his role of Judge of Israel, he ordered that a census be taken of all world Jewry to facilitate the emigration of the young and enterprising; he levied a capitation tax of three shekels in silver on every Jew; and amid a host of other directions, prudently abolished polygamy among the Jews of Asia and Africa. He enjoined all the luminaries of Israel, such as the Grand Rabbis of Paris, Bordeaux, and London, and the Herren Drs. Gan and

Professor Zunz of Berlin, to carry out these instructions.

After the reading of this proclamation, Noah, divested of his costume, returned to New York. The cornerstone lay outside the church for some time. It finally landed among the curios of the Buffalo Historical Society.

Noah is believed never to have set foot on Grand Island. The laying of the cornerstone in an Episcopal Church in Buffalo both opened and closed the Ararat chapter. A less sanguine man would have been disheartened by the storm of protest and ridicule evoked by his singlehanded efforts to arrange a happier destiny for Jewry, but Noah did not surrender his attempt to solve the Jewish question.

In 1837 we find him lecturing on "The Evidences of the American Indians being the descendants of the Lost Tribes of Israel" and suddenly making his strange anthropological discoveries a point of departure for stating his belief that:

"Under the cooperation and protection of England and France, this re-occupation of Syria within its old territorial limits is at once reasonable and practicable."

"From the Danube, the Dniester, the Ukraine Wallachia and Moldavia the best of agriculturists would revive the former fertility of Palestine."

And in 1844 came his famous "Discourse on the Restoration of the Jews."

When one remembers that one purpose of Ararat was to qualify the Jews for "the great and final restoration to their ancient heritage," one is not surprised to discover that Noah's American territorialism winds up in pure Zionism. The "Discourse" is a weird document addressed to the gentile world whom he urges to aid in the pious task of restoration. His arguments are a mixture of rhetorical exhortation and shrewd political judgment. With charming impartiality he points both to the constellation of powers in the Near East and to the star of Bethlehem. On the one hand, "England must possess Egypt as affording the only secure route to her possessions through the Red Sea"; on the other hand, abandoning the crasser considerations of world diplomacy, the Christians had better help the Jews to fulfill the Messianic prophecies. Christians who believe in the Second Coming of Christ must arrange a suitable reception, else where, cries Noah persuasively, is He to come? Noah is grateful for all Christian interest in the temporal and eternal welfare of Israel. He is even grateful for the concern displayed by the Society for Evangelizing the Jews, but these societies will best fulfill their duty, suggests Noah innocently, in view of their lack of success, by restoring the Jews to Zion in their *unconverted* state. "The Second Advent, Christians, depends on you." And who better suited for this task than American Christians, descendants of the Pilgrims?

Among the minor charms of the "Discourse" is an original interpretation of the eighteenth chapter of Isaiah, which cleverly indicates, according to Noah, that America was forseen as the land which would aid in the restoration. No less entrancing is Noah's description of Palestine. "The climate is mild and salubrious," Noah assures his enraptured audience. All things bloom in profusion—wheat, barley, rye, corn, oats, the cotton plant. Tobacco grows on the mountains. Delectable fruits such as oranges, figs, grapes, peaches, apples, plums, nectarines, flourish all over the place, and the coffee-tree, not to be outdone, "grows almost spontaneously."

Noah's final plea, "Let the first movement for the emancipation of the Jewish nation come from this free and liberal country" probably made a greater impression on his gentile hearers than his summons to Ararat did on the Jewish world. Most of Noah's Jewish contemporaries viewed his struggle with the "goluth" as a harmless oddity to be overlooked in an eminent writer and Tammany man. When he died in 1851 *The Asmonean* was moved to characterize him as "the most graceful paragraphist in the United States." We must forgive *The Asmonean* for this critical lapse, just as we must pardon the composer of the obituary for not knowing that he was writing of one of the most picturesque and original of Herzl's precursors.

NAZI KULTUR IN YORKVILLE

An extraordinary pilgrimage has been taking place in Yorkville during the past few weeks—a pilgrimage which bids fair to continue for some time unless stopped by the proper authorities. The Mecca is a German movie house, and the object of worship, *Sieg im Westen*, the Nazi film record of the conquest of Western Europe. What is interesting is not the picture, which by now has little new to offer to those familiar with Nazi propaganda techniques, but the audience. The throngs that wait in line to get in, that pack the house show after show, raptly watching the progress of the swastika, are a phenomenon which no democracy can afford to disregard. To minimize the significance of this outpouring as a "handful of Nazis," who can be taken care of at the right time, is to follow a pattern of error whose fatal consequences are visible in every headline.

I went to see *Sieg im Westen* on a Friday afternoon. Everybody knows what a typical 3 pm movie audience consists of—women and children for the most part. This audience, on the contrary, was overwhelmingly masculine, with a sprinkling of women and a few small boys brought in by painstaking fathers. The men I saw were no old gentlemen or retired businessmen killing an afternoon in a sentimental, nostalgic observance of the progress of the "Fatherland"; they were obviously not poor, unemployed loungers seeking a few hours' shelter and diversion. These men were husky, well-dressed Germans of all ages. When I came in, no seat was vacant, so I had ample opportunity to observe the rows of short-cropped heads and burly backs before me. The first question that arises in the mind of a spectator is: who are these men? Why do so many vigorous, prosperous looking men apparently have no regular hours of employment?

These are questions which every official in a government committed to a defense program and the preservation of democracy might well ask himself, since it is apparent from the character of the *Sieg im Westen* spectators that they constitute no aggregate of the curious, nor even of vaguely pro-Nazi movie-goers, but an inimical force, meeting in the heart of the city.

It is customary for truant officers to descend on the Paramount or similar temples of temptation, during school hours, to search for truants. The officers take it for granted that few lads of school age are lawfully enjoying the enticements of Benny Goodman or Hedy Lamarr at 1 pm of a Wednesday. I do not mention this circumstance because I think it would be desirable for the police to descend on suspicious movie houses and take members of the audience into custody. A picture which is permitted to run will naturally be witnessed, and mere attendance at such a film can hardly be construed as a subversive act. I merely wish to stress the parallel, however, that audiences largely composed of mature men, gathered during the work day to witness the mechanics of warfare, puzzle the beholder as inevitably as when sixteen-year-olds survey the charms of Dorothy Lamour during school hours. It seems the "tourist" season has begun in America.

When I finally got a seat I had a closer opportunity to observe the reactions of the audience. I am not referring to the cheers for Hitler, nor the jubilation when the swastika rises over the Eiffel Tower. These may be taken for granted. Germans who go to see pictures like *Sieg im Westen* don't foregather to deplore the prowess of German arms; nor do they arrive to boo at Hitler. They may be expected to rejoice audibly when the Nazi legions march past the Arc de Triomphe in Paris, or when Hitler, smiling smugly, enters the ancient Cathedral of Notre Dame to the peal of organ music. I am referring to something else. I have never been in an audience which seemed to have such a craftsmanlike appreciation of the techniques of warfare as this one.

The picture shows very little actual carnage. The victorious Germans advance, the epitome of might and discipline, invading land after land, but the slaughter is not seen. One witnesses a kind of righteous martial progress, implacable but just, as a force in nature. The German text announces that to forestall the evil machinations of the Poles, the Norwegians, the British or whatever the case may be, the "peace-loving" Germans are obliged to march forward, and we see the Nazi columns tramping across new territories, crossing fresh boundaries. Ruin and devastation are shown only to be presented as the fiendish work of the British. German soldiers may be seen with their huge guns in the process of taking aim and shooting, but the destruction wrought by the successful shot is rarely presented. What is stressed is the technique of the shooting itself.

Repeatedly I heard around me grunts of appreciation for what was presumably a particularly talented handling of gun or cannon. One was conscious of a competent understanding of the skills involved. It reminded me of the spontaneous enthusiasm elicited in American vaudeville audiences by a particularly adept tap dancer, when some brilliant step brings down the house. On those occasions, I have never been quite sure as to what was so good in the performance but I was always aware that some especially impressive exhibition of skill had just been witnessed by people able to judge the talent involved. In the same way, in this Yorkville theatre, whenever military maneuvers were being shown, artillery brought into position, or new kinds of military equipment employed, I felt the presence of large numbers of people who were connoisseurs, though not of dancing. Similarly, the numerous charts and maps showing the convergence of troop movements and the whole strategy of the campaign were watched with fascinated attention. If this was a lesson in tactics and maneuvers, it had apt pupils.

Since I had arrived in the middle of the picture I could watch one audience file out while another filed in during the intermission. The second audience had a few more women in it, but the predominance of men held good. The overwhelming majority, judging from all the German spoken, were Germans, but there were a few exceptions. Several Japanese were impassively watching the exhibition put on by their Axis partners. In the back row sat two Negroes. They could hardly have relished the obscene bit in the film where French Senegalese troops dance a grotesque jungle dance for their Nazi captors.

During the first performance I had near me one of those military connoisseurs whose grunts and *sotto voce* cluckings helped me give true skill its due. I don't know whether audible indications of emotion are especially typical of Nazi audiences, or whether just coincidence provided me with two particularly expressive neighbors. Perhaps the overwhelming impact of the great victory broke down the supposed Aryan reserve. My second neighbor was equally vocal, though in contrast to his predecessor, who had been a formidable looking fellow, he seemed the prototype of the good-natured, mild Hans of a German storybook. He sighed in genuine deep distress whenever the cruelties inflicted on poor, helpless Germans by such persecutors as Czechs or Poles were depicted. He laughed in innocent merriment at the discomfiture of weak-kneed British Tommies surrendering to the thin tune of "We'll hang our washing on the Siegfried Line." I was conscious of him, taut, reverential, when the Führer made one of his few haloed entrances on the screen. I am sure Hans was a simple, likable fellow who believed all he saw implicitly and uncritically—which made him not one whit less potentially dangerous than the harder-headed specimens I saw about me.

When I left, with the peal of Hitler's entry into Notre Dame and the promise of greater things to come ringing triumphantly in my ears, it was nearly six o'clock. A long line stretched outside the theatre. Directly in front paced three pickets—Aryan Germans, citizens of that other Germany which lives in exile. They carried placards: 'Watch the Fifth Columnists," "Here is the Trojan horse," "See your Nazi neighbors enter this theatre"—but the line waiting for tickets grew longer. The pickets, obviously intellectuals, men who perhaps had played a part in the German republic, kept walking resolutely, knowing well what might be expected of Bund hoodlums lurking in the offing, though police were on hand to prevent disorder.

Herr Goebbels must have moments of good, clean fun when he meditates on New York policemen, whose salaries are provided by American tax payers, earnestly standing guard over *Sieg im Westen.* Unless there is a definite change of policy on the part of our government we may assume that after this picture will have run its course in New York and elsewhere, it will be followed by other gifted productions of the Nazi propaganda machine. One can hardly designate such a state of affairs as tolerance, freedom of assembly, or any other of the four famed freedoms. Leading government officials have made it abundantly clear that they consider America gravely imperilled, nor have they kept secret the direction from which danger threatens. So aware are we of extraordinary circumstances confronting us that we have introduced conscription and a heavy armaments program. Yet at a time when we are sending boys to military camps to prepare not against some mythical enemy but a specific menace whose reality even isolationists concede, we permit the existence of rallying points for the open concentration of Nazi sentiment. The swastika enrolls its volunteers while Uncle Sam stands watch at the door.

There are anti-democratic forces at work in the United States that are difficult to corner. An organization like the America First Committee obviously has in its midst honest isolationists as well as treasonable pro-Nazis. It may be hard to disentangle each group from amid the folds of the American flag to which both cling. Though we understand the significance of gatherings which boo Roosevelt and England, yet can't muster even one mild hiss for Hitler; though we perceive the orientation of elements which decline to sing "God Bless America" because Irving Berlin is the author; nevertheless such evidence of intent is tenuous. But when avowed Nazi groups are allowed to flourish unrestrained and to propagandize the population not subtly but with a sledge hammer, then it is time to suggest that government agencies investigating subversive activities stop picking at herring, red, black or any other shade, and take a poke at the whales spouting under their noses.

(June 1941)

LOOK LOCATES A JEW

Look, of January 27, 1942, has an article on anti-Semitism by Vincent Sheean. Yet perhaps "article" is a misnomer because Sheean is brief, unpretentious and does not undertake to probe the fundamental causes of this much-analyzed affliction. He says some good things on the danger of "social" anti-Semitism, which is generally viewed as a fairly innocent deviation from absolute tolerance. He drives home the point that even "social" anti-Jewish discrimination can be a menace to democratic institutions because it provides the "psychological soil" for reactionary movements of every kind.

This is no news to most of us. The thesis has been expounded more than once by more than one Jewish publicist, but it is good to read such forthright, sensible words in a general magazine with the circulation of *Look*. One rather hopes that every gentile reader of *Look* will take the Sheean warning at its value and become aware of the connection between private prejudices and public political movements

In addition to Vincent Sheean's remarks, the industrious reader will discover a neat box which tabulates "Facts—Not Fancies—About Jews." There he will encounter reassuring statistics about the role of American Jews in American life. He will be heartened to find out that of 60 top officials in the large radio chains only five are Jewish, and that of 19 banks in the New York City Clearing House, but one is Jewish-owned.

Up to this point, *Look* has done a good job and deserves the thanks of all concerned. But not content with this achievement, the magazine really goes to town on the subject of anti-Semitism in the section coyly headed "Why Hate Ben Kaufman?" In these two-and-one-half illustrated pages, *Look* presents a "flesh-and-blood Jew: citizen, father, friend of man." The editors are clearly actuated by the noblest of motives. Their intentions are of the best. They know that statistics carry no punch. Even the intriguing data about the country's 1,974 daily newspapers of which only 15 are owned by Jews, may misfire. Nor can reliance be placed on Vincent Sheean's persuasive pen alone. They have a better scheme up their camera.

As an antidote to malicious and unfounded prejudice, *Look* proposes to show pictures of a real Jew, not a "mythical Jew" created by Nazi propaganda. Let the American public but get a slant of that rare bird, an authentic Jew, photographed in his customary habitat amid native fauna and flora, and everybody will perceive what an inoffensive, tractable specimen it really is.

So *Look* sent a Marco Polo to the recesses of darkest New Jersey who returned with pictures of a Jew, a regular guy, bright Ben Kaufman. Let the folks gather round. Here we have him caged at last, a "flesh-and-blood Jew" shown in his kindly roles of "citizen, father and friend of man." We see Ben visiting the American Legion headquarters—he never misses a day. We see him talking with filial devotion to his old mother, whose long life has embraced Russian pogroms and final success in the land of the free. We see him working tirelessly in his office, always ready to lend a helping hand. Here he is at the family dinner table with his wife and daughter, and there again you spot him discussing a difficult problem with his rabbi. And don't think Ben is just a plaster saint. Just to show he's human, you get a shot of him buying a cigar, or sitting down for a game of rummy at the Elk's Club. And to top it all, Ben has a Congressional Medal of Honor, one of the 72 given for valor in World War I. So Ben really rates a write-up. These boys who went down to New Jersey bagged some pretty good game. Small wonder that they returned triumphant with their trophy, and headed their offering "Why Hate Ben Kaufman?"

Well, I for one, "hate" Ben Kaufman. I hasten to add that I have nothing but respect for the actual gentleman, and if I had come across him as part of the American scene occasionally subjected to candid camera enthusiasts, I would have thought him the nice fellow he undoubtedly is. But I hate the symbol "Ben Kaufman," the spectacle put on by a national magazine to enlighten those who don't know much, but know what they dislike.

There is one picture in the collection that stays in my memory. It is the one of Ben and his eighty-six-year-old mother. We are informed that she worked as a janitress so that her children might get an American education. Her boy made good. He got a scholarship to Syracuse University. True, he didn't become an electrical engineer because the field offered "few opportunities to one of his faith." But he made good. Aren't there two big pages of pictures to show him happy, successful and meritorious? Perhaps the old lady will be pleased when her friends call her up to congratulate her on the signal honor finally bestowed upon her son—to be exhibited as a "flesh-and-blood Jew." But perhaps she will wonder sadly why her son is being displayed under the ominous title: "Why Hate Ben Kaufman?" She may even be perplexed by this strange denouement of the great American Dream. A sardonic epilogue to the flight from Cossacks, from whom she "hid in cellars in Russia"!

And how about the sweet-faced daughter and wife who are shown with Ben decorously gathered round the supper board? How do they relish the extraordinary publicity suddenly beating down on their clean linen? Why hate Rita, the daughter who is so obviously a fine girl? Why hate Gertrude, the good wife? Why hate the old Mrs. Kaufman who smiles with maternal pride and tenderness upon her son? *Look* is showing them to you as a community service—so you'll see the breed is harmless, just plain folks like everybody else.

When some fifty-odd years ago a Jewish family I knew settled in a small town in upper New York State, the minister came to call, expressing great eagerness to meet a Jew. He had never seen a son of Israel. He honored Biblical patriarchs, but he had heard that modern Jews had horns. He asked in all innocence if the newcomers boasted any such interesting excrescences, small, rudimentary ones perhaps, but still horns. This tale is not apocryphal, nor too hard to believe. In due time the family in question won its way in the community. They prospered; the neighbors stopped looking for horns; eventually the daughters even had to be sent to New York City so that they shouldn't fall in love with agreeable and susceptible young *goyim*. And the story of the horns became an amusing family legend.

Apparently the horns are back again. That is the only explanation for *Look*'s extraordinary illustrated supplement on the Jewish question. The sole object of every picture exhibiting the amiable Ben is to convince skeptics that Jews have neither horns nor tails. They work, they marry, they love their wives and children, they have mothers, they smoke—in short, by all objective data, they qualify as members of the species, optimistically named *homo sapiens*. Characteristically, *Look* chose no pictures of eminent Jews—men distinguished in science, art or literature— for its crusade. The editors were careful not to produce a Brandeis, an Einstein or a Freud in their gallery, because such figures would merely stress the horn motif of modern demonology—the weird and wonderful Jewish brain from which fabled miracles project.

I find the curious minister of half a century ago easier to fathom and less depressing than those modern Americans for whom the *Look* illustrations are obviously intended. After all, that minister had never seen a live Jew, but was willing to believe the evidence of his senses. When he examined the heads of my friend's family and discovered no suspicious protuberances, he was prepared to admit that he had been misinformed. Unless of course, he said that these particular Hebrews were an exception, and would henceforth be rated among his best unhorned acquaintances.

But today the American public cannot plead this artless ignorance. Jews, good and bad, prominent and obscure, are not exactly an unfamiliar sight. Jews have even been known to get into the papers. Their countenances, personalities of all varieties, achievements, etc., are not precisely *terra incognita.* And if, despite all the evidence, there are beings who still require demonstrations of the "Why Hate Ben Kaufman?" variety, they are hardly suitable material for conversion. Rather than such abject attempts, I'll take a chance on the Jews blowing their own horns.

(February 1942)

THE CASE OF JACOB GOLDSTEIN

S uppose you are Mr. Jacob Goldstein, or Mr. Lester Goldstone, according to your taste in nomenclature. You are an average American Jew with the virtues and limitations of average human beings everywhere when they have been neither debased nor exalted by special incitements. You are just run-of-the-mill; that is to say, you do not belong to that ardent minority among Jews whose intellectual prowess and idealistic fervor is a constant irritant to the professional anti-Semite. Until the advent of Hitler, you evinced no active interest in Jewish causes of any kind, except, of course, Jewish charities, because you were so essentially confident and at peace in the America of which you were an industrious, law-abiding and ambitious part.

Now, naturally, being a normally sensitive and decent person, you are deeply troubled by the catastrophe that has overtaken other Jews in the Hitler-dominated countries. You cannot read of the massacres of the helpless and the innocent without a special horror and anguished astonishment. But, after all, the terror of which the newspapers bring you inescapable reports is taking place in Europe—the nightmare Europe where a new barbarism holds sway. And you, Jacob Goldstein, are a grateful citizen of a powerful democracy whose vision of a free world in which human instead of animal values prevail has never seemed so precious and so good as at this turning point in history.

It is after Pearl Harbor, and you are anxious to do your bit. You have grown a trifle portly—you were more limber "over there" in the last shindy, as your membership in the American Legion testifies. But you still have plenty of grit. So you get yourself enrolled as an air-raid warden. Your wife, in the meantime, is ringing all the doorbells in the apartment house and trying to sell war stamps. She also explains graphically how ladies should jump up and down on tin cans to flatten them for Uncle Sam.

You are so full of patriotic zeal you even get the superintendent to call a tenants' meeting in the basement, and, since no one seems anxious to talk, you make a speech to start the ball rolling. You don't happen to live in a

Jewish neighborhood, but that does not dampen you spirit. Aren't we all out to lick Hitler and the Japs? For the first time, you can voice your sentiments about the menace of the Nazi plot for world domination without feeling you must add apologetically, "Don't think it's because I'm a Jew." In terse, original phrases you urge your fellow tenants to keep them rolling and flying, to enroll as air-raid wardens, to sign up as nurses' aides. In short, there are no limits to your ingenuity and enthusiasm.

Then, one evening as you trudge dutifully up and down your block, you hear some passer-by mutter: "Another one of those damned Jewish air-raid wardens." And when you report the incident to your cronies, you discover several others have also encountered this curious complaint "too many Jews are air-raid wardens." It hurts you in a special way. Of late, even in the United States, you have become accustomed to hearing "too many Jews are doctors," or lawyers, or bankers, or storekeepers, or politicians. You have even heard some wag remark that too many Jews were Nobel Prize winners. When your younger boy—not the one now in an Army camp on the West Coast—came home with an excellent report card, your pleasure was faintly tinged with concern, for you had recently read an article which indicated too may Jewish children strove for high marks.

But this is something different, or at least it seems different to you. You can fathom some motive in the other "too many's"—motives of economic rivalry, or envy, or unreasoning libelous prejudice—but "too many Jewish air-raid wardens" is beyond you. Everybody knows you receive neither money nor honor for your promenade. And there is all the room in the world for more wardens. Your particular district is clamoring for volunteers and not getting the required number. Nevertheless, someone has raised the evil whisper "too many Jewish air-raid wardens."

You wonder if you should resign. Should you hand in that white arm band and take it easy in the evenings? Should you tell your wife to make less noise about the tin cans that must be salvaged for the war effort? But then "they" will say you are not cooperating. You can already hear the swelling mutter "too few Jews are air-raid wardens; too few tin cans. . . ."

Yes, Mr. Goldstein is in a tough spot. And when he looks for counsel, he is increasingly confused. He reads neither the Anglo-Jewish nor the Yiddish press, where the "Jewish problem" is debated back and forth with unrelenting thoroughness. He does not understand Yiddish, and his subscription to the Voice of Israel is listed among his charities. He hardly ever gets around actually to reading an issue, though he is always planning to find the time. However, though he lacks theoretical equipment, he has a practical knowledge of certain aspects of anti-Semitism. He has long been familiar with some forms of social discrimination, but these do not agitate him too much. He has no morbid longings for clubs or resorts which do not welcome him. Economic discrimination is more serious, and though he personally has not been affected by it, he is ready to fight with all he has for equality of opportunity.

But the virulent, pathological anti-Semitism of Nazi propaganda is something Mr. Goldstein had not expected to witness in these "enlightened" times. Still, once he perceived the character of this systematic onslaught on all civilized values, it became a phenomenon that, after a fashion, he could understand, just as he could understand the venom in a serpent's poison sac. It was the nature of the beast. Even when Mr. Goldstein would, shudderingly, come across a copy of Social Justice or the mouthings of William Dudley Pelley, he understood. This was the enemy, trying to get a foothold in America, in the time-honored way, by exploiting lusts and prejudices. It was not America. And America had scented the danger. *Social Justice* was no longer being hawked on street corners; the lads of the Pelley stripe were finding their way behind bars as traitors and Nazi agents. By this time, thought Mr. Goldstein, everybody would have figured out that anti-Semitism was the first and cheapest device of the pro-Fascist demagogue. Since this was now obvious to even the meanest intelligence, nobody would let the war effort be jeopardized by such a vicious and palpable trick. And Mr. Goldstein was comforted—until the air-raid warden incident. Apparently the poison was still at work, despite the war.

Today Jacob Goldstein is wondering.

Mr. Goldstein is intellectually confused for still other reasons. He is familiar with the sting of his enemies—that is an old affliction whose total cure he expects when the ideals of a civilized world prevail—but he is increasingly baffled by the exhortations to which he is subjected by his friends. He is startled to find himself, in ever-growing measure, the subject of discussion and analysis. He had assumed he was taken for granted as one of the country's constituent religious and national strains; yet now hardly a month passes in which some solid magazine does not devote space to his unspectacular existence.

He has been a pretty faithful reader of *The Saturday Evening Post* for years, for instance—likes their wholesome "American" fiction (none of your Faulkner or Hemingway for Mr. Goldstein)—and he was uneasily astonished to discover a series of three articles on the "Jewish problem" in that safe, familiar territory. All were written by Jews, and all volunteered different analyses and offered different panaceas.

Judge Jerome Frank, in "Red, White and Blue Herring" (December 6, 1941), advocated the thesis that if Jews were given half a chance, they would vanish in the "melting pot," leaving no trace behind. In fact, according to Judge Frank, Jews in their zeal to merge swiftly and anonymously with the American scene were post-haste throwing overboard all the spiritual and cultural baggage acquired through the centuries, including their great ethical and religious heritage. "Most Jews born in American regard as their significant heroes Jefferson and Lincoln, not Moses and David." Mr. Goldstein was uneasy. He hesitated to take issue with a Justice, but he did not consider allegiance to Lincoln and Moses mutually incompatible, and he rather resented being deprived of figures whom he had always viewed as among the chief glories of his people. He couldn't figure out the Judge's mathematics—according to which his value would increase if he reduced himself to a colorless zero.

Then a few weeks later (March 21, 1942), Mr. Goldstein came upon "The Jews Are Different" by Waldo Frank, which went off on quite a different tack. The second Mr. Frank pictured the Jews as bearers of the "democratic tradition of the prophets"; far from growing remote from the moral passion of the Bible, as the Judge adduced, they were all "different" because, consciously or unconsciously, Jews carried the fire of the democratic ideal.

Though the mantles of prophecy sat uneasily upon him, Mr. Goldstein found the second article more attractive than the first. At least it left him the holy books, though perhaps in more potent and immediately effective doses than he had been accustomed to imbibing. But when the next week his eyes fell upon "The Case Against the Jew" by Milton Mayer, he began to feel a little sick. After the first sentence: "The Jews of America are afraid their number is up—if not today, then tommorrow or the next," Mr. Goldstein, though generally a peaceable man, experienced somewhat less than affection for the author. And though Mr. Mayer went on to indicate that Jews would be saved if they mended their ways, and returned "to the radical righteousness of Isaiah," Mr. Goldstein was intensely skeptical of the constructive nature of Mr. Mayer's contribution to the Jewish question.

By this time, all Mr. Goldstein's friends were debating these various points of view with intense agitation, not because of the intrinsic merits of the attitudes indicated but because they had been expressed in a large American magazine. (Similar articles in the Anglo-Jewish press would not have caused the slightest ripple.) *PM* periodically carried huge headlines on relevant themes, and by June Mr. Goldstein was already psychologically attuned to reading "Jews, Anti-Semites and Tyrants" by Stanley High in Harper's. Ordinarily Mr. Goldstein did not read Harper's; he thought it a bit highbrow, but the title attracted him as he scanned the current magazines at a newsstand. Mr. High's opinions, especially since they were those of a Methodist not a Jew, gave the Goldstein entourage quite a lift. It was inspriring, if a little disconcerting, to read: "Anti-Semitism is a recurring form of reaction against the struggle of Western man for religious, political, and economic emancipation. The Jew has been hated because the sources of that struggle are in large part Jewish." Mr. and Mrs.

Goldstein looked upon each other with a touch of mutual awe when they discovered "The heaviest responsibility that the Jew has to bear is his gift to the world of the Old and New Testaments, the Prophets and Jesus. Encompassed in those gifts are the form and substance, the life and breath of the struggle for freedom which the powers of the world have most desperately fought to suppress." This made the role of both Hitler and Goldstein crystal clear. Thus reinforced, Mr. Goldstein felt that even the loudest chorus of "too many Jews are air-raid wardens" would be unable to keep him from the completion of his appointed rounds.

But along came the *Reader's Digest* (September 1942) with an article entitled "The Facts About Jews in Washington" by W.M. Kiplinger. Again there were headlines in *PM*, plus an article by Pearl Buck. Mr. Kiplinger made plain that Jews in government employ were hard workers who had won their jobs by passing civil service examinations. He also stated that young Jews were attracted to Washington because, through the automatic functioning of the civil service rules, they escaped the discrimination they met in private employment. Yet Mr. Kiplinger's conclusion was, nevertheless, that since Jews were only four percent of the population, they should not have more than four percent of the positions. If not for Pearl Buck's beautiful rejoinder, Mr. Goldstein would have had a bad time of it. After all, man cannot live by prophecy alone, and if Jews were to be kept out of considerable sectors of private employment by discrimination, and out of civil service by such a voluntary *numerus clausus*, Mr. Goldstein did not see how the home fires would be kept burning.

The psychological difficulties of Jacob Goldstein are by no means unique. They are shared by many American Jews who until the past decade had had no special Jewish self-consciousness and no acute awareness of Jewish problems as such. But no shield, either of willful ignorance or of apathy, can be stout enough to withstand the batterings of anti-Semitic attack or pro-Semitic apologies to which Jews are now being subjected. The ordinary Jew looks aghast at the costumes with which he is now being furbished. On the one hand, he sees the Satanic vestments, complete with horns and cloven hoof, of Hitler demonology, dragged out of some primordial abyss of madness and bestiality. On the other, he beholds the Messianic robes and martyr's halo neatly laid out in readiness for a final holocaust. And he is oppressed by the melodramatic character of the roles to which he is assigned. He is bewildered at finding himself alternately cast as Ormazd or Ahriman, as the cardinal principle of good or evil. He would like a part more in accordance with his real talents—the part of a simple human being, judged according to his particular merits or demerits.

It is just this part which is becoming increasingly hard to get, even in the United States. Too many Jews feel themselves under psychological compulsions which curtail their freedom of action and freedom of expression. Before the war, many Jews deliberately refrained from denouncing the international menace of Nazism as vigorously as they were inclined, because they were afraid of the charge of warmongering. The charge was raised anyhow, because anti-Semitic propaganda is never dissuaded from launching an accusation because it is false. The fact remains, however, that the leading American interventionists counted few Jews in their midst. It was considered an asset for the interventionist camp that its most articulate figures, from Dorothy Thompson up to President Roosevelt, were overwhelmingly non-Jews. Yet the circumstance that the Jews had front seats at the Nazi carnival of death should not have made their testimony less telling. It was as though a man whose home and family had just been destroyed by incendiaries bent on starting a general conflagration should hesitate to give the alarm or point to the criminals for fear of being accused of arson.

Since America's entry into the war, Jews are again aware of malicious whispering campaigns to the effect that Jews are getting special consideration from draft boards, are getting desk jobs, etc. All the hoary, thousand-times disproven libels about Jewish participation in the war effort, part of the stock in trade of anti-Semitic propaganda, are being hauled out anew. Consequently there are Jews who catch themselves noting the Jewish names in casualty lists with the dismal hope that the neighbors will not fail to observe the number of Cohens and Levys cited. Part of the pathos of this hope is that no matter how impressive the figures are, or how heroic the exploits recounted, not a single anti-Semitic jibe will thereby be stopped. Hitler found it very simple to efface all Jewish names on monuments to the war dead in Germany, and the fact that the proportion of Jewish soldiers in the German army in World War I was greater than their proportion in the population in no way affected the success of his campaign. The same holds good for milder manifestations of the disease of anti-Semitism.

There is another fear from which some Jews suffer. We are living in a period which is witnessing the most savage persecution of a minority in the history of mankind. The systematic massacres of Jews staged by the Nazis make St. Bartholomew's Night child's play in comparison. But while some American Jews are outraged by the comparative indifference with which civilized mankind is viewing the physical annihilation of a people, others feel that no undue fuss should be made about the martyrdom of the Jews. The same people who shared in the general outburst of indignation at Lidice—an outburst which found dramatic and moving expression— take for granted the silence which shrouds the prolonged Lidice of European Jewry. In this silence is a tacit admission that Jews are different, that their sufferings are different, and that the compassion and fury which should be the rational reaction to these sufferings, unparalleled anywhere in scope and intensity, would somehow be unseemly.

Yet the impulses to express indignation, to suffer, to arouse the sympathy of one's fellows, should not be subject to a kind of self-imposed censorship for fear of arousing antagonism. Such a censorship, whether in the emotional, political, or economic spheres, is a surrender of fundamental human rights.

Suggestions that there be a voluntary *numerus clausus* for Jews in government employ are an indication of an alarming trend, all the more so because they are frequently put forward in good faith. Jacob Goldstein, the average Jewish citizen of the United States, has the right to expect that his efforts in any field will be judged only by his competence and his honesty. Any other interpretation of his rights is, on the face of it, discriminatory. Particularly when the country is engaged in a life and death struggle, it can ill afford to be wasteful of the ability or industry of its citizens in order to cater to prejudices which are the antithesis of our professed ideals.

The open rabble-rousing and hate-mongering of obvious Fascist elements is a danger which cannot be minimized, and which is being faced by everyone intelligently concerned with the future of our country. But there is a more insidious danger, not so readily recognized, but equally potent. That is the creation of a psychological atmosphere in which the individual is divested of his particular attributes, be they good or evil, and made into an impersonal category answerable to some fiction in the popular mind. That is the first step in the dehumanization of Jacob Goldstein and the substitution of a tribal symbol. It is also the beginning of a psychosis, alien to the spirit of America, whose development if unchecked would threaten the fundamental structure of our democracy.

(1943)

CONFERRING IN BERMUDA

Bermuda is a pretty place, especially at Easter time. There are lilies, sunshine, and fine sea bathing. Tired businessmen, school teachers and tourists used to make their reservations at the excellent hotels which the island affords, particularly during Easter week when the Atlantic retreat is at its loveliest. Since the war, things are different. It is not so easy to get to Bermuda these days, unless, of course, you happen to be a government representative on an official mission. Then you can still go to Bermuda. You can still admire the lilies on Easter Sunday on the way to Church. You also have a chance to get away from it all under the pleasantest surroundings. No one will be able to follow you to Bermuda—no one who may ask embarrassing questions, no one whose voice is too tense with agony, no one whose face may haunt you afterwards.

The gentlemen at Bermuda have had their vacation. They were blessedly undisturbed by any "pressure group." They were guarded from the representatives of Jewish organizations who had worked out concrete plans for the possible salvation of the remaining human beings marked for murder in Hitler's slaughterhouse. They were protected from representatives of American labor who indicated their desire to participate in the humanitarian enterprise of the Conference. Both Philip Murray of the CIO and William Green of the AFL have made public the refusal of the government to admit officers of these great American labor organizations to the deliberations.

One voice from which the individuals who participated in the Refugee Conference were particularly careful to insulate themselves was that of the hundreds of thousands of helpless men, women and children doomed to be murdered in cold blood by the Nazi executions. While the Bermuda Conference was in session, the secret Polish radio appealed for help in an underground broadcast from Poland. The broadcast pleaded: "The last 35,000 Jews in the ghetto at Warsaw have been condemned to execution.

The Bermuda Conference on Refugees opened on April 19, 1943.

Warsaw again is echoing to musketry volleys. The people are murdered. Women and children defend themselves with their naked arms. Save us . . ." At this point, the station went dead.

"Save us . . ."—that cry did not reach Bermuda. Even before the Conference made its report, consisting of a "number of concrete recommendations," none of which has been made public, it was obvious that no serious rescue program was under consideration. This was plain from the outset. It was plain from the locality selected for the deliberations, from the exclusion of the representatives of those most concerned, and from the secrecy. Above all, it was plain from the funereal croakings which accompanied the deliberations. The delegates chosen for a mission to save lives in the most literal sense went at their task in the spirit of undertakers.

From the first day of the Conference, the meager press releases warned against any high hopes for refugee aid. The United States and British delegations agreed at once that any large-scale migration of refugees was out of the question. Mr. Richard K. Law, head of the British delegation, stated that "one must not be betrayed by feelings of humanity and compassion into a course of action which will be likely to postpone the day of liberation." Dr. Harold Willis Dodds, President of Princeton University and head of the American delegation, announced that "The solution to the refugee problem is to win the war." These are impeccable sentiments; unfortunately, their relevance is not clear.

No one disputes the fact that the successful prosecution of the war is the first objective of the United Nations, and that nothing must be done to impede victory. However, none of the detailed rescue programs presented by responsible organizations to the Bermuda Conference could in any way be viewed as conflicting with the primary purpose. Would opening the gates of Palestine beyond the restrictions of the White Paper harm the war effort? Would the granting of havens in neighboring countries hurt anyone except the Nazis? Would the adequate utilization of the United States immigration quotas permitted by law "postpone the day of liberation"? Only a small fraction of the 153,000 persons who may be admitted annually into the United States have actually entered. Only 39,389 persons were admitted during 1942. A hundred thousand more human beings could have entered without increasing the total number of immigrants permitted by the present immigration restrictions, if the procedures had been relaxed to permit the application of an unused quota from a given country to that of another where refugees are begging for help. If cargo vessels which now return from their destinations with empty bottoms were to be used for the transportation of human beings each one of whom, depending on age and sex, would be a passionate worker and fighter for democracy, would that be injurious to the cause of the United Nations?

The questions answer themselves. The trouble with the gentlemen at Bermuda was not that they were too martial, but that they were not martial enough. They were afflicted not only with inhumanity, but with timidity and the fatal appeasement blindness for which the world has already paid so dearly. Enough of the proceedings at the Bermuda Conference has leaked out to enable us to gauge the course of events.

At first the Conference apparently discussed the possibility of setting up temporary havens in French North Africa, Cyrenaica and Ethiopia. But at the last minute, even this compromise decision was scrapped. According to *The New York Times* (April 28), "It could not be learned whether the American delegation had refused to allow settlement of refugees in French North Africa or the British had rejected the idea of providing a temporary refuge in Cyrenaica and the Divedawa area of Ethiopia. These were the three regions the delegates were understood to have discussed."

So there we have it. Keep the doomed from the Jewish National Home because Arab Fascists might not like it. Don't let them into the United States within the quotas permitted because Hamilton Fish and Father Coughlin might not like it. Scrap even the possibility of sanctuaries in French North Africa because pro-Vichy anti-Semites, who have been so notable an asset to the battle against Hitler, might not like it. Disregard the protests of the Christian church, of American labor, of every decent, liberal element in the country; disregard the conscience of civilized mankind now on trial, and cower before the howls of notorious pro-Fascists. That is the way to win the war, and to make victory worthwhile.

There was one Jew at the Bermuda Conference—Congressman Sol Bloom, Chairman of the House Foreign Affairs Committee. He was a safe, helpful Jew for the gentlemen of Bermuda to have in their midst—a political observer who, it is alleged, has frequently stated that "there is no Jewish Problem." Obviously, a Jew blessed with this astigmatism was the ideal spokesman of a tortured people. Congressman Bloom cast no discordant note into the sell-out at Bermuda. Referring to the carefully worked out proposals for rescue presented by the Joint Committee on European Affairs, Bloom sagely remarked: "You can't settle such problems in a Madison Square Garden Mass Meeting." Now the gentlemen at Bermuda can claim before the world that a representative of the chief victims of Nazi savagery concurred in their deliberations. Was not Congressman Bloom speaking for the children gassed daily in the lethal chambers and shot down in the narrow ghetto streets? When his voice joined the chorus of undertakers, was not that the sanction of the martyrs themselves? The living, as well as the dead, were buried in Bermuda, and the Jewish Congressman added his spade of earth.

Hitler has won another victory at Bermuda—a moral and political victory in which Nazidom rejoices. Every reactionary who wants the purposes of the United Nations defeated has triumphed in the failure at Bermuda. The so-called Refugee Conference has made a mockery, not only of the agony of millions of helpless human beings, but of the great cause of liberation to which the democratic world is committed, and which alone makes the horror of our time understandable and endurable.

(May 1943)

FREE PORT

President Roosevelt's announcement that the United States would admit a maximum of 1,000 refugees to be housed at Fort Ontario, has aroused emotions ranging from bitter indignation to restrained jubilee. The properly indignant view the proposal as piddling to the point of being offensive. The jubilant, on the other hand, profess to see great "symbolic" merits in the readiness of the United States to participate in the task of providing havens, even if on so slight a scale. However, even the most enthusiastic can hardly escape the feeling that the mountain labored precious little, and brought forth a very small mouse.

For the past couple of months the press has carried on an agitation for "free ports," the term coined by Samuel Grafton to designate temporary havens for refugees. Havens have been advocated for over two years by most organized bodies concerned with the problem of rescue, but Mr. Grafton's phrase caught the public's fancy more effectively than previous demands for emergency shelter. It is somewhat difficult to understand why the concept of "free ports," according to which human beings are viewed as cargo to be stored temporarily while in transit to other eventual destinations, should have touched the imagination of the American people more keenly than a cry for "sanctuary." No doubt a sociologist of the future will find cause to speculate on the psychology of an industrial civilization which would be more readily stirred by the notion of fellow men as portable and transportable goods than by appeal to mercy and the ethical obligations of religion implicit in the word "sanctuary." However that be, the fact remains that the first tangible result of the pressure for havens has been the President's recent announcement.

Among his instructions to those engaged in selecting the fortunate 1,000, President Roosevelt took care to include the following provision: "In choosing the refugees to be brought to the United States, please bear in mind that to the extent possible those refugees should be selected for whom other havens of refuge are not immediately available. I should, however, like the group to include a reasonable proportion of various categories of persecuted peoples who have fled to Italy." In other words, the 1,000 at Fort Ontario are to provide a kind of assortment of Europe's persecuted. We will be able to point to a few samples of each variety with pride, and take note that no favoritism has been shown. Above all, it will be impossible to level the awful charge that the measure was undertaken to save European Jews from certain slaughter by the Nazis.

It would be idle to pretend delight with this contribution toward the salvation of European Jewry. If Fort Ontario represents the full extent of direct American participation in rescue, then it means that at most a few hundred European Jews will be saved by the richest and most powerful democracy in the world. After the preliminary fanfare and build-up, it is difficult to reconcile oneself to such a conclusion. If the 1,000 refugees to be housed in Fort Ontario will actually prove to be the total number admitted, then the free port so established is impressive neither as a practical measure of alleviation nor even as a gesture.

There is, of course, the hope that the President's announcement was a trial balloon and that prodding by the American people may result in an extension of the original scheme.

No doubt the President was influenced by the fear of an unfavorable public reaction to a more magnanimous offer. There is no denying that there is a sizeable degree of anti-alien sentiment in the country which a responsible leader of the nation must take into account when shaping his policies. The bugaboo of a "foreign" invasion of refugees has been thoroughly exploited by reactionaries of all political persuasions, and the President cannot ignore its existence. Even if this were not an election year, the leader of a democracy must keep his ear to the ground. This is not necessarily ignominious. It is of the essence of representative government: there cannot be a sharp dichotomy between public sentiment and executive action.

Nor can the fact that November is around the corner be truthfully dismissed as irrelevant. If the President were to alienate a considerable body of his followers by an act completely out of harmony with the desires of the American people, no adherent of his policies would wish him to embark on such a course without due consideration. The President's political astuteness is well-known. In the present instance, nevertheless, one may venture to ask whether Roosevelt has accurately gauged the spirit of his supporters—present and prospective.

The bigots, the pro-Fascists, the isolationists, the lunatic fringe, the tories, will be as antagonized by 1,000 refugees as by 1,000,000. Three zeros more or less are nothing in their eyes, and they are congenitally more sympathetic to decimation than to any five intervals of the decimal system. As soon as the Fort Ontario project was made public, Westbrook Pegler promptly made known that his heart was in the usual place, and concluded a characteristic screed against the proposal with the typically malodorous statement that as far as he was concerned, only "native Americans" should have the right to vote. This invitation for the disfranchisement of a sizeable proportion of the American people appeared not in a scurrilous leaflet circulated by subversive groups but in a reputable American newspaper, and was elicited by the alarming possibility of the admission of 1,000 refugees.

Obviously such are not the men and women whose views President Roosevelt must take into account. These are the enemies not only of an enlightened foreign and domestic policy but of the democratic institutions which the President is sworn to safeguard. There is no appeasing the Coughlinites, the Rankins, or the Peglers. By the time a columnist whose writings are syndicated from coast to coast feels bold enough to suggest that the ballot should be reserved for "native" Americans, the *sub rosa* stage is over; the frontal assault on American democracy is on, and its protagonists are no longer skulking under cover. That they should constitute the most vociferous opponents of havens in any form is only to be expected, just as it is to be expected that they should promptly couple their attack on any potential future citizens with an open offensive against naturalized citizens.

Foreign-born disciples of these gentry have food for thought. Once anti-alien psychosis is permitted to develop unashamedly, it is obviously a short step to extending it to citizens who didn't manage to get born in the United States. At which point are Mr. Pegler and his ilk prepared to stop? Will the "native" Americans be native enough if they are first generation specimens, or will there appear the additional qualification of "native" parents or grandparents? How long will it take before the howl that only "white Protestants" be eligible to vote is heard in the open? It is the howl that follows logically after the anti-Semitic howls, the anti-alien howls, and the "native American" howls.

Is this jungle howl the *vox populi*? Must it be listened to by the shapers of American policy? These are not rhetorical questions. A candid evaluation of the situation is essential before one can presume to criticize President Roosevelt's offer.

What indications of the reactions of the American people toward the plan to provide temporary asylum for refugees in the United States are available? Everybody knows that prominent liberals, churchmen of all faiths, and organized labor have long been on record as favoring the establishment of havens. Recently, CIO and AFL leaders have again renewed their demand for free ports. Apparently, American labor is no longer haunted by the terror of immigrant competition, a fear which was originally partly instrumental in the shaping of our immigration laws.

Labor's humane and enlightened attitude toward the refugee problem must surely be taken into account in any honest estimate of public feeling.

It would be a mistake to assume that support for havens is limited to humanitarians enrolled under the banner of Henry Wallace. It cuts across party lines and may be discovered in wholly diverse quarters. The governors of 18 states—practical politicians—recently endorsed free ports. The unpredictable Clare Booth Luce has added her 100 percent Republican voice to that of the supporters. To top it all, the Hearst press has called on the United States to "lead the way, and set the example for allied and neutral countries, in the establishment of temporary havens or 'free ports' for refugees" (New York *Daily Mirror*, May 13, 1944).

That the Hearst press, which can hardly be accused of dreamy-eyed idealism, has seen fit to throw its weight behind the movement for havens is an indication that popular support for the idea may be found among much wider segments of the population than might have been anticipated. One thing is clear. Not only the foredoomed champions of lost causes are conscious of America's moral obligation to take part in the work of rescues. Hard-headed political realists have not been frightened off by the prospect of unfavorable repercussions. Apparently they judge the spirit of the American people more charitably, or more justly, than the administration.

Four million human beings who might easily have been saved have been murdered in the Nazi slaughterhouses. The word "easily" is used advisedly. There was a period before the war when Jews could have escaped their butchers. There was room in the wide world—plenty of room. There was ample warning as to the fate of those who would remain in Hitler's hands. The generations of the future will find much about our era incredible. They will find the human abattoirs, the lethal chambers of the Nazi killers unbelievable. They will find the conduct of the civilized nations which refused admission to women and children faced with certain murder equally so. It will be hard to explain the meaning of "visas" and "quotas" under such circumstances, and the "red tape" of consular offices will acquire a new etymology; it will mean red with blood.

At the present moment, there are still approximately one million Jews alive in the Balkans. We know what is in store for them. We know it with a measure of circumstantial detail which does not bear repeating. If anyone assumes that Nazi sadism has been assuaged by the extermination centers of Poland and occupied Russia, that Nazi bloodlust has been sated by less than the total murder of the Jews of occupied Europe, he is an optimist. We have just had direct word from Hungary. No less a personage than the Hungarian Premier, Doeme Sztoyay, saw fit to broadcast by shortwave to the United States. He wanted to explain the massacre of Hungarian Jews to

Hungarians in America: Jews were being exterminated to provide "room for American Hungarians to return to their native country after the war." The Hungarian Premier had learned the Nazi murder lesson well. He had assimilated the teaching of his masters so thoroughly that he even bettered his instructors in the clarity and economy of his explanation. Goebbels would have counseled against such candor. Americans are still insufficiently enlightened to appreciate all the direct applications of Nazi doctrine.

The Hungarian Premier was probably nonplussed by the indignant reception his information elicited among Hungarian Americans who shortwaved back a denunciation of his policies. Nothing could indicate the demoralization of our time more vividly than this dialogue through the ether. It sounds like a Satanic fantasy composed by Swift or Voltaire and entitled "Conversations in Hell." But the words were spoken, a few weeks ago, across the Atlantic. The Hungarian Premier is as much a senseless instrument of destruction created by the Nazis as the robot plane, and the noise of both sounds savagely and idiotically through the air. As one listens to that evil whirr—"we kill to make room"—one waits for a human voice. It is time for man to speak.

One is tempted to say: let us cast aside all the statistical arguments which prove that the United States instead of being overrun with immigrants since 1933 has actually admitted a *million fewer* immigrants than would have been permitted by the quotas if they had been filled. Essentially these calculations should be irrelevant. However, it is impossible to yield to this temptation. We must point out again, that if the permitted quotas had been merely re-allocated among the various countries, if the procedure of granting visas had been expedited when that was still possible, a million human beings could have been saved within the numerical restrictions of our immigration laws.

Now, it is futile to use the terminology of visas and quotas. We have no consuls in Nazi Europe who can ponder over the credentials to salvation of some helpless human being. But we are under obligation to offer sanctuary to whomever can escape. Countries like Turkey, which adjoin the Balkans, will not admit refugees unless assurance is given that the United Nations will provide asylum. We cannot urge Turkey to provide temporary havens unless we are prepared to do so.

If the United States can permit itself to declare to the world that its maximum contribution to the refugee problem is the admission of 1,000 people, what answer can be expected from smaller and poorer nations, who have coped with sporadic streams of refugees for years? If the United Nations really accepts the moral responsibility of offering sanctuary to Hitler's victims, then only one principle can be viewed as valid. We will provide free ports, or temporary havens to whomever can escape, and we will do all in our power to assist in this escape. Everything else is a mockery.

There has been so much bloodshed, so much slaughter, that unfortunately even if we were to provide for every Jew remaining alive in Europe we might still not consume unused quotas of the past decade.

As the struggle sharpens, President Roosevelt will be fought by every obscurantist element on each large and liberal issue. The cleavage between him and the Neanderthalers will grow wider and deeper. He cannot hope to bridge the gap except by a capitulation which would make any momentary victory meaningless. Every measure conceived now is a token of the peace in the making. President Roosevelt from the outset ranged himself on the side of the brave, new world. He must have the courage of his own faith, and the faith he has inspired. He must have the courage to have his voice be heard above the animal snarls and howls, and the imbecile mechanical clatter.

(July 1944)

AT FORT ONTARIO

I spent a day at Fort Ontario, one month after the opening of the Shelter to 1,000 refugees. Now they are no longer called "refugees"; the official designation is "residents," and the change is symptomatic of the genuine desire of the administrative staff to handle understandingly the complex and delicate problems inevitable in the situation.

Twelve hours at Fort Ontario is a long time. I shall remember my visit as one of the longest days of my life. I mention this to dispose of the easy jibe at journalists who poke around for a few hours, and then run back home bursting with revelations. A week would have been better and a month would have been still better, but time is stretched by the fullness of experience, and no normally sensitive person can visit the Shelter without feeling that he has peered into each of the several circles of hell into which Hitler has sub-divided Europe. The children chattering in three or four languages apiece—German, Italian, French, Polish, Yugoslav—bring greetings from each.

How do the former denizens of the inferno fare as "residents" on American soil? How charred is the brand plucked from the burning? When questions so dreadful have to be asked, small wonder that some of the answers are, in their way, dreadful too.

First, as to the physical aspects. The Shelter is beautifully located on the shores of Lake Ontario. There are broad, well-kept green lawns, shady walks, and plenty of space for recreation and rest directly facing the lake. The first impression, after one has passed the gate, is that of a pleasant summer camp. Even the housing (barrack dormitories for the single people and small houses arranged into apartments for families) carries out the adult camp note.

The appearance of the people was an agreeable surprise. I had seen pictures of the refugees taken immediately upon their arrival—gaunt, harrowed faces, tattered clothing. I had also read subsequent reports which indicated that the elementary problems of adequate food and clothing had as yet not been satisfactorily solved. When I visited the Shelter, a month had already elapsed, and much of the earlier criticism was no longer valid. The men, women and children looked, on the whole, as well-dressed as any group of similar numbers outside the wire fence. Very shabby or inappropriate wearing apparel was the exception rather than the rule. I should also say that the people seemed, at first glance, about as healthy a group as the average. Had I not known where I was, I should have missed noting many still-ravaged faces and worn bodies. As it was, even a month of fresh air, sunshine, and regular feeding had clearly accomplished a transformation. Only the children appeared markedly below par. They were thinner and paler than American children; after I had learned the ages of some, it was clear that many were undersized, stunted in growth. But the total first impression was that of a middle-class community, not prosperous but decent, with an exceptionally large percentage of men and women whose faces indicated refinement, intelligence, and a high level of culture.

However, when one leaves the lovely promenade around the green lawns with children playing in the sunlight, and goes off among the wooden barracks, many other aspects come to the fore. One begins to realize that one is among human beings tormented and bereft beyond the mind of man to imagine; one is among the deeply wounded and these wounds have not lessened their needs nor their desires. These men and women are still capable of wishing and wanting and hoping—that is the miracle. That is also the tragedy under the present circumstances.

I think it is only fair to state at the outset that the government is doing its utmost to deal justly with the refugees. They were brought to Fort Ontario outside the quota for the duration of the war, on the understanding that they would be confined to the grounds with no possibility of working outside the camp. Each refugee signed a statement agreeing to these conditions. The government undertook to provide the basic needs of food, clothing, shelter and medical care, plus a small allowance of a few dollars a month for incidentals. These conditions are being kept. It is true that the refugees did not arrive to a smoothly functioning Shelter, where all preparations necessary for the reception of 1,000 people had been made. The amount and type of food required had not been gauged accurately. As one member of the staff put it to me, "We did not know that they would be so hungry!" The phrase threw light on the starvation and malnutrition of years which could not be at once assuaged. However, by now there seemed to be general agreement among the refugees that the food was ample and satisfactory. Some to whom I spoke did not like the unaccustomed style of cooking, but these were minor and minority complaints. Obviously, mass-cooking does not make for the tastiest fare, but the extent to which the administration of the camp is anxious to suit the particular preferences of the residents may be judged from the fact that pumpernickel and rye bread are brought in daily from bakeries in an adjoining town because the local bakeries carry chiefly white bread which the refugees dislike.

As to clothing, that question too is being adjusted. Each refugee is provided with his basic needs. Women, for instance, are entitled to two dresses, two slips, two panties, etc. In other words, provision is made for the garment worn and for one change. Some of the refugees had a few garments when they arrived, but most had nothing save the nondescript rags they wore on their backs. One could see old men in shorts donated by an English or Yankee soldier in Italy. To fit out 1,000 people with even minimal clothing requirements is no slight task, particularly as the staff wisely decided to grant each individual a cash clothing allowance and permit him to make his own selection in the town of Oswego. Each day 75 people are given passes to go to town and buy what they urgently require. In order to maintain local good will, whose importance is obvious, all purchasing is done in Oswego, even if better values might be obtainable elsewhere. This creates a sympathetic contact between the local community and the refugees. However, the town is not equipped to handle a mass descent of 1,000 people, and rotation is necessary. This prolongs the process of essential equipment. By this time, the majority have received elementary necessities, particularly as a great many have received gifts from friends, relatives, and residents of the town of Oswego.

Shelter, again, is on a simple, subsistence level. If one thinks in terms of a Palestinian *kvutzah*, the standards are luxurious from the point of view of space. If one thinks of an average New York apartment, no sensible comparisons are possible. I saw the living quarters of several families. Each consists of a very long room which has been partitioned off into bed-chambers and living room, according to the number in the family. One room in each unit has running water. Each room is provided with essentials: cots, a table, some chairs, and shelves for clothing and books. Despite the bare wooden planks of walls, floors, and furniture, the effect is not dismal because the small rooms are clean, sunny, and the plain unpainted furniture is obviously fresh from the carpenter's workshop.

In addition, a canteen has been opened. B'nai Brith has furnished a recreation hall with attractive wicker furniture, games, and a radio. There is an auditorium and a small house of worship. In short, the basic elements of existence have been provided. Much still has to be done, but there is no point in listing lacks or deficiencies which are steadily being corrected.

The real problem lies much deeper than three meals a day and a clean place for sleeping. It lies even deeper than security from murder. These are the thousand saved. They are grateful for salvation. Person after person gave passionate thanks in my presence for the opportunity to live. One beautiful old woman with a saintly face—she had been a physician in Vienna—said to me: "I praise God every hour for America, for the American people, for this place. I want to write it to the President." And when I mentioned the fact that I had heard a few complaints, she added bitterly: "They should be ashamed." Others spoke in a less ecstatic vein but were equally indignant at the notion of any critics in their midst: "Some people are never satisfied. They should be glad they are alive."

But voiced or unvoiced, one desire troubles all—freedom. There is a barbed wire fence around the camp. No one can come in or go out except by special dispensation. One of the most poignant scenes imaginable is the sight of the refugees lining up towards evening at the fence, while the residents of Oswego stand on the other side of the barbed wire and engage them in conversation. At first there used to be a tremendous turnout of townsfolk peering curiously at the strange beings in the camp, and compassionately throwing them food and clothing. By now fewer come, but the people behind the barbed wire are still a local spectacle. Similar age-groups seemed to be attracted to each other. I saw a little blonde American girl looking wide-eyed at the little blonde German Jewish girl directly on the other side of the wire, who stared at her in equal fascination. Two American boys of about 15 were laughing about something with a couple of refugee boys of their own age. I wasn't close enough to discover in what language they spoke to each other, but there was an obvious mutual interest. Older people were talking earnestly and were being earnestly listened to by sympathetic citizens. Who knows what tale of grief and horror they were unfolding to the free Americans outside the barbed wire? One wonders what goes on in the minds of the citizens of Oswego as they peer through the barbed wire at those penned in. One does not have to wonder at what goes on in the minds of those seeking to touch the world from which they are shut out.

Earlier in the day, I had approached two young girls who told me that they were Hungarian. They spoke German. One was 18 years old; the other 16. I asked them how they liked their new life. "It is nice," the younger one said, "but we have always been in camps. And now again a camp." For the last six years these girls had been shipped from one concentration camp to another. Almost since they could remember, their lives had been detention in "camp." Fort Ontario was naturally a paradise in comparison with their previous experiences, but it was still a far cry from freedom. They spoke wistfully rather than rebelliously, almost as though they accepted the strange fate which had made them innocent yet perpetual prisoners.

A sixteen-year-old boy was less quiescent. He was a handsome, well-built lad, and his blue eyes flashed resentfully at the monstrous situation he was not docile enough to accept. His father said to me regretfully: "I should have let him go to Palestine. He had a chance, but I was selfish. I wanted him with me." And the boy offered no contradiction.

Fortunately for the young, however, the authorities will permit children of elementary and highschool age to attend the public schools in Oswego. During my visit—the week before school opened—public school teachers from Oswego had volunteered to instruct the children daily and aid them in getting ready for American public schools. For many children who had spent their young lives in flight and hiding, this was to be the first taste of formal schooling. The teachers, who were offering a part of their vacation as a social service, told me that the children were agreeable and responsive. I watched several groups being taught. Little kindergartners were painstakingly singing "Oh what a beautiful morning" and "Three blind mice." Older ones were doing the usual business with the rudiments of English. The children impressed me as well-disciplined and cheerful, which, in view of their background, was reassuring.

S chool will, paradoxically, mean liberation for the young. For a number of hours daily they will be able to lead a normal existence outside the barbed wire. The adults have no such prospect, unless the terms of their detention are liberalized.

We know that the refugees were brought in outside the quota, and we can imagine the hue and cry that would be raised by reactionaries if they were released on the responsibility of friends or relatives. It is therefore idle to start discussions of this type. The refugees are under federal jurisdiction, and their residence must be Fort Ontario. This, presumably, need not preclude eventual visits to friends or relatives. Some of the older refugees have children now established in the United States—children for whom the precious visas had been secured years before. As I was at the Shelter on visiting day I had occasion to witness several touching reunions. One mother was embracing her young soldier son wearing the uniform of the United States Army. The boy had been given a furlough to see his mother before leaving for overseas. I was told that there were several such cases.

Another proviso was that the refugees were not to work lest they compete with American labor. However, a local situation has arisen which makes a more generous interpretation of the conditions feasible. Oswego is located in a fruit area. Neighboring farmers are begging for help in harvesting their peach, apple and pear crops. Far from resenting refugee labor, they keep appealing to the Shelter for workers. If the United States Employment Service were to certify that no other labor is available, it might be possible to permit the refugees to work provided they were paid the prevailing wage scale so as not to undercut wage standards. The same holds true for some tank factories in the vicinity.

The chief objection to refugee labor is the fear of competition. Where a labor shortage exists, such objections are no longer tenable. If the refugees were allowed to work in the immediate area, the Shelter would still be their residence. At the same time, the refugee would have an opportunity to regain his self-respect and independence, not to mention the fact that he would be helping to relieve the manpower shortage in the vicinity.

Undoubtedly such a step might be resented in a period of unemployment. Now, unexpectedly enough, ill will is being created because the refugees are *not* working. A friend of mine summering in Orange County—Hamilton Fish's bailiwick—reported a conversation with a local farmer. He complained that the refugees were leading a lazy, parasitic life at government expense—playing tennis—while he could get no help. He also insisted that the refugees were receiving a munificent allowance of $10 a week. The fact that the refugees would consider themselves lucky if they received that much a month is beside the point. Distortions of the truth and malicious rumors are unavoidable. It would seem, however, that merely from the aspect of public relations—apart from the questions of benefit to the country or justice to the refugees—it would be psychologically sounder to let the refugees be self-sustaining. This is said not in criticism of the government, which is carrying out the terms of its commitment as originally conceived, but in the hope that experience will dictate a revision of these terms after taking into account all factors.

The government is fulfilling its initial responsibilities. The same cannot be said for the various Jewish organizations. They came òn the scene with too little, and too late. It is impossible to overestimate the psychic shock to the wanderers caused by the lack of a festive reception. They should not have had to depend on the kindness of the Oswego townsfolk for a brief taste of lavish and luxurious America, thrust to them through the barbed wire fence. Precisely because these human beings had been utterly despoiled, they should not have been further pauperized by the donations of clothing from individuals they had never seen. The several Jewish organizations might have had the foresight to prevent this additional pain through communal action.

One woman said to me with a moody eloquence: "We thought they would meet us with flowers." She had fled from horror after horror. Her two small children were left behind in a Belgian convent. By a miracle, whose reality she could hardly grasp, she had reached the United States, the shores of Lake Ontario. "That it should be I," she kept repeating. "That of all the hundreds of thousands, it should be I." And because she was Lazarus risen from the dead, she had expected a hosanna of welcome from those who could so easily have shared her destiny, or that of the slaughtered she had left behind.

"I used to think I would never want anything again," she told me, "but now I want to forget, I want to live, I want to build a home for my children." As I sat with her, I could see an infinitely pathetic demonstration of how she could "want," a demonstration of which she was completely unaware. Throughout our conversation she kept painstakingly scalloping toilet-paper. She had no runners or doilies, and she wanted to cover the bare unpainted boards. She was making a home, so she was scalloping toilet-paper; the "fine tissues" which she had probably not seen for years, looked decorative to her.

This may be viewed as symbolic. One of the "thousand" should not have to scallop toilet-paper. There are enough Jewish women's organizations to provide needs above the bare subsistence level. This applies to clothing, home furnishings, and the various requirements of a tolerable life. Above all, let there be no hand-me-downs. What is not good enough for a man or woman living comfortably in New York is surely not good enough for people who for years have known only the rags in which they escaped from the Nazi robbers and murderers.

The responsibility of the Jewish organizations extends beyond the provision of necessities such as have been mentioned. One must bear in mind that in the Shelter are 1,000 human beings confined together. They must be given the means of developing an active cultural and social life. At present, the refugees are organized into national blocks according to their countries of origin—Yugoslav, Polish-Russian, German and Austrian, with a scattering of Greeks, Turks, etc. Each block is represented on a General Council. Bickering and rivalries have already developed among these blocks. There is no use in moralizing about this, or exclaiming piously that people who have endured so much should have a sense of their common bonds instead of their differences. Suffering rarely makes saints. It is more likely to shatter the nerves even when it fails to shatter the body. To expect the refugees to be beyond all human frailties just because they have been stretched on a rack is impudent and stupid. It is as unimaginative as to expect a person whose nails have been ripped off to display a well-polished manicure.

A charming German woman said to me, "Why don't some women's organizations come in and start social activities among the women? The women don't care about the men's politics. That will bring us all together."

Another refugee to whom I ventured some remarks about the obligations of cooperative living made the significant comment, "Cooperative living! That makes sense for Palestine. There it's for an ideal. But what is the ideal here—just to live?"

Phrases like these indicate the immensity of the psychological problems which must be faced—problems of healing, of spiritual revival. In this field lies the natural province of the Jewish organizations. The many complex questions will not be solved by one philanthropic visit, or by a sporadic donation now and then. A concrete program must be worked out immediately by all interested bodies. B'nai Brith has done something constructive through the furnishing of a bright, cheerful recreation center. The gentile teachers of Oswego are doing something through their volunteer instruction of the children. It is the duty of every Jewish organization—and none is free from blame—to make the rescued "remnant" feel less bereft. Most of their losses cannot be made good, most of their griefs are past solace, but as long as the refugees are behind the barbed wire fence, we must come to them not patronizingly, as occasional benefactors, not curiously, as critical investigators, but humbly and devotedly, as brothers.

(September 1944)

ON HEBREWCIDE

The word "atrocity" is acquiring new connotations. The generation that grew up after the first world war knew clearly what "atrocity stories" were. They were the inventions of unscrupulous propagandists, and the more dreadful the tale, the less truthful the content. This state of mind about "atrocities" was a great boon to all those not concerned. From 1933 on people could nod their heads knowingly whenever some report of Nazi infamy reached their ears. That was a good deal more comfortable than accepting the information as *bona fide*. Even when accounts whose credibility could not be disputed began to appear in the general press, the ingrained reluctance to believe, as well as lack of imagination, prevented people from reacting adequately to the reports they glanced at as they turned the pages of their daily paper.

But now "atrocity stories" are in better repute. The extermination centers have been photographed. Films of Majdanek, of Buchenwald, and other concentration camps have been made by the United States and by Russia. The public has had a chance to see the mounds of charred bones and the faces of the survivors. The "atrocities" have been on display. For 35 cents anyone could go to a newsreel theater and look into the depths. Even the general motion-picture houses carried shorter versions of the Signal Corps releases so that the American public might at last "believe."

Eisenhower had asked that America familiarize itself with the truth. Of course, not all theaters complied with this request. Radio City excused itself on the grounds that its public was too sensitive—women and children of tender years. Besides it might have been difficult to devise suitable pirouettes for the subsequent ballet of the Rockette maidens. Most of the motion-picture houses that showed the "atrocity" pictures were careful to omit those reels which might prove too shocking. The condensed versions—those most commonly shown—were not cut with a view to retaining the most revelatory material in the briefest compass. They were cut to attenuate rather than to abbreviate. The American public was spared the spectacle of the mingled mass of dead and dying which appeared in the original Signal Corps films. The sight of an arm or leg twitching here and there among mounds of corpses was not permitted to harrow the audience. The editing was considerate. Furthermore, at the beginning of the reel the spectators were enjoined to look away if they did not have strong stomachs. They could close their eyes for 15 minutes, and then look calmly at the entertaining feature that followed.

However, despite these successful attempts to lessen the impact, enough remained to convince the public. America saw the furnaces and the carefully contrived equipment used to burn human beings. It saw the methodically assorted piles of shoes, of eyeglasses, of children's toys, belonging to the murdered. It even saw the faces of a few survivors, carried out on stretchers by their liberators. It saw enough to understand that "atrocities" could be reinstated as a word in good standing. Thanks to these films something of the nature of Nazi crime has belatedly begun to seep into the American consciousness.

Nevertheless there is something which these pictures—whether the Russian or the American—will not help America to understand. An audience can sit through one of these films, gasp with horror or compassion at some given moment, and leave without any comprehension of the fact that the extermination centers were created for the primary purpose of murdering Jews, that the faces they had seen were Jewish faces, that the dolls and babies'shoes lying in their appropriate heaps belonged to Jewish children. This may also be due to editing. Perhaps the original versions did not think it necessary to soft-pedal this essential element: that the victims were slaughtered because they had Jewish blood. Wherever the blame may lie, the fact remains that just as the public has been sheltered from the most poignant and terrible scenes in the films, so it has been protected from the realization that this was the end-product of anti-Semitism.

Admittedly, other nationalities also were led into the murder factories, but the overwhelming majority was Jewish. Whether the proportion be 90 percent or 99 percent, we know whose bodies fed the crematoria.

I saw the picture of Majdanek filmed by the Russians—the gray house of murder where no one living remained, only the testimony of skulls and ashes and the neatly catalogued belongings of the dead. There, among other mounds, lay heaps of passports, some of which the narrator held up, as he recited: French, Polish, Czech, Greek, Russian, etc. He did not add: French Jew, Polish Jew, Czech Jew, Greek Jew, Russian Jew. That item of information was omitted as irrelevant.

A funeral service is shown in the Majdanek film—a service held by the townspeople in commemoration of the "exterminated." It is a Christian service, with crucifixes and priests. I do not begrudge the Christian victims of Majdanek the rites of their faith or the symbols of their religion. Had there been but one Christian martyr in Majdanek, it was fitting that his ashes and memory be honored with all solemnity. But a film of Majdanek which showed the cross should have shown another symbol too. Where was the Star of David? Where was the rabbi to mourn the countless thousands of Jewish dead? That is a question that cannot be waived.

An uninformed audience which sees the Majdanek film will remember the cross. It will recall the cosmopolitan enumeration of all the peoples of Europe. It will have no inkling of the identity of those who came in sealed wagons to fill the gas chambers. The memory of the Jewish martyrs has been annihilated in death, just as their bodies had been annihilated in life. That is a sacrilege as well as a bitter travesty of the truth.

The American films mention "Jews" in their listing of nationalities, but without any special emphasis. I shall not forget the faces of some of the "Poles" I saw carried out by American soldiers. It is hard to establish contact with piles of ashes and bones, with masses of bodies in mass graves. One stares at bone and ash almost as if one were already dead oneself and past feeling. But the eyes of the living—the half-dead, some of whom may survive and more of whom have been freed too late—cannot be evaded.

A young man, carried out on a stretcher, looked out at the audience directly. The gaunt face, the immense tragic eyes of this "Pole" or "Frenchman"—there was no mistaking them. We looked at him with horror and astonishment. He looked at us, the passive spectators, with horror too—a profounder horror than ours.

I have seen newsreels of men dying on the battlefield, and God knows there is no lack of agony on those young faces, but there is a difference between even the intensest suffering and the mute boundless horror one sees in the eyes of those who were rescued from Oswiecim or Buchenwald or Treblinka. It proceeds from levels of experience previously not known to man, and it encompasses not only the devils who tortured them but the whole strange, incomprehensible and uncomprehending world outside the barbed wire.

Only Jews know this horror—the horror of a people chosen for wholesale extermination—in the heart of Europe, in the light of day, with the active collaboration or tacit knowledge of other men and women.

What are the reasons for this calculated attempt to prevent the full realization of Jewish martyrdom from reaching the public? Is it feared that less indignation will be aroused if it becomes clear that most of the victims in the extermination centers were Jews? Or do the authorities decline to differentiate between Christian and Jewish nationals of various countries on the grounds that this would be a form of anti-Jewish discrimination?

No doubt both factors enter, and the second reason is, superficially viewed, the more creditable of the two. The Allies do not wish to emulate the Nazis in drawing distinctions between a German gentile and a German Jew. In fact, they are so logical that in some instances German Jewish victims have been imprisoned as enemy aliens. That is the *reductio ad absurdum* of this position. However, no ratiocination can cover up the bald truth that when human beings have been murdered solely because they were Jews, their martyrdom cannot be commemorated as that of Poles, or Frenchmen, or Germans, or Russians. It cannot be lamented with priests and crosses.

The Nazis have made of the murder of Jews a specific and singular crime. It does not fall into the category of the killing of prisoners of war; it cannot be classified as the killing of civilians of occupied countries, because German and Austrian Jews as well as other "enemy" civilians were exterminated as completely. It does not even fall under the heading of religious persecution, like the massacre of St. Bartholomew, because converted Jews were murdered just as ruthlessly. In all previous historic periods a Jew could have escaped through baptism and assimilation. The Nazis barred every door.

The twentieth century has seen the addition of a new crime to the bloody roster of man's sins. We have known homicide, fratricide, deicide, regicide. The quality of each killing has its name. We can now add Hebrewcide—the murder of a human being neither because of a misdeed he has committed, nor because of his political convictions, nor his religious faith, nor his economic class, nor his membership in an "enemy" people, but solely because he belongs to the people of Israel. This murder has been stripped pure of every other impulse which might conceivably enter into the calculations of the murderer. Rich and poor, young and old, male and female, bright and dull—nothing affects the outcome save the crystalline fact—Jewish birth or ancestry.

The crime is *sui generis*. Jews have been murdered before. There have been pogroms in Czarist Russia and in Mohammedan countries, but be it remembered that conversion could buy life. That is why what the Nazis have done has no parallel. We are faced with a new reason for murder—a reason which has cost five million lives in the space of five years.

Anti-Semitism is an old and complicated disease, but the enormous crime to which it led is new and simple. You kill a fellow being because he is a Jew; that is all. No other motive need enter into the act, and there can be no appeal from this motive. It is not an act of individual hooliganism, nor that of professional murderers. On the contrary, it is connived at and participated in by diplomats, by scientists, by average citizens—in short, by what we are accustomed to view technically as the non-criminal class.

There is no escaping the implications of this fresh and awesome reality. Those who object to blinking at the truth, to the hush-hush policy applied to the identity of the dead, do so not because they wish to establish the

Jewish pre-eminence in suffering. They do so because they know that this phenomenon must be openly recognized if its recurrence and appearance in other parts of the world is to be prevented.

Even some Jews feel that it is wiser not to stress the extent to which the victims of the extermination camps were Jewish. Otherwise, there may be resentment at a "war to save the Jews." The public may be less sympathetic; the Nazis may be viewed with less loathing, etc. We are familiar with the whole sorry argumentation whose plausibility is an indictment of all mankind. Were we to grant that people will view the murder of Jews more calmly than that of Poles, Greeks, Frenchmen, or any other group, what does that prove? Does it mean that we are to accept so monstrous a concept? The same individuals who are rightly troubled by discrimination in a job or a pleasure resort and carry on energetic campaigns for the removal of legal disabilities are prepared to make terms with the most extreme and most terrifying "discrimination"—exclusion from the realm where the moral law of mankind functions. That is the final and inevitable meaning of the desire to prevent a general recognition of the nature of the "atrocity" that our generation has witnessed.

The specific and ancient evil which we call anti-Semitism has found its logical and ultimate expression in an equally specific crime—the systematic extermination plan directed only against the Jew. It is dishonest to confuse the issue with talk of the Nazi savagery towards other national groups. Of course, not only Jews suffered from Nazi bestiality. The conquered peoples were subjected to every brutality, including mass murder. The whole world has heard of Lidice. However, Lidice was destroyed in punishment for an act of resistance. Quislings among all the occupied peoples could live. Those who collaborated, who were docile to the new order, might be enslaved, might be degraded, but they could exist. Despite outbreaks of violence directed at individuals, those who submitted were permitted to exist as peoples. The slaughter of Czechs, and Greeks, and Russians is not less foul than the murder of Jews, but it is different. It is essential that this difference be perceived rather than deliberately glossed over.

There are tribes who practice infanticide, yet who would view matricide as a sin. It would obviously be idle to seek to stamp out infanticide in their midst without a specific attack on the specific crime. Those well-intentioned men and women who urge the soft-pedalling of the Jewish issue in the discussion of Nazi atrocities are themselves removing the onus from Hebrewcide and making its repetition psychologically easier. They are helping to put Jews outside the pale where concepts of right and wrong operate.

No restitution can be made to the five million Jews who have been murdered. "Retribution" in any real sense is a meaningless word. What adequate retribution can there be no matter how many "war criminals" should be executed? One realizes the impotence of vengeance when one watches the trial of war criminals filmed by the Russians, or the pictures of the killing of Mussolini. The bodies of the Germans—minor officials—hang from their gibbets; Mussolini's disfigured flesh is kicked by an infuriated mob, but the very kicks are a sign of the hopelessness of amends, of punishment.

What is involved is not a question of retribution. The pathological forces unleashed by Fascism have not yet spent themselves. They must be fought in all their manifestations openly and without evasion. Otherwise the "extermination center" for Jews may again be admitted by some nation as the logical instrument of a philosophy, instead of rejected as the obscene symbol of mankind's greatest crime.

(July 1945)

MAKE THEM CRY!

NOTES OF A FUND RAISER

The various worthy causes with which I have been associated in the course of the years have had one thing in common: they were always in need of funds. Affluent causes may exist somewhere, but I can recall no publication, institution, social project or political group with which I ever had any dealings which did not require an immediate cash transfusion to keep it from expiring. If it was a new enterprise, it had to be enabled to take its first hopeful steps. Consequently, I have often been requisitioned to expound a crisis.

Once upon a time the technique for gaining support was comparatively simple. I remember the remote days when sympathizers or disciples would gather at a meeting and a comrade passed a hat, or a blue and white box. Sometimes a more energetic individual would make a list of the "paper donations," starting with an impressive dollar bill. The clink of dimes and quarters would be set going by earnest remarks, not few but heartfelt. Whether it was bail for Eugene Debs or a Workers' Fund to redeem the Emek, comprehensive ideological exegesis would be the sole requirement to start the trickle of coins and promises. Usually, the enlightenment would be supplied by on-the-spot talent. If a guest speaker was imported, assuming that the coachfare could be raised, he would generally spend the night in a bed hospitably shared by a local enthusiast.

Sometimes, at intimate gatherings, a glass of tea and sponge cake would be served. Once in a great while, some imaginative spirit, fired by the wonders of private initiative, would undertake to organize a boat ride or a picnic. These expeditions were rarely as profitable to the sponsoring cause as originally anticipated and were viewed by the more ascetic as a form of self-indulgence.

After World War I, when Jewish relief assumed a scope that could no longer be met by the zeal of idealistic amateurs, the whole approach to fund-raising changed. It became a science with its special lore and mysteries. As a result of our higher knowledge, several paradoxical developments took place. The most startling of these was Law I, which declared that the more agonizing the need to be described, the more sumptuous the surroundings in which it must be detailed. I have spoken of Treblinka at flower-festooned banquets, and of rain-swept immigrant tents at exquisite luncheons. The elegance kept pace with the rising distress. Like my betters, I have delivered some of my most bloodcurdling reports while suitably adorned with a corsage of orchids.

Whatever original misgivings I might have nurtured have long since vanished under the instruction of specialists in the art. "That's human nature!" announced the masters who pointed out the stern necessity of a gala atmosphere. I must confess that the sacrifice was not hard to make. Orchids and attendant trimmings do not require much indoctrination.

Those of us brought up in the glass-of-tea tradition learned the soft way that you had to spend money to make money, and that to extract a sizeable contribution you first had to lure your prospect into a Grand Ball Room; when things really got tough there was always the Waldorf-Astoria. Undoubtedly, the experts who keep a practised finger on the donor's pulse have hit on some psychological truth which it would be folly to disregard. If roast beef gets results, there is no use in moralizing about a vegetable plate.

There was another notion of which one had to be disabused. I had held a naive belief that some situations spoke for themselves, and were far more eloquent than any phrases I could produce. After the crematoria had become common knowledge did one really have to wrap up the plea in oratorical effects? Was it not more seemly to keep the emotional barrage muted? The provision of information was legitimate, but did one really have to embroider the misery of the DP camp or the heroism of Israel? It seems one did.

I am not likely to forget the briefing I received before setting out on a fund-raising tour not too long ago. "Make them cry!" ordered the boys who knew. "Wring their hearts and leave them limp!" The wisdom of these alarming instructions was fully borne out by subsequent developments; the direct ratio between tears and cheers (expressed in pledges) was incontrovertible. There was no escaping the sequence: the way to the pocketbook led first through the stomach; then through the tear ducts. The first part of this process offered no serious obstacles. It was simple enough to arrange a banquet or dainty sandwiches according to the occasion, but how make them cry?

I regret to say that my personal success in this endeavor was of the most modest. My audiences generally left under their own power and though they seemed to listen to my remarks with a fair degree of interest, few had to look for an extra handkerchief. In fact, after one of my most emotional appeals—so I thought—a lady tripped up to me smiling cheerily and said, "Thank you for not making us cry; they always make us cry."

This sobering compliment left me no illusions as to my own gifts, but in the course of my experiences I had occasion to observe what worked. And since this study can prove profitable, I offer it to my fellow campaigners. Naturally, I do not include in my observations the effectiveness of internationally acknowledged leaders whose influence derives from their moral authority. I am speaking of the lesser fry who as volunteers or professionals are engaged in the task of making American Jewry do its duty.

Some of the most successful tear-jerkers in my experience operate on the theory of no holds barred. Their assault on the emotions is neither subtle nor exquisite but it is amply justified by the flutter of checks as well as handkerchiefs; the proof of the pudding is in the meeting. As everyone has surely witnessed one of these performances he can supply his own sob-line. I prefer to describe an affecting gathering that falls into a different category.

I had been shipped to a sizeable midwestern city where I was assured everything was in the doldrums. The campaign was a flop; the big givers were cutting. Whether you called it a depression or a recession, business was bad; the public was tired, etc. And what was my job? I had to produce the rabbit out of the hat which would make hardheaded businessmen forget their last conference with their accountant. The headlines in the daily papers did not matter; the news was "remote." In short, I had to make them cry.

The scene of the proposed miracle was a brunch at a first-class private club. When I arrived I found some 40 prosperous-looking gentlemen of assorted sizes, none of whom had ever heard of me but who accepted me courteously as one of the inevitable accompaniments of these bleak occasions. I gathered from a tactful hint that these were busy men, that they all knew the "story," and that if "Mrs. Circus" would not extend herself unduly, it would be appreciated by all concerned.

The local campaign manager, aware of the avowed determination of those present to give less than the year before, had brought reinforcements in the shape of a prominent businessman from a neighboring community. In addition to being a forceful speaker and a devoted worker, this gentleman had the distinction of not having "cut"; in fact, he had increased his pledge. I was in favor of abdicating completely so as to give this hero more time, but the manager was obdurate. When he was not engaged in making a tally of the missing—big givers who had failed to show up—he would mutter to me: "We're in a tight spot; give them the works."

During the brunch I tried to get my bearings. My neighbor to the right seemed less formidable than his sleek, well-groomed fellows. He was giving me the inside "dope." The community had been squeezed dry; there were local needs; and besides people were losing money. He knew the boys; they were big-hearted and had done more than could be expected; but they were all going to cut this year; he was going to cut too; I shouldn't be disappointed. After all, one could not be expected to give out of capital.

It all sounded ominously familiar. I could barely eat the excellent chicken liver omelette before me, though my neighbor, a wholesale butcher, assured me that I need have no misgivings; his concern had provided the chicken livers.

The brunch over, the proceedings went on as ordained. The campaign manager indulged in the usual combination of flattery, grief and exhortation. The volunteer spoke as businessman to businessmen about the need for plus-giving. He was earnest and direct, and I was much moved. So was the manager. Sensing the frost, the volunteer directed me, "Not more than fifteen minutes; or they'll start leaving."

I spoke as well as I knew how about what I had seen in Israel. When I sat down every eye except the volunteer's was dry. I was afraid to look at the manager.

The moment of calling the pledge cards had come. The chairman of the meeting, to whom this delicate task had been entrusted, was a kind-looking elderly man who had lost heavily during the current season. Everyone present knew of his financial reverses and sympathized with his difficulty; he was chairman of the drive and yet he would have to cut—a bad example.

After a few routinely harrowing remarks which elicited no more response than those of the previous speakers, the chairman stopped for a moment; then he resumed, his voice quavering: "Boys, I shouldn't do it, but let be what will be. God will help me." At this point, his eyes filled with tears and, overcome with emotion, he was unable to continue. He turned to his handsome young son: "Let Jim tell you." Jim arose, and also obviously laboring under extreme emotion, declared: "You know my dad. You know the kind of heart he has. His children are behind him. Boys, he is not going to cut; he is going to give out of capital."

At this point the hard-boiled businessmen who had listened with exemplary self-possession to my tales of Dachau and Cyprus turned to each other misty-eyed. My sympathetic neighbor, the wholesale butcher, wept unabashedly into a large handkerchief. The ice was broken. Man after man, shaken to the depths, raised his pledge in the chairman's honor. The chairman himself kept repeating, "God will help."

The campaign manager alternately mopped his brow and his eyes, and kept exclaiming, "This is terrific. I tell you this will make history."

Finally it was all too much for me and I began to cry too. By the banks of capital, we sat down and wept; aye, we wept when we remembered interest.

I should not like to leave the impression that the cut into capital is the unkindest cut of all. Jews, the most philanthropic of peoples, do most of their weeping when they remember Zion. But the Gods of our economic system are exacting, and have worshippers of all creeds. After my instructive brunch, I had a better understanding of a society which accepts the conscription of its sons more philosophically than of its wealth, and is apparently more agitated by the prospect of an excess profits tax than by the possibility of atomic warfare. I also finally understood why one depression winter I paid income tax while a world-famous American millionaire went scot-free. He would have been obliged to dip into his "capital."

(December 1950)

HAVE AMERICAN JEWS
A JEWISH FUTURE?

I should state at the outset that I view the problems of Jewish existence
and Jewish survival from the angle of the secular Jew. The truly religious
Jew, for whom Judaism is an absolute and supernatural faith, has, I assume,
no problems in regard to his Jewish identity. He may have insoluble
economic or social or political problems but none in regard to the nature of
his Jewish commitment or his Judaism. He *knows*—in the declarative
mode. But most American Jews cannot be included in that category of
assurance, no matter how encouraging the statistical reports in regard to
growing congregations and increased attendance at temples in suburbia.
What chance for survival, in significant Jewish terms, is there for this
Jewry, no longer deeply rooted in Orthodox Judaism?

No other group has a like problem. An Irish Catholic can disregard his
ethnic origins, become an unhyphenated American and remain a Catholic.
His children need never trouble themselves about Erin if such is their wish.
Should he move in another direction and become a renegade Catholic, he
can still remain a proud Irish nationalist. The peculiar dilemma by which
abandonment of either the faith or the people becomes total apostasy is a
unique Jewish predicament or blessing, depending on how you view the
matter. This is hardly news. Intellectually, of course, we know that there
are atheist Jews, just as at the other end of the spectrum there exist
Americans of the Mosaic persuasion; but neither the infidel, nor the
member of the Council for Judaism, can effect a convincing *partial*
severance. As long as a man says, "I am a Jew," he is involved in a whole to
which, whether he likes it or not, his allegiance must be dual. No matter
how he may chafe at the bond, his very cries of outrage are a measure of his
involvement, and his release can only be through assimilation or
conversion. The latter are few and dramatic departures; the corrosion of
assimilation, however, in its various forms—from red to red-white-and-
blue—is increasingly constant in our society. I venture on this statement
despite the scarcity of conclusive statistical evidence, and despite the
impressive contrary evidence of synagogue enrollments and crowded
Jewish centers with their manifold activities.

There is no point in moralizing about this. If many American Jews attend their temples more out of social conformity than out of spiritual exaltation they are no more reprehensible in this than their gentile neighbors. From synagogue to golf course they faithfully reproduce the institutional pattern of their environment and, though it is customary to speak of the invisible ghetto in which the American Jewish community dwells, within those well-cushioned walls no special Jewish character or culture emerges. The cultural assimilation of American Jewry is almost complete. Despite the biological cohesion of his group, the American middle-class Jew is indistinguishable from his gentile counterpart. If some hotel is restricted, he builds another just like it or better. If some country club is bigoted, or Palm Beach is exclusive, there is always Miami.

And why not? There is nothing remarkable in the fact that a group adopts the values of its society and environment. Or that an able, energetic people creates a comfortable or luxurious life for itself when the opportunity permits. What troubles one is the question of how long will biological cohesion *suffice*, or—more alarming still—how long can it *continue* without impelling intellectual or spiritual drives which are specifically Jewish?

These may be familiar croakings whose gloom should be dissipated by the uncontested sprawling vitality of a prosperous American Jewry whose children are attending Jewish schools of some type in larger numbers than a generation ago, and whose energies expressed through Jewish communal affiliations display a redundant vigor. We may well ask: are the symptoms so deadly if the patient is alive and kicking? Perhaps we make exaggerated demands; perhaps the present status indicates that a Jewry may be wholesome and viable without the zealous religious or ideological commitments which we have associated with spiritually flourishing Jewries in the past. Why must Jews be more self-conscious as Jews than other groups in their religious or ethnic identifications? Why can't a Jew just be a Jew passively, without heart-searchings or head-scratchings or lengthy discussions about Jewish survival?

Assuming that a bovine Jewishness—placidly chewing the cud of conformity—could exist for any appreciable period, it would be highly questionable if such existence were in itself a cause for congratulation. But the hypothesis is academic. Such a Jewry could not perpetuate itself beyond a generation or two. One need merely reflect on the tremendous shocks which galvanized American Jewry within the last two decades and stirred it to the self-awareness now expressed in the circuit of its current activities. Catastrophe, however, in whatever part of the world it might occur, cannot be a people's hope. It is too heavy a price for self-awareness. Besides, while to perish for the Name was an act of heroic affirmation in former centuries of persecution, the solidarity of meaningless suffering—

meaningless because the individual has not elected his martyrdom—can prove only a temporary cement. Already we have a generation that knew not Hitler, and there are Jewish parents who cannot bring themselves to tell their children of the fate of the six million. Not only Germans but Jews cannot bear to make the fearful explanation. How does one tell a contented child that he belongs to a people which only a few years ago was rounded up for extermination? How does one explain a gas chamber and a slaughterhouse to the potential victim—to the one who might have been there? The horror of this confrontation is intolerable and I understand the successful young Harvard professor of my acquaintance who tries to keep such knowledge from his ten-year-old son. The reluctance has a deeper reason even than sheer horror. The young professor is a Jewish intellectual who is already one stage beyond suburbia. The values he brought from there are no longer meaningful in his present world. His Jewish attachments are of the most tenuous; consequently, he cannot weigh down his child with a burden of irrational, zoological suffering which only a profound religious or national piety can transmute into the endurable. And both are lacking.

I live in Cambridge, in an academic community where I meet young Jewish intellectuals represented in the graduate schools and faculties of a number of great New England colleges and universities. I appreciate the danger of offering personal observation as sociological data and I make no such pretense. But, in a situation so fluid that reputable Jewish sociologists come up with separate profiles for American Jews of the thirties, the forties, and the fifties, perhaps one may detect, by local sampling, a trend for the sixties. Intermarriage, among the *intelligentsia*, is one of them. And indeed what rational argument can one offer an emancipated intellectual against intermarriage? He will not accept the supra-rational religious interdict, and any other appeal savors of tribal savagery. The children of these marriages are to be free, free as the parents. It is hardly necessary to indicate how most of them go. Involvement in the majority culture results in a painless assimilation. Within a generation, the Jewish origin of a gifted parent becomes only a piquant curiosity with no relevance for his descendants. Much Jewish talent and intelligence are quietly departing from the Jewish people at the present time—more than the sociologists with their variable figures of intermarriage rates indicate.

And supposing these able second-generation or third-generation American Jews—bred in American schools and colleges, well on the way to intellectual achievement and professional success—do not intermarry? What is their present active bond with the Jewish people, the Jewish faith, or both? Frequently none. Their hour of disquiet comes when their children are old enough to ask for explanations: What is a Jew? Why are they Jews? I have watched scenes of near-panic in which the parent tries to evolve a mutually satisfying answer. He can no longer take refuge in the village atheism fashionable among Jewish immigrants, or first-generation, intellectuals—an atheism often propounded in an excellent Yiddish—nor has he the compensating secular nationalism of that group. The solution appears to consist in a hodgepodge of folklore and ceremony observed not for itself but to fill an otherwise uncomfortable void. Hanukah is the antidote to Christmas and Barton chocolate menorahs consolation for the glittering star of Bethlehem.

Not so long ago, I was present at a Hanukah party bravely contrived by a few college women—all the wives of academicians in the Cambridge community. Each of them would have scorned affiliation with a local temple; at the same time, they had no resources of their own. Despite a devout pilgrimage to the local Barton's candy store, the songs and games were artificial. The children were not deceived by the synthetic holiday. One bright lad was clearly worried; he wanted to know if the current merriment was being offered as a substitute for Christmas, and when mamma to cheer him up promised Hanukah presents, he promptly announced that the Hanukah presents he most wanted were nice ornaments for his Christmas tree. I did not invent this anecdote—the point is much too obvious for fiction. The child was not being deliberately impudent. With a sublime unconsciousness, he had formulated the dilemma of many American Jews. The most agreeable Hanukah gift is something that will trim the Christmas tree.

Despite all that has so recently been endured and achieved, American Jewish intellectuals keep drawing further away from the forces which shaped them and from identification with a Jewish future, though they do not deny their past. But in failing to make common cause with their people in its pain and in its hope, in rejecting the present they reject the future.

I speak of the intellectuals who appear as problematic—whose relationship to Jewish life is tenuous or hostile—because they are omens. As a rule youth rejects the establishment—that is one of its trademarks. Whether he be opposing the political or social structure, or casting off his religious tradition, or both, the intellectual's rebellion against aspects of his society is as commonplace as his conformity. Why then should there be the current agitation and concern? Are Jews unduly sensitive in this regard? Do they display an absurd unwillingness to accept the inevitable by-products of what is called enlightenment? Why do they appear to be more alarmed on this score than other communities who may deplore the irreverent paths taken by their children without feeling cut to the quick, except insofar as particular individuals may be affected?

The answer is probably that only in the case of the Jews does rejection become total; it is never piecemeal. Joyce may turn his back on Dublin and its beliefs, and remain authentically Irish. Lenin may reject Czar and God and remain profoundly Russian. Both remain within their community, if one uses the term in its largest sense. They may criticize, or daringly reshape it, but they and their descendants can continue to be Irish or Russian. When Boris Pasternak, however, rejects both his religious tradition and his ethnic community, he has made a complete breach. We call it assimilation. The Russian, Irish or gentile American intellectual can turn his back on significant aspects of his world without a surrender of identity. The Jewish intellectual has no such alternatives. If he cuts both the *religious* and the *ethnic* tie, the severance is total. Even if he continues to call himself a Jew statistically, there is a good chance that his children will not; the data on intermarriage on the college level appear to indicate this. Consequently, Jewish concern about the alienated intellectual is not exaggerated. No organism, with a normal will for survival, can unprotestingly accept the loss of some of its best elements.

At the present time in the United States we are in a paradoxical situation. The Jewish intellectual has become a kind of new American culture hero. Disintegrating on the analyst's couch, uprooted, erotically mobile, he becomes the prototype of the wanderer in the modern Wasteland. Jewish characters, Jewish themes, Jewish environment with a sauce of Yiddish, are in style. Any best seller list of the past decade reveals the truth of this statement. Furthermore, Jewish writers who deal with Jewish themes have scored great critical as well as commercial successes. There is fame as well as money in the exploitation of Jewish material. Bellow, Roth and Malamud come to mind among the many novelists; they in turn are reviewed by literary critics of note who are accused of forming "the New York establishment," an unsubtle euphemism for Jewish. And on Broadway "Fiddler on the Roof," with its saccharine evocation of the *shtetl*, is a huge success.

But the situation is paradoxical because at a time when Jewish writers, far from being indifferent to their background, appear to be obsessively preoccupied with it, many Jews on the other hand are engaged in deploring their estrangement and view their preoccupation as a morbid symptom rather than as an evidence of vitality. The report we receive from the ablest Jewish writers about American Jewish life—the Jewish community—is anything but reassuring. Each in his fashion, allowing for variations in talent and style, if he is a serious American Jewish writer of the second or third generation, describes a middle-class existence oppressive in its vulgarity, without ideas or ideals, and without genuine commitment to the religious or social values it professes. The fictional characters who inhabit the scene are gross and trivial, as are their activities and ambitions. Allowing for obvious exceptions, this is not an unfair generalization.

Of course, a satiric view of any class or segment of society is a legitimate exercise of the creative faculty. What is troubling about the contemporary American Jewish writer's stance is that what he sees from his angle is monotonously negative. One suspects he is engaged in a valedictory. This is his farewell to a world from which he has emerged and is leaving. And the mood of his farewell is distaste rather than nostalgia.

Those concerned about this rupture, be it demonstrative or silent, ask themselves whether the fault lies in the eye of the beholder or in what he beholds. Is American Jewish life so arid and impoverished that it has nothing to offer to some of its brightest sons? Or does some perversity of vision afflict some of our keenest minds?

I go on the assumption that the valedictory is premature, that there exist specific Jewish challenges which are neither parochial nor ignoble, and which transcend the tribal and the hidebound. I am now using the favorite adjectives in the vocabulary of rejection. When intellectuals fervently proclaim that they are not "joiners" and that they have an energetic contempt for organizations, they of course mean the organizational patterns of the American Jewish community. They do join, with considerable zeal, any number of organizations and movements—civil rights and peace movements come to mind. The contemporary intellectual, particularly the Jewish one, is *engaged*. He is likely to be ardently committed rather than cynically withdrawn. He is aware of the surge of world problems and of the interrelated human family. We applaud this involvement; unfortunately there is too often one exception to the all-embracing sense of social responsibility. If our idealist joins the Peace Corps, he would feel cheated were he to find himself shipped to the Negev rather than the Congo. At a time when he is personally affected by the national liberation movements of various African or Asian peoples, he views Jewish nationalism as restrictive. This is an old story since the emancipation. *Nihil humanum mihi alienum est* provided it's not Jewish. And our task is to convince him that his human dimension is increased not lessened by his espousal of the Jewish cause among the great causes he shoulders—that it, *too*, is *his* cause.

These are unhappy realities, and there are no villains in the piece. At the same time those concerned about this trend must ask themselves—not too soberly—what can be done? For the Jewish intellectual in the United States is least subject to any of the reminders which may affect other sectors of American Jewry. No perceptible five o'clock shadow falls on academia or Bohemia. The invisible walls are rolled back and if there is to be any authentic impulse to use this freedom in its fullness without a repudiation it must come from positive sources.

Unless there is a determination to the contrary, the more completely an American Jew is drawn into the pattern of American life the fainter becomes his Jewish identification. We are witnesses of the Jewish decline—from the urban immigrant ghetto to middle-class suburbia to the emancipation of the young intellectuals to undramatic effacement. The progress may be rapid or slow; it may skip a step or prolong a given stage, but it is there as steady march or unconscious attitude. And there is no point in moralizing, no more than there is point in moralizing about warmth in Florida or cold in Alaska. Such is the climate. And the road is to ultimate assimilation. Many second- and third-generation American Jews are on that road, unaware perhaps of their destination.

What is there in American life to keep Jewish identity vigorous? Intense religious commitment, the apparently inexhaustible source for generations? In a secular, liberal age Jews, no more than other groups, can pretend to passionate pieties. At best, there are observances which blend innocuously into the general scene. The rare zealot when he appears is an irritant, in Williamsburg as in *Mea Shearim*. The enlightened tolerance of American democracy at its best, which except for fundamentalist pockets is characteristic of our culture, amiably encourages attendance at the church or synagogue of "your choice" because the choice is no longer a matter of life or death for Christian as well as Jew.

If one seeks to be honest one must face the paradox that whereas all American slogans appear to encourage what we loosely call "cultural pluralism," American reality opposes it. The Irish may parade on St. Patrick's Day, the Ukrainians may dance folksily in colorful costumes, the French may remember Lafayette—all to the accompaniment of general applause and speeches reminding us that the American heritage is richer for its many strands. But unless there is an inner compulsion within the minority culture to maintain itself, despite all the affectionate ancestral memories, it will dissolve in the general stream. To maintain a culture without territorial boundaries within which the culture is operative is a difficult and complex endeavor. The Soviet Union is an example of various ethnic groups with their own languages, mores, etc. continuing to dwell as units on their own soil. Contemporary Russia is a synthesis not an integration of these units; it follows the logic of its history. Obviously, nothing could be more antithetical to the American spirit than such a system. Only the Communists and the Black Muslims—in their several plans for separate Negro states—have suggested disintegration as a program.

There is a more amorphous territorial unit within which a minority culture can also flourish—the ghetto. The Yiddish-speaking East Side of a generation ago was an example. But the ghetto, too, is contrary to the best in American life. It is an immigrant refuge to be deserted as soon as adjustment to the new world can be made. The shadowy "gilded ghettos" of which we speak in reference to the social segregation in American life are another matter. These so-called ghettos have no special Jewish character or dedication; they are merely segments cut from the uniform slab of American middle-class culture.

Several years ago a small boy I know well returned from the first grade in the admirable public school he attends on the West Coast with a drawing suitable to the season. The subject was "We celebrate Christmas in many ways." One way indicated—due I am certain to a thoughtful teacher's vigilance—was Hanukah, suitably illustrated by a boy lighting a menorah. The transformation of the festival in honor of the Maccabees into one of the exotic ways of celebrating Christmas will perhaps be of interest to some future anthropologist. In the meantime, the confusion should not be blamed on the well-intentioned teacher or the ill-instructed child. It is the sign of the crossroad at which a minority culture falters before abandoning the struggle to maintain an independent course.

A year later the same child told me that his new teacher had an even brighter idea. She solved the problem of the celebration of Christmas in the public school by urging her two Jewish scholars to substitute the word Hanukah for Christmas in any carol in which the latter was mentioned. Ring out, you Hanukah bells! This seemed to her a logical compromise and unless the Jewish families in that city of the far West were particularly vigilant or concerned, we may assume that both Christian teacher and Jewish pupil remained happily unaware of the absurdity—if not worse— that had been perpetrated. I happen to know that in this same American town the small Jewish community had been seeking adequately trained Jewish teachers for its few Jewish Sunday school classes, without success. Obviously the Jewish education and possibly Jewish future of the children growing up in that fresh Western air would be determined by how much will to persist the community displayed—which is not quite the same as a fierce conscious will. Otherwise a less dramatic alienation than that of the intellectuals is on the way.

I spoke of writers because they formulate their disenchantment in words. Among other sectors of the intellectual community, there is a less demonstrative, passive fading away. What can be opposed to this painless assimilation, the conviction that to remain a Jew is no longer important? In a secular, rationalist age the appeal to religious faith has lost its force except for a few. Our intellectuals will not become *Hassidim*, despite their exotic charm, and the light of Franz Rosenzweig or Martin Buber will illumine only a special group.

I know that this is not the whole picture. Most American Jews have profited sufficiently from attendance at their temples and community centers possibly to forestall the debacle I have described. But danger signals cannot be estimated merely by their numbers. Their significance must be judged by the condition they indicate.

There is nothing peculiar or wicked about this condition. In a secular society where religion has become a sign of conformity rather than of blazing difference, where it creates categories of respectability within which the decent citizen and his family operate, there is no reason to expect a higher temperature among emancipated American Jews than may be found among their neighbors. And in this atmosphere of tolerant air-conditioning many cool chambers beckon—Unitarian, Ethical Culture or Jewish Christian Science.

There remains the other great source of Jewish identification—the sense of Jewish nationalism, the awareness that one belongs to one people. East European immigrants who came at the turn of the century—many of them demonstratively irreligious and triumphant in their newly acquired emancipation—created a world of their own with its own language and folk customs. For a decade or two the New York East Side, and in a lesser degree other urban centers, bore witness to cultural pluralism successfully practiced on the American scene. With the integration of the immigrant into American life, that transplanted culture vanished. What remains of Yiddish? Courses in the language have been introduced in a number of universities and I am told that students have enrolled in a Yiddish course offered in the Harvard Hillel Society. There are courses in Yiddish at Brandeis. Yiddish is exotic. It is already so remote from the contemporary young American Jew that it is no longer embarrassing. He will not be tempted to hide a Yiddish newspaper inside an English one, as his still self-conscious father or grandfather might have done.

In that former world, there also developed the several parties of the Zionist movement which, each in its own way, sustained the sense of Jewish purpose and identity. Our common experience of that flourishing and decline is sufficiently recent to obviate any need for recapitulation. Not only for Herzl was Zionism the Sabbath of his life. It was the Jewish Sabbath in the lives of innumerable Jews in whose homes no candles were ever lit on Friday night. They knew that they were Jews in their hope of a common future even more than in their memories of a common past and their dread of a common fate. But what about the post-Hitler American Jewry, soon to come of age, for whom the climactic experiences of our century already have the distance of history? Can Zionism play the role in their lives that it did in the hearts of two previous generations? They have been spared the terrible prods of persecution and discrimination. They are integrated into the pattern of American life, content in their technological paradise, and proudly at home as Americans. It is for Jews a new and singular experience—this natural inclusion in a society in which difference in religious practice invites no serious disability and where ethnically homogeneous groups revolve naturally around their centers of worship. All this, and public approval, too!

Only the absurdly sensitive would find a cloud in the sky. I doubt if, under the impact of the recent raising of the religious issue during an election campaign, many Jews are breaking their hearts because no Jew is likely to be elected president of the United States in the foreseeable future. After all, let's be sensible! And now that under the spur of Sputnik and the baying of Laika in the outer heavens academic quotas are crumbling and bright young Jews offer their high IQs to the faculties as well as student bodies of the country's great colleges, what grievances remain? There is still the kind of petty social discrimination immortalized in "Gentlemen's Agreement" but Jews have shown such talent in creating more than equal, if separate, residential areas and country clubs that it is difficult to appeal to outraged Jewish pride on that score. Social discrimination does not subject the Jew, like the Negro, to a lower standard of life. The only complaint that one hears seriously voiced is the dread of "social ghettoization": Jews do not have enough social, as distinct from professional and political, contact with their gentile neighbors. The self-respecting Jew might well counter with the question: Why does not the gentile feel ghettoized? Why is the Protestant who sees no Jews in his home after office hours in less of a seclusion than the Jews whom no gentile visits? There are differences, of course, which it is needless to belabor, and only a recklessly affirmative Jew would appreciate the query.

It becomes increasingly difficult to come with the Zionist call of salvation when there is no clear apprehension of the danger from which one is to be saved. Formerly, the perils were not metaphysical. The wounds, individual and national, required no demonstration. Whether one dwelt in the safety of America or suffered in the Europe of a Czar or Hitler the need for a redemptive solution was clear and immediate and involved the best spirits of the Jewish people.

We are in a different historical case in the United States today. I decline to speculate on what changes might take place in the event of a serious economic crisis or on the hypothetical seizure of power by an emergent native Fascism. Theoretically, anything can happen; here as well as there. But the nightmares of history cast no light of augury on our present.

In this present, it is idle to assume that Zionism can again be the motive power for Jewish life that it has been—not because American Jews are less idealistic but because they are in a different historical situation. In this sense, the crisis for Zionism is also a crisis for Judaism. A great stream of energy is drying up for which no outpourings of good will for Israel are an adequate substitute. Friendly benevolence and passionate identification are not the same thing. I speak now from the point of view of the American Jew not from that of Israel. Israelis who perceive no distinction between a contributor to the United Jewish Appeal who does not settle in Israel and a

Zionist, probably a lesser contributor, who also does not settle in Israel, may be right when they consider the immediate objective effect on Israel. The subjective difference to the American Jew, however, is enormous. It goes beyond nomenclature to emotion. When *Zionists* turn into *friends*, Jewishness, if not Israel, has lost.

Such a view is not a negation of the diaspora. It is merely a realistic acceptance of what may be demanded of a diaspora existing under the happy and favorable conditions of the American diaspora in the twentieth century. Nor do I seek to suggest that American Jews will vanish as a group in the next generation or two. On the contrary, there seems to be every indication that despite intermarriage and falling away on an increasing scale, the bulk of American Jewry will continue on its present course—the pattern that we see today. There will be Jews and Jewish centers. The core will remain, but it will not be the saving remnant: neither in its ethnic culture nor in its religious intensity will it be significantly Jewish. It will be American, as it must be. Folk memories may be cherished, but memories and sympathies are not a substitute for a full Jewish life.

In this period of history, a complete Jewish life can only be led in the Jewish state. There the secular Jew and the religious Jew, the radical kibbutznik and the rigid fundamentalist, whatever their violent differences and disputes, are both engaged in the creation of a Jewish land and a Jewish life with all the scope the terms permit. In language, in culture, in purpose, there the one people emerges. There parents need not fear that Jewish symbols and festivals will pale into invisibility before the brilliance of the Christmas candles. In that full and unself-conscious Jewish world, a holiday may be celebrated as a rejoicing or a solemnity—not as a strategy. And memory need not be stimulated by artifice nor attachment by catastrophe.

The greatest Jewish achievement of modern times—the creation of the State of Israel—was the achievement in the main of secular Jewish nationalism, yet in that process all aspects of Jewish life were revivified. I said before that the crisis of Zionism was also the crisis of Judaism; by the same token, Zionism *fulfilled* becomes the chief nourisher of Judaism.

At an Ideological Conference in Jerusalem several years ago, Golda Meir made a paradoxical statement. In the course of one of those inevitable debates about Israel and the diaspora she declared: "When I meet my American friends, women who are my contemporaries, I am sorry for them. They worry about their grandchildren. My grandchildren are in Revivim, a kibbutz in the Negev, but I am absolutely sure about them." Of course, we understand the nature of her confidence. Grandchildren in the Negev may pose many serious problems in the matter of sanitation or safety, physical survival in the grimmest sense, but none in the matter of their "Jewish" survival. Of this Mrs. Meir could be more sure than her American friends. She might have to worry about the strategy of defense against invaders but not at all about the strategy of keeping them Jewish.

This Jewish life which once more has full opportunity to flourish has its rich Jewish spiritual character whatever the nature or absence of formal religious commitments. The vision of a social justice which animates Israel's founding fathers stems more from the Prophets than from Marx, or perhaps it would be truer to say that in Israel Socialist doctrine has been divested of its alien materialist guise. The rift between the faith and the people, which gapes ever wider in the contemporary diaspora until it threatens to become the abyss in which both will be swallowed, has been closed in the Jewish state.

I should not like to be misunderstood. I do not believe that the existence or well-being of American Jewry is threatened. Nor do I believe that the only good life for a Jew is in the Jewish state. American Jews certainly know the good life—and I use the term not ignobly—as equal participants in American democracy. But a complete life as a Jew can only be experienced in full sincerity in the Jewish state.

(January 1961)

JEWS AND BLACKS

One of the paradoxes of the Jewish condition in the United States is that although Jews number little more than two percent of the population they do not qualify as a minority. However recent their immigrant struggles, they have by now achieved middle-class status as a community. Yet, regardless of their incontestable economic and professional success, they still retain the long memories and apprehensions of a persecuted minority. They cannot forget that throughout their history periods of ease have monotonously alternated with catastrophic reversals. Hence they are wary. A change in the rules by which they won emancipation appears as a threat not merely to their comfort but to their existence. Unless the intensity of this nervousness is appreciated the conflict between Jews and other minorities cannot be understood. The unhappy breach between Jews and blacks is not primarily a reaction to black anti-Semitism, painful though that be. Sporadic instances of black anti-Semitism kept cropping up even when the Jewish-black alliance in the civil rights struggle seemed firmest. Charges against Jewish "slumlords" and exploitative Jewish storekeepers were periodically raised. (Often the Jewish storekeeper had bought his store before the black influx into the neighborhood, and was the only white merchant who failed to join the white flight.) And more than one black spokesman (Imamu Baraka, for example) indulged in the grossest anti-Jewish incitement at the very time when idealistic young Jews were facing the guns of the Ku Klux Klan in the South. These familiar manifestations met with the usual responses: Jewish and black organizations united in deploring the sins of both sides; overreaching tenement owners should be fought as landlords not as Jews; and black extremists should be brought to account.

The current rift is more fundamental. It has been caused, not by the real or hypothetical derelictions of some Jews or by the rhetorical excesses of some blacks, but by the ongoing re-evaluation of the original goals of the civil rights movement. Jews blushed at the presence of "Mr. Goldberg," owner of a Harlem or Watts tenement, even if he was no worse or better than other landlords, just as they urged the relocation of Jewish storekeepers stranded in a hostile ghetto. But attempts to dismiss a public school principal or teacher ("We have too many Mr. Ginzbergs in our schools") solely on the ground that he was Jewish was another matter. Capitulation in this instance would have meant the abandonment of the principle whose observance had assured Jewish equality before the law. The open confrontation between Jews and blacks that followed Andrew Young's dismissal and Jesse Jackson's espoused support of Arafat was only the climax of a conflict that had been brewing since the social aims of the sixties were replaced by radically different objectives.

Education was the earliest battleground and has remained a prime area of contention. One of the first shocks came in 1968 when black leaders in New York City launched an unprecedented attack on the public school system. Criticism of educational methods and institutions was no novelty. Since the twenties public schools beset by the problems of mass education have routinely been accused of stunting the development of their charges. Exponents of John Dewey or followers of Robert Hutchins agreed on the deficiencies of pupils, mainly white, tested in various sections of the country.

What distinguished the black onslaught on the public schools was not only its ferocity but its nature. For the first time public schools were being accused not of stupidity or incompetence—the traditional complaints—but of "cultural genocide" of black pupils. Furthermore, this "genocide" was willed. It was a deliberate conspiracy to destroy the minds of black children. Jewish teachers were singled out as the conspirators. These extraordinary accusations could not be dismissed as the fabrications of irresponsible demagogues; they were the declarations of respected community leaders. A black conference on urban education held under the chairmanship of Rhody A. McCoy, administrator of the Ocean Hill-Brownsville demonstration school project, issued a statement (March 1968) declaring, "It is no longer reasonable to expect that black people will. . . . submit to a genocidal system." A spokesman of Brooklyn CORE had no hesitation in stating that "certain teachers have conspired to miseducate black and Puerto Rican children." And in a notorious article, "Anti-Black Jews," John F. Hatchett, a black educator, wrote of "the cultural genocide daily practiced against my people by a group of people whose entire history should have told them no." These denunciations were but a few of many samples.

In addition to the bitterness and indignation generated by such libels, Jewish teachers, heavily represented in the public schools since the establishment of the merit system, saw their hard-won right to teach threatened. Until the institution of uniform examinations, whose passage impartially determined placement on teachers' lists, Jewish teachers had effectively been excluded. The establishment of the merit system had been viewed as a glorious victory for equality of opportunity. Jews could no longer be kept out because of prejudice or a school administrator's preference for a crony. Now this progress was to be set back by demands for "community control" that meant the scrapping of an unbiased method of teacher assignment. Instead, schools in black neighborhoods would be staffed by black supervisors; white teachers would be dismissed or transferred.

None of this sounds wildly revolutionary today. But when first propounded the notion of community control went far beyond the provision of compensatory education or of equal opportunity in the accepted sense. It was the first of the salvos directed against what had been viewed as the sacrosanct principles of democratic education: no racial or religious quotas for teachers or pupils; no certification of teachers except on individual merit. The battles of the Teachers Union on behalf of these principles, the refusal of white teachers, mainly Jewish, to acquiesce in arbitrary transfers or dismissals precipitated the earliest in a series of continuing encounters.

With amazing rapidity a new educational jargon challenged what had been traditional concepts. Among these were that standard tests of achievement and ability were suspect because they were not "culture free"; that it was progressive to determine advancement on all steps of the educational ladder by racial quotas; that civil service examinations were *ipso facto* biased because some groups were "disproportionately" adept at passing examinations to the detriment of minority candidates. By now the radical departures of the sixties have become current cliches, in some instances embodied in law, and enjoying ideological approval if not popular acceptance. "Merit," no longer meritorious, has become a pejorative term, and what began as a local dispute has evolved into a fundamental re-examination of individual vs. group rights with all the far-reaching implications of such an ideological shift.

Though white communities throughout the country became involved on both sides of this re-appraisal, and though the classic cases of Bakke and Weber were brought before the Supreme Court by gentiles, Jews ironically became the targets of black resentment. Precisely because Jews had been at the forefront of the civil rights struggle, blacks, on the one hand, expected automatic support for their demands from Jews, and Jews, on the other hand, were particularly sensitive to being strictured as betrayers of their liberal commitments. However, the source of the schism lay not in a change of heart among Jews but in the change of direction taken by the black movement.

In the bad old days when liberals marched against *de jure* segregation in the South, it required no particularly delicate conscience to be outraged by Southern racial legislation. The passion with which Northerners enlisted in the civil rights struggle was authentic. Today many of those who hailed the triumphs of the civil rights movement are deeply troubled at being cast as opponents of what now passes for the liberal agenda. One Presbyterian minister formulated his moral dilemma in a mini-sermon: "How could a minister live with himself upon recalling how his feet had marched through Alabama tear gas in 1965, only now to find his fingers walking through the Yellow Pages toward the heading that reads, 'Schools— Private'?" (*Los Angeles Times*, April 10, 1977). The clergyman resolved his difficulty by concluding that each man must act according to his conscience. In 1965 he would have had no doubts as to what course conscience dictated.

Was the sympathy of Northern liberals for the black struggle against segregation in the South merely a cheap readiness to applaud at a safe distance? Are Jews who now fight quotas and mandatory busing akin to the bigots who barred blacks from schools and colleges? Those who equate *de facto* with *de jure* segregation, and equality of opportunity with "equality now" have a ready answer. Others, no less honorably concerned with the social issues involved, reject the equation as false. "Reverse discrimination" is not a neat slogan hatched by an unscrupulous copywriter. It genuinely raises fundamental questions about the nature of justice in a democratic society—questions which for Jews are not abstractions. The historic experience of the Jewish minority is not irrelevant to an understanding of Jewish attitudes in the present confrontation with the much larger black minority.

Jews have consistently interpreted emancipation as meaning equal civil rights and free access to the opportunities a society offers. If in the exercise of these rights most of their fellows in schools and neighborhoods turned out to be Jews, none except assimilationists viewed such fellowship as a diminution of privilege or dignity. Social and economic advance followed rapidly upon the fall of legal barriers. Once quotas were formally disavowed, the immigrant neighborhood school became the portal to colleges and professional schools from City College to Harvard. To be free of quotas, of legal restrictions, was what Jews had sought and found in America. Consequently, the looming forfeiture of individual rights to group demands strikes a particularly sensitive nerve among Jews. It bodes the return to a legal confinement from which they had escaped through the basic assumptions of American democracy. An integrated society, as it was conceived by its most idealistic proponents, was one that assured equality before the law and equality of opportunity for all its citizens regardless of race and religion. That these principles were frequently violated in practice did not lessen their significance. The progress of American democracy seemed assured through the passage of the Civil Rights Act, which at last brought all the disenfranchised within its fold. By the same token any program that invoked race or religion as determinants of action appeared ominous. The reluctance of whites, Jews among them, to support current escalating black demands is not evidence of unreliability when the chips are down. Much of the murk surrounding black-Jewish relations arises from the conviction that the present turn of the black revolution is neither morally defensible nor practically feasible.

Mandatory busing, in view of its inflammatory nature, is a case in point. The urban centers of the country, from Boston to Los Angeles, have been rent by this issue. Black spokesmen, protesting predominantly black public schools, dismiss the attractions of the "neighborhood school" as a device to compound the ills from which they suffer. At some point the vicious circle of segregated housing leading to segregated schools must be broken. How? School districts whose zoning lines were deliberately drawn to ensure segregated schools lend themselves to the obvious remedy of redistricting. But what about schools where no such intent existed? In New York City for instance, the public schools I once attended with other immigrant children are now predominantly black or Puerto Rican. The Manhattan high school in which I once taught Irish and Italian working-class whites has undergone the same change. The process was gradual, reflecting population shifts in the city. Suppose that in the fifties when the influx of minority students began to increase, some provident administrator had ventured to suggest that the number of black or Puerto Rican students in a given school be limited. It is not hard to imagine the outcry that would have met any attempt to discriminate according to race or ethnic origin. Such a proposal would have had no chance of adoption. Yet only the arbitrary imposition of a racial quota—an unthinkable solution at the time—would have prevented the transformation now deplored.

The change in the school population was evidence not of ghettoization but of black mobility in every borough of the city. The schools altered as the city altered. Blacks were not confined to Harlem, nor were Puerto Ricans restricted to a given sector. That whites moved out when blacks moved in, just as gentiles had moved out when Jews arrived, in no way affected the achievement of mobility. Whites, too, exercised this right. There is no point in reciting the litany of urban ills that prompted the exodus to the suburbs. White families could no more be kept forcibly in the South Bronx or parts of Manhattan than minorities could be compelled to stay within particular enclaves. Today many urban centers, like New York, have overwhelmingly minority populations. It may be Manhattan, Detroit or Los Angeles; the minority has become the majority. Furthermore, because of the higher birth rates of blacks and Hispanics, the ratio of white to minority children keeps falling even without white flight. Elaborate plans drawn up by court order to overcome *de facto* segregation are generally defeated within a few years by demographic factors. In Los Angeles a large Mexican influx steadily transforms the composition of the schools. No mathematical magic can prevent this process unless white children are to be brought in from increasingly distant localities. In addition, many Hispanics object to busing on the grounds that it weakens the cultural cohesion of the community and diminishes its political clout.

Yet despite the inherent difficulties of achieving a suitable racial mix by legal decree these could perhaps be overcome by incorporating remote suburbs with the central city, provided the populations affected were persuaded of the good sense of the new laws and of social and educational benefits to be derived. Such is not the case. The neighborhood school is deeply embedded in American educational practice. Millions of Americans graduated from elementary schools whose student bodies were largely Irish, Polish, Italian, Jewish or true Wasp. The open door of the public school never gave an automatic guarantee that a cross-section of the nation would be represented in the classroom in statistically accurate proportions. No matter how theoretically desirable such representation might be, the fairness of a democratic school system could only be judged by its admission of qualified pupils with no racial or religious restrictions. In the civil rights struggle of the sixties the fight was for the open door. The significant victory of James Meredith, for whose admission into the University of Mississippi the federal government marshalled its full authority, was entrance into the university. That bigoted white students chose to transfer as a result in no way impaired the completeness of that victory. The crucial right established was free access to institution, not to the presence of a particular student body. It is this distinction that has been obscured by much of the contemporary fracas.

Let me use an extreme example. Were the city in which I live to order the creation of separate "Jewish" sections in subways or buses I would fight this discrimination with every means available to me; such a fight would presumably enlist the sympathy of non-Jews, just as the black struggle in Montgomery, Alabama, aroused white support. But suppose I were to discover that most of my fellow passengers were Jews. Depending on residential patterns, such a situation is readily conceivable. Would I then be justified in protesting *de facto* segregation in public conveyances? Or suppose I were to discover that something more deliberate than the accident of residential patterns was responsible for the preponderance of Jews in my train: non-Jews had decided to boycott trains to which they and I had equal access. Would I then have cause to demand the forcible travel of a certain proportion of non-Jews in public conveyances? The suggestion is obviously nonsensical, for though I may rightly deplore the imbecile prejudices of my fellow citizens, my right is to the non-discriminatory use of the subway, not to the society of the passengers.

Through this *reductio ad absurdum* I wish to raise the larger question of how meaningful a protest against *de facto* segregation can be for any

Marie Syrkin

minority. Even more seriously, in what degree does the confusion between *de facto* and *de jure* segregation erode the civil rights of all groups? As a Jew I am completely familiar with *de facto* segregation. At various periods I have lived in almost exclusively Jewish neighborhoods and have consequently attended public schools with predominantly Jewish student bodies. A common term to designate the social life of the middle-class Jews is the deprecatory "gilded ghetto." Another is "five o'clock shadow," the hour that separates Jew and gentile at the close of the business day. The world of the arts and the academy is for Jews and blacks an exception to the rule. However, whether Jews lived in wretched East Side tenements or later in prosperous suburbs, they matter-of-factly accepted Jewish residential concentration as a natural pattern of communal life. Having from the Middle Ages to the Nazi era known literal ghettos that imprisoned them by law (as well as enforced residence in the Russian "pale") they were in no danger of blurring the line between *de facto* and *de jure*. They never considered a preponderance of their own people in their environment evidence of discrimination, or at any rate, of a discrimination to which they could object with any grace. In their constant struggle for equality of opportunity in employment, housing and education their emphasis was on "better." Though formal quotas have fallen, many administrators of prestigious private schools admit that Jewish enrollment beyond a modest percentage means a departure of gentiles. Some private schools that have refused to institute a silent quota have become largely Jewish as a result. Few Jews viewed the result as cause for agitation. The presence or absence of gentiles was irrelevant to the major purpose, which was the quality of education rather than the quantity of non-Jews in the school. This attitude was dictated both by self-respect and reason.

In the battles about mandatory busing, resentment centers around "mandatory," with its accompanying specters of racial or ethnic selection. Voluntary busing is for the most part welcomed. Many communities opposed to mandatory busing encourage parents to bus their children out of their neighborhoods to schools of their choice. The argument that voluntarism fails because more black than white parents avail themselves of the opportunity hardly holds water. It makes sense to transport children to a better school; the reverse is nonsense. Since much of the rationale for busing lies in the claim that black schools are short-changed financially, the remedy lies in improving them, not busing unwilling children. Since so far no objective study has shown that busing brings positive results, parents who decline to make their children pawns in a self-defeating numbers game are not "racist." James Coleman, of the famous Report on the Equality of Educational Opportunity, now questions the effectiveness of busing as a social or educational tool; predictably, he has been read out of the liberal canon.

284

Those who in good faith joined the crusade against legal discrimination are not apostates when they oppose the establishment of a new system of *de jure* discrimination through the imposition of quotas and a disregard of legal safeguards for the individual through the scrapping of the merit system. Polls and popular initiatives in cities and states show that the overwhelming majority of voters oppose busing and quotas though they approve compensatory education and training for under-privileged minorities. Ironically, considering the obloquy to which Jews have been subjected, studies show that Jews are still preponderant among the white minority that supports busing and quotas. In a recent survey of the Los Angeles Jewish community (numbering 472,000), researchers Neil Sandberg and Gene Levine sadly reported that while 88.5 percent of their respondents favored racial integration "only 40 percent approved busing." From all indications this is a higher percentage of approval than would be found in any other ethnic group. Martin Lipset, on the basis of his studies, has concluded that despite the hue and cry about the hypothetical Jewish retreat from liberalism, "It is the liberalism or leftism of Jews that should be commented on and explained, not their conservatism."

In this regard the voting record of the 23 Jewish members of the House of Representatives is instructive. In votes on 18 key issues selected by the Congressional Black Caucus as "of concern to Black and lower-income persons" the Jewish congressmen voted correctly in accordance with the standards of the Black Caucus in strikingly greater measure than the other members of the House, with the exception of the Black Caucus itself. Though only six percent of the House, the Jewish members constituted 42 percent of those with perfect records of support for measures advocated by the Black Caucus. The issues included funding for lower-income persons, Rhodesia, school desegregation and affirmative action. It should be added that most of these congressmen had few or no black constituents in their districts.

Analyses of voting records in municipal and federal elections put Jews squarely in the liberal column. Despite their concern for Israel, they by and large vote against increased defense budgets. And they consistently support social welfare programs. The proportion of Jews in the virulently anti-Israel Left remains high. The charge that economic prosperity has dampened traditional Jewish social idealism is not borne out by the record. Though "self-interest" is no more ignoble a motive for Jews than for blacks, sizeable categories of Jews remain perversely free of its influence. In the Bakke and Weber cases, both plaintiffs and defendants had Jewish supporters. What blacks resent is that Jewish support for their revised program is no longer total.

The identification of blacks not only with the Third World alliance against Israel but more notably with the PLO, while aggravating black-

Jewish relations, is not the basic cause of division. The attraction of the Third World for blacks is self-explanatory; so is the lure of petrobillions lavishly promised by Arab representatives in exchange for black support in the United States. Inevitably, Jews will deplore the political opportunism of blacks as of whites, and will be less generous with contributions to the black organizations involved. But this is not the issue either.

In the ongoing revision of the social consensus in the United States, at stake for the Jewish minority is not how large a piece of the national pie will be theirs—the favorite analogy of commentators—but the method by which the pie will be apportioned. According to the new dispensation, will competing ethnic groups jostle each other for slices corresponding to the group's size, or will the old democratic dream that each person will give and receive as an individual prevail? The abrogation of individual rights would mean curtailment of free entrance into the professions and sciences in accordance with ability and intellectual zeal. If pursued to its logical conclusion such curtailment would drive most Jews back to the role of petty entrepreneurs from which they had escaped through immigration to the United States. Obviously, "self-interest" urges adherence to the articles of the democratic faith as first proclaimed; at the same time, it is misleading to characterize supporters of individual rights as greedy backsliders from commitment to social progress. Rightly or wrongly, they still believe that protection of the individual holds the best promise for meeting the needs of all minorities within a democracy.

(1979)

HOW ISRAEL AFFECTS
AMERICAN JEWS

W hat common denominator can be found in the impact of Israel on the veteran Zionist who rejoices in the dream fulfilled, on the middle-aged big contributor to UJA determined to make Israel a going enterprise, on the idealistic member of a youth group going on *aliyah*, on the campus Leftist waving the banner of Fatah, or on the average mass of the vaguely sympathetic or indifferent? I do not believe that a mathematical mean will provide the answer, for the impact of Israel on American Jewry involves the total position of Jews in the diaspora and is in some degree independent not only of the views, but of the desires of those affected.

A striking instance of the effect of Israel's emergence on popular attitudes is that for the first time in generations a code word for Jew is no longer the medieval "wandering Jew" or "rootless cosmopolitan" but "Zionist," the individual fiercely rooted in his soil—the exact opposite of the former stigma. The epithet of "Zionist" may be bestowed on an unwilling designee: a Polish Jew who insists that he never strayed from the Communist fold and who still prefers exile in Denmark to settlement in Israel, or an Abbie Hoffman, named as "Zionist" by black extremists despite this Yippy's enthusiastic courting of Arab terrorists. Any Jew, no matter how remote from or antagonistic to Zionism, may find himself so described both by anti-Semites reluctant in the post-Hitler era to employ the classic vocabulary of Jew hatred, and by well-intentioned gentiles who matter-of-factly assume that Jews are naturally Zionists.

I n this sense, the existence of Israel compels Jewish identification, whether through acknowledgment or rejection, for rejection, too, is an admission of a bond even though the individual may demonstratively decline to honor the connection. With Israel constantly in the headlines, evasion becomes psychologically as difficult for a Jew as physical escape from the omnipresent fundraiser. Denial must be declared—a process that inevitably stimulates Jewish self-awareness even if negatively.

Obviously this kind of Jewish consciousness represents a Pyrrhic victory holding good for only a minority whose presence, however, should not be ignored in the total assessment. For a much larger group, Israel is a source of affirmative Jewish awareness, the chief alternative to assimilation available to American Jewry.

The cultural assimilation of American Jewry is almost complete. Whether he lives in an ethnically homogeneous middle-class community in Forest Hills or a small town in the Middle West, the home of the American Jew differs in no significant way from the society of which he is a part. It has no distinctly Jewish character. In a secular society, religious faith—the force which for nearly two millennia had been the major cohesive element in the life of Jews—is obviously waning. The current spurts of religious revival cannot reverse this trend, and even infusions of fashionable *Hassidism* from Williamsburg will not appreciably alter the situation. And now even the biological cohesion of American Jewry is threatened by intermarriage—the inevitable consequence of the weakening of spiritual cohesion.

What then remains? The second great impulse to Jewish identification, other than religion, had been Jewish nationalism, the awareness of belonging to one people. In the United States it for decades sustained East European immigrants, many of them demonstratively irreligious and triumphant in their newly acquired emancipation from the fetters of tradition. But Zionism as an ideological current could not flow indefinitely in the kindly American diaspora without being fed by new sources. These were provided by the agony of the Holocaust and the emergence of Israel. The reality of a Jewish state prevented what had been a powerful sentiment from dwindling into sentimentality, at best a vague attachment to a hope not seriously held, like a mechanical repetition of "Next year in Jerusalem" by the irreverent young at *seders* in the time before these words had again assumed immediacy and could arouse passion. Today, because of Israel, ceremonial phrases and remote Biblical place names have the sharp relevance of the day's headlines. The forgettable past has reappeared as the inescapable present. Speaking of a Jewish state, Herzl declared to the Jews, "If you will it, it is no fable." The Jewish state in turn assures the vanishing diaspora Jew, "If you will the Jewish people to remain, it is no fable." In this rekindled awareness lies the chief influence of Israel upon American Jewry, as upon Soviet Jewry in this hour or perhaps Argentine Jewry tomorrow.

Of this truth the Jews of catastrophe provide the most dramatic examples, but even comfortable American Jewry, despite its affluence, is visibly troubled by increasing challenges to the democratic consensus. Jews in the United States are no longer confident that the democratic doctrine by which an individual could prosper according to his accomplishments and ability is unassailable. While among American Jews there is no apocalyptic surge to the Jewish homeland as took place briefly in Soviet

Russia, in Europe at the close of the Hitler era upon the establishment of Israel, American Jewry shows signs of unease in American Zion. And instinctively many turn to the actual Zion for an answer. For the first time in centuries Jews have a viable alternative to benign assimilation, discrimination, or active persecution. This revolutionary turn in Jewish history looms so large that its very immensity makes comment superfluous. Yet reduced to its essence that is what Israel is all about and what its brief existence has meant to American Jewry.

How many American Jews will embrace the alternative is another question; what matters is that a choice exists. And its presence seeps into the consciousness of numberless Jews who have not the slightest intention of going on *aliyah* and who are not even affiliated with the various Zionist or pro-Israel organizations engaged in good works. The emotional involvement of Zionist sympathizers may be taken for granted. I am thinking of the larger numbers who without any ideological commitment find themselves considering, if fleetingly, Israel as the solution to a real or hypothetical difficulty. We have all met them. Let me mention a few: the elderly woman afraid of muggers who tells me in dead earnest that she will settle in Israel because the streets are safe there; the restless youth dissatisfied with his life style who thinks that a kibbutz may offer a more meaningful existence; the nervous professional who fearing himself threatened by an emergent quota system begins to wonder whether he should not explore possibilities in the one land where he is sure that his Jewish identity will not expose him to any form of discrimination—direct or reverse; the parent who thinks that the bracing moral climate of Israel may be wholesome for his problem child. And, on another level, I might mention figures as diverse as convicted Communist spy Soblen or a Meyer Lansky who mistakenly assumed that the Jewish homeland would prove their asylum.

None of the types I have mentioned are Zionists in the accepted sense. In actuality, the lady afraid of crime will probably remain in her luxury apartment on the New York West Side. The boy who goes so far as to try a summer in a kibbutz may find that the rigors of cooperative living as practiced in Israel are not for him. The teacher whose specialty is Henry James may get a letter from the Hebrew University regretfully informing him that there are no openings in his field, and the parents of the problem child will learn that Israel guarantees no instant reclamation. What is significant in these apparently trivial instances is not the frivolity of the impulse but the state of mind they indicate—a pervasive awareness of wholly new options in the life of the Jewish people, including American Jewry. For in each case, except for committed Zionists, the choice of Israel as a possible solution to a particular problem is paradoxical. The lady in search of a quiet haven surely knows what dangers constantly threaten Israel. The professional understands how precarious his career in a pioneer country may prove, and so on. But somewhere in each of these individuals lurks the feeling, perhaps unformulated, that for a Jew the ultimate assurance lies in a Jewish land.

The role of Israel in nurturing committed Zionists, whether the comparatively few who go on *aliyah* or the hundreds of thousands actively working for the well-being of the Jewish state and the still larger periphery that rallies to its defense in a crisis, is self-explanatory. I think it is no longer possible to visualize a vital Zionist movement in the diaspora without the substance of Israel to nourish it.

I have mentioned the two major and obvious effects of Israel's existence on American Jewry: the development of a sharpened sense of Jewish identity and the provision of an alternative to assimilation. These were the objectives of Zionist doctrine and they have been fulfilled.

There are other, subtler ways in which the impact of Israel may be felt. I refer particularly to the new imagery about the Jew that Israel has introduced into the popular mind. Not everyone may be charmed by cartoons depicting an aggressive Israeli fighter, but there is no denying that they represent a new stereotype. Of course, the anti-Semite is not disarmed. He put the same long nose on his Jewish "aggressor," even if he be as snub-nosed as Dayan, as he did on the cringing Jew he formerly enjoyed depicting; but by and large images of vigor and independence have replaced those of cowardice and obsequiousness in the consciousness of the gentile world.

The change did not take place suddenly with Israel's victory in 1967. Less dramatically the process was at work from the time of the first pioneer settlements in Palestine. Let me illustrate from personal experience. In the forties, during the Hitler years, I taught English in a New York highschool with very few Jewish students. When the latter would be absent on Jewish holidays I would be asked what the Jews were celebrating. I soon discovered that these opportunities for enlightening my students about the customs of their Jewish classmates were less rewarding than I had assumed. What was Passover? The Jews were persecuted in Persia. No matter how stirringly I spoke of Egyptian bondage and deliverance, or how gaily I explained how Esther circumvented Haman, I sensed what my pupils were thinking, and sometimes expressed with youthful brutality: "So Hitler isn't the only one. They have always been hated. There must be a reason."

Any historical explanation became a tacit appeal for compassion, for comprehension. In that atmosphere it was painful to teach *Ivanhoe*. The one German refugee in my class would wince visibly each time the cringing Isaac would get another taunt or buffet. And the noble Rebecca was too clearly the unreal creature of romance to be of much help. Today this aspect of *Ivanhoe* would no longer be traumatic: the modern Rebeccas are on the front pages and the Isaacs have become sturdy Itzhaks. They provide a more effective refutation than a learned disquisition on medieval barbarism and the status of the Jews in the days of stout King Richard.

On the other hand, when in connection with a novel about midwestern pioneers my class discussed the general subject of pioneering ventures, some lone soul generally mentioned Jewish pioneers in Palestine; the kibbutzim offered spectacular illustrative material so dear to every teacher's heart. During such moments the Jewish pupils did not look miserably self-conscious—the eternal victims—and the gentile students were free from the disagreeable obligation of having to sympathize or to understand; they could quite simply admire.

I n addition to changing gentile stereotypes, the comparatively few decades of Jewish independence have given new symbols to the national imagination. The Jews of the diaspora proved curiously unable to create forms to express the central Jewish tragedy of our time. This impotence was a psychic malady of the Hitler years, a poverty of spirit of which we were aware. Israel, in being or in becoming, created the poetry as well as provided the actuality of resistance. Let me give one instance. At the height of the Holocaust a Palestinian youth group marched to the Dead Sea and ascended Masada some years before that fortress had been excavated to become a tourist attraction. It was a tough march. At the top of the hill they erected a monument to which they affixed a tablet engraved with the words, "If I forget thee, O Diaspora."

The words, "If I forget thee, O Jerusalem" had been conceived centuries before in Babylon. They continued to live in the imagination of the Jewish people as the ultimate expression of sorrow, remembrance and determination. I think that it is not far-fetched to believe that among the illuminating images of our epoch is the ascent to Masada of these Palestinian boys and girls. They were able to express imaginatively what no other contemporary Jewry found the inner strength to phrase—the indictment of an era: "If I forget thee, O Diaspora." Only those reared on the soil of Jewish independence could have given this metaphor to the Jewish people.

Another aspect too should be stressed. Small, struggling Israel, by virtue of being the Jewish state, has become the spokesman and champion of the Jewish people. It is no accident that the only Jewish community that ventured actively to rescue Hitler's victims was that of the 600,000 Palestinian Jews who viewed themselves as a people and, regardless of size or power, alone assumed the prerogatives of a people. Similarly, only Israel could call an Eichmann to account. Were Jews of any other country to track down a Nazi criminal it would be an understandable act of individual retribution. Only Israel could bring in a national verdict which became a universal ethical judgment. Through the Eichmann case Israel compelled the world to re-examine the tangled question of individual moral responsibility. And at the present time, Israel is the advocate of the right of Soviet Jewry to emigrate. She is not merely a passive asylum.

Not all American Jews are pleased by Israel's arrogation of this position. Who appointed Israel as Defender of the Jewish people? Some complain of Israel's undue interference in the internal affairs of American Jewry. These charges were sharply made in the last presidential campaign and many Jews insist that not everything that is good for Israel is good for the Jews, particularly American Jews, whose concerns and interests extend beyond the periphery of the Jewish state. We can observe various attempts to create a dichotomy between Israel and the diaspora. This must be noted as a reaction to the extraordinary pull of Israel which not through ideological declarations at Zionist Congresses but through its shaping of modern Jewish history occupies a central role in the life of the Jewish people.

Finally, in considering the whole of Israel's impact on American Jewry, we should not omit the many who are self-consciously nervous about Israel's errors and imperfections. Everyone can make his list of failures as well as successes: social inequities, deprivation among Oriental Jews, the seemingly endless struggle with the Arabs. Where is the dreamed Utopia which would give the answer to social and national ills?

Though I am an unlearned, secular Jew, permit me in this connection to quote Maimonides. In describing the hoped-for days of the Messiah Maimonides writes:

> *"Let no one believe that when the Messiah will come anything in the world will be destroyed, or that there will be some change in Creation. This will not be so. The world will go on even as it had before. The* Tannaim *said that there will be no difference between the present day and the days of the Messiah except for the fact that the Jews will cease to be subject to alien domination. That is all."*

The one condition for the ideal time set down by the medieval sage is independence—the ability of a people to act according to its lights. From this all else follows: the rescue of victims of persecution, the building of a cooperative society or whatever else the vision may inspire. But the precondition is the sovereign right to act. The *capacity* for the search for solutions marks the days of the Messiah, not their attainment. Perhaps the chief impact of Israel on the diaspora lies in the realization that at last through Israel's existence the Jewish people has this capacity. "That is all."

I said earlier that without Israel it would be difficult to visualize a continuing vital Zionist movement. I shall go further. Without Israel it is no longer possible to visualize a diaspora meaningfully committed to Jewish survival. At some point hope deferred becomes pathology and the will sickens. That is how the phrase "the centrality of Israel" should be understood. It is not an ideological manifesto but an acknowledgment of a reality of contemporary Jewish life.

V.
SOME
BOOKS

DIARIES OF THE HOLOCAUST

One year I undertook to give a course on the Literature of the Holocaust at Brandeis University. The attempt to define the scope of the course for the university catalogue and to draw up a book list indicated the peculiar problems which beset such an endeavor. The difficulty lay not merely in the lack of familiar guidelines: the absence of well-tried texts, comfortable anthologies with notes and critical studies of the period. While any course in a fresh field might present this challenge, its content would be determined by more or less defined criteria.

The literature of the Holocaust, however, eludes the usual classifications because of the very nature of its theme. The accepted literary categories— novels, plays, verse, essays—are unsatisfactory because they assume a measure of formal achievement to warrant consideration; there are minimal standards for even the smallest of the Elizabethan or Victorian small fry. But when we deal with the Holocaust—an event too awful for our imagination and too close for critical perspective—the whole jargon of literary criticism seems an impertinence. In another generation perhaps, it will be possible to judge novels and poems which deal with Hitler's extermination of European Jewry as coolly as we do fictional accounts of the massacres of Jews during the Crusades or the persecutions of the early Christians by the Romans. Well-documented—but is it art? But as long as both readers and writers are still participants, sharers of the same history if not of the same fate, the necessary perspective is absent. Reader, writer, critic, are for the present too much engaged.

We hesitate to apply the usual canons to the immense mass of written material about the destruction of the Jews already available and still being produced in various languages. Our qualms inhibit judgment, yet we. continue to read not only because we are in search of some supreme artistic expression but because we are still grappling intellectually and morally with what happened. From the first raw accounts of the victims to more deliberate works composed by survivors who recollected, though not in tranquility, we seek first of all knowledge, not knowledge of the outward circumstances of which by now we have the graph, but an understanding of what animated killer and killed. For the photographs, the descriptions, the documentary films bewilder us as much as they inform.

Great literature, they tell us in school, deals with universals. We close the *Iliad* with an understanding not only of the ancient battles of warring chieftains but of Priam and Achilles in their full terror, suffering and humanity. We are introduced to experiences which, however heightened and extraordinary, are, in the deepest sense, familiar. The reverse is true in our reading of the Holocaust. We have learned a special vocabulary—Auschwitz, gas chamber, crematorium, transferpoint; if need be, we could draw diagrams to illustrate the definitions, yet killer and killed, except for rare glimpses, remain alien and singular.

Though this new vocabulary colors the consciousness of modern man none of it has been assimilated. Despite our superficial familiarity with the events—we know not only the outcome but the whole sequence of episodes in wearying detail just as we know the huge cast and how it will behave—we remain estranged. There are five years in contemporary history—1940-1945—for which we have no emotional map though we can fill in the place names in the correct localities.

And yet there is no dearth of those who have tried to communicate the nature of what they experienced. Leaving aside the reports of survivors and the testimony of witnesses, printed and unprinted (countless manuscripts still lie unpublished in such institutes as the *Yad Vashem*), a conscious, sustained effort to give form to what they endured was made by many Jews in Hitler's Europe. The manuscripts that have been found are evidence of probable larger numbers not recovered.

First of all there are the diaries. Anne Frank was not alone. In nearby Brussels another sensitive adolescent, Moshe Flinker, was keeping a Hebrew record, which, like Anne's, would be found after his death in Auschwitz. In Warsaw another teenager, Mary Berg, was making notes in Polish while Emmanuel Ringelblum, the historian, and Chaim Kaplan, the Hebrew educator, were writing their respective scrolls of agony for the judgment of history. With the exception of Mary Berg, who reached the United States in 1944 in a prisoner exchange because her mother was an American citizen, the writers were killed by the Germans; their diaries, dug up after the war, remain abrupt, incomplete, ending at the threshold of Treblinka or Bergen-Belsen.

Despite the differences in the persons and circumstances of the authors, the diaries have one quality in common which partially explains their effectiveness: they are written in innocence. Whatever the degree of foreboding—and the mature men in the Warsaw ghetto have few illusions or hope—the impact of events is registered without benefit of hindsight;

the reader knows what is hidden from the writer. This tragic irony makes the diaries peculiarly moving, and differentiates them from the many circumstantial accounts which will be written by survivors after a lapse of years.

The unfinished diaries affect us for still another reason. Not only Anne, the delightful little girl, but the baffled, suffering men are still within our grasp. Their questions, doubts and accusations are ours; we understand them as with the most desperate effort we do not understand what the survivors of the crematoria tell us. The experiences of the diarists are still in the main human, and when in the Warsaw ghetto they cease to be so, the immediate horror and amazement of the writer expresses what we feel. Our ability to sympathize with the diarist is due not merely to the fact that an individual moves us more readily than an anonymous multitude, but rather that his sufferings wear a recognizable shape: they evoke fellow-feeling. This sense will paradoxically lessen when we enter the charnel house. The more direct the assault upon our sensibilities, the swifter the aversion, the turning away.

Perhaps it is too early for art to impose its order upon this chaos. As yet no great imaginative work has appeared though the temptation to deal with the theme grows constantly greater, as the number of books on the subject testify. The initial silence of diffidence has give way to a flood of memory. I write "memory" advisedly for many of those who use fiction are for the most part reliving rather than imagining. At any rate, there is by now a huge body of published writing which informs if not illuminates. I shall deal with only a few representative diaries, choosing those that impress me for one reason or another.

The three diaries of the Warsaw ghetto are complementary, dealing with the same brief span of time—1940-1943—and with the same tight, confined existence. From November 1940, the creation of the ghetto, to July 22, 1942, the beginning of mass deportations from the ghetto, the chief events are recorded by each diarist writing in secret; each crucial date in the ghetto's history is marked by an entry. The facts are the same. Students of the period who scan the available data for confirmation of particular incidents will note that except for occasional differences of a day or two in the dating of an occurrence, there are no contradictions in the factual record. More surprising, in view of the different characters and ages of the writers, is the similarity of their reactions to what is happening. The social historian trained in political thought and action, the Orthodox Hebrew scholar, and the fifteen-year-old schoolgirl move from a confused hopefulness to hopelessness in the same baffled progression. Though they differ greatly in emotional intensity and intellectual resources, their basic responses are as tragically alike as the events they describe. Their unpreparedness, the comparatively long duration of their initial unawareness, indicate the state of mind of European Jewry, and help explain its inability to read the signs. Literacy came late to the wisest.

Emmanuel Ringelblum (born in Galicia in 1900), an active Labor Zionist deeply involved in party work and the organized communal life of Polish Jewry, is obsessed from the first with a sense of social responsibility. In his "Notes" he is meticulously writing history as well as an indictment; he trains a secret society of fellow reporters whose records and interviews of refugees from other ghettos will in time form a priceless underground archive, composed and concealed at the peril of death. These records, some smuggled out in Ringelblum's lifetime, others found in milk cans after the war in the ruins of the Warsaw ghetto, were to prove, as Ringelblum anticipated, major source material for the history of the catastrophe. His society of scribes, using the deceptive name of *Oneg Shabbat* (Sabbath celebrants) painstakingly keep the record of the Nazi Witches' Sabbath, the saturnalia of blood which engulfs European Jewry, until the "celebrants" themselves perish.

Chaim Kaplan (born 1880 in White Russia), a Hebrew teacher, has, like Ringelblum, spent his adult life in Warsaw. But unlike Ringelblum he is something of a recluse, more concerned with books and Hebrew manuscripts than with social action. He, too, is possessed with the need to "record," but his is a solitary voice, a personal cry to his God for a reckoning. He is less concerned with the drama of a dissolving society than with judgment for the malefactors, Jews as well as Germans. Ringelblum, aware of Kaplan's diary, notes: "Several times I implored Kaplan to let me preserve his diary, assuring him that after the war he would get it back." But characteristically Kaplan refused, offering merely to let it be copied rather than transferred to the archive. Ringelblum was convinced that the diary was lost. Fortunately, it was discovered years later by Professor Abraham I. Katsh and published in 1965.

Mary Berg, less introspective and anguished than her elders, has a keen eye for detail. Perhaps because she is young and healthy, biologically incapable of authentic despair, she has left extraordinarily vivid glimpses of the life rather than the death of the ghetto. When both the social historian and the stern moralist cry out, "The ghetto dances," the girl's account of how the young still seek ordinary pleasures appears as a corrective.

At the outbreak of the war Kaplan writes stubbornly (October 26, 1939): "Our existence as a people will not be destroyed. Individuals will be destroyed but the Jewish community will live on. Therefore every entry is more precious than gold, so long as it is written down as it happens, without exaggerations and distortions." At this stage Kaplan's optimism is hardly surprising. Seven months later (May 27, 1940) Ringelblum declares even more categorically: "If the war were to last as long as the Jews can hold out, that would be bad, because the Jews can hold out longer than the war can last." As defeats multiply, the ghetto continues to follow the fortunes of the war in the expectation of deliverance. On December 9, 1941, Mary Berg writes: "America's entry into the war has inspired the hundreds of thousands of dejected Jews in the ghetto with a new breath of hope. The Nazi guards at the gates have long faces."

Today we read these diaries no longer in the expectation of learning new facts, whose further compilation only adds to the known, but to share in the education of the authors. We are concerned with the education of Ringelblum and of Kaplan, for theirs is still our education. The progressive discoveries they make about Germans, Poles, fellow Jews and about themselves confirm us in our darkest misgivings about the nature of man and offer new dimensions for the exploration of his condition. Throughout, both men, the secular liberal and the Orthodox Hebraist, suffer almost as much from the spiritual decline of all about them as from their own physical extremity. One of Ringelblum's early entries (May 9, 1940) is of an eight-year-old child who goes mad, screaming: "I want to steal, I want to rob, I want to eat, I want to be a German." And he notes (September 9, 1940) that at the madhouse Jewish lunatics praise Hitler and give the Nazi salute.

Kaplan is engaged in a more direct theodicy. As a religious man he interrogates God rather than society. His shift of mood can be gauged from two entries: during the first Hanukah of the war (December 9, 1939) Kaplan writes: "A simple old woman asks me each day: 'Why is the world silent? Does Israel have no God?' I wished to comfort her in her agony, and so I lit four Hanukah candles. And as I kindled the lights I felt they were as humiliated as I." Less than a year later (October 24, 1940) he will permit himself the Job-like outcry: "But He Who sits in Heaven laughs."

Ringelblum, using a different vocabulary, will reach the same despairing conclusion. Before this clarity is achieved, however, we get a graphic picture of the confusion in the ghetto as it is being established. Nobody understands the Nazi design because all insist on having the design make sense in terms they can rationally apprehend. Its cold logic is rejected for normal human explanations. That is why each new act of German savagery, each new decree continues to surprise the inhabitants. The Poles too are unclear about the fate of the Jews. The ghetto situation abounds in macabre ironies. There is a period just before the establishment of the ghetto when Poles masquerade as Jews so as not to be seized for forced labor for the Reich. And Polish parents hide their children in the homes of Jewish friends because the Aryan blood of gentile children is useful for plasma for soldiers of the Reich. The gallows humor of these masquerades is lost on neither diarist, both of whom faithfully record grim ghetto jokes, among them that Jews who managed to escape return of their own free will to Warsaw. Kaplan writes of "tens of thousands of Jews who fled to Russia" who come back (1940) in the belief that the worst is over.

The agony accompanying the establishment of the ghetto is tempered by recurrent illusions. Perhaps with this sundering of the Jews from the rest of the world the Nazis have achieved their purpose and the Jews will be allowed to exist undisturbed in their wretchedness. Kaplan writes sardonically of the Jewish police (December 21, 1940): "The residents of the ghetto are beginning to think they are in Tel Aviv. Strong bonafide policemen from among our brothers to whom you can speak in Yiddish." Mary Berg is one of the simple souls whom Kaplan scorns. The Jewish policemen with their badges with a Star of David give her pleasure: "I experience a strange and utterly illogical feeling of satisfaction when I see a Jewish policeman at a crossing," (December 22, 1940) and she describes the "cordial" attitude of the ghetto dwellers to the Jewish police at this stage. Two months later (February 19, 1941) Ringelblum comments on the fact that in an altercation popular sympathy is with the Jewish police: "You would have minded a Polish policeman so why don't you mind a Jewish one?"

Within a year the Jewish police will be the most execrated element in the ghetto, but in the beginning the policeman strutting with his badge is a symbol of Jewish authority. Kaplan's bitter observation ("they think they are in Tel Aviv") has its kernel of truth.

In a more sophisticated fashion, Ringelblum, too, nurses dreams of national revival within the enforced solidarity of the ghetto. Writing a few days before Mary Berg and Kaplan make their diverse comments on the Jewish police, he expresses another hope: "Today I was at a concert in the Judaic Library. Jewish artists appeared and sang in Yiddish for the first time. The program was entirely in Yiddish. Perhaps this is a beginning of a return to Yiddish." Ringelblum's optimism about the revival of Yiddish is premature. In May 1942 he will report that "Jews love to speak Polish." And he explains that very little Yiddish is heard in the streets because speaking Polish is a psychological protest against the ghetto.

In the grim parody of autonomy the Jewish Council plays the grimmest role. At first Kaplan, enumerating all the tasks that have been delegated to the Council by the Germans, observes mildly enough (September 23, 1940), "The *Judenrat* has turned into a Jewish government, and by order of the conqueror it must now perform governmental functions it was never prepared for." Since the Jewish Council is responsible for food distribution, sanitation, schooling, work selection, tax collection, and housing, not only the Jewish Council but the ghetto inhabitants are under the illusion that the Council's activities are ways of prolonging the ghetto's life; the initial fury of the Council's critics is directed at the Council's failures in securing more food, more adequate medical help or more tolerable living quarters in the destitution of the ghetto. As late as April 20, 1941 Mary Berg expresses sympathy for Adam Czerniakow, President of the Council, who must deal with the "Germans every day and at the same time bear with the complaints and the reproaches of the starving, embittered and distrustful population."

Ringelblum makes short shrift of the composition of the Jewish Council from the outset (December 10, 1940): "Ruffians, nice boys all of them, wearing high shoes, have taken the reins at the Jewish Council. . . . Some of the leaders of the Council are honest people but without understanding of social problems." A year later (January 1942), when the ghetto is dying of typhus and starvation, he attacks "the inhumanity of the Jewish upper class" and the Jewish Council as its instrument. Those with money are faring better; bribes can secure not only bread but exemption from the dreaded labor camps. Up to a certain point the poorest of the poor will fill the quotas required by the Germans.

The charges that the members of the Council are weak, cowardly and venal increase in vehemence as the agony of the ghetto approaches its climax. In this connection, Kaplan's evaluation of the composition of the *Judenrat* should be noted. He makes it abundantly clear that the members of the Jewish Council are not acknowledged Jewish leaders with moral authority in the community (October 27, 1940): "The *Judenrat* is not the same as our traditional Jewish Community Council which wrote such brilliant chapters in our history. Strangers in our midst, foreign to our spirit . . . the President of the *Judenrat* and his advisers are musclemen who were put on our backs by strangers. Most of them are nincompoops whom no one knew in normal times. They were never elected, and would not have dared dream of being elected as Jewish representatives; had they dared they would have been defeated. All their lives until now they were outside the Jewish fold."

Kaplan complains that for a while "even my Zionist friends" tried to get close to the seat of power to get jobs, but "generally our members ran from the *Judenrat*." He quotes an unnamed Zionist who declares: "We have a Zionist tradition to uphold and will never be a party to this criminal gang called the *Judenrat*."

It is apparent from the foregoing, as well as from Ringelblum's accusations, that while the administration of the ghetto by Nazi edict is delegated to the Jewish Council and the Jewish police, the leadership of the ghetto is in other hands. Imposed functionaries, at first the butt of Jewish demands they cannot fulfill, finally loathed as the executors of the Nazi deportation orders, unable to save themselves or their families, they are tragic, ambiguous figures. One thing is not ambiguous. With few exceptions the members of the Council neither were nor became Jewish leaders.

Yet when Adam Czerniakow, realizing at last that his fulfillment of the Nazi deportation orders meant not the partial salvation but the total annihilation of the ghetto, committed suicide on July 24, 1942 rather than sign the German decree, the three diarists exhibit varying degees of sympathy. Predictably young Mary writes of his "great courage and energy till the last moment"; Ringelblum has only a brusque note: "too late, a sign of weakness—should have called for resistance—a weak man." Kaplan, who has been Czerniakow's and the *Judenrat's* most savage attacker, writes unexpectedly, "His end proves conclusively that he worked and strove for the good of his people; that he wanted its welfare and continuity even though not everything done in his name was praiseworthy."

This ambivalence of judgment is not merely the suspect charity of an obituary. It reflects the basic dilemma of the ghetto—that it had to live and die by quota if it were not to perish at once. At first the Council honestly believed that it was the buffer between the Nazis and the ghetto; its allocation of the little available, including work, would be kindlier than the dispensations of the stormtroopers, each of whose intrusions filled the ghetto with terror and littered its streets with corpses. The ghetto shared this view. As long as they hoped for survival, the ghetto dwellers were each engaged in selection for life. Long before the deportation to the gas chambers, the choosing had started.

Among the most harrowing pages in Ringelblum's diary are his accounts of starving and freezing children. In November 1941 he writes: "Tonight, the 14th, I heard a tot of three or four yammering. The child will probably be found frozen to death tomorrow morning, a few hours off. Early October, when the first snows fell, some seventy children were found frozen to death on the steps of the ruined houses. Frozen children are becoming a general phenomenon." Death lies in every street: "In one courtyard the children played a game tickling a corpse." Kaplan and Mary report similar scenes of mass misery and the growing insensibility of the people to their own and others' suffering.

These are "natural" deaths—of hunger, cold and disease. Ringelblum listening to the cry of a dying child is no monster. He has nothing to share. Mary Berg, who has eaten that day, turns away weeping from a child "with big blue eyes" who cries, "I am hungry," and Kaplan records the hardening of the heart of all about him. From the start each lives at the expense of another. To give is to die oneself or to choose death for one's own child. Ringelblum puts it plainly (May 30, 1942): "What are we to do? Are we to dole out spoonfuls to everyone, the result being that no one will survive? Or are we to give full measure to a few—with only a handful having enough to survive?" And he proceeds to meditate on the categories that should perhaps be saved from death by starvation. This terrible choosing, demanded by every ramification of the Nazi scheme, will find its ultimate expression in the "selections" of the Jewish Councils but is implicit in every Nazi order from 1939 on. There will be degrees of guilt and horror but only degrees.

The ghetto's will to live expresses itself not only in the struggle for bare subsistence. Ringelblum has counted over 60 "night-spots." Kaplan mentions the "frivolity" in the ghetto despite sporadic slaughters and constant starvation, yet he adds, "It is almost a *mitzvah* to dance. The more one dances, the more it is a sign of his belief in the 'eternity of Israel.' Every dance is a protest against our oppressors." But secret dancing is the slightest of the protests; the ghetto's extraordinary intellectual and spiritual vitality glows until the end.

Young people take vocational courses given by the ORT. Mary Berg reports that "we" are urged "to study as hard as possible and to share among ourselves not only our bread but our knowledge." Ringelblum not only trains his underground research workers, the members of *Oneg Shabbat* whose studies will result in the history of the ghetto, but participates in the organization of forbidden schools and lecture series. The question of language in the schools is debated: "There are to be three languages of instruction—Yiddish, Polish and Hebrew." A few months later, however, he reports the decision to concentrate on Yiddish. The Jewish Culture Organization organizes a whole courtyard in which only Yiddish will be used for lectures and instruction. "There is an intense cultural activity. More than 99 courtyards have conducted Mendele academies—Yiddish schools." (February 27, 1941). And Kaplan records how cleverly Jewish children learn in secret: "In time of danger the children learn to hide their books. Jewish children are clever—when they set out to acquire forbidden learning they hide their books and notebooks between their trousers and their stomachs." (February 15, 1941).

Mary Berg, many of whose friends are budding painters and musicians, describes the concerts and art exhibits of her fellow students. At an exhibition of the work of her school, "still lifes" are the most popular. "The spectators feast their eyes on the apples, carrots and foodstuffs so realistically painted." Few people linger before the drawings of beggars. A particularly popular feature are the architectural designs for post-war houses surrounded by gardens: "The visitors at the exhibition look with pride at these housing projects for Poland of the future . . . which of us will live to see it?" (September 28, 1941).

While some dream of a free Poland, others are assiduously studying English in preparation for emigration after the war; at the same time

Marie Syrkin

Jewish scientists conduct scientific studies as best they are able, among them an investigation of the nature of hunger. As might be expected, the various political parties, Bundists, all shades of Zionists, and Socialists, are particularly active. The underground press publishes papers and leaflets which are openly distributed because for a while the ghetto believes the Nazis are indifferent to its intellectual turmoil. "Bloody Friday" (April 18, 1942), when the publishers and distributors of the underground publications are executed, dispels this notion.

When the Jewish Council tries to suppress ideological debate on the grounds that continued political activity will invite further massacres and deportations, the timid agree, but according to Ringelblum, some believe that the ghetto has been morally "rehabilitated": "This is the first time that Jewish blood has been spilled for reasons of political—not purely personal—activity." These are the beginnings of the debate on resistance which will soon shake the ghetto.

At which point do the diarists become aware of the Final Solution? In April 1941 Ringelblum is still able to write that the "news from the camps is not bad." Another year will pass before the knowledge of what is euphemistically called "resettlement" by the Nazis becomes inescapable. In July 1942 Warsaw has already received information as to the nature of Treblinka, but Ringelblum tells us that the Jews of Western Europe still think it is a work camp. They go to the death trains carrying "brand new valises." And almost to the end the rumors which fly through the ghetto minimize rather than exaggerate reality. At a time when massacres in Vilna or Lodz run into the thousands during a single "action," reports in Warsaw tell of 50 or 60 victims. Jews escaping from other ghettos in Poland flee to Warsaw because they have heard that it is an independent "paradise." Not only the trickery of the Germans, with their blandishments of marmalade and bread for deportees who peaceably report to the transferpoint is responsible for these delusions. The Nazi propaganda campaign, calculated to lull the fears of the deportees so as to facilitate the process and prevent information from reaching the outside world, is only one element in the deception of the ghetto. The other is self-deception—the inability to believe what until then had been unbelievable. Ghetto rumors of atrocities lessen rather than exaggerate the truth, to reduce the events to psychologically manageable proportions. The new idiom of the twentieth century—extermination center—has not yet been learned.

When the truth is finally assimilated, the diarists lament the failure of the ghetto to resist. Kaplan, through the figure of a mythical Hirsch, appears in the guise of stricturing prophet (June 16, 1942): "My Hirsch is screaming: 'Cowards. . . . You delude yourselves out of hope that the evil will not reach you . . . Protest, alarm the world! Don't be afraid. In any case

306

you will end by falling before the sword of the Nazis. Chicken-hearted ones, is there any meaning to your death?'"

Yet it is Kaplan who describes the results of two attempts at resistance: a mother refuses to surrender her baby. "They immediately grabbed the baby and hurled it out of the window." During a deportation two porters, "virile men," struggle with their captors. The next morning "the Nazis avenged the mutiny of two porters with a hundred and ten Jews." Not only foolish hope but a sense of collective responsibility restrains the young and still vigorous. The others, the old, women, children, the sick—that is to say the bulk of the ghetto—are impotent, reduced by hunger and disease, and unarmed. On July 30, 1942 Kaplan adds another detail: "People come to the transferpoint voluntarily, saying 'Take me out of the quagmire of the ghetto. I will die anyhow.'"

As early as August 1941 Ringelblum comments on the passivity of the Jewish masses who die unprotestingly: "Why are they all so quiet? Why does the father die, and the mother, and each of the children without a single protest?" He gives two explanations; the fear of mass reprisals which will hasten the destruction of the ghetto; and, equally significant, physical weakness, a "direct result of hunger," which keeps the starving people inert and incapable of moral or physical reaction.

The diaries begin with "why" and end with "why" though the object of the query keeps changing. At the outset the writer tries to find rational explanations for the Nazi program which in the beginning is viewed not as a new mode, *sui generis*, but as an atavistic throwback to the familiar persecutions of the past. An ancient, much-enduring people can find comfort in historic parallels. When Ringelblum and Kaplan read the riddle of the Nazi Final Solution, they abandon the quest for understandable motives, economic or political. The first stage in the education of the diarists—and they reflect presumably what is felt obscurely and less consciously throughout the ghetto—is the recognition of the existence of motiveless evil. Ringelblum poring over social causes, Kaplan, Job-like, mourning over the innocent in the hands of the unrighteous, at last stop asking why the murderer—German, Ukrainian, Lithuanian and Pole— murders. They are reduced to the simplest formulation: he murders because he is a murderer. This explanation, too primitive for a psychologist and too unsophisticated for a sociologist, is finally the only one the victim accepts.

The second "why" deals with the behavior of the world outside the Nazi realm of death and depravity. Why do Polish neighbors loot and betray the victims? Where are the "good" Germans? And, above all, what of the outraged conscience of the democracies when they learn about the fate of

European Jewry? There is a jubilant moment in June 1942, when Ringelblum records that the "world knows." The British radio has been broadcasting information about Polish Jewry: "For long, long months we tormented ourselves in the midst of our sufferings with the questions: Does the world know about our suffering? And if it knows, why is it silent?" Now that the world has been alerted measures to aid the tortured Jewries will be found. He rejoices particularly in the role of his OS reports smuggled out of the ghetto, in giving the alarm: "We have struck the enemy a hard blow. We have revealed his Satanic plan to annihilate Polish Jewry, a plan he wished to complete in silence." The realization that the world will accept the annihilation of European Jewry as one of the vicissitudes of war and make no special intervention in its behalf dissipates his short-lived euphoria.

Kaplan, with fewer expectations of the social conscience of mankind, is at this time worrying about Rommel's successful drive in Africa; he permits himself a note on current Allied efforts unwonted in its bitterness even for so tart a commentator as Kaplan: "Perhaps here too Israel is at the heart of it. Our luck has caused it. You don't go into partnership with *idiots* and *failures*."

After the world has been despaired of, the last "why" is addressed to the Jews. Ringelblum puts it directly (October 15, 1942): "Why did we let ourselves be led like sheep to the slaughter? Why did everything come so easy to the enemy?" In another entry he declares: "Now we are ashamed of ourselves, disgraced in our own eyes, and in the eyes of the world, where our docility earned us nothing." And he urges resistance.

It is apparent that the questions historians would pose two decades later were asked in bitterest soul-searching by the sufferers themselves. No cool retrospective critic, wise in hindsight, could write more indignantly than Ringelblum or Kaplan with his outraged cry of "Chicken-hearted ones!" However, the total effect of the diaries negates the self-castigation of the authors. Unlike the armchair commentators of the future, they are the agonized voices of the ghetto storming against itself. And, despite their self-contempt and anger, the image of helpless suffering they record provides the answer to what they ask.

For the last question can be asked only after the first two have been answered. As long as the Jews believe that Nazi barbarism is accidental, outside the norms of human behavior, they cannot credit a savagery beyond their imaginations to conceive. It is obvious from the ghetto's shock at each murderous action in the ghetto streets that they view these slaughters as episodes, to be explained by the viciousness of a particular German commander or a passing Nazi mood. The evil is piecemeal, as it has always been, and the killers, no matter how numerous, are individual. Hence the Jewish struggle to triumph over the accidental and to circumvent individual caprice. When the Jews reach the abyss of realization at the rim of the mass grave or the door of the gas chamber, they will be too worn down for any gesture of resistance. Similarly, as long as they believe that an outraged world will intervene in their behalf, every effort to defeat the will of the killer by remaining alive, whatever the conditions, seems meaningful.

"Why did we not resist?" the third question, is asked only when all hope has been abandoned, and hope in this context is more than the expectation of personal survival. When hope in man—German, Polish, American, English—is lost, the call to resistance is made. For at no moment do those who organize it nurture the illusion that resistance can achieve more than the death of most Jews and a few Germans. "To die with honor" becomes the slogan of the Jewish Fighters Organization. The notion that dismembered European Jewry had tangible means of resistance against the Nazi war machine is part of the mythology of hindsight.

Six months before the ghetto's last stand, Mary Berg describes the appeals of the Jewish underground (September 20, 1942): "The population is summoned to resist with weapons in their hands and warned against defeatist moods . . . 'Let us die like men and not like sheep' ends one proclamation in a paper called *To Arms.*"

We know from other accounts that the ghetto had no arms and that a few pistols and homemade grenades were smuggled into the ghetto with enormous difficulty through purchases from the Polish underground. The diaries of Kaplan and Ringelblum stop before the ghetto's uprising, and Mary Berg, already in France by April 1943, can offer only a hearsay report. Though Ringelblum puts special emphasis on recording the history of the underground movements for his archive, his diary devotes little space to their efforts. Yet knowledge of these heroic activities is as essential for a total view of the ghetto as Ringelblum's disenchanted picture of the brutalities of the Jewish police and the timidity of the Jewish Council.

However, at one point Ringelblum allows himself a paean to the heroines of the underground which obliquely casts a light on an aspect of the ghetto he does not generally dwell on. He writes: "The heroic girls, Chajke and Frumke—they are a theme that calls for the pen of a great writer. Boldly they travel back and forth through the cities and towns of Poland. They carry Aryan papers identifying them as Poles or Ukrainians. One of them even wears a cross, which she never parts with except when in the ghetto. They are in mortal danger every day. They rely entirely on their 'Aryan' faces and on the peasant kerchiefs that cover their heads. Without a murmur, without a second's hesitation, they accept and carry out the most dangerous missions." The girls travel from ghetto to ghetto bringing information, maintaining links between the severed Jewries and smuggling arms. Ringelblum concludes with unwonted enthusiasm: "The story of the Jewish woman will be a glorious page in the history of Jewry during the present war." Girls were more suitable for the role of emissaries between the ghettos than even blond young men since a physical examination would betray the latter.

To the end the remaining Jews of the ghetto worry about "the eternity of Israel." Ringelblum reports a debate about a proposal to rescue a few hundred children by hiding them in Polish monasteries which have agreed to accept them. The argument which ensues indicates the stress still laid on saving a few lives as a way of ensuring the people's survival. The fear that these children will be converted and that their numbers will be too small in any case to alter Jewish destiny is countered by the view that in a time of mass slaughter every Jew is precious as the possible preserver of Jewish peoplehood. Even the danger of conversion must be risked: "Sending a handful of Jewish children into monasteries will enable us to rescue those who will be the creators of a new generation of Jews."

The Ringelblum archives contain invaluable material on the history of the Jewish Fighters Organization as well as on all aspects of Jewish self-help and resistance in Warsaw and other ghettos. This must be borne in mind as one reads the last despairing, fragmentary outcries of the "Notes." Ringelblum will take part in the ghetto's uprising and survive it only to be discovered and executed by the Germans in 1944. Before his death he will succeed in smuggling out an account of the underground intellectual life of the ghetto which will be its noblest memorial. In his valedictory he will write to his comrades proudly, "Know then that the last surviving educational workers remained true to the ideals of our culture. Until their death they held aloft the banner of culture in the struggle against barbarism." But in the diary written in staccato notes, half-completed sentences, during the death throes of the ghetto, there is no time to applaud the brave or recount their deeds. There remains only the throb of horror.

Kaplan's last entry (August 1942) expresses envy of the 5,000 Jews who went to the transferpoint of their own accord: "They had had their fill of ghetto life which is a life of hunger and fear and death . . . Would that I could allow myself to do as they did." These are his penultimate words. His last sentence is, "If my life ends what will become of my diary?" He managed to assure its preservation before his extermination in Treblinka.

Despite the fury of the writers and their unsparing criticism of their fellow Jews no one can read these diaries—and this includes the less analytical account of young Mary Berg—without the conviction that the fortitude of ghetto Jewry sprang from a fierce will for national as well as personal survival. Anyone venturing to pass moral judgments on the conduct of European Jewry in the charnel house must marvel more at the good than at the base. Nothing more eloquently brings home Jewish helplessness in the Nazi vise than the self-accusations of its bravest spirits. No matter how vehemently or how often the diarists may stricture the "criminal Jewish police" or the "criminal Jewish Council," the very nature of their condemnation enables us to perceive the gulf that separates the ghetto's inner life and its acknowledged leaders from the so-called "authorities," appointees of the Nazis. And even the moral failures who fulfill the Nazi bidding in the vain hope of saving themselves and their families are not wholly excluded from the circle of compassion. Weak and corruptible though they may be, indignant though the writer be, the fallen are presented as part of the Jewish tragedy and as fellow victims.

In Western Europe Nazi persecution was more circumspect. Though the anti-Jewish laws were imposed on the Jews of the occupied countries, the drama of the Final Solution was in the main enacted in the East and in Central Europe where public opinion was more tractable and less squeamish, if not openly sympathetic to the Nazi program. Mass slaughters did not take place in the streets of Amsterdam nor were mass graves dug in the heart of Brussels. The chief exhibitions of violence were the roundups of Jews for deportation East. In the prison that was Nazi Europe the West appeared to provide a larger cell with more opportunities for escape than the closed ghettos. Two remarkable diaries tell of attempts to hide in the West.

Both are the diaries of the very young. Unlike Mary Berg, whom the brutality of ghetto life forced out of the private world of adolescence, the diarists write to communicate what they feel rather than to record the history of the time. No doubt many other young souls were keeping diaries to express their troubled emotions, their personal responses to the wonder of growing up and to the terror of being a Jew in Nazi Europe.

The most famous of these is, of course, that of Anne Frank, whose diary, started in her Secret Annex in Amsterdam when she is 13 years old, begins on June 14, 1942 and ends on August 4, 1944. Anne and her diary have been thoroughly publicized; the facts of her fate are familiar. That she has become the symbol of the Jewish tragedy for the non-Jewish world, to be viewed in motion pictures, is understandable. The bright little girl's humor, curiosity and unquenchable hopefulness beguile the reader. He is not obliged to face the meaning of her incarceration. Through her words he shares in an adventure in which the individual quirks of the participants are amusing, and Anne's adolescent longings poignant but not painful. When the diary concludes with Anne's expectation at the age of 15 that "I may yet be able to go back to school in September or October" (June 6, 1944, D-Day), the reader is mercifully spared the need to follow her to Bergen-Belsen. He can, if he wishes, muse on her innocence and faith in man without being forced to consider what happened to that innocence and faith on the following day. Anne can be sentimentalized and gushed over by the unimaginative.

In her hiding place Anne is not unaware of what is happening. On October 9, 1942 she writes: "Our many Jewish friends are being taken away by the dozen. . . . We assume that most of them are murdered. The English radio speaks of their being gassed." But she is 13 years old, with a quick-silver vitality and eagerness. She may be "terribly upset" but her moods shift and immediately after her reports of the doings "outside," she is able to write: "How fortunate we are here, so well-cared for and undisturbed. We wouldn't have to worry about all this misery were it not that we are so anxious about all those dear to us whom we can no longer help."

The lucky Franks, aided by courageous Christian friends in Holland who risk their lives daily to keep them provided with food and minimal comforts, come to the same end as the Jews in the ghettos of Eastern Europe. Anne, caught in the turmoil of adolescent dreams, dwells occasionally on the possibility of capture, but her age and temperament enable her to create a world of make-believe in the attic with Peter. Her natural illusions require no explanation as do those of the ghetto dwellers.

At the same time, while involved primarily in the tremors of her own springtime and praying that "surely the time will come when we are people again and not just Jews," she cannot help meditating on Jewish fate in general: "Who knows, it might even be our religion from which the world and all peoples learn good, and for that reason and that reason only do we have to suffer now." And while declaring passionately, "I love the Dutch, I love this country," the young girls adds, "We can never become just Netherlanders, or just English, or representatives of any country for that matter, we will always remain Jews, but we want to, too."

Bruno Bettelheim in *The Informed Heart* blames the Franks' destruction on their desire to continue their private life "as usual." Had they tried to escape to the free world or tried to fight Germans instead of hiding passively, they might have survived. Anne should have gone to live with a Dutch family as their child. They should have had a gun to shoot down the police when they came for them. Bettelheim concludes that Anne died because her parents could not get themselves to face the facts of Auschwitz.

Judging from Anne's account it is probably true that the family tried with incredible ingenuity to live "as usual" in their hiding place. They read,

studied and sought to remain human. Bettelheim's other strictures hardly
bear examination. The Franks had fled from Germany to Holland in 1933,
though they would have been wiser to have tried to get on the American
immigration quota. They had no more foreknowledge than the rest of us.
The notion that Anne could have been hidden with a Dutch family is
dispelled by a glance at the photograph of the dark-eyed, dark-haired little
girl. Aryan-looking small children were sometimes concealed in remote
villages. Anne was too old and too marked a Jewish type for so public a
solution. True, the family could perhaps have acquired a pistol, though it is
not clear which member of the family would have been able to employ it.
The only probable result of resistance would have been the death of the one
survivor of the group, the father. In any case Anne, like other Annes in the
Polish ghettos, would have perished.

The assimilated, well-educated, middle-class Franks living in Holland
decided that their best chance to escape the Nazis was to hide in a secret
apartment until the end of the war, however long that might be. Another
well-to-do family in Holland decided on a contrary course. At about the
same time that the Franks went into hiding, Polish-born Eliezer Flinker,
an Orthodox businessman living in Holland, fled to Belgium with his seven
children in 1942, to live openly in Brussels on an "Aryan" permit. During
Passover 1944, the Flinkers, betrayed by an informer, were seized by the
Gestapo. In their home was found the fatal evidence—*matzot*, prayer
books, ritual food. The family was sent to Auschwitz where the parents and
the oldest son, eighteen-year-old Moshe, were killed; the six younger
children survived. Like Anne, Moshe kept a diary which was discovered
after the war in the basement of the Flinker apartment and published in
Israel in 1958.

It is idle to speculate on why the Flinkers chose Belgium as their refuge,
just as it is pointless to re-argue the decision of the Franks. Both the Franks
and Flinkers, by trying to escape the deportations to Eastern Europe,
displayed exceptional enterprise if not perspicuity. Each family had a plan
of action—the Franks relied on the goodness of a few trusted gentile
friends; the Flinkers speculated that survival might better be achieved in
an environment where they were unknown and where their money would
secure the necessary residential permits. Each family managed to live for
two years before capture and each family left an extraordinary testament in
the diary of one of its children.

Young Moshe's Diary is written in Hebrew. Three years older than
Anne, Moshe begins his diary when he is 16. As precocious and intense as
Anne, he has none of her childish gaiety or effervescence. Brooding,
scholarly, obviously an *Ilui* (a prodigy), he engages in a theodicy which
rivals that of Kaplan in its probing. And yet he is a schoolboy with the good

pupil's concern for marks. His first entry (November 24, 1942) deals with school. In 1940, when the Germans came to The Hague, he entered a special highschool for Jews. Restrictions multiplied; he had to turn in his bicycle; then Jews were forbidden to ride on streetcars: "However, I continued going to school during those last days because I wanted to get my report card and find out whether I had been promoted to the next class."

In Brussels, unable to attend a Belgian school, Moshe spends his days reading Hebrew and Yiddish books which he borrows from a still-existing Jewish lending library. He starts resolutely to study Arabic because after the war he intends to be "a Jewish statesman in the Land of Israel." He studies diligently despite the difficulty of getting adequate textbooks; at one point he acquires an Arab-French grammar which necessitates the purchase of a French dictionary since his French is not as good as his German. But he perseveres for, "It is obvious that we shall have to live in peace with our brothers, the sons of Ishmael, who are also Abraham's descendants." While he mourns his inability to take special courses to qualify him for his future diplomatic career, he trusts with deep conviction that "the Lord will help me when my own intelligence is inadequate."

He reveals his plan to become a "Jewish statesman" in December 1942 when the fortunes of the war and of the Jews offer little reason for such extravagant anticipations. But the boy is not indulging in an idle fantasy; he is a believer waiting for Redemption. On the secular plane he is able to analyze the military situation, the political tensions among the Allies and the prospects for the Jews with an unblinking clarity rare among his elders. Comparing the present persecution of the Jews with those of the past, he understands that for the first time in history the whole Jewish people may face destruction. He early warns of "a coming war between England and America on one side and Russia on the other." He foresees the danger of "the final assimilation" of the surviving Jews after the war, and because of this menace he decides: "I am preparing from now on to emigrate to my homeland, and as soon as possible I shall try to do so, the Lord willing." This is five years before the establishment of Israel.

At no point does he lessen the horror of what is taking place. The boy receives its full impact, escaping only to the diminishing solace of his Hebrew studies. What sustains him in the midst of a sharply realistic appraisal of global catastrophe is his faith that these are the birth pangs of the Messiah. Amid such abominations salvation cannot come from the victory of one side or the other but only from God. The very intensity of his apocalyptic vision of the world's evil leads him to disdain human solutions. When the roster of sins is complete, the Lord will grant deliverance: "I think that this war will end with the downfall of most of the world because all have tortured our people. As I see it, the only thing that is delaying the approach of our salvation is that certain countries have not committed enough sins to blacken their names completely. The most important of these nations are England and America (the sins of Germany and Russia are now sufficiently enormous). Now, when England and America every day drop bombs on defenseless towns, on women, children and the aged, their list of sins must be getting longer. . . . But it is as yet impossible to be saved for the American has not amassed his quota of sin." (June 13, 1943).

Despite this passage, Moshe is no religious zealot complacently waiting for the Americans to fill their quota. While he never questions divine justice or divine wisdom, he pleads for divine help for his people. He is consumed by a sense of guilt because he is not sharing the sufferings of his fellow Jews. Once while still in Holland, he was asked why he did not try to flee to Belgium or Switzerland: "Any girl or boy who can flee from the Germans is saved for our people and can be a hope for the future." In his Belgian refuge he writes: "Now I feel that I have not been saved for the future of my people; on the contrary, I see myself as a traitor who fled from his people at the time of their anguish."

On the day (June 22, 1942) that he learns of the extermination of Jews sent East he turns to his Bible but finds no consolation, "not in the Pentateuch with its lofty commandments" nor in books of the Prophets. He chants the *Lamentations* and among his sorrows is that "I have done what I said I would do—study the Bible each day—but I have found nothing in it." Yet even as he ventures on this blasphemy, he blames himself rather than the Book.

At the same time, he is a lonely boy who wants friends, remembers a girl he knew in Holland, and watches the gaiety of the young Belgians from afar: "I see in the streets that the gentiles are happy and gay and that nothing touches them. It is like being in a great hall where many people are joyful and dancing and also where there are a few people who are not happy, and who are not dancing. And from time to time a few people of this kind are taken away, led to another room and strangled. The happy dancing people in the hall do not feel this at all. Rather, it seems as if it adds to their joy and doubles their happiness."

Moshe reports family quarrels; the mother wants to cross the border to Switzerland; the father refuses because a family of seven children is not mobile or likely to go undetected. The capture of a friend who made the risky move silences the mother.

The boy appears curiously indifferent to the question of escape to a neutral country. He is chiefly troubled by the premonition that the sufferings of the Jews will prove meaningless; the survivors will reject redemption: "I have often asked my Jewish acquaintances what they think the state of affairs will be after the war and I have always received the same answer—that everything will be as it was; we shall continue to stay where we now live and life will go on as before" (November 30, 1942). But this is not God's will, he declares firmly. The Jews were driven from their homes and cities to return to the Land of Israel. Such is the religious rationale of his hope, even while he soberly recognizes the human obstacles to its realization.

Was Moshe a victim of his family's passive acceptance of its doom? Bruno Bettelheim's suggestion that Jewish families could have saved their children by distributing them among friendly Christians presupposes the existence of numerous Christians ready to harbor a Jewish child. Nothing in the record warrants such an assumption. The Flinkers felt safer with their large brood in strange Brussels than in Amsterdam, their home town. Courageous, self-sacrificing Christians who ventured to conceal Jews were rare individuals. The glimpses Anne and Moshe give us of seizures of Jews in the midst of a silent, cowed population show the Jews isolated in the West by the apprehension of the bystander as in the East by ghetto walls.

The diaries of the Holocaust that I have discussed are not primarily emotional outbursts. A victim's lamentation, unless he is a great poet, can become tiresome even to the sympathetic reader. These hurried notes from Hell are precise in observation as well as eloquent, though apparently written without any self-conscious effort at restraint or "discipline," and differing in style and mood. The authors and their world emerge sharply etched. The quizzical little girl in her Annex, the passionate historian and the sardonic scholar "recording" in the ghetto, and the possessed boy wandering on a Brussels street, come terribly alive; the unfulfilled futures of the wonderful boy and girl, reminders of what has been destroyed, tease the mind. Candid, acute, articulate, each writer bares more than his heart; he reveals, often unwittingly, how tightly shut was the trap in which Jews of Europe perished and how few passers-by even bothered to glance at the bars.

(May 1966)

Warsaw Ghetto, by Mary Berg, edited by S. L. Shneiderman, 1945. L. B. Fischer.

Notes from the Warsaw Ghetto, by Emmanuel Ringelblum, translated from the Yiddish and edited by Jacob Sloan, 1958. McGraw-Hill.

Scroll of Agony, by Chaim A. Kaplan, translated from the Hebrew and edited by Abraham I. Katsh, 1965. Macmillian.

Anne Frank: The Diary of a Young Girl, translated from the Dutch by B. M. Mooyaart, 1952. Doubleday.

Young Moshe's Diary, translated from the Hebrew; edited by Shaul Esh. Published by Yad Vashem in Hebrew in 1958; in English in 1965.

NELLY SACHS

The award of the Nobel Prize to Nelly Sachs has drawn attention to her not as a German poet to be considered in the context of German literature, but primarily as the poet of the Jewish Holocaust. She is now acclaimed as the voice of *Das Leiden Israels*, the suffering of Israel, by which she means not the land but the Jewish people, and her work is measured by the magnitude of her theme.

There is no lack of poems on the Holocaust. By now a huge body of poetry on the subject exists in a variety of languages. Even Yevtushenko produces his Russian *Babi Yar*, more notable for its political statement than its poetic achievement. Many single poems, poignant or powerful, have been printed but, with the possible exception of Yiddish poems of Jacob Glatstein, no body of work in some fashion commensurate with its theme has appeared. The usual explanation has been that the agony was too great for any cry. Only a major poet, a Shakespeare or a Dante, could write of such events without lessening them. And, certainly, most of the poems on the Jewish experience in the Nazi era leave us dissatisfied even when they move us. While we may be moved by the individual poet's pain or indignation, we are so largely because we read already sharing the emotions of the writer, and most of the time our own unshaped feeling exceeds what has been expressed.

Many poems written in the ghettos and camps have come to us in scraps, preserved by chance or smuggled out, as ghetto diaries have been. Among the most notable of these is the Yiddish "Song of the Slaughtered Jewish People" by Yitzhak Katzenelenson, whose wife and children were exterminated in the early deportations from the Warsaw ghetto, and who was himself killed not long after he managed to bury two copies of his elegy. The poem, of about a thousand lines, makes no pretense to literary artifice. There are no striking images or words. Simply, literally, often in hackneyed phrases, he describes what has befallen him and his family—the

---

The translations of Nelly Sachs's poems in this essay are my own.

loss of his wife and sons, the procession of children marching along the ghetto streets to the transferpoint, the trains that wait to be filled: "Just yesterday they started out, and now I see them stand, once more upon the transferpoint." Or he addresses his dead wife:

> *You hear. You hear. In my great misery*
> *You comfort me, my wife.*
> *I fill you with my anguish as with seed;*
> *Bear my accusing words as once my sons,*
> *Bear them and carry them from world to world.*

The Yiddish poem is in rhymed quatrains of uneven quality. Katzenelenson is too terribly in earnest to be mawkish, yet what he writes about is too terrible for his rendering. He can communicate only the nature of his personal anguish, not its immensity. We know his loss, his horror, his fury, but nowhere are we content that this chaos of feeling has found form. We are left with the event, not its transmutation. The refinement of raw experience into art has not taken place.

I mention Katzenelenson's poem because it demonstrates so clearly the limitations of even an affecting literal statement. To the extent that such a poem is descriptive or narrative it adds little more than the pulse of rhythm to a prose record. To the extent that it is lyrical, that is to say a subjective expression, it is inadequate to what is felt. Often a successful poem can transform a minor incident—seeing a bed of daffodils or observing a hedgehog—into an authentic experience. Major themes have the reverse effect: they dwarf the attempt unless the writer is a great poet.

Collections of ghetto poems, such as I have seen, are for the most part painfully poor. Not because the poet is insincere or fails to depict an actual emotion in complete, devastating honesty. Not even because he necessarily lacks literary craftsmanship. He may name the place, the circumstance—be it Auschwitz, the gas chamber, or an SS man in action—without achieving the impact of a fresh news report. During a visit to the DP camps I was startled by many of the songs composed in the concentration camps and sung by survivors. The lyrics, in most cases, were starkly banal, popular in the worst sense, but at least the words made no attempt to prettify a horror they were unable to communicate. But the melodies were often familiar, mildly plaintive Russian tunes; sometimes they were even sentimental Austrian waltzes. The contrast between the grim content and the music was something of a shock though the singers, who should presumably have been most sensitive to the impropriety, or at any rate inappropriateness, of the lilting tunes appeared to feel no dissonance. It had to be said or sung somehow. The one great chant of the death camps, the *Ani Ma'amin,* "I believe that the Messiah will come," makes no overt reference to the situation of the singer. "Look in thy heart and write," the classic counsel of a good poet to his fellows, is unfortunately not enough for the making of poetry, as the earnest doggerel of the lovelorn and the bereaved constantly testifies.

The literary virtue of Nelly Sachs is that she has managed to transmute personal anguish into personal vision. Using sophisticated literary techniques, daring, often surrealist images, she composes her lament for a people. Long before the rest of the world took cognizance of her, Germany had been aware of the Jewish refugee poet in Sweden writing German poems. Born in Berlin, December 10, 1891, Nelly Sachs fled with her mother to Stockholm, Sweden in 1940 through the help of the Swedish novelist Selma Lagerlöf—the rest of Nelly Sachs's family perished in Germany. As everybody now knows, on her 75th birthday she shared the Nobel Prize with the Israeli novelist Shmuel Yosef Agnon. But one year earlier, in 1965, she had been awarded the Peace Prize of the German Book Trade in Frankfurt. (In 1960 Nelly Sachs returned to Germany for the first time after 20 years to receive the Droste-Hulshoff poetry prize.)

According to the terms of the Frankfurt Peace Prize, it is awarded for "encouragement for the conception of peace, of humanity, and understanding among peoples." Her citation read: "The poetical work of Nelly Sachs speaks for the fate of the Jews at a time of bestiality and reconciles German and Jew without contradiction. Her poems and lyric descriptions are masterpieces of German, works of forgiveness, salvation and peace." Why did the poet who most powerfully presents *Das Leiden Israels* receive such an award from Germans? Why is she viewed as a poet of reconciliation? Certainly not because she in any way seeks to lighten the weight of what has been endured or the evil of the perpetrators. Nor is there any murky confusion between victim and evildoer in her moral universe. Rather, her horror is so immense that it transcends the puny wickedness of individuals. Evil becomes a mystery, just as good is a mystery, painfully understood.

This ability to transcend without sentimentalizing lies at the heart of her poetry. In its Job-like sense of mystery and in its consecration of the martyr her poetry has a religious element. At the same time she never ignores the nature of martyrdom; her transcendence never loses sight of the intimate reality of pain. She neither takes refuge in abstractions nor confines herself to notations of bestiality. In much of the writing about the Holocaust the description of the degradations endured becomes a degradation of the victim. The bestiality of the acts suffered reduces the sufferer to a zoological level. A free verse play such as Peter Weiss's "Investigation," for instance, in which witnesses recount in concrete detail the myriad torments and indignities to which they have been subjected, has the paradoxical effect of further assailing the dignity of the beings to whom such things happened. The stench of the latrine and the odor of decaying flesh cling to the living and the dead, and the sad shifts for survival define the moral climate of the concentration camp. This naturalistic verisimilitude equates the tormented with the nature of their torments. To the extent that it is only a partial truth, it becomes a betrayal of the truth, and the dehumanization of those who perished becomes their further violation.

A too rarefied sublimation can prove as meaningless as a total concentration on physiology and scatology. Nelly Sachs maintains a delicate balance in her search for reality. She can be simple, almost matter-of-fact, as in her "Lullaby":

> *Night of weeping children*
> *Night of death-marked children—*
> *Sleep may not enter here.*
> *Dreadful nurses*
> *Watch instead of mothers;*
> *They clutch treacherous death in their muscular palms;*
> *They sow it in walls and rafters.*
> *Brooding horror nests everywhere.*
> *Fear suckles the little ones.*
> *Only yesterday a mother,*
> *Like a white moon, drew sleep close.*
> *Into one arm*
> *Came a doll, red-cheeked, faded with kissing;*
> *Into the other*
> *A stuffed animal, grown live through love.*
> *Now only the wind of dying*
> *Blows the shirts over hair*
> *That no one will ever comb again.*

Yet even the homely pathos of this nursery scene is stirred by "the wind of dying" and by the image of the "dreadful nurses." The exactness of the nursery terminology—the stuffed animal, the red-cheeked doll—is lifted to another dimension by the central image of maternity in Hitler's Reich: "Fear suckles the little ones." Despite its apparent simplicity the tension of paradox permeates the poem. It is a lullaby for those who cannot be put to sleep.

On the other hand, she can compress the whole history of the Jewish people into a tight poem like "Sand":

> *But who emptied the sand from your shoes*
> *When you had to rise for dying—*
> *Sand Israel brought home,*
> *The sand of its wandering?*

Burning sand of Sinai
Mixed
With the tongues of nightingales,
With the wings of butterflies,
With the serpent's dust of desire,
With the wormwood's bitter secret
Mixed.
Fingers,
That emptied the sand from the shoes of the dead,
To-morrow you will be dust
In the shoes of those to come.

The sand of Israel's wandering is first of all the sand of Sinai, the holy mountain where the religious character of the people was formed. It has been mixed with much else through the centuries, alien temptations dubious as the serpent's desire, lovely as the song of the nightingale, bitter as wormwood, but the essence remains the burning sand of Sinai with its inevitable suggestion of dedication. The "fingers," sacrilegious, ominous "fingers," will in turn become dust, but not consecrated as the sand of Sinai.

In her youth in the pre-Hitler years Nelly Sachs, the daughter of a well-to-do German industrialist, wrote neo-romantic poetry about Nordic myths and figures; she was interested in the arts, particularly the dance. In the thirties she presumably came under the influence of Gershom Scholem and his studies of Jewish mysticism. Her later work is permeated with Jewish tradition and scholarship—a store of learning not wholly acquired in the post-war years of exile, since she was nearly 50 years old when she fled to Sweden in 1940. What for lyric poets is a lifetime of creativity was already behind her. But from 1940 on, the delicate poet writing German expressionist verse like many of her contemporaries became possessed of her great theme. Her bibliography indicates that as early as 1921 she had published a volume of verse with the pleasant title *Legends and Tales*. Her next volume did not appear until 1946; its name is *In the Abodes of Death*.

In a letter to a fellow exile in Stockholm, Professor Walter A. Berendsohn, (May 15, 1946) Nelly Sachs wrote: "My life is so torn in pain that each time I plunge into fire to find words for the unsayable. Often I am overcome by irresolution which makes me mute before the overpowering, but then nights come when I am overpowered, and trembling I must dare. I will not stop following step by step the path of fire and flame and star of our people and I will bear witness with my poor being."

In the same letter she indicates that bearing witness, as she understands it, includes not only lament and accusation. It is that and more. For she writes further: "When each of the peoples of the earth seeks for meaning, why should not Israel again offer mankind a draught from its own ancient source? I do not think it is enough to win fruit and home from our inherited earth when it is in our power together to fulfill the ancient call of our people—new and purified by suffering." (*Aufbau*, October 28, 1966).

Among her first works on *Das Leiden Israels* is her mystery play, *Eli*. She raises the central questions of the Holocaust—why do the innocent perish, why is Israel martyred? *Eli* consists of 17 brief scenes set in the market-place of a small Polish town destroyed in the war. A few Jewish survivors work among the ruins trying to rebuild the houses. The theme is the death of eight-year-old Eli whose murderer is sought by Michael, a survivor who may be one of the 36 righteous men on whom the world rests. The murderer, when discovered, is destroyed by his own sense of guilt, not by any outer vengeance.

A mystery play is a medieval form dealing with sacred and Biblical themes; in medieval writing Jews, unless they are the Biblical patriarchs, are of course the villains, and in medieval ballads and folklore a recurrent theme is the murder of a Christian child by Jews. Chaucer's "Prioress" recounts the tale of a holy child slain by "cursed Jews." In her twentieth-century mystery play Nelly Sachs deals with contemporary history not as dark myth. The events have just taken place. It is too soon for any reassignment of guilt and there is no doubt as to who is the innocent victim. To the medieval fable is counterpoised an actual moment in a Polish town in the 1940s.

It is estimated that of the six million Jews who perished in the Holocaust, one million were children. Though the literature of the Holocaust is filled with glimpses of the intolerable pathos of these deaths, no words have been as moving as the photographs and documentaries we have seen. No one is likely to forget the picture of the bewildered little dark-eyed boy with upraised arms herded by stormtroopers along a ghetto street. Nelly Sachs's Eli is not that frightened child. She writes:

> *And when Eli saw*
> *With his eight-year-old eyes*
> *How they drove his parents along the cow path, the cow path*
> *He took his pipe and piped.*
> *He did not pipe as one pipes to cattle or in play.*
> *He threw his head back*
> *As the deer, as the roe,*
> *Before they drink at the spring.*
> *He turned his pipe to the sky,*
> *He piped to God, this Eli.*

He is killed by a soldier, angered by the child's audacity in thrusting his head back and piping high to heaven. As her "Lullaby" and other poems indicate, Nelly Sachs knows fully the helpless terror of children; she does not romanticize their destruction by endowing it with metaphysical consolation. But a mystery play may by definition allow the miracle. Eli is the innocence of Israel attacked throughout history because of a divine dedication. In a subsequent scene, the music of Eli's pipe is echoed in the blast of the *shofar*, described as the *Heimholerhorn*, the horn that calls us home. And one of those listening to the blowing of the *shofar* says:

> *In my ear is a sound*
> *As though someone were near*
> *To pull the thorn out of the wound,*
> *The thorn that sticks in the middle of the earth.*
> *Someone takes the halves of the earth apart like an apple,*
> *The halves of today and yesterday—*
> *Takes out the worm and puts the core together again.*

This is the basic faith of the poet to which is opposed another voice crying out: "I tell you, the new Pentateuch / Is written with the mold of fear / On the walls of the cellars of death."

Eli is uneven, perhaps, because of its form. Nelly Sachs is a lyric rather than dramatic poet and some of the stage effects in *Eli* are strained. But the central conception of Israel as the consecrated martyr, not the helpless victim, is clearly defined. The child Eli defies the brute world with his divine piping. The world is not transfigured by his death. Nelly Sachs offers no easy salvation. However, the sound of the pipe is an affirmation; it echoes somewhere, just as the sound of the *shofar* summons to homecoming. These too are realities: human, Jewish notes in the cacophony of evil. In Nelly Sachs's poems we are most aware of this human voice, mourning, questioning, praying.

The collection of poems entitled *In the Abodes of Death* was written at about the same time as *Eli* in the years immediately after her escape to Sweden. Living in poverty with her old mother, she described the conditions under which she wrote: "Since I dared not turn on the light in the one room in which we live—I could not interrupt the rare, precious rest of my mother—I tried to repeat and repeat in my head all that was enacted in that atmosphere, there, where night had been torn apart as a wound. In the morning, I wrote what I remembered as well as I could."

In these poems are recurrent images of dust, stones, smoke and stars. The first section, "Your Body in Smoke Through the Air," has as its epigraph a verse from Job: "And when after my skin, this is destroyed, then without my flesh I shall see God." While the chimneys "through which the body of Israel rose dissolved in smoke" are inescapably literal, the chimney sweep is "a star that turned black" and the chimneys are called "Freedom paths for the dust of Jeremiah and of Job."

The chimney is of stone, its function conceived by men never named: the Germans who place brick upon brick. The dust, however, is that of Job and Jeremiah to be received by a darkening star. In a pantheistic universe, these are the transformations of the world of which she will write again and again.

At the same time she is capable of intimate tenderness. In a poem on the survivors she wrote:

> *We, the rescued,*
> *Beg of you:*
> *Show us our sun slowly.*
> *Lead us step by step from star to star.*
> *Softly let us learn to live again.*

Though she never mentions the Germans they do not remain anonymous. In a powerful poem on Hitler, the subject is unmistakably described though he is not named: "What secret desires of the blood . . . let the dreadful puppet player arise."

> *Arms up and down*
> *Legs up and down*
> *And the setting sun of the Sinai people*
> *As the red carpet under his feet.*

> *Arms up and down*
> *Legs up and down*
> *And on the moving ash-gray horizon of fear*
> *The star of death stands gigantic*
> *Like the clock of the time.*

In these images meaning is compressed and heightened without explication. The metaphors are not elaborations of ideas; they are the ideas.

The poetic method of Nelly Sachs is seen at its best in the poem on Hitler, the puppet player who manipulates the "stage of his deed" around which his "foaming mouth" has blown an "ash-gray moving horizon of fear." On the stage are *Staubhügel*, heaps of dust, pulled by an evil moon, as in nature the tides of the sea are drawn by the moon. Presumably, though this is not stated, the *Staubhügel* are the Germans. There is an implicit comparison between the great waters and the dust to which human beings have been reduced, so that not only the murdered become ash, but the murderers are themselves puppets of dust, mechanically going through spasmodic motions, "arms up and down, legs up and down"—automata without will or capacity for revolt.

Another series of images in the poem reinforces the surrealist setting. The red carpet of the stage of the puppet show is the glowing light of the "setting sun of the people of Sinai." And, while the arms go up and down and the sun sets, another luminary is seen: the huge star of death, which replaces the sun as the clock of time. Instead of the sun to measure the passage of days and hours, the fateful star of death shines on the ash-gray horizon of fear.

What has the poet said in her image of a puppet show with its oddly luminous setting? Through the economy of imagery—for imagery here is not decorative but the substance of the poem—she suggests the frenzy of Hitler and the mechanical submission of the Germans, neither of whom are named. Only the Jews are identified, but they do not appear as abject victims; on the contrary, they are a glory—a setting sun. To the principle of life and light which the sun represents are opposed two cold luminaries. The first is the evil moon—we must recall the relation of lunacy to the moon—whose influence is baleful. The second heavenly body is the gigantic star shining on an ash-gray horizon. By the fading of the people of Sinai the world is left to death and terror. The sign of the age is death. Because of its compactness and suggestiveness this poem is more satisfying than the looser lyrics to which I have already referred.

A nother poem which merits analysis is the enigmatic "In Flight." Nelly Sachs has many references to flight in her poems beginning, in a poem written immediately after her escape, with the "fugitives of smoke" (the title) who rise through the chimneys of the death factories. "In Flight" was published a decade later and illustrates a deepening metaphysical streak in her poetry. The first lines are a striking paradox, when one considers the objective reality behind them: "In flight, what great welcome underway." This "welcome" holds no offer of human hearth or hospitality. The fugitive is wrapped in a blanket of wind—of all cloths least suited for a covering; her feet are in shifting sand, sand that is allied to fin and wing, to fish and bird; and a stone that comes into her hand bears the inscription of a fly. The conclusion of the poem comes with tragic force: "In place of home [*Heimat*] I hold the transformation of the world [*Verwandlung*]," the processes in the cosmos through which inorganic nature and organic life are united. In earlier poems Nelly Sachs has written of stones that they are a "coffer full of lived life," billions of aeons and petrified memories from genesis onward. They are Jacob's pillow, the Wailing Wall, pre-history and history; and they are constituted of the same particles as the stars, for the stars are "wandering, shining, singing dust" (*Chor der Sterne*).

The consolation of the fugitive, her welcome, is this pantheistic awareness of the oneness of the universe and the metamorphosis of its many forms, and her acceptance of man's place in a universe that encompasses more than man—the universe of stone, butterfly, sea and star. Yet this is not an abstract, metaphysical statement which might just as readily be given in a banal prose essay. The human need of the beginning— the anguish of flight—and the renunciation of the conclusion—"instead of a home"—gives the intellectual statement the intensity of poetic feeling and perception; the idea is developed solely through images, not declarations. The exegesis is that of the commentator.

The image of dust, the common denominator in the universe, recurs more simply in a poem about the suffering of animals, whose "fate turns with small steps, like the second hand on the dial in the unredeemed hour of mankind." Nelly Sachs does not hesitate to write of the calf torn from its mother, the mute fish, the bloody flesh of a horse on a battlefield. She is not afraid of the triteness of straightforward compassion, nor in this poem does she seek unusual symbols for its expression. However, in the midst of poetic commonplaces there occurs the magnificent line: "How much creeping and feathered dust clings to the soles of our shoes, which stand like open graves in the evening." The "graves of air" of the Jews of Europe do not obscure the leather graves in which we tread on life, that "creeping and feathered dust."

This oneness with all forms of creation appears poignantly in "Prayer for a Dead Bridegroom." The shoes torn from his feet remind her that they were made of "calf-skin once stroked by the warm tongue of the mother-animal before it was torn off." Now that skin is torn off again in a second killing, that of her love.

The interrelationship in the universe, not only in the organic world of man and brute but in the cosmos, as seen in the poem "In Flight," finds another striking image in "He who comes from earth to touch the moon." The lyric is not a tribute to the marvels of modern technology. This astronaut will discover celestial mineral substances penetrated by explosive human longings: "Craters and dry seas filled with tears move through starry stations on the journey through the eternal." The German is *"Fahrt in das Staublose,"* "journey into the dustless," an impossible rendering. Equally impossible to translate is *"Überall die erde baut an ihren Heimwehkolonien,"* "Everywhere the earth builds her colonies of nostalgia." The universe of Nelly Sachs is not remote or alien. Its atoms in all their transformations include man and his spirit. The exile, the fugitive, from a given hostile spot in a specific geographical location we call earth stresses the kinship of all matter in its changes and evolutions not from a materialist view, but religiously and personally. "In the hand of God, sand becomes light."

This retreat into the metaphysical, this journey into the *Staublose* is, however, poetically fastened to an inescapable reality. No cosmic consolation exists in her powerful metaphor for total desolation after the death of all she loved: "Superfluous is the embrace of emptiness, a circling ring that has lost its finger." ("*Übrig ist die Umarmung der Leere / ein Kreisender Ring/ der seinen Finger verlor.*") And the poems, already quoted, that deal directly with the dead and the survivors are rooted in the agony of the actual experience, though branching out from it in a variety of images.

In her poems on Israel, the people and the land, she is simpler and almost conventional. Her sense of Israel's spiritual uniqueness is uncompromising. In the poem "Abraham" she writes: "You from whose foreboding blood, the butterfly-word 'soul' sprang as from a cocoon." ("*Aus dessen ahnenden blut/ sich das Schmetterlingswort 'seele' entpuppte.*") There is no satisfactory English rendering of *entpuppte*.

And in "Israel," he who beheld the angels, she writes: "Israel, zenith of longing, heaped about your head lies wonder like a storm to break at last on the *Schmerzgebirge* [mountain peaks of suffering] of your time." Again we are in trouble in search for an English equivalent for the concentrated *Schmerzgebirge*, but the sense offers no difficulty. The highest reach of spiritual desire will be paid for by centuries of pain, and to the zenith of longing is opposed the "mountain peak of suffering."

Just as Israel, the people, appears consistently as one early blessed and cursed by a spark of the divine, so her poems on the land of Israel stress the relationship of the people to its spiritual history. The poems are full of Biblical references, yet in the plethora of Biblical allusions a superb personal note transforms what, except for the poetic skill of expression, might be traditional tributes to the land to which its people come weeping from all the corners of the earth "to write anew the psalms of David in your sand." Suddenly comes the illuminating personal line: at the solemn harvest of fulfillment "there stands perhaps a new Ruth, holding her gleanings in poverty, at the crossroads of her wanderings."

Whether she writes of the people or of the land she prays: "Lay on the field the weapons of vengeance/so that they grow still/For iron and corn are kin/In the womb of the earth." And she addresses herself to all peoples in a poem on words: "Peoples of the earth/ Do not destroy the universe of words/ With the knife of hate . . . and let no one mean 'death,' when he says 'life'/ and not mean 'blood,' when he says 'cradle.'"

The Germans have honored Nelly Sachs as the poet of reconciliation despite her concentration on the Holocaust as the central event of her life and of her time. Some critics have questioned her failure directly to accuse the Germans or to demand a reckoning, and are impatient with the metaphysical, pantheistic assuagement she offers. The only valid question in a literary appraisal concerns the effectiveness of her method—not the correctness of her position, which may be argued in a political forum.

She does not cast imprecations on her persecutors like the great poet who by the waters of Babylon cried: "Blessed be he who will take thy little ones and dash them against the rock." In its compactness, precision, and savage fury, "By the waters of Babylon" is perhaps the greatest single expression of a people's demand for retribution. Nor, like the contemporary Yiddish poet Jacob Glatstein, does she turn her back on a brutalized world to return to the moral sanctuary of the Jewish ghetto. She continues to seek for meaning in a universe that she refuses to view as hostile despite the smoke of the death chimneys drifting across its skies. And she finds religious answers. She dares to proclaim: "We dead of Israel say to you/ We reach one star farther/ Into our hidden God." Neither does she veil experience in metaphors and abstractions when she writes: "The crooked line of suffering/ Gropes fumblingly after the divinely lit geometry/ Of the universe." Such is her belief: the universe has its God-inspired plan to be discovered through pain.

Despite her failure to describe the minutiae of the atrocious, as Picasso does in the Guernica mural, or to take the greatest example, as Dante does in the Inferno, there is no evasion in her poems. In her fixation on the star of death she is not heedless of the stacked piles of dying flesh and blood. The suffering children in her "Lullaby" are real. And her human pain, her personal bereavement, find expression in a series of "Epitaphs Written on Air" for murdered friends and relatives with no gravestones to be inscribed. The delicate restraint of these poems indicates another aspect of her talent, almost classic in its grace.

Nelly Sachs escaped the physical experience of the concentration camp. If one can imagine that her frail body and extraordinary sensibility might have survived Ravensbruch or Auschwitz, perhaps her poetry would have had an earthier character. But that is a meaningless supposition. Her poetic way is through the illuminating image, not the catalogue of carnage. She is neither photographer nor chronicler of documentaries. And she is resolutely unstylish. She ventures to be hortatory, impassioned, exalted— all the adjectives smacking of eighteenth-century romantics rather than the trends of modern poetry. But such is her skill, the intellectual toughness of her imagery, and the tenacity of her personal vision, that while she may not be a "modernist" she is a voice of the twentieth century, not fashionably disenchanted, but daringly at home in the transformations of the world.

When one writes of Nelly Sachs it is difficult to ignore Gertrude Kolmar, her marvellously gifted contemporary who perished in a German extermination center. A more sensuous, vivid poet than Nelly Sachs, Gertrude Kolmar is the great German Jewish poet whose poems stop at the threshold of the death camp. She is a measure of what has been lost, just as Nelly Sachs is a measure of what has been saved by the accident of a Swedish novelist's intervention.

It was given to Nelly Sachs to become both elegist and celebrant—elegist of the martyrdom and celebrant of the martyred. That is what gives her work scope. Moreover, she poses in her fashion the question mark which hangs over our century, the mystery of its moral collapse. This question is her accusation, more far-reaching than the rhetoric of denunciation.

One of the guests who spoke in her honor at Frankfurt, Dr. Werner Weber, characterized her poetry in these terms: "In the preface to one of her poems, Nelly Sachs states that the number of Torah commandments corresponds to the number of bones in the human body, the number of prohibitions to the number of veins. 'Thus, the whole law covers the whole of the human body.' And we may also say that this law also covers the poetry of Nelly Sachs. And now, perhaps, we are in a position to understand how it was possible that a human being of this day and age, violated by the apocalyptical evil of this day and age, can find words which do not know hate, which do not propound the idea of revenge, which complain full of dignity, and refrain from indictment. They are words governed by the law. The Talmud gives a comparison of unforgettable strength here. It states that when the people received the commandments on Sinai, God held the mountain like a barrel with the open side pointing downward over the people. What does that mean? Leo Adler interpreted it in the following manner in one of his sermons: 'The spirit of Torah is like a utensil with the opening pointing towards the earth. That which remains in the vessel is the content of true religion, but that which falls out is transitory and mortal, drawn down by the earth, just as it derived from the earth.' Within the frame of such a religion, Nelly Sachs was able to bring the evil of the time into her poetry, without the word itself becoming evil in the process. Man-hunting extermination camps, trenches full of corpses—she has the strength to say all these things; and the unspeakable misery of the facts can do nothing to her, cannot pull her down. For her security is in the law."

This law extends to the universe whose divine geometry she seeks to ascertain. In her poetry Nelly Sachs has created her individual symbols—sand, stone, smoke, butterfly, star—for its discovery. The scenery of her world, despite its muted colors and shifting outlines, is as unmistakable as that of Chagall or Blake. Her flight, beginning with her actual flight from Germany, becomes a larger exploration in which exile is no longer possible. But it is no ecstatic euphoria. In the last poems she has published, "Glowing Riddles," are to be found the full heartbreak of solitude: "This night/ I walked along a dark sidestreet/ around the corner/ my shadow lay

Marie Syrkin

down in my arm/ this tired garment/ wanted to be carried/ and the color
Nothing addressed me:/ 'You are in the other world' " (*Jenseits*).

But her more characteristic mood is still that of the spiritual searcher for
new discoveries "shining in darkness, deep under the snow."

(March 1967)

THE FUN OF SELF-ABUSE

P *ortnoy's Complaint* has been hailed as wildly funny, brilliantly bawdy and as the ultimate in the depiction of Jewish neurosis. A *New York Times* review entitled, "A Portrait of the Artist as a Young Jew," sets the tone of the critical reception. Philip Roth, according to the accolade, has outdone himself in explaining the Jewish condition in the American gilded ghetto. Since I found the novel occasionally amusing, frequently nasty, and Jewish only in its unabashed collection of Jewish jokes as well as stereotypes, I comment on it because the book is being heralded as a scintillating interpretation of the modern Jew. The unwary reader might believe that he was about to purchase another *Herzog*. The reviewers have dusted off the same adjectives with which not so long ago they acclaimed Bellow's marvelously funny and subtle portrait of a Jewish intellectual. But let there be no illusions. The distance between Portnoy's lengthy dribble and Herzog's self-analysis is that between antic exhibitionism and hilarious self-revelation.

Not that *Portnoy's Complaint* isn't funny. Roth is a gifted mimic with a superb ear for the intonations of dialogue. He milks the comic possibilities of Portnoy, age 33, (the age of the proverbial sacrifice, incidentally), remembering mamma on the analyst's couch, to the full. The Jewish mother, possessive, protective, urging, *ess, ess, mein kind*, has been good for a laugh since the days of Milt Gross. Terrified of germs, dubious of hamburgers, repelled by lobsters, and concerned for all that goes into and out of her offspring, she has long been a veteran prop for the comic; an old reliable who has finally made it to *The Ed Sullivan Show*. Though Roth's detail is far brighter, it is the same routine. Even allowing for the obsessive quality of Portnoy's recollections—after all he is letting go on the analyst's couch—the Jewish mother as the explanation of all that ails him begins to pall despite the supportive role of the constipated daddy, her spouse. What keeps the extravaganza going is the author's virtuosity in heaping up corroborative detail like the "whole" can of Chicken of the Sea tunafish generously provided for the *shvarze's* lunch, or mamma at the ironing

board applauding her darling's rehearsal of his role as Christopher
Columbus for the third-grade school play. When so much is superficially
accurate, what could be false?

Yet despite the reassuring minutiae, authentic in their realism, the
caricature turns vicious. Sophie, the mother, is not even a plausible type, let
alone an individual. She is a synthetic production, an amalgam of clichés,
with touches from the Orthodox *shtetl* alternating with bits from middle-
class suburbia. Mamma veers from a fixation on Orthodox ritual, perhaps
true of her mother, to lack of decorum in her intimate behavior in the
presence of her son which would be a travesty of grandma. Roth manages
to endow the lady with both earlier taboos and later license, so offering the
worst of both worlds. A collection of gags, recognizable in the more
amiable creations of Sam Levenson or the blacker humor of Myron Cohen
or Bruce Friedman, Sophie, by virtue of Roth's transforming malice,
becomes a grotesque festooned with dirty toilet-paper, the whole held
together by a thick glue of elementary as well as alimentary Freud. Roth's
chief contribution to the Jewish mother routine is the picture of mamma
threatening her son with a long breadknife to make him eat. To make sure
that this maniacal bit is viewed as characteristic of the type rather than as
an individual aberration, the Jewish ladies who come to play mahjongg
applaud this technique in child care. Since symbolic castration is too dime-
a-dozen in the depiction of a mother-son relationship, Roth enlivens the
scene by putting a literal knife in mamma's loving hand.

The puny father whose throne-room is the toilet seat, Uncle Hymie who
treacherously destroys his son because the lad is in love with a *shikse*, the
whole bunch of singularly unattractive relatives and friends, form the
restrictive environment—a hollow shell of outward decencies—from
which the adolescent Portnoy seeks refuge in his solitary sport. For him too
the toilet is his sanctum.

Sophie with the breadknife, the father defecating, the son masturbating,
complete the trinity of the Jewish family as painted by Roth. These are the
revelatory attitudes perceived through the keyhole which is Roth's camera.
Nor does the author ever let the reader take refuge in the notion that this
particularly unappetizing family just happens to be Jewish. Roth is
relentless in driving home the thesis that the factors responsible for
Portnoy and his ways are peculiarly Jewish. When Portnoy cries out, "Dr.
Spielvogel, this is my life, my only life, and I'm living it in the middle of a
Jewish joke. I am the son in the Jewish joke," he is chanting Roth's theme
song.

Yet Roth's stunning verisimilitude in trivia too often disguises a failure in
truth. The failure does not consist in the satirist's legitimate exaggeration
of his characters. It is more fundamental, for under the cartoon of the

Jewish joke leers the anti-Jewish stereotype. Portnoy polluting his environment is one such. When he graduates to the fascination of female "apertures and openings," his penis never loses its Jewish consciousness. Like Julius Streicher's Satanic Jewboy lusting after Aryan maidens, Portnoy seeks blonde *shikses*: "What I'm saying, Doctor, is that I don't seem to stick my —— up these girls, as I stick it up their backgrounds; as though through —— I will discover America. Conquer America, maybe that's more like it" (my omissions).

He boasts of "another gentile heart broken by me," a heart belonging to a New England patrician. The scene in which the swarthy Jew gloats in the contrast between his body, "at least half of which is still undigested halvah and hot pastrami, from Newark, N.J.," and that of the Botticelli-like maiden, "all Republican refinement," from New Canaan, Connecticut, is a sample of the Roth technique. The halvah and hot pastrami, diverting touches, obscure the baleful stereotype which emerges from under the banter. The dark Jew seeking to defile the fair Nordic is standard stuff. While Goebbels would leave out the humanizing halvah, there is little to choose between his and Roth's interpretation of what animates Portnoy. In both views the Jewish male is not drawn to a particular girl who is gentile, but by a gentile "background" which he must violate sexually.

Nor do the male *goyim* escape Portnoy's malevolence. As a member of the staff of a House committee investigating television quiz scandals, he is able to expose an "ur-WASP." Portnoy rejoices: "Yes, I was one happy yiddel down there in Washington, a little Stern gang of my own, busily exploding Charlie's honor and integrity, while simultaneously becoming lover to that aristocratic Yankee beauty whose forebears arrived on these shores in the seventeenth century. Phenomenon known as Hating Your Goy And Eating One Too."

Strikingly this is one of Portnoy's few, if not only, expressions of joy. Is this "happy yiddel," destroyer and defiler, and cast from a familiar mold, the same chap as the guilt-ridden *shlemiehl* whose cavortings inspire a belly laugh? Let the real Portnoy stand up. Apparently Roth has not made up his mind as to his creation and uses him as the vehicle for his several furies. Or is Portnoy both the medieval demon-figure and the contemporary funny fellow obsessed by mamma? Since the character is too slight to bear such a burden, the reviewers have concentrated on the cartoon and ignored the stereotype.

However, even as a cartoon Portnoy is not convincing. An emancipated Jew does not invariably refer to gentile girls as *shikses*; his vocabulary and imagination are more flexible. Mamma might so describe her son's loves and deplore the choice, but the son would not constantly ape her terminology. Nor would he refer to himself as "one happy yiddel." A less-than-friendly observer might so describe him. Roth's ventriloquism, by which he pretends that the hostile voice of the author is that of the character, is a fundamental weakness in the conception. At one point, Portnoy screams, "Jew, Jew, Jew, Jew, Jew. . . . I happen also to be a human being."

H ere is the crux of the trouble. For all the broad caricature and abundant visual realism, Portnoy never becomes a human being. We are told that little Portnoy always had As in school, that he graduated first in his class in law school, that he is Assistant Commissioner of Human Opportunity in the City of New York, engaged in investigating racial discrimination in the building trades. Another one of those brilliant Jewish liberals; a "closet socialist" he calls himself. But no trace of any intellectual or social concerns is permitted to smudge the contour of Portnoy as sketched by Roth. His scholastic excellence and the post he occupies do not serve as amplifications of his personality; instead they are further Jewish demerits hung on him like tags: Jews may be smart students and be interested in social causes but beware what is within. Roth's scalpel exposes not only the dirt behind the respectable façade of the Jewish family, but the wretched creature cowering behind the much-touted Jewish intelligence and devotion to liberal causes. At any rate Portnoy never voices an idea or expresses a generous emotion. A total phony, presumably, and a rebuke to all those Jews who get high grades and profess to be socially involved.

Portnoy's Complaint is described by the author as "a disorder in which strongly felt ethical and altruistic impulses are perpetually warring with extreme sexual longings, often of a perverse nature." Without being a Dostoyevsky a writer setting himself the task of describing this affliction might have tried to suggest the psychological complexity of his supposed theme. "Acts of exhibitionism, voyeurism, fetishism, auto-eroticism and oral coitus" are plentiful, but where are the other symptoms? Where is a single scene in which the patient suffering from this conflict appears as an ethical or moral being? The reduction of Portnoy to a series of compulsive sexual practices dehumanizes him, and the author's chief way of redeeming his hero from anonymity is to label him "Jewish."

Some reviewers have been so undiscerning as to place Portnoy beside Herzog in the gallery of contemporary Jewish heroes of fiction. Nothing highlights Bellow's triumph and Roth's limitations as much as this juxtaposition. Herzog is Jewish, neurotic, lecherous, intellectual, with powerful family attachments. Though he can be "wildly funny," he is not a farcical cartoon; he is a complex human being with relationships with fellow human beings. Where Portnoy is involved only with "openings and apertures," each of Herzog's loves is a deliciously portrayed individual. Who can forget the Japanese girl, the aging Bohemian or the pseudo-intellectual wife? Whereas Portnoy, despite his high IQ appears to exist in a vacuum, Herzog's moral intensity is conveyed as vividly as his erotic misadventures. And where Bellow has rich humor, Roth must make do with farce. The comparison with Bellow helps to define Roth's quality as a writer—his strength as well as his weakness.

For the farce is often effective. In the concluding scene of the novel, Portnoy appears in Israel. First, he discovers that "here we're the WASPs," then, more originally, that in Israel he is impotent. A kibbutz lass, Naomi, "that hardy, red-headed, freckled, ideological hunk of girl" tells him off. After lecturing him on a just society, the common struggle, and a socially productive life, she enumerates his shortcomings: he is a self-deprecating, self-hating Jew, a typical product of the diaspora. She bids him go home; his obscene wooing fills her with loathing. "Tell me please why must you use that word all the time," she wants to know. Finally, to be rid of him, she kicks him "full force with that pioneer leg just below the heart," leaving the unchastened Portnoy writhing on the floor: "Ow, my heart! And in Israel! Where other Jews find refuge, sanctuary and peace, Portnoy now perishes! Where other Jews flourish, I now expire!"

The clash of clichés, wholesome *sabra* versus ghetto Jew, is funny. In a shrewd stroke Roth puts the obvious criticism of Portnoy into the mouth of a *sabra*, so disarming the opposition. Naomi's blunt description of Portnoy as a self-hating Jew takes the edge from anticipated accusations and enables the author to appear above the battle. To quote Roth against Roth would be a *reductio ad absurdum*. In a recent *Times* interview, Roth has already dismissed expected Saturday morning sermons on self-hating Jews: "After all, rabbis have got their indignation to stroke, just as I do."

In the same interview Roth tells us that he deliberately concluded his novel with Naomi's question, "Why must you use that word all the time?" He did so "to raise obscenity to the level of a subject." Roth explains that Portnoy's compulsive obscenity is his theme: "Why he must is what the book is all about." So it's not farce; it's serious. Roth appears to be in dead earnest about the deeper significance of his obscenity. Portnoy may urge light-heartedly, "Put the id back in Yid," but he is portentous for all that. In fact, the whole extravaganza must perhaps be taken without salt, kosher or *treif*.

First as to obscenity. As a subject it has been around a long while. Its literary practitioners, defenders, and opponents constitute a notable list. Some Greeks objected to Aristophanes; some Romans to *Trimalchio's Dinner*. Shakespeare had endured his expurgators, and so on through *Ulysses*. These are among the great examples. Of minor titillators, the host is too huge for mention. Certainly, in our present complacent climate, anyone can pick his favorite exponent of graphical sexual postures at any drug store with a shelf of paperbacks. Philip Roth is hardly breaking ground in this sphere. While adolescents may get excited, and adults bored or charmed according to their taste, in 1969 we are accustomed to the explicit in description. Nor is Roth's vocabulary daringly novel. Current best sellers as well as the placards of our college revolutionaries have completed the education of middle-aged squares who used to be embarrassed by four-letter words; now only the cops flinch. It is therefore hard to understand what new dimension Roth believes he has given to the public usage of obscenity.

At the same time a lack of originality is no guarantee against lack of taste. Judge Woolsey's classic decision exonerating *Ulysses* from the charge of obscenity includes the following comment: "In many places it seems to me disgusting, but although it contains, as I have mentioned above, many words usually considered dirty, I have not found anything that I consider to be dirt for dirt's sake." And *Lady Chatterly's Lover*, a novel which seems very innocent to contemporary readers, uses the famed Anglo-Saxon monosyllables romantically rather than obscenely.

Intense sexual passion circumstantially described is not obscene, as any number of literary works demonstrate. Obscenity is achieved when the writer shows not human beings animated by emotion but merely organs in friction. This contemptuous dismemberment of personality Roth aims for and achieves *ad nauseam*.

But what makes this a fresh theme? What has Roth raised to the level of a "subject"? The notion that obscenity is liberating and, as campus demonstrators never tire of stressing, exposes the hyprocrisy of the Establishment, is also hardly news. To give the old business an unexpected twist, we must get back to the Jews, the Jewish mamma, the Jewish taboos. By combining *kashrut*, the ultimate in ritual purification, with the most extreme in obscene speech and behavior, we get a situation calculated to startle, particularly when represented as cause and effect. Each urge repressed will surge expressed, we learn in the psycho-analytic primer. Roth's contribution is to exhibit the sty under the abstention from pork. Once the lid is lifted seething Portnoy is revealed. Yet Freud simplified and with a Jewish angle is only part of what the book is "all about."

We are still left with the "happy yiddel," merry only when destroying a male gentile or possessing a New England "background." And we still have to fit the Jewish getter of high grades, the professional idealist, whose only recorded action is cruelly malicious, into the Jewish mamma routine. Somewhere the comedy does not gell. Individual sentences are funny; Jewish turns of speech ring true. The externals of Jewish middle-class life—be it the cooking or the Anti-Defamation League—are neatly caught. Jewish mores, the hero's *tzores*, all in one jolly brew.

Or is it jolly? My objection is not primarily to the superficiality of the treatment since Roth is innocent of any effort to suggest the depth and intensity of the Jewish experience in the modern world. You can't judge Al Capp by Rembrandt. But there are all kinds of cartoons, some funny, some vicious. "Spring me from this role I play of the smothered son in the Jewish joke," cries Portnoy. Roth's hero need not worry. He also plays another part. Within the trappings of the old-hat Jewish joke lurks a savage anti-Jewish stereotype, even more old-hat, and not at all funny.

(April 1969)

VI.
THE
SOCIALIST
ROOTS
OF
ZIONISM

THE SOCIALIST ROOTS OF ZIONISM

In revolutionary movements the role of Jews is as paradoxical as in other aspects of the social scene. Whether it be Czarist Russia, or pre-Hitler Germany or the contemporary United States, Jews enjoy a prominence both relative and absolute. If you take the New Left in the United States as an example, a small minority of the Jewish population may be involved but this small minority represents a larger proportion than that contributed by other groups. Furthermore, positions of leadership within the movement, from the intellectual authority of Herbert Marcuse to the clownings of Abbie Hoffman or the mysteries of Marc Rudd's Weathermen, are often held by Jews. This involvement has endeared the Jews neither to the Right nor the Left. That the Right exploits the activities of Jewish radicals for the propagation of anti-Semitism is traditional. But that the non-Jewish radicals have often proven to be openly anti-Semitic and that Communist movements as in Eastern Europe have spewed out their zealous Jewish disciples has been perennially surprising to the Jews affected. Even more so when these Jewish Communists or radicals could truthfully claim that they had themselves subscribed to the anti-Jewish disparagements of their masters. All this is drearily familiar and each day brings renewed evidence of this state of affairs.

Yet familiarity, while it may lessen the shock, does not explain. Each thread in this tangle bears looking at. First, why are Jews over-represented in revolutionary movements? We know the usual answers. In countries of persecution a despised minority will naturally join the rebels hoping that the social revolution will bring the remedy for its sufferings. Such an explanation certainly held good for the oppressed Jews of Czarist Russia. But then how do we account for the preponderance of children of affluent middle-class and upper-middle-class Jews among the ranks of SDS and other extremist groups in the United States? Is there among Jews a higher measure of social idealism, the "heritage of the prophets," which predisposes them to take up the banner of universalist redemption through Socialism? It is a tempting thesis often propounded. But then what about Jewish over-representation at the other end of the spectrum? The peddler who becomes a successful merchant is as authentic a Jewish stereotype as "my son, the revolutionary," so lending plausibility to the classic dual charge of anti-Semites that Jews are at the same time capitalist exploiters *par excellence* and Communist subverters of the social order.

Without seeking to probe the reasons for Jewish ubiquity at the forefront of many fields of endeavor, it is apparent that in any country of free opportunity, untrammeled by quotas or artificial restrictions, Jews surge forward far in excess of their numbers in the general population. And they surge forward in a variety of occupations and preoccupations. Their revolutionary ardor is no more characteristic than their penchant for chess, physics, finance or violin-playing. If Fascist movements did not by their nature exclude Jews, no doubt we would have to deplore an excessive number of Jewish names among such gentry. The only safe generalization that can be made is that Jews are even-handedly attacked for their excessive presence regardless of the field in which this is displayed.

Zionist thinkers, Socialist and bourgeois, have made this Jewish "excess" a cardinal element in their ideology. The Socialist stressed the excess of middlemen. Herzl, on the other hand, was troubled by an over-production of individuals of "*mittlere intelligenz*" who in their frustration will become revolutionaries. He explains how a Jewish homeland will deflect these potential firebrands from social revolution because the Jewish return to Palestine will be led "by our middle-range intellectuals whom we have produced in such overabundance and whom persecution in their present places of residence is turning into proletarian socialists. No, I am much rather inclined to think that in the countries where the Jews are disliked— and even in other countries—we shall be given credit for rendering a patriotic service if we finally solve the burdensome old Jewish problem, if we divert the superfluous Jews, and thus remove the threat of a revolution which is supposed to start with the Jews and end heaven knows where." (Address at the Maccabean Club in London, July 6, 1896).

Herzl's obsession with the excessive number of these "middle-range intellects" obviously did not stem from a concern for their intellectual caliber. Rather he was troubled by a proliferation of middle-class professionals—doctors, lawyers, teachers, journalists—who, unable to participate freely in the societies of which they were a part, joined revolutionary movements. One of Herzl's favorite talking-points to the gentile world, an argument which he reiterated as often as his solution, is the promise that a Jewish homeland would siphon off restless Jewish spirits and, by normalizing the Jewish situation, reduce revolutionary tensions in European countries.

What would Herzl have made of the current scene in which Jewish intellectuals, middling or otherwise, with full access to the available opportunities in their countries, certainly not victims of discrimination in the sense that Herzl deplored, nevertheless join the rolls of Maoist, Stalinist or Trotskyite sects? Particularly puzzling to a prognosticator like Herzl would have been the current development in which the Jewish homeland instead of proving the hoped-for safety valve has instead become the particular target for concentrated attack by the so-called revolutionary forces.

Yet the anti-Jewish, let alone anti-Zionist, bias of the Socialist movement is a matter of record. That international Socialism, committed to a vision of universal brotherhood, should have dismissed Zionism as a form of petty nationalism and proscribed its teaching made sense within the terms of its ideology. However we may evaluate the conclusions of the old nationalist-internationalist debate, it had the integrity of a sustained position. The same cannot be said for doctrinaire Socialist hostility to Jews, be it Marx's notorious essay on the Jewish question, in which he states that the essence of Judaism is the profit motive, or Proudhon's view that the Jews are the spirit of finance, or the statements of such German Social Democrats as Franz Mehring, or Wilhelm Liebknecht.

In this script the Jew appears as exploiter and middleman, and anti-Semitism is explained in economic terms as the revolt of the oppressed. August Bebel refers to Jewish loan sharks; Karl Kautsky in a striking passage writes: "The decaying artisan fights against big industry and jobbers; the deeply-indebted farmer against the loan shark and trader, especially the cattle and grain dealer. All these groups attack the Jews who appear to them as the real exponents of money and commercial capitalism, and who furthermore are represented among the professions by numerous and efficient individuals." (*Neue Zeit*). Franz Mehring spoke of the Jewish usurer who drives the peasant from the land.

There is very little to choose between such estimates and those of the reactionary Czarist government which justified anti-Jewish pogroms by explaining that the Jews, an unproductive mercantile class, exploit the productive Christian peasantry. In fairness one must add that unlike the Russian *pogromchicks* the Socialist ideologists, German, French, Russian, were concerned with cause and effect in the terms of their analysis of capitalist society. They were not engaged in justifying anti-Semitism and they assumed that the Jewish question would be solved through the social revolution and Jewish assimilation. At the same time, by virtue of their analysis they could not bring themselves to condemn anti-Semitism in the straightforward fashion that might have been expected. On the contrary, their analysis inevitably led to the conviction that anti-Semitism was a useful stage in the development of revolutionary consciousness.

A resolution of the Social Democratic Party formulated by Bebel declared that "The Social Democratic Party fights anti-Semitism as a movement which is directed against the natural development of society but which, *in spite of its reactionary character, and against its will, is bound to become revolutionary*" (Cologne Conference, 1893) [my emphasis].

A Jewish Austrian Socialist, Heinrich Braun, at the same time, wrote even more explicitly: "The socio-political job which anti-Semitism is doing today in overcoming the century-old idiocy of the peasants; in creating passionate commotion in this most indolent stratum of the population; in propagandizing the small artisans, the petty officialdom, and other groups not easily accessible to the Social Democracy—this job can, in the perspective of a revolutionary development of society, hardly be over-estimated." And another scribe writing in *Vorwarts* hailed anti-Semitism as *"cultural manure for socialism in the truest sense of the word"* (June 26, 1893) [my emphasis].

These appraisals appeared after Russian pogroms a decade earlier had alerted the world to the full possibilities of modern anti-Semitism. The extremist *Narodnaya Volya*—the party to which the young Trotsky and Lenin had been attracted—viewed pogroms as an educational instrument, a prologue to revolution. In 1881, during the pogroms, the Executive Committee of the *Narodnaya Volya* went so far as to issue an appeal urging the people to march against the Jews, the landlords, and the Czar: "Arise, workers, avenge yourselves on the landlords, plunder the Jews, and slay the officials." Though the appeal was repudiated by soberer members of the Executive the theoretical view of the pedagogic utility of pogroms was maintained. While the German ideologues did not formulate the uses of anti-Semitism with the untrammeled ferocity of the Russian revolutionaries, their intellectual positions are not too far apart.

I refrain from quoting vicious, anti-Semitic utterances of French Socialist ideologues (Proudhon, Fourier, etc.) which may be interpreted as expressions of personal prejudice from which Socialists, like other men, are not exempt. More significant are the theoretical conclusions cited no matter how unconsciously motivated by irrational bias. These conclusions could not fail to be bitterly disheartening to self-respecting Jewish Socialists or liberals. *Narodnaya Volya's* incitement to pogroms disenchanted many Russian Jews, among them Pinsker and Smolenskin. They were not the first.

Twenty years earlier, in Germany, Moses Hess had already found himself at odds with Socialist comrades in regard to the Jewish question. When Moses Hess died in Paris in 1875, representatives of the European proletariat gathered round his grave to honor him as the "father of German Communism." No Zionist district sent a delegate to hail Hess as the "father" or at least "grandfather" of modern political Zionism though he had anticipated political Zionism by some 25 years.

How significant a figure Hess was in the Socialist movement of his time can be judged from the fact that the *Communist Manifesto* devoted several valuable pages to excoriating the theories of Hess, who had converted Engels to Communism and had influenced Marx. The amount of vitriol he rated in the great Communist classic is a good indication of his importance. His own generation viewed him primarily as a Socialist theoretician and leader, while his pioneer formulation of Jewish nationalism was hardly noticed by his contemporaries. Time, however, has reversed his role. Only students of the history of Socialism know the name of Moses Hess. In the history of Jewish nationalism the opposite has been true. The reputation and influence of Moses Hess has kept pace with the development of Zionism. His title to fame is two-fold. He was one of the earliest proponents of political Zionism—his *Rome and Jerusalem* appeared in 1862; Herzl's *Judenstadt* in 1895. Still more important, he was the first Jewish Socialist to view Jewish nationalism not as an expression of bourgeois reaction but as a means of revolutionary fulfillment.

Hess himself states that his interest in nationalism finally took form due to his scientific studies of race—a study to which he devoted himself after his exile to Paris. This interest was strengthened by modern national movements such as the Italian war of liberation. He became convinced of "the ultimate disappearance of any particular race dominance and the necessary regeneration of all oppressed peoples." Naturally enough the problem of the Jewish people began to absorb his chief intellectual energy. His conclusions appeared in *Rome and Jerusalem*.

Rome and Jerusalem is a curious work. Its great virtue is the daring and imagination, as well as shrewd political vision, with which it approaches the Jewish question. At the same time it is a strange combination of philosophical theorizing, science, quaint sentiment and rhapsodic enthusiasm. It is impossible to estimate the book's true worth unless one understands its background, and the forces against which it was directed.

Hess's first problem as a Socialist was to demonstrate that nationalism could be a progressive and not a reactionary force, that true internationalism meant not a standardized cosmopolitanism but an opportunity for the free and harmonious development of the races and nations which constitute the human family. He was the first Socialist of his day to attempt a reconciliation of nationalism with the theory of Communism. His second problem, after demonstrating that the Jews were a nation whose spirit was expressed in Judaism and not merely a religious persuasion, was to evaluate the special racial genius of the Jewish people.

According to Hess, dubbed "Communist Rabbi Moses" by his associates, Socialism was not a question of bread alone, but of moral values, the dignity of the human spirit. Communism was the law of love applied to social life. The "true Socialists" protested against those who believed Communism was solely the concern of the proletariat and against those who over-emphasized the force of economic interests. For the class struggle they substituted an humanitarian appeal to culture, social justice—to ideal rather than material motives. The struggle for human freedom and social security must be waged not in the name of the proletariat, but in the name of humanity.

One can readily see how this idealistic "true Socialism" won from Marx the kindly designation (*Communist Manifesto*) of "speculative cobwebs, embroidered with flowers of rhetoric, steeped in the dew of sickly sentiment" because it was mistakenly concerned with Truth and Man in general, rather than with the proletariat. Much later, in *Rome and Jerusalem* Hess was to make the heretical, un-Marxian statement that the race struggle, rather than the class struggle, was primary.

What finally caused Hess, caught in the vortex of the "international Socialism" of his time, to develop a sense of Jewish nationalism? In 1840, the ritual murder case of Damascus aroused Jewry somewhat as the Kishineff pogroms, or the Dreyfus case, or the Nazi persecutions did subsequently.

Moses Hess was stirred to a sudden Jewish consciousness. Writing in *Rome and Jerusalem* 25 years later, he relates, "Then it dawned upon me for the first time, in the midst of my socialist activities that I belong to my unfortunate, slandered, despised and dispersed people. And already, then, though I was greatly estranged from Judaism, I wanted to express my Jewish patriotic sentiment in a cry of anguish but it was unfortunately immediately stifled in my heart by a greater pain which the suffering of the European proletariat evoked in me." It is interesting to compare this reaction with the outburst of the schoolboy Lassalle who recorded in his diary on May 21, 1840: "A people which endures this, is terrible. It should avenge or suffer this treatment . . . Cowardly people, you deserve no better fate . . . you do not know how to die, to destroy, you do not know just vengeance—to perish with your foe—You are born to be slaves."

Nevertheless, "the suffering of the European proletariat" engaged the undivided attention of Lassalle until his death, and of Hess until 1862, when he published *Rome and Jerusalem*. Not that Hess's Jewish consciousness could remain wholly dormant. There were the innumerable occasions when his Socialist comrades, even Marx, referred contemptuously to that "Jew" Hess. There was the letter from Nicholas Becker, author of "They shall not possess it, the free German Rhine." In an outburst of patriotic emotion, Hess had sent a musical composition to the German poet, only to receive a chilly, formal reply with "You are a Jew" written in a disguised script, on the back. There was the constant pressure of German anti-Semitism, directed with equal virulence against the loyal veterans of the "War of Liberation," the "enlightened" Jews who strove to become "wholly Germanized" or the Orthodox observers of the faith.

Against Hess's advocacy of nationalism were arrayed the "class struggle" zealots and the brotherhood-of-man humanitarians. One must remember this in order to realize how essentially original and revolutionary were many of his apparent commonplaces. The historic background becomes still more important for an adequate comprehension of his hyper-fervid insistence on the exalted character of Judaism and the sanctity of its national mission. The leading German intellectuals of his day had evaluated Judaism contemptuously. The philosopher Feuerbach had dubbed Judaism as "the religion of egoism . . . The Jew is indifferent to everything which is not directly related to his own welfare." Bruno Bauer, in an exposition which won the praise of Marx, had expounded the doctrine that the essence of Judaism was animal cunning, and that Jews had always opposed historical progress. Marx himself had diagnosed Judaism as an anti-social element whose secular cult was buying and selling, and whose secular God was money.

Such were the reasoned verdicts not of ignorant fanatics, but of the liberal intellects of the period—men whose contributions to philosophy and sociology had influenced Hess profoundly. In the light of this absolute condemnation, one begins to understand the passion of Hess's praise. What would otherwise appear as uncritical rhetoric becomes plausible when viewed as a challenge and vindication.

Hess's conception of the individual worth of every race develops naturally not only from his ethnological studies, but from his general philosophy of history. History, as well as natural science, has exact laws, a plan according to which it develops. We can determine the principles governing the phenomena of the organic world experimentally, but we can only infer the laws governing the social progress of man intuitively, because humanity, as a social organism, is still in the process of growth. Here Hess introduces his curious term "the Sabbath of History." Nature, the organic world, has had its Sabbath. The completed creation of the natural world was celebrated symbolically by the "natural Sabbath." After seeing that it was good, God rested on the seventh day. But history, the social world of man, has yet to celebrate its Sabbath. Man has yet to see that his way of life is good. "The historical Sabbath will begin only after the complete development of social life, after the creation of a harmonious social organization in which production and consumption will be in a state of equilibrium."

And who is to usher in the final Messianic epoch when man's spiritual and ethical development will reach completion? Hess has no doubts about that. "The special field of operation of the Jewish genius is the social sphere." Judaism is not "anti-social." On the contrary "the national-humanitarian essence of the Jewish historical religion is the germ out of which future social creation will spring." The Jewish mission, which began with great religious creation, will not end until humanity has reached its highest form of social development. Judaism is not concerned with the salvation of the individual. It is concerned with the salvation of mankind. Judaism links the individual, the family, the nation, all humanity, into an integrated whole whose noblest expression will be found in "the coming regenerated state of human society." The special calling of the Jew is to convey to the world "revelations affecting the social life-sphere," an elegant way of formulating the familiar charge "All Jews are Reds."

Hess's particular view of the Jewish mission led him directly to Zionism. National regeneration must precede social redemption. In order to participate adequately in the revolutionary struggles of humanity, the Jewish people must have its own fatherland. Regenerated on its own soil, the Jewish people will be able to fulfill the mission appointed it by history—to usher in a new social order.

When the main threads of Hess's thought are disentangled from the sentimentality and enthusiasms which frequently obscure it—his almost maudlin digressions on the noble revolutionary French people, spiritual kin of the Jews, are a case in point—one finds that he has made several original contributions toward the definition of Jewish nationalism.

His insistence on a Jewish nation at a time when it was customary to speak of the Jewish faith; his belief that race formed social institutions (therein he differed from Marx); his specific evaluation of a revolutionary character of the Jewish people; his advocacy of a Jewish state in Palestine based on productive labor, remain vital and stimulating conceptions, even if one discounts his Sabbath of History or his high-flown view of the exalted mission of Jewry.

The ideas of "Queer Duck" Hess had little practical influence in his time. Over 35 years were to elapse before Jewish Socialist thinkers were again to assert the revolutionary character of Zionism as a movement of national and social redemption. When Nachman Syrkin began to formulate the synthesis between Socialism and Zionism at the close of the last century he was less concerned with defending the nature of the Jewish psyche against Socialist detractors than with opposing the traditional notion that Socialism and nationalism, particularly Jewish nationalism, were incompatible. In 1898, a year after the publication of Herzl's *Judenstadt*, he writes in *The Socialist Jewish State* that Socialism is "the opposite of pseudo-internationalism" and declares that "each national emancipation movement finds its moral support in socialist ethics and socialist concepts of freedom." And he comments bitterly that "The bearers of the idea of national emancipation among all oppressed nations are generally the *intelligentsia*, the socialists and the proletariat. Only in the case of the Jews, among whom everything is topsy-turvy, have the socialists inherited assimilation from the bourgeoisie and made it their spiritual heritage."

According to Syrkin, the Jewish proletariat is consciously and unconsciously the bearer of a "specific Jewish protest." As the great protest movement against Jewish suffering, Socialism will become the possession of all Jews since every class of Jewry, proletariat, bourgeoisie and *intelligentsia* suffer as Jews. Therefore Socialism is "the movement towards which Jews are driven by political instinct and human dignity. But they must accept socialism as Jews freeing it from assimilationist sham."

The next step is, of course, Zionism but "the Jewish state can only come about if it is socialist; only by fusing with socialism can Zionism become the ideal of the whole Jewish people." Because the Jews must establish a homeland they will be the first to realize the Socialist vision. "What is utopian for others is a necessity for the Jews." In the process the Jews will become "the most revolutionary of peoples."

The difference between such a conception of Zionism and that of Herzl, who hoped that Zionism would reduce revolutionary unrest, is fundamental. Syrkin's attacks on bourgeois Zionism attest to the cleavage. Reviewing the course of the movement Syrkin himself offered a resumé of the arguments he presented when he was fighting for his new idea:

> *The Jewish proletarian masses constantly under the pressure of Jewish political and economic need and migration from land to land are the natural fulfillers of the Zionist idea; they are driven to Zionism by necessity. Their historic redemption depends on the establishment of a free Jewish land of labor and socialism. The acquisition of civil rights by the Jews of Eastern Europe and emigration to America result in the transformation of the Jewish working class into a middle class. In the Diaspora a productive working class is created only under the pressure of necessity; the productive class changes into a non-productive one as soon as this pressure is released. Zionism is therefore the complement and requisite of Jewish socialism, and becomes the ideology of the conscious Jewish socialist. Similarly, assimilation becomes the concern of the Jewish bourgeoisie, and the ideology of Jewish defeatists, escapists and traitors.*
>
> *The Zionism of the Jewish masses is more than the colonization projects of Hoveve Zion with its bourgeois limitations; it is more than the longing for a "spiritual center" which is the national ideology of the* maskil; *it is more than the philanthropic Zionism of the West Europeans. The Zionism of the Jewish masses is social, and bound up with the ideal of a new society.*

Ber Borochov, a younger contemporary of Syrkin, provided the Marxist underpinnings for Syrkin's Utopian Socialist Zionism. Using the terminology of dialectical materialism and stressing historic determinism

349

rather than Syrkin's voluntarism, Borochov stiffened the texture of the Socialist Zionist idea and gave it an economic-sociological base of particular appeal to contemporary Jewish youth with both radical and nationalist leanings. Borochov's striking concept of the *"stychischer prozess"* (an almost untranslatable term meaning an inevitable dynamic force) with its vision of hosts of Jews driven from their countries by implacable economic and social forces culminates in the prophecy: "The land of spontaneous concentrated Jewish immigration will be Palestine."

The *halutzim* of the second and third *aliyah* were more likely to be disciples of the humanitarian Socialism of Syrkin than of Borochov's Marxism, not to mention the assorted Tolstoyans or other Utopian devotees of communal living in their midst; however Borochov's apocalyptic vision of an inevitable world drama involving Jewish destiny was to be enacted during the Nazi period when Jews of all classes and political persuasions were desperately trying to enter Palestine. But the concept was to prove its validity not only in a period of apocalyptic catastrophe. It should also be noted that by the time Borochov was composing "Our Platform" from which I have quoted, he had added the factor of *will* to his determinism. Spontaneous Jewish immigration would have to be directed and organized "by the conscious Jewish proletariat." This would ensure "proletarian Zionism" the only possible road to the realization of Zionism.

For *bona fide* Jewish revolutionaries like Rosa Luxemburg and Leon Trotsky, Socialist Zionism, regardless of the Marxist trimmings, was another bourgeois deviation no more palatable than the Bund. Rosa Luxemburg, who in one of her most moving letters from prison mourned the pain of the water buffaloes hauling wagons in the prison courtyard, rejected the notion of any special interest in Jewish suffering with such vehemence that one is tempted to suspect that of all suffering to which she responded with such extraordinary passion and sensibility, she found Jewish suffering the least painful. And everyone knows Trotsky's early disclaimer of any narrow Jewish concern which might deflect him from the world revolution. Rosa Luxemburg was murdered before the Nazi Final Solution. Trotsky, who was not killed until 1940, was compelled to ponder on "special Jewish sorrows" during his exile. In an interview with Jewish correspondents in Mexico in January 1937, he admitted that his original prognosis that the Jewish question would be solved through assimilation and the social revolution had not been confirmed. While still maintaining his negative view of Zionism, he now allowed for the possibility of national territorial groupings under Socialism: "The dispersed Jews who would want to be reassembled in the same community will find a sufficiently extensive and rich spot under the sun. The same possibility will be opened for the Arabs as for all other scattered nations. *National topography will become part of the planned economy.*"

And in an article written in February 1937, he wrote, "The Jewish question never occupied the center of my attention, but that does not mean that I have the right to be blind to the Jewish problem which exists and demands solution." He went on to suggest: "Are we not correct in saying that a world socialist federation would have to make possible the creation of a *Biro-bidjan* for those Jews who wish to have their own autonomous republic as the arena of their culture? It may be presumed that a social democracy will not resort to compulsory assimilation." Though he views Palestine as a "tragic mirage" and the actual Soviet *Biro-bidjan* as a "bureaucratic farce" he no longer excludes a territorial solution. (*Termidor and Anti-Semitism*, New International, February-May 1941) In 1940 he cries out in words reminiscent of Borochov: "Today decaying capitalist society is striving to squeeze the Jewish people from all its pores: seventeen million individuals out of the two billion populating the globe, that is less than one per cent, can no longer find a place on our planet." (*Manifesto of the Energy Conference of the Fourth International*, Socialist Appeal, June 29, 1940). It is pointless to speculate on how Trotsky would have envisaged the Jewish question, which had begun insistently to trouble him, had he escaped the assassin's bludgeon and beheld what was to come in Europe and Palestine.

For a brief moment the Holocaust of European Jewry appeared to shake the anti-Zionist front of doctrinaire Jewish Marxists—Isaac Deutscher, for instance. And in 1967, when Israel appeared to be on the verge of destruction, some misgivings were expressed by Herbert Marcuse and others. Today the picture has again changed. The New Left, the Third World champions, the black militants, are vociferously anti-Israel and anti-Semitic. Whether they follow the Russian or Chinese line, the result is the same. And many Jewish radicals accept the furious anti-Semitism of their comrades as unblinkingly as in the nineteenth century their predecessors accepted the anti-Jewish onslaughts of revolutionary spokesmen. Perhaps they even subscribe to it. Certainly, they appear to find no difficulty in extending a hand of fraternal comprehension to exponents of Jewish genocide. I refer not merely to sympathizers of El Fatah and the like whose programs may be explained in the framework of the Arab-Israeli conflict but to such figures as the black militant leader Imamu Baraka, otherwise known as the poet LeRoi Jones. Nowhere have I noted a word of rebuke by Noam Chomsky or I.F. Stone or Herbert Marcuse or any other prominent Jewish Leftist for LeRoi Jones's open call for a pogrom in a style more reminiscent of Streicher than even of *Narodnaya Volya*. Let me quote as a sample from a poem—the literary merit is irrelevant—which appears in a collection of Jones's recently published verse: "Selling fried potatoes and people, the little arty bastards talking arithmetic they sucked from the arab's head. Suck you pricks. The best is yet to come. On how we beat you and killed you and tied you up. And marked this specimen 'Dangerous

Germ Culture.' And put you back in a cold box."

The full litany of the crudest anti-Semitism is here contained. There is no point in multiplying the examples. What is significant here is that this is no idiosyncratic utterance by a discredited rabble-rouser but the considered statement of a black spokesman. This call for a pogrom, instead of being repudiated by its author since its original publication, has been reprinted by him. And neither have the spokesmen of the Left repudiated Jones.

The pattern is now familiar. Jews wholeheartedly enter revolutionary movements. At a given stage, the revolution, like capitalism at a given stage of its development, spews them out. Sometimes, not always, Jews may maintain a shaky foothold at the price not only of assimilation but of total identification with the anti-Jewish campaigns. Whether Jews are persecuted as rootless cosmopolitans or as chauvinistic Zionists such has been the pattern in Czechoslovakia at the Prague trials, in Soviet Russia and in Poland, whose exiled Jewish Communists were disconsolately sitting in Denmark to prove that they were wrongly charged with Zionism. In the United States the heavily Jewish Left is in no position to cast out a large proportion of its members. Nevertheless, like its forebears of the *Narodnaya Volya*, it makes peace with black anti-Semitism as a form of revolutionary ferment, and the Negro civil rights movement has proclaimed its emancipation not only from white supporters in general but particularly from Jewish supporters who once flocked to the cause.

Where does all this leave the Socialist Zionist thesis? There is a disheartening sense of *déjà vu* in the whole scene with one significant difference. In the nineties Syrkin's chief struggle was with the internationalists. Today national emancipation movements, no matter how minuscule or newly hatched, are idealogically respectable. Once the Left or champions of the Third World affix the label of "liberation" movement, any nationalism is kosher. The diaspora Socialist Zionist or the Israeli *Mapainik* or *Mapamnik* who, seeking admission to this conclave, points to Israel's unique social achievements in the kibbutz, *Histadrut* and political democracy and cries "me too" finds his rejection hard to swallow. Logically, his indignation is justified. But the Left is not convinced on the intellectual plane, just as in the sphere of the bloodily irrational there can be no meeting ground with the pseudo-revolutionary cabal of Arabs, Japanese, Germans and blacks who, as in the Lydda massacre, focus on Israel as the object of their hate much as the Nazis focused on the Jews.

In America something of Borochov's cumbersome "*stychischer prozess*" seems to be gathering steam. The minuscule Jewish minority was able to flourish in the United States as long as the democratic consensus in regard to the rights of the individual held good. How spectacularly Jews advanced in a liberal democracy which allowed the individual to progress in accordance with his zeal and ability we know. Today, as the democratic consensus is being shaken or reinterpreted to substitute ethnic group rights for individual rights, Jews are obviously threatened. It is not primarily a question of a Jewish landlord or a small Jewish merchant in an urban ghetto. More ominous is the displacement of Jewish teachers, Jewish doctors, Jewish civil servants, and Jewish students from the institutions to which they won admission honorably in open competition. The attack on the merit system, the sole safeguard of equal opportunity in a democracy, is a crucial stage in the displacement of Jews. Though it has become fashionable for liberals to sneer at "meritocracy" as if there were something ethically disreputable in successfully meeting objective qualifications for given posts, most Jews are not likely to regard ethnic quotas as a form of social equity. Rather they will insistently cling to the belief that quotas are a return to blatant racial and religious discrimination, all too reminiscent of Czarist Russia.

Jews became teachers in New York or won entrance into American universities in far larger numbers than their proportion of the population only when the fight against such discrimination appeared to be won and Jews were judged by their standing on civil service lists or college board examinations. This golden day seems to be drawing to a close. Hardly a week passes in which some Jewish organization is not protesting the violation of what were basic tenets of American democracy. It seems to be a losing battle not only because of growing social pressures but because too many are no longer convinced of the justice of what they once upheld. Whereas not too long ago liberals and radicals opposed quotas as reactionary, today some fervidly champion representation in the social structure according to race or ethnic origin.

The fact that American *aliyah* to Israel, small as it is, increased dramatically in the last few years is probably not unrelated to the uneasy sense of dislocation which the American Jew is beginning to feel. He is being challenged on the ground he thought most firm in the United States— his very virtues—intelligence and industry. Again he hears that there are too many Jewish doctors, scientists, university professors, literary critics, college students. Even schools such as the Bronx High School of Science, which chooses its students by impartial entrance examinations, is under attack because the students do not reflect the correct urban racial mix. There are too many Jews and too few blacks and Puerto Ricans. Even our Jerry Rubins and Abbie Hoffmans who profess their allegiance to El Fatah have been rejected as "Zionists" by the Black Panthers, though they earned that particular designation as little as the Polish Jewish Communists. The social upheaval in the United States is already claiming Jewish victims and initially not among entrepreneurs but among impeccable "productive" members of society.

Supposing then that the Socialist Zionist analysis is correct in its assumption that economic, political and social pressures in the diaspora will combine to dislocate Jews even in the liberal democracies. Such dislocation need not be the result of gross anti-Semitism or Nazi-style persecution. On the contrary, it may take place in the guise of a higher social morality to which many Jews themselves energetically subscribe. As the status of Jews changes, what should be a revolutionary response on the part of the Jews affected? They can with high-minded or masochistic enthusiasm—depending on your evaluation—(1) accede in the demolition of the positions they achieved, or (2) they can dig in and fight the erosion of their legitimate rights by the means available to them under the political system of the country in which they live, or (3) they can emigrate to Israel. In Soviet Russia the last is being attempted by some and few will question the revolutionary nature of such action both from the Jewish and Russian point of view.

In the United States the American Jewish community is embracing the second alternative. It rejects current reinterpretations of democracy in which the rights of ethnic blocs supercede those of the individual citizen. At present Jews must conduct this struggle handicapped by the knowledge that their former liberal allies now accuse them of impeding the triumph of the true democratic ideal. In theory America still reverences the old democratic pieties; in practice the good society is being cast in a contrary mold whose shape liberals increasingly accept and radicals applaud.

Paradoxically this means that whenever the abilities of individual Jews lead to group disabilities, Jews in the diaspora must protest the new dogmas. They must oppose the notion that progress demands that American democracy be fragmented into competing ethnic blocs, each of which stakes out its own pad. And despite the anti-democratic position of the Left on this question Jews must not surrender their faith in a humane, democratic Socialism despite the mockery such concepts now evoke.

At the same time the most revolutionary segment of the Jewish community will emigrate to Israel. Such an act is revolutionary in its impact whether it be the product of choice or of a "*stychic*" drive, and regardless of the political attitudes of the individual concerned. By virtue of his move, whether he likes it or not, the immigrant is involved in a radical personal and national transformation. This is true not only of the Labor Zionist who advocates an advanced social program but of the Orthodox zealot, the political Rightist, the backward and the advanced. Willy-nilly each is thrown into a retort which breaks up and recomposes social attitudes.

By its very being the Jewish state plays a revolutionary role. Its emergence has galvanized an inert Middle East not only through the enmities it has aroused but through the emulation it has invited. To survive, Israel has from the outset been compelled to initiate daring social, economic and ecological experiments and to design radical blueprints for integrating diverse elements into a would-be egalitarian society. Needless to say, Israel's failures are as manifest, if not as numerous, as its successes. Yet, whatever the failures, Jews for the first time in centuries can take part in hammering out the contours of their social vision without being stigmatized as treasonable dissidents, or Jewish capitalists, or peripheral aliens even by their ideological fellows. They may be dissidents or they may be capitalists but they are not aliens, and their shortcomings will not be viewed as the expression of the Jewish spirit. This great liberation is bound to free suppressed energy. The problems of Israel are at once so intimate and so immense that none of its citizens can escape their impact. Whatever his inclinations, each citizen must face and grapple with the perplexities which bristle at every turn. If you like large definitions you may call these the class struggle, the race struggle, the social struggle, or whatever; if you incline to humbler terminology, they are the problem of a society in the making.

At a recent Zionist Congress I listened to a group of self-styled "radical" students fulminating against the Jewish establishments of the countries from which they came—the United States and England—and to which they were returning. Naturally they did not spare the "establishment" in Israel from which they demanded a larger allocation of money. A weather-beaten kibbutznik listened to them for a while; then he shrugged his shoulders and said to the young people making free with the rhetoric of revolution: "You know, the most revolutionary thing you could do would be to go on *aliyah*."

Judging from the evidence, we may conclude that at some point revolutionary movements in the diaspora, no less than capitalist regimes, reject the Jewish minority. Sometimes the Jew may remain at the price of abject self-denial or at best, painless assimilation. For many diaspora Jews involvement in radical movements has been a deliberate escape from an oppressive Jewish identity, the modern equivalent of a trip to the baptismal font. Since assimilation may be successful for individuals, but not for the mass, the most forthright involvement in the social and national struggle will have to take place in the Jewish state. It is this opportunity that constitutes its essentially revolutionary nature, and the revolutionary nature of Zionism.

CONCLUSION:
ZIONISM TODAY

In one of the entries in his *Diaries* Herzl comments on what he calls the "egg dance" of his difficulties in launching the Zionist movement. He wryly enumerates the various "eggs" he must delicately juggle: the Orthodox Jews; the modernists; the Austrian super-patriots; the Christian sects; governments such as Turkey and Russia; envy and internal friction within the Zionist movement. Today read "Leftists" for what Herzl calls "modernists," substitute 100 percent Americanism for his "Austrian patriotism," replace Turkey but not Russia in the Great Power game, and the list, drawn up over 70 years ago, has a disturbingly contemporary ring. Those wrestling with the problems of governing an actual Jewish state would recognize each item with the immediacy of experience, and they would have to make substantial additions to Herzl's semi-humorous count.

The first of these would be Arab opposition—an egg not yet hatched at the time when Herzl began to dream. Herzl did not stupidly or callously ignore the existence of a native population, as Arab propagandists like to charge. On the contrary, he drew an extravagant picture of happy coexistence of Arab and Jew in his Utopian fantasy, *Altneuland*. Like other Zionist thinkers, he assumed that the benefits resulting from the transformation of Palestine's arid wastes through Jewish labor and settlement would ensure Arab friendship and cooperation. This conclusion seemed to him so eminently reasonable as to be inevitable. With a romantic's faith in the triumph of good sense and good will he anticipated no other outcome. Early Zionism continued to share both his hope and his error.

But perhaps Herzl's greatest mistake was in assuming that the creation of a Jewish state would wholly solve the Jewish problem. In speech after speech, article after article, throughout his brief, intense career, he predicted the disappearance of anti-Semitism once host countries were relieved of the Jewish "irritant" in their midst through the migration of impoverished Jewish masses to a land of their own. An independent Jewish state would meet both the need of the suffering Jews and disarm the prejudices of the non-Jews. He was obsessed with the logic of his vision.

A crucial part of Herzl's prognosis came to pass in larger measure than even he anticipated. Not even Herzl's active imagination could have foreseen the extremity of the Jewish condition during the Hitler decade, or the extent to which Israel served to rescue the survivors of the Holocaust. The category of "survivors" would have to include not only those who had escaped physical extermination but Jews throughout the world, including American Jews, for whom the massacre of the six million would have been unendurably traumatic if not for the rise of Israel. The existence of a flourishing Jewish state gave Jews who had either personally endured or witnessed the Hitler era the psychic stamina to continue as a people. But the expectation held by Zionist theoreticians, from Moses Hess to Pinsker to Herzl, that a Jewish state would dispose of anti-Semitism proved illusory. Anti-Semites merely changed their vocabulary and direction. Zionism and Israel became a convenient focus for the hatred formerly spent on the wandering Jew.

This development has been one of the most painful in the history of Zionism. From the outset of the pioneer venture danger and physical hardship were taken for granted, in fact were cause for pride. Moral approbation was assumed; and it was forthcoming. The young zealots who drained marshes before and after the Balfour Declaration may have been dismissed as naive sectarians, foolhardy and probably foolish, but they were admired. By the time Israel was established in the face of Arab attack enthusiasm for the valiant young state was still dominant. In the rhetoric of the time, an historic wrong had been righted and justice was being served. Though Arab propaganda campaigns began to erode this sympathy, public opinion was strongly with Israel. Russia's switch from the ranks of Israel's supporters to that of her foes was correctly interpreted as an exercise in *Realpolitik* in the thrust for Soviet penetration of the Middle East. In 1967 when Israel, abandoned by a regretful President Johnson and other democracies that had guaranteed her security, emerged victorious over the combined Arab armies in a dazzling coup, hurrahs for the small country that had withstood such odds single-handedly were loud and generous. Zionism was still in good odor.

But the climate was to change. New Arab strategy in which agitation for Arab refugees gave way to the irredentist claims of a displaced Palestinian people provided an ideological vocabulary for the Left and a potent slogan for undermining the very basis of Zionism. Elsewhere I have discussed how shrewdly the new tactic was exploited. Not unexpectedly many a good friend became honestly troubled by complexities he had not foreseen, and by the emergence of a militant Israel no longer to be automatically regarded as more sinned against than sinning.

Obviously Zionism could not be insulated from the dynamic of contemporary events. The alliance of the Third World with the Communist and Arab blocs was a bitter disappointment to a country that had fashioned close bonds with emerging African states. In 1957, as Israel was approaching its tenth anniversary, Foreign Minister Golda Meir could express gratitude to the General Assembly of the United Nations for the understanding and help of its member states: "Many of these countries are without direct interest in our area. But their appreciation of the moral, social, historic and religious factors involved led them to profoundly held convictions which they have maintained with staunchness and courage . . . It is a satisfaction and a joy that with many of the new countries that have joined the United Nations in the meantime we are linked in bonds of friendship, of understanding and of mutual aid."

Today these words have a sardonic ring. The UN, which hailed a gun-toting Arafat on its rostrum and passed a resolution equating Zionism with racism, produces an instant majority for any measure sponsored by the Arab-Soviet combine and its adherents. Abstract justice has small chance among the clash of racial antagonism, appeals to Moslem religious solidarity, competing national ambitions—all within the geo-political frame of Great Power rivalry. The isolation of Israel has clearly little to do with its supposed derelictions. It would be naive to enumerate the monstrous regimes whose practices never elicit remonstrance; the list keeps growing.

The measure in which anti-Zionism has become the rallying cry of groups ranging from the extreme Right to the Left in every part of the globe is one of the curiosities of our time. It cannot be explained by a surge of compassion for the purported sufferings of Palestinian Arabs. Assuming even that full credence were given to the depiction of their plight as described by their champions, the condition of Palestinian Arabs is obviously idyllic in comparison with the experiences of current refugees, be they boat people from Vietnam, ethnic Chinese, Cambodians or fugitives from tyrannical states whose excesses are reported daily. Yet Germans, Japanese or Italians are not devoutly training in military camps in Lebanon or Syria to come to their aid. Recruits of the West German Bader-Meinhoff Gang, the IRA, the Italian Red Brigade and the Japanese Red Army are not rallying to these suffering, uprooted millions. The terrorist internationale, whose nucleus and spearhead is the well-financed PLO, has magnified Israel into the chosen target for "revolutionary" outrage, pretty much as the Nazis made of the individual Jew the epitome of evil. And the success of the technique must be measured by how loudly the crash of explosions reverberates in the more respectable corridors of diplomacy.

Awareness of the crass political and economic motivations of either support or censure has made it possible for Zionists to endure the pariah role thrust upon them by a sizeable sector of the world community, if not with equanimity then with no diminution of self-esteem. On the contrary, each manifestly absurd accusation, each threat to Israel, has heightened the sense of solidarity which comes to the fore in extreme danger. However, this awareness simultaneously increases a realistic perception of Israel's exposed and perilous position. To despair is no counsel, neither is a headlong optimism. How can the situation be assessed?

From the outset there were two trends in Zionism. The "practical" (strange adjective to describe the pioneer zealots) Zionists who advocated the creation of "facts" through the purchase of land and its reclamation by Jewish settlers; and the "political" Zionists who sought "legitimacy," Herzl's favorite slogan. By the time the Balfour Declaration was issued in 1917 both groups could point to considerable accomplishments. Kibbutzniks were ploughing in the Emek and the "legally assured home" so passionately sought by Herzl had been granted. With the passage of the Partition Resolution in 1947 "legitimacy" had been conferred on an independent Jewish state whose borders, though encompassing much less territory than the envisioned home, closely followed the areas of actual Jewish settlement. Both trends had been proven right.

But with every Arab assault on Israel's legitimacy, her right to exist, new facts were created, notably in 1948 when Egypt occupied Gaza, and Jordan seized the West Bank and East Jerusalem, and in 1967 when Israel re-united Jerusalem and re-occupied the West Bank and Gaza. The Yom Kippur War and the negotiations with Egypt resulted in further changes. The one constant throughout these fluctuations has been the continued attempt to undermine Israel's legitimacy.

One unfortunate result of Israel's solitary struggle in an atmosphere of irrational malevolence has been Zionist wariness of giving comfort to the enemy by questioning Israeli government policies. This dilemma has been particularly acute since the election of the Likud government, whose domestic and settlement program has aroused considerable opposition among Zionists outside of Israel, as well as in Israel itself. However, the real difficulty besetting Israel is not the wrong course of a particular administration, though that may compound the trouble; party control in a democracy is temporary and may be repudiated. The unhappy truth is that the real problem is posed by the *post facto* attack on Israel's legitimacy by the very midwives who assisted at her birth and in their espousal of the pretenders to that legitimacy.

Granted the need for a Jewish state and the justice of its establishment, (as I have argued in various essays in this book) have these initial assumptions been invalidated either by the positive results of the Zionist enterprise or by the negative consequences of assaults upon the state? Let me illustrate: before the passage of the Partition Resolution Zionist partisans—to answer the charge that Jewish settlement had displaced Arabs—kept demonstrating by reference to impeccable British census reports that the Arab population of Palestine had doubled during a period when the populations of neighboring Arab states had declined or remained static; while native Arabs enjoyed a higher rate of natural increase because of improved health services, Arabs from Syria and Jordan kept pouring into Palestine because of opportunities provided by the developing Jewish national home. Yet in a catch-22 situation adversaries of Zionism cited this population growth as an argument for stopping Jewish immigration.

In a further catch-22 variant, the Law of Return whose terms allow any Jew to enter Israel as of right has been attacked as discriminatory. The Law, promulgated immediately upon the establishment of Israel, proclaimed to a world that had closed its doors to Jews fleeing from gas chambers that at last there was one spot on the globe that Jews could claim as home; non-Jews could become citizens after a period of residence. The Law of Return was an essential instrument for creating an independent Jewish state. What point had the Partition Resolution if its intent could be nullified by the easy device of an uncontrolled Arab influx into the small Jewish area? Israel had come into being to cure the specific affliction of Jewish national homelessness. The Arabs—and it should again be noted that until the sixties the argument was with Arabs not with then non-existent Palestinians—enjoyed vast territories and 21 independent states. The Law was not only a dramatic declaration summoning those rotting in DP camps or enduring persecution in Arab lands: it was affirmative action to redress long-standing inequity. Once the need to create a Jewish state had been granted, the tiny state had to exercise its primary function—to be a Jewish, not a multi-national, homeland. Only by denying the legitimacy of Jewish nationhood could criticism of measures to ensure this nationhood have meaning.

As I have already mentioned, despite accusations of "genocide," Palestinian Arabs in Israel and in the occupied territories have one of the highest growth rates in the world. Whereas Israeli Jews have some three children, Israeli Arabs have more than six per family. In the occupied territories the Arab fertility rate reaches nine. Israeli Arabs who did not join the Arab exodus in 1948 together with those who returned under provisions for the reuniting of families now number 500,000, approximately 15 percent of the population. Their villages are mainly in Galilee, a still sparsely settled region and the site of legendary kibbutzim. Should present demographic trends, abetted by the failure of the Likud government to encourage settlement in Galilee rather than on the contentious West Bank, go unchecked Jews might within a decade become a minority in a region with a special aura in the history of Zionist pioneering. There is reason to hope that a more intelligent settlement policy will reverse this trend. Supposing, however, that this should not prove to be the case. Would the unwillingness of Jews to breed at the Arab rate mean relinquishment of a vital part of the Jewish state? I raise this hypothetical question because murmurs for eventual Arab "autonomy" in Galilee have been heard. This nibbling at the small state erodes the confidence of its citizens. Yet the independence of any part of Israel cannot be viewed as conditional even if Jews have two children instead of six, any more than Los Angeles can lose its status as an American city because Mexican immigrants become a majority. In principle the legitimacy of Israel cannot be forfeit to demographic fluctuations or to circumstances arisen since the establishment of the state.

Perhaps the most vivid illustration of how the ideological assault on Israel depends on superimposing later events on the landscape of 1948 may be seen in the treatment of the Palestine problem. Apart from the recent emergence of Palestinian nationalism there is the matter of numbers. Today the press refers routinely to three or four million displaced Palestinians. But in 1948, according to the cautious estimates of United Nations commissions, not more than 600,000 Arabs joined the flight from the part of Palestine that became Israel. Assuming the later figures to be accurate due to an extraordinarily high rate of natural increase, the accretion to the UNRRA rolls of indigent Arabs in the countries of residence, and the refusal of the Arab states to allow the normal resettlement of the original number, how does this deliberately contrived Palestinian diaspora impugn Israel's moral position? Not long ago, Iraq, underpopulated and in need of labor, advertised in Egypt for workers who might settle in Iraq, but specified that "Palestinians" were not acceptable—the "homeless people" argument should not be weakened.

Admittedly assertions of principle offer a spare diet on the international scene. In the search for peace, the Palestinian problem, whatever its origins, must be solved. On one point Israeli opinion, except for minuscule Leftist groups, is united: opposition to the establishment of a third state within the borders of historic Palestine. Spokesmen of the previous Labor government declared repeatedly that there was room for only two states, one Jewish and one Arab, within the territory originally encompassed by the Balfour Declaration—an area that includes Jordan. However, the Labor government differed substantially from the Begin administration in its readiness to withdraw from most of the populated West Bank in accordance with security provisions such as those offered by the Allon plan.

The reasons for Israeli opposition to a PLO-dominated state are familiar. The political program of the PLO, aiming at the destruction of Israel in two stages, remains unchanged. The Palestine National Council spelled out the tactics to be pursued: first, to establish a "national, independent and combatant authority" on any portion of liberated Palestinian authority territory (read West Bank); second, to use this state as "only a step toward the realization of the strategic objective, namely, the establishment of a democratic Palestinian state" once the "Zionist entity" (Israel) has been liquidated.

Candor can go no further, nor has this program so far been repudiated in any detail. The PLO cannot be accused of subterfuge. A West Bank ministate would be a "point of departure," an "arsenal" and "combatant." Should anyone harbor the hope that such a strategy could be contained by agreements or controls, Hawatmeh, also under the PLO umbrella, disposed of that notion: "No supervisory system of the kind that may be set up by the UN will prevent us from exploiting every opportunity to transform the entire country into an arsenal."

Repeatedly proponents for the recognition of the PLO have assured the world that "moderates" among the PLO are prepared to grant Israel's right to exist. They have detected signs to that effect. Yet no sooner does some zealous negotiator appear with the tiding that Arafat is softening than a chill blast from Cairo or Damascus dissipates that hope. The case of retired Israeli Major General Peled, chairman of the Israel Council for Israeli-Palestinian Peace, is instructive. Peled announced to a press conference in Tel Aviv that he and an unidentified "top figure" in the PLO had on January 1, 1977, in Paris, signed a document in which the terrorist organization accepted Israel's right to exist. No sooner had this "historic breakthrough" been announced by an enthusiastic Peled than Farouk Kadoumi, head of the PLO's political department, energetically denied the story *in toto*. And from Paris, scene of the rapprochement, came a formal PLO statement assuring the world that it would never recognize the "Zionist entity" and re-affirming dedication to the sanguinary resolutions of the PLO covenant. So it has gone since then. "Disguised dialogue" and "Gambits," terms used by PLO apologists who think it indelicate to demand a straightforward repudiation of the covenant, are hardly acceptable substitutes for an explicit commitment to co-existence. Israel cannot make policy by consulting a Ouija Board, and currently the most industrious reading of signs and omens in the manner recommended has failed to reveal a change of heart in the PLO command. Peace agreements are not made by signs but by the kind of tough clarification that went on in the Camp David negotiations. In a curious article entitled "On the Importance of Reading Signals" (*New Outlook*, October 1976) Peled explains his method. He and those like him who still insist that Israel is missing an implicit affirmative in the PLO's explicit negative response are not likely to convince many Israelis. The new test for literacy devised by PLO sympathizers can enjoy popularity only among soothsayers.

While negotiations with the PLO as at present constituted would be as profitable as a discussion of civil rights for blacks with the Ku Klux Klan, Israel has come to recognize the existence of a new nationalism on its doorstep. The old Zionist conviction that Arab nationalism would be amply satisfied by the Arab states established by the Allies in liberated Turkish territory, and that the Arabs would not grudge "the small notch" reserved for the Jewish state has given way to the realization that, however inequitable the distribution of lands and resources between Jews and Arabs, the Palestinian demand can no longer be ignored. How can it be met without suicidal concessions?

It should be noted that even an Israeli very sensitive to the rights and wrongs of Palestinian Arabs such as Lova Eliav, wrote in his much publicized book, *Land of the Hart*: "It must be stressed that the partition as a possible solution to the problem of Israel and the Palestinian Arabs does not mean dividing *Eretz Israel*, historic Palestine, into more than two states. In other words I do not have in mind a Palestinian state in the administered areas separate from the state of Jordan: I am speaking of one state which will contain the majority of the Palestinians."

In this respect the dovish Eliav is not too far removed from what was official Israeli policy as stated by the former Meir government, including the supposedly hawkish Golda Meir, and subsequently of the Rabin cabinet. The Likud government's change of direction bodes little good for a solution to the Palestinian problem. Fanatical insistence on the retention of the West Bank—Judea and Samaria—as Israel's religious and historic patrimony has only sentiment to recommend it. The claim that from 1920 to 1946 the territories on both banks of the Jordan were integral parts of Palestine and that in 1946 Great Britain arbitrarily established the kingdom of Transjordan (later renamed Jordan) on 80 percent of the original territory of Palestine—hence Jordan is Arab Palestine and no further truncation of the remainder should take place—could probably be sustained in international law. Nevertheless, whatever the justice of this contention, the historic claim and contemporary demography are here at odds. Judea, Samaria and Gaza have an indigenous Arab population of over a million. Together with the sizeable Israeli Arab minority the incorporation of an additional million Arabs would threaten its identity as a Jewish state as effectively as an Arab military victory. Begin's formula, "autonomy for the people but not for the land" is obvious sophistry. And the prospect of indefinitely administering a reluctant citizenry would not enhance Israel's well-being or physical safety.

Begin's provocative settlement policy on the West Bank is defended by his supporters, who in the past derided the establishment of kibbutzim, as a continuation of the authentic pioneer tradition. Did not the practical Zionists establish "facts" by founding classic communes like Degania or Revivim? Admittedly Elon Moreh, set up near Nablus, is a fact, but one wholly antithetical in meaning and purpose to what those who preached the religion of labor had intended. Degania was established on arid land purchased by the Jewish National Fund. That was the legal title; the moral title was conferred by the productive toil of the settlers. Elon Moreh is on expropriated, not purchased, Arab land. It is occupied, not worked, by a handful of zealots who earn their living inside the green line, in Israel. To call a military outpost in occupied territory a "fact" in the sense of the term as originally conceived is a travesty. Unfortunately, pressure for a PLO state makes the dismantling of these outposts problematic.

The evidence of such pressure is all about us. How long the United States will remain firm in its commitment not to negotiate with the PLO as long as that organization cannot bring itself to revoke its covenant is a matter of conjecture. The potency of oil blackmail, indignantly rejected in 1973, is apparent. Since the fall of Iran, Saudi Arabia must be wooed, and Saudi Arabia demands the execution of the PLO program under the milder rubric of "Palestinian rights." While some brave voices in Congress and the administration still proclaim independence and stress the danger of allowing the United States to become the captive of OPEC in its domestic and foreign policy, the pro-Arab tilt in the press, TV, and various statements of public figures is getting steeper. The prompt brandishing of the oil weapon by black organizations immediately after the resignation of Andrew Young and their unabashed attempt to transform the incident into a Jewish-black issue shows how readily and in what unexpected quarter this technique will be employed. And in Europe, the Socialist International, long the friend of democratic Israel, bestowed the accolade of respectability on Arafat, through its officials, West German Willy Brandt and Austrian Chancellor Kreisky.

Declaiming against the gross expediency of these maneuvers is useless. By the time the proponents of a pro-Arab shift admit that since the Arabs sit on a large portion of the world's oil American interests must first be considered, there is little point in appeals to conscience or memory. But what are American interests? The notion that the piecemeal abandonment of Israel will blunt Arab appetite is illusory. The oil wells of the Persian Gulf and Libya will not gush more liberally for the United States once a deal is made. Syria will still covet Lebanon. Iraq will still worry about Syria, and Jordan will fear them both. And Russia's drive to the Middle East will have been accelerated through the creation of a solid pro-Soviet base in any PLO state. OPEC will lack no incentives for raising its prices as it pleases and maintaining its stranglehold on the West. The United States exaggerates the disinterested idealism of the oil potentates if it believes otherwise. After a brief respite sound reasons from the Kurds to Pakistan, from Angola to Ethiopia, will be discovered by various members of the combine for fresh extortions. Iran's seizure of the American Embassy provides dramatic evidence of how specious is the linking of oil to the Palestinian issue, despite the obligatory anti-Zionist rhetoric. As a long-term policy capitulation to oil blackmail is too costly. Such appeasement will lead not to Fortress America but to America Forfeited, inwardly corroded and ringed by totalitarian states. President Carter's promise that America will not become the prisoner of OPEC has more than election rhetoric to recommend it.

At some point, presumably, a peace settlement will be negotiated in which Israel will be assured of "secure and recognized borders" and Palestinians will achieve independence in a viable state federated with or including Jordan. Barring a catastrophic war, in which case the fates of large as well as small states become uncertain, there is no going back to a "homeless" Jewish people. This Zionist fact has been seared into modern consciousness and has achieved a radical transformation in how Jews are viewed. Without Israel there will be no Jewish people, only rapidly assimilating or vanishing Jews. So that the destiny of Jewish peoplehood rides on the existence of Israel. To this article of faith I hold.

As I look back upon the decades of Zionist struggle it is hard to renew the early exaltation. Not because of disenchantment with Israel's failure to become the ideal commonwealth "based on the principles of social justice" and egalitarian Socialism of which her founders dreamt. Were certificates of good conduct passed out on the international scene as the price of existence, how many countries would pass? And in any fair grading Israel would rank far higher than most of her detractors and all of her foes. In any case a distinction should be made between what Israel demands of herself and what a less than even-handed world demands of her. The talent of Israelis for self-criticism shows no abatement since the time of the prophets. The clamor within Israel against materialism, corruption, bureaucracy, inefficiency and social injustice to Jew and Arab merit full regard and is evidence of a stubborn idealism still flourishing in the harshest of outward circumstances. Intolerable, however, is the readiness of world opinion to judge Israel by standards set for no other people. None of the charity displayed for young countries battling vast internal and external troubles is in evidence if Israel strays. Floodlights of publicity that manage to miss brutality and oppression on a monstrous scale in Asia, Africa or Eastern Europe illumine every Israeli infraction. "More" is expected of Israel we are told. This disproportion is discrimination rather than tribute and a dangerous compliment. When Castro fervidly assures the non-aligned countries meeting in Havana that "nothing in recent history" parallels the Nazi genocide of Jews more than the Zionist "genocide" of Palestinians one again appreciates the perverse arithmetic by which the extermination of six million Jews is equated with the rapid multiplication of Palestinian Arabs. That this comparison was made before a conference debating the respective merits of two Cambodian regimes, one of whom won undisputed recognition as Hitler's successor in mass murder, adds to the perversity.

Awareness of this fundamental inequity, seen also in the bland calculations according to which military experts in their allocation of arms coolly expect three million Jews routinely to equal 100 million Arabs clouds the future. Are Zionists engaged in a labor of Sisyphus? Will every victory turn into defeat? How many more miracles of daring and ingenuity must Israelis perform before they can get off the tightrope of their existence and have the chance to lead ordinary lives without spectacular feats? These are troubling questions that strike at the heart of the problems of emigration and lack of large-scale immigration that beset Israel. For though Israel was the creation of an extraordinary few, the elementary human right to be ordinary is one for which Zionism must soberly struggle without the Messianic transport of 1948. Yet the paradox of Jewish existence is such that the very notion seems extravagant, even scandalous, particularly to diaspora Jews who themselves live at a lower pitch.

For the time being the precious right to be ordinary has as yet not been achieved. Peace is the prerequisite just as peace is the prerequisite for a decent life in an impoverished Arab state like Egypt as Sadat has realized. Given peace, the energies squandered on war can be engaged in building a good, not necessarily ideal, society. Israel, in surrendering the buffer of the Sinai, has taken large risks for that hope. Ben-Gurion dreamt of making the whole desert, not only a few kibbutzim, fruitful. Sadat has offered to pipe water from the Nile through the Sinai to the Negev. Are these mirages? Perhaps the fury of the rejectionist Arab states will succeed in undermining the peace process. The possible scenarios for disaster are plentiful. On the other hand, if the United States remains firm in asserting its independence of the oil cartels, belligerent Arab states will have lost their main lever. In such a situation the peace initiative begun by Egypt may develop to include other Arab states and the Palestinians. It should be remembered that not so long ago Egypt seemed hopelessly intransigent. And even the fiercest rejectionist states appreciate the risk of pushing Israel too far, for if the image of David no longer holds—Goliath may win—then the figure of Samson looms. There will be no Auschwitz in the Middle East. But there is no point in indulging in apocalyptic nightmares. A blueprint for peace exists and an accommodation that will satisfy the needs of Israel and the Palestinian Arabs is a practical possibility.

Would the Utopian visionaries of the past have lost heart had they foreseen how it turned out? I think not. Herzl would add another slippery egg to his collection of difficulties and after a view of Haifa continue, inspirited. Modern technology and imagination had produced the wonders he had prophesied for that city. The author of the Socialist Jewish state, after noting that it had taken more than four hours daily to get the houses built and the fields plowed, would rejoice that the class struggle could be waged on home territory. Above all, the marvel of an achieved Jewish state would vindicate their urgent fantasies.

Jewish national independence, so hard-won, must still be defended. While the tug of geo-political forces is unpredictable, in one sphere Jewish will is paramount yet remains unexerted. The ingathering confidently anticipated by the founders of Israel has not taken place. The Jews of catastrophe came; the Jews of comfort, except for handfuls, evaded the harsh challenge of full partnership in building the Jewish state. That is the inner wound of Zionism. Golda Meir, moved by the sight of young American Jews rushing to Israel in a time of crisis, asked directly, "You are ready to die with us; why do you not live with us?" Obviously, there was no satisfactory answer. But that readiness to die was the plainest testament to the meaning of Jewish national independence even for lucky American Jews. Obscure historic memory warns against its loss. One task of Zionism today is to prod that memory.

(1979)

Composed in Garamond by
19th Street Graphics
Washington, DC

Printed and bound by
The Maple Press
York, Pennsylvania